Data Analysis with Mplus

Methodology in the Social Sciences

David A. Kenny, Founding Editor

Todd D. Little, Series Editor

www.guilford.com/MSS

This series provides applied researchers and students with analysis and research design books that emphasize the use of methods to answer research questions. Rather than emphasizing statistical theory, each volume in the series illustrates when a technique should (and should not) be used and how the output from available software programs should (and should not) be interpreted. Common pitfalls as well as areas of further development are clearly articulated.

RECENT VOLUMES

ADVANCES IN CONFIGURAL FREQUENCY ANALYSIS
Alexander A. von Eye, Patrick Mair, and Eun-Young Mun

APPLIED MISSING DATA ANALYSIS
Craig K. Enders

DIAGNOSTIC MEASUREMENT: THEORY, METHODS, AND APPLICATIONS
André A. Rupp, Jonathan Templin, and Robert A. Henson

APPLIED META-ANALYSIS FOR SOCIAL SCIENCE RESEARCH
Noel A. Card

PRINCIPLES AND PRACTICE OF STRUCTURAL EQUATION MODELING, THIRD EDITION
Rex B. Kline

DATA ANALYSIS WITH MPLUS
Christian Geiser

INTENSIVE LONGITUDINAL METHODS: AN INTRODUCTION TO DIARY AND EXPERIENCE SAMPLING RESEARCH
Niall Bolger and Jean-Philippe Laurenceau

DOING STATISTICAL MEDIATION AND MODERATION
Paul E. Jose

Data Analysis with Mplus

Christian Geiser

Series Editor's Note by Todd D. Little

THE GUILFORD PRESS
New York London

Originally published in the German language by VS Verlag für Sozialwissenschaften, 65189 Wiesbaden, Germany, as "Geiser—Datenanalyse mit Mplus—978-3-531-16393-2".

A Division of Guilford Publications, Inc.
370 Seventh Avenue, Suite 1200, New York, NY 10001
www.guilford.com

Printed in the United States of America

This book is printed on acid-free paper.

Last digit is print number: 9 8 7 6 5 4

Library of Congress Cataloging-in-Publication Data

Geiser, Christian.
[Datenanalyse mit Mplus. English]
Data analysis with Mplus / Christian Geiser.
pages cm — (Methodology in the social sciences)
Includes bibliographical references and index.
ISBN 978-1-4625-0245-5 (pbk.) — ISBN 978-1-4625-0782-5 (cloth)
1. Multivariate analysis—Data processing. 2. Mplus. I. Title.
QA278.G4513 2013
519.5′35028553—dc23

2012033585

Series Editor's Note

I'm very pleased to introduce Christian Geiser's book to you. This book was originally published in German by Springer Verlag. I felt it was so important to bring the book to a broader readership that we secured the rights to produce it in English as part of The Guilford Press series Methodology in the Social Sciences. Given that Christian is a very talented multilingual scholar, I knew that rendering this excellent work in English would be both easy for him and an important contribution. Special thanks go to the legal and contracts team at The Guilford Press who worked diligently to secure the English-language rights to Christian's book and to Whitney Moore, whose assistance in bringing this book to fruition was above the call of duty.

Why am I so pleased to bring this book to you? Simply, it is the most thorough and accessible book available on how to use Mplus for all manner of statistical analysis procedures. Mplus is a popular software package that is capable of estimating a wide variety of useful analyses. Figuring out how to get Mplus to do most of the analyses, however, is both challenging and frustrating if you rely on the Mplus User's Guide. Christian's book is clearly organized, covers a wide variety of analyses that Mplus can estimate, and is easy to follow.

In other words, *Data Analysis with Mplus* fills an important gap. It is not focused simply on a cookbook model of how to run the various analyses in Mplus. Because it is written for the applied researcher and not the quantitative analyst, the models are accessible. Christian explains each analysis model step-by-step. He does not presume that you will have used Mplus before. In fact, he actually begins with how to prepare and bring in data. This feature is a rarity and an important one because it is an essential step to master *before you can do any of the fun analyses!*

A wide variety of different analyses are described in this book. In a clear and methodical manner, Christian explains what the syntax means, teaches you very useful Mplus tricks, and actually alerts you to the defaults that exist (which can be a mystery sometimes). Because of his skillful syntax pedagogy, new users will feel comfortable knowing what the syntax means and not be intimidated about using it, which is important for new researchers who do not have much exposure to the world of writing syntax for data analyses.

Christian's focus on different types of analyses will help build your knowledge and understanding of Mplus syntax. For example, some analyses are presented first as manifest variable techniques before the complexity of a measurement model is added. This piecewise exposure helps avoid the overwhelming effect of presenting both manifest and latent variables in the same model and allows for highlighting important differences in the required syntax. Christian does a terrific job of explaining Mplus syntax in bite-size pieces so that a reader without prior knowledge can understand it. This aspect of his book is essential, I think, because often it is the failure of nonquantitative users to grasp a simple, or basic, concept that results in their not understanding the following steps. The chapter-specific recommendations focus on the applied researcher.

Christian's book is an excellent resource manual for anyone wishing to use Mplus for advanced statistical data analyses. It is a terrific complement to Rex B. Kline's *Principles and Practices of Structural Equation Modeling*, Timothy A. Brown's *Confirmatory Factor Analysis for Applied Research*, as well as my forthcoming book, *Longitudinal Structural Equation Modeling*.

TODD D. LITTLE
Berlin, Germany

Preface

Multivariate statistical methods with or without latent variables are more and more frequently used in virtually all areas of social science research. One reason is that many studies examine research problems that involve complex relationships among a variety of manifest and/or latent variables. Multivariate statistical approaches with latent variables are particularly useful—and are becoming increasingly popular—because they allow researchers to explicitly take errors of measurement into account, thereby avoiding bias in parameter estimates and standard errors (Bollen, 1989).

The computer program Mplus allows the analysis of a wide variety of multivariate statistical models with or without latent variables in a single comprehensive modeling framework (Muthén, 2002; Muthén & Muthén, 1998–2012). A special feature of Mplus is that it allows for both the estimation of models with continuous latent variables (e.g., confirmatory factor analysis, structural equation modeling, item response theory) and models with categorical latent variables (so-called latent class variables). Latent class models (see Chapter 6) can also be combined with models for continuous latent variables (see Chapter 3), for example, in the analysis of *factor* or *growth mixture models*.

In addition, Mplus is flexible in handling data situations that violate assumptions of common methods of parameter estimation, such as maximum likelihood (ML). For example, ML estimation requires multivariate normality of the variables. The assumption of multivariate normality is often violated in practice, for instance, when items with ordinal-scale level are used as indicators of latent variables (Finney & DiStefano, 2006). In addition, many statistical procedures require independent observations drawn from random samples. Many empirical studies, however, make use of cluster samples in which individuals are nested within groups (e.g., children nested within school classes). Such cluster sampling violates the assumption of independent observations and requires the use of the multilevel modeling techniques implemented in Mplus (see Chapter 5).

Mplus offers a variety of robust methods of parameter estimation so that ordinal, otherwise non-normal, and clustered data can be properly analyzed. In addition, Mplus can be seen as a relatively user-friendly program. Even though models have to be specified via syntax commands in Mplus, the Mplus syntax is fairly straightforward and easy to learn. Complex models can be specified with relatively few lines of code, and the user does not necessarily have to be an expert in programming or matrix algebra to be able to specify a complex latent variable model.

The present book provides an introduction to multivariate data analysis with Mplus as well as to the theory and practical application of different types of multivariate statistical methods that are particularly relevant to social science research: cross-sectional structural equation models (SEMs; including regression, confirmatory factor, and path analysis; Chapter 3), longitudinal SEMs (including latent state, latent state–trait, autoregressive, latent change, and latent growth curve models; Chapter 4), multilevel regression analysis (Chapter 5), and classical latent class analysis (LCA; Chapter 6).

Because the goal of the book is to introduce readers to statistical computing in Mplus in an application-oriented and user-friendly way, empirical data examples are used throughout the book. Many of these examples reflect typical analyses carried out in the social sciences and can thus be directly transferred to a user's own research questions. Numerous screen shots and output excerpts guide the reader through the analyses and the interpretation of the Mplus output in a step-by-step fashion. Furthermore, all data examples and input, output, and other files are available on the companion website (*www.guilford.com/geiser-materials*) to further facilitate the use of the techniques discussed. All syntax files are annotated, making it easy for the user to connect the statistical model to the syntax specification in Mplus. Many of the examples are limited to six or fewer variables so that they can be reproduced using the free Mplus demo version that is available for downloading at *www.statmodel.com/demo.shtml*. This has the advantage of making most examples available for teaching without requiring students to purchase the full Mplus program version.

The book starts with the question of how to prepare a data set for use in Mplus. Given the great popularity of SPSS in the social sciences, I chose to demonstrate the key steps in data preparation and data export using this general statistics program. The basic principles can be easily transferred to other statistics programs, such as R, SAS, STATA, STATISTICA, and Systat.

The book is meant to be more than a pure Mplus syntax guide, and it is not a replacement for the Mplus User's Guide (Muthén & Muthén, 1998–2012; *www.statmodel.com/ugexcerpts.shtml*). My goal is not only to show the reader how to specify different types of models using Mplus syntax, but also to provide guidelines for useful modeling strategies and the interpretation of the results. Furthermore, the book also points out some typical caveats in the analysis of complex multivariate data (e.g., the question of how to assess measurement invariance in longitudinal SEMs or how to avoid local likelihood maxima in LCA) and how to properly address them. Specific issues and solution strategies are discussed in various text boxes throughout.

Despite the focus on application, the theory of each of the statistical approaches is briefly reviewed at the beginning of each chapter. It is important to note that the book is not a replacement for relevant statistics textbooks or for specialized literature. Therefore, key references to relevant literature are provided at the beginning of each chapter and for the discussion of specific problems, such as the question of how to most appropriately test the mediated effect in path analysis (see Section 3.5 in Chapter 3).

The choice of statistical methods was made on the basis of my experiences as a lecturer for numerous statistical workshops, focusing on what seemed to be the needs of a large number of empirical scientists. I hope that the selection of methods and models presented in this book will be useful for researchers who want to use these techniques in their research. The use of more complex statistical methods is discussed in Geiser, Crayen, and Enders (2012).

The present book evolved from my seminar and workshop teaching experiences. I am grateful to my students and to the participants in my workshops for the feedback provided in these courses. In addition, I would like to thank Martin Corth, David Cole, Mark Roosa, and the Deutsches Zentrum für Altersfragen (German Center for Gerontology) for letting me use data sets as examples in the book. I also want to thank Christopher Marx for his help in preparing and analyzing the data set used to illustrate path modeling and mediation analysis in Section 3.5 as well as for his helpful comments on the draft of Section 3.5. Furthermore, I thank Claudia Crayen for creating some of the figures and for helpful corrections, as well as Henriette Hunold, Anne Janssen, Tanja Kutscher, Maike Luhmann, Natalie Mallach, and Tabea Reuter for their careful proofreading of the German draft and for their useful comments. I am grateful to C. Deborah Laughton and Todd D. Little for their faith in this project and for their great support, and Whitney G. Moore at the University of Kansas for her substantive and extremely helpful review of the manuscript. All of these individuals have contributed significantly to making this book more comprehensible and user-friendly and to eliminating errors. All remaining errors, omissions, and weaknesses are my sole responsibility. Please contact me at *christian.geiser.78@gmail.com* if you find errors or have suggestions for improvement. I wish all readers the best of luck with their own analyses using Mplus and for successful publication of the results.

CHRISTIAN GEISER
Logan, Utah

Contents

The companion website *www.guilford.com/geiser-materials* provides all data sets and Mplus input and output files, as well as additional materials discussed in this book.

1

Data Management in SPSS

In this chapter, I explain how to prepare an SPSS raw data set for use in Mplus. The procedure is demonstrated in the program SPSS, because it is one of the most widely used general statistics software packages in the social and behavioral sciences. The essential steps shown here can be transferred easily to other common programs, such as R, SAS, STATA, STATISTICA, SYSTAT, etc.

Mplus cannot directly read data sets in the common SPSS data format (*.sav). However, it is easy to export a data set as a simple text file (a file with the typical file extensions *.txt or *.dat) from SPSS or another general data management program. Such a text file can then be used for statistical analyses in Mplus. In my experience, the text file format that works best is a simple tab-delimited format. *Tab-delimited* means that each column (typically representing a variable) in the text file is separated by a tab symbol. Reading data in other formats is possible (see *Mplus User's Guide*; Muthén & Muthén, 1998–2012), and one may also use summary data (e.g., covariance matrices, correlation matrices, means, and standard deviations) instead of raw data, as described in Section 2.2.

In the following sections, a convenient procedure for preparing and exporting a raw data set from SPSS is demonstrated, step by step, using the sample data file **KFT.sav**. It should be noted that the method described here is not the only possible way; other procedures yield the same results. The sample data file as well as an SPSS syntax file with the relevant commands can be found on the companion website.

BOX 1.1. *Sample Data Set* ***KFT.sav***

The data set **KFT.sav** contains data from $N = 455$ German high school students who were tested with a German intelligence test battery, *Kognitiver Fähigkeitstest* (*Cognitive Abilities Test*, KFT; Heller, Gaedicke, & Weinläder, 1976). The KFT is frequently used to measure school achievement in German-speaking countries. Subtests in the present data set included verbal material (variables **kft_v1** and **kft_v2**), numerical ("quantitative") material (variables **kft_q1** and **kft_q3**), and figural ("nonverbal") material (variables **kft_n1** and **kft_n3**). The data set contains the sum scores of the students for each of the six KFT subtests.

1.1 CODING MISSING VALUES

It is recommended to assign a numeric missing value code for all missing values prior to importing data into Mplus, including SPSS "system-defined" missing values (i.e., empty cells with a dot in the SPSS data view). Saving SPSS system-defined missing values into the *.dat file can cause errors when reading the data file in Mplus. Therefore, system-defined missing values should be recoded into user-defined missing values using a numeric missing value code. It is recommended that a numeric missing value code be used—that is, a number such as "–9," "–99," or "999"—to clearly identify any missing values in the data set. Of course, the missing value code needs to be chosen in such a way that the number cannot occur as a valid score on a variable. In our example, the number –99 is used as missing value code for all six variables. A score of –99 cannot occur as a real value for any of the six KFT subscales.

It is important to note that one should refrain from deleting missing values in the raw data set. Mplus has excellent capabilities for dealing with missing values (e.g., full information maximum likelihood [FIML] and multiple imputation; e.g., see Enders, 2010; Geiser et al., 2012). In addition, listwise deletion is also an option available in Mplus; hence, there is no need to delete missing values before analyzing the data in Mplus. (*Listwise deletion* means that only cases with complete data on all variables are included in the analysis.)

System- and user-defined missing values in SPSS can be recoded easily into a unitary (user-defined) missing value code using the point-and-click option **Transform → Recode into same variables**. This is shown for the KFT data example in Figures 1.1 through 1.4. The use

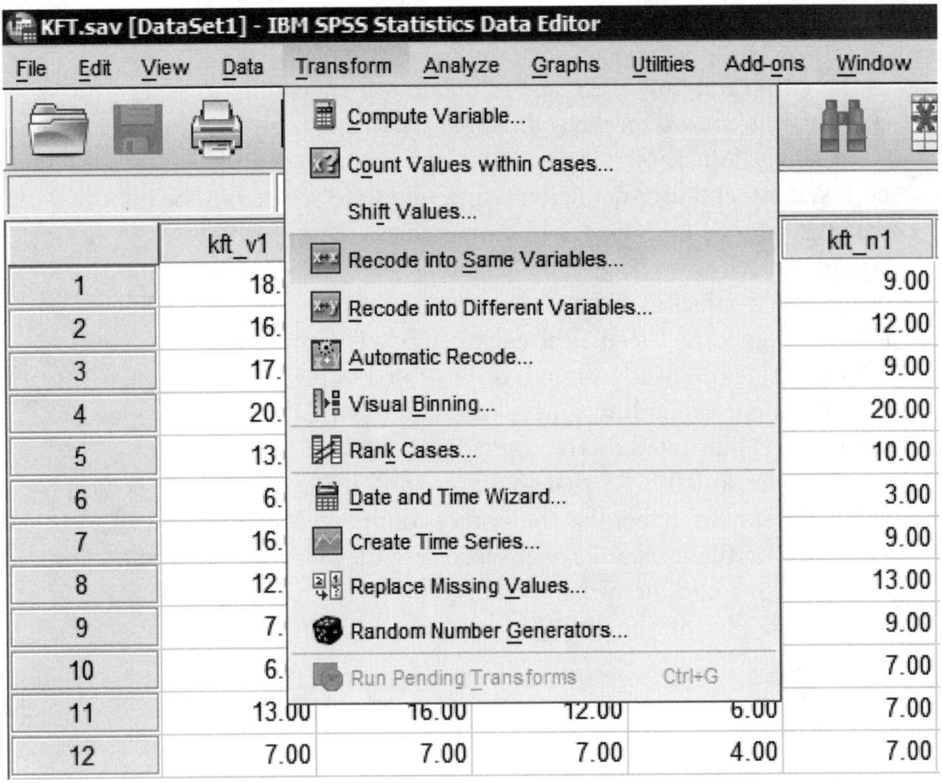

FIGURE 1.1. SPSS option **Transform → Recode into Same Variables**.

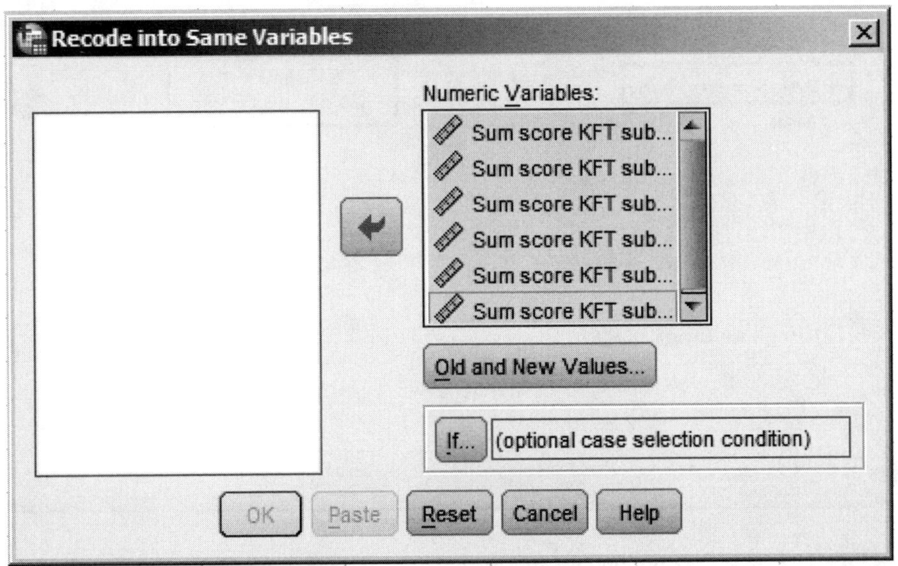

FIGURE 1.2. To assign (or change) a numeric missing value code, all variables are transferred to the window on the right-hand side.

of the corresponding SPSS syntax command for coding missing values (RECODE) is shown on the companion website.

Caution: After assigning a single user-defined missing value code to both system- and user-defined missing values, SPSS needs to be informed that the new code indicates missing values. (Unfortunately, SPSS does not recognize this indication by default.) Otherwise, SPSS would treat the newly coded values as if they were actual scores (i.e., –99 as a valid value) leading to incorrect statistical calculations. The procedure for defining missing values explicitly as such is illustrated in Figures 1.5 through 1.8. Use of the corresponding syntax command (MISSING VALUES) for the same goal is illustrated on the companion website.

In order to tell SPSS that –99 now indicates a missing value for all variables, one can either use the syntax command MISSING VALUES, as illustrated on the companion website, or use the following point-and-click options in SPSS: In the variable view, go to the first variable, then Missing Values, and click on the three little dots on the right of the cell, as shown in Figure 1.6.

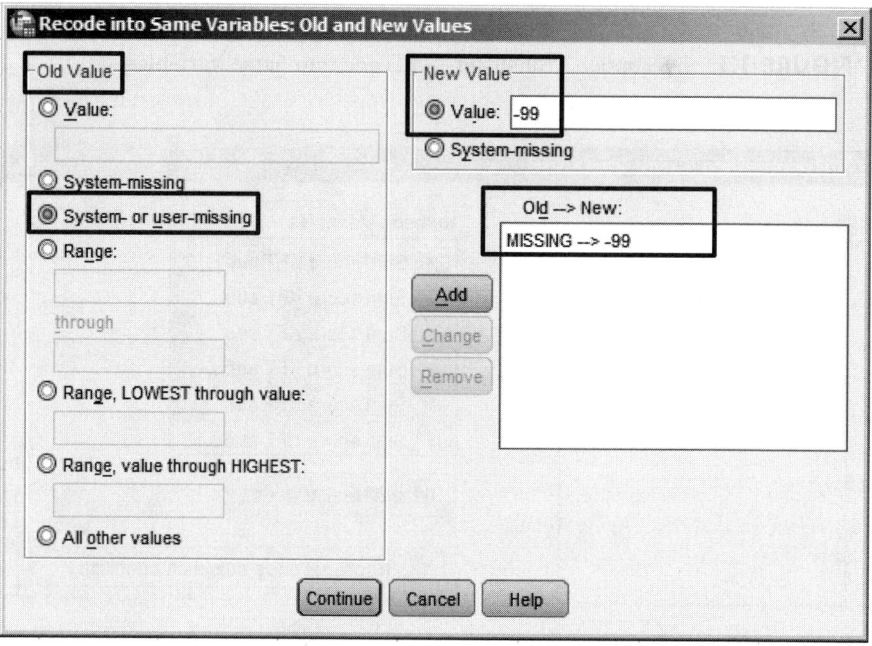

FIGURE 1.3. The option **Old and New Values** is used to recode system- and user-defined missing values into the same numeric code, here –99.

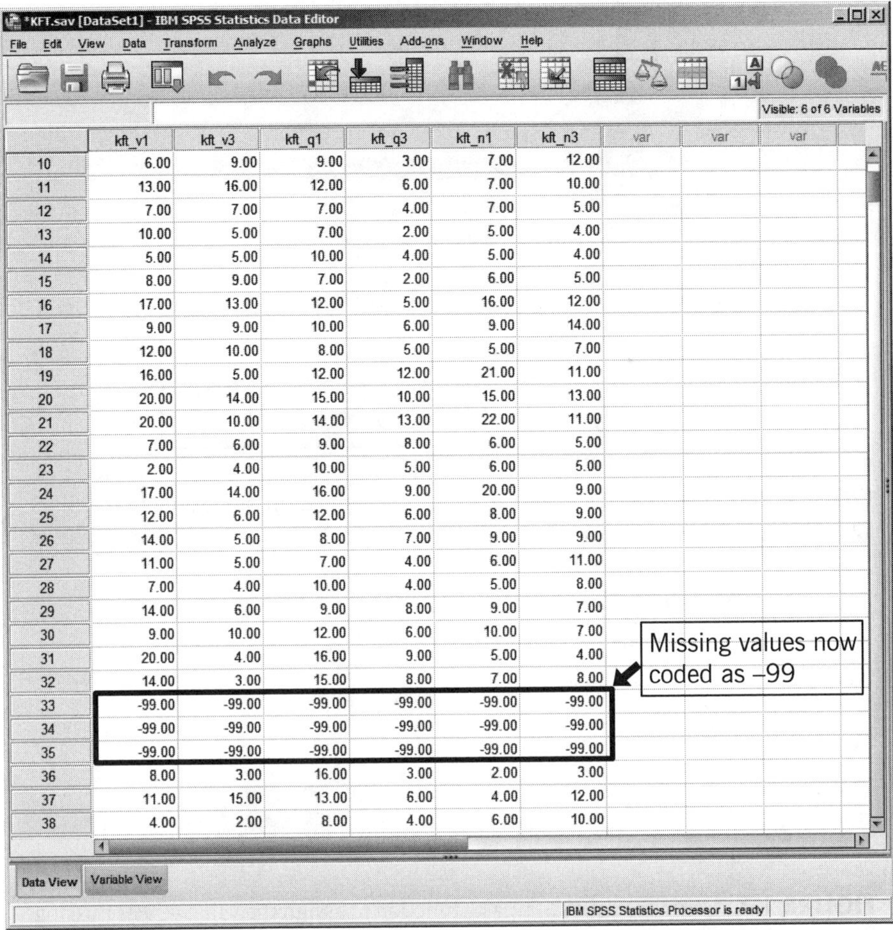

	kft_v1	kft_v3	kft_q1	kft_q3	kft_n1	kft_n3
10	6.00	9.00	9.00	3.00	7.00	12.00
11	13.00	16.00	12.00	6.00	7.00	10.00
12	7.00	7.00	7.00	4.00	7.00	5.00
13	10.00	5.00	7.00	2.00	5.00	4.00
14	5.00	5.00	10.00	4.00	5.00	4.00
15	8.00	9.00	7.00	2.00	6.00	5.00
16	17.00	13.00	12.00	5.00	16.00	12.00
17	9.00	9.00	10.00	6.00	9.00	14.00
18	12.00	10.00	8.00	5.00	5.00	7.00
19	16.00	5.00	12.00	12.00	21.00	11.00
20	20.00	14.00	15.00	10.00	15.00	13.00
21	20.00	10.00	14.00	13.00	22.00	11.00
22	7.00	6.00	9.00	8.00	6.00	5.00
23	2.00	4.00	10.00	5.00	6.00	5.00
24	17.00	14.00	16.00	9.00	20.00	9.00
25	12.00	6.00	12.00	6.00	8.00	9.00
26	14.00	5.00	8.00	7.00	9.00	9.00
27	11.00	5.00	7.00	4.00	6.00	11.00
28	7.00	4.00	10.00	4.00	5.00	8.00
29	14.00	6.00	9.00	8.00	9.00	7.00
30	9.00	10.00	12.00	6.00	10.00	7.00
31	20.00	4.00	16.00	9.00	5.00	4.00
32	14.00	3.00	15.00	8.00	7.00	8.00
33	-99.00	-99.00	-99.00	-99.00	-99.00	-99.00
34	-99.00	-99.00	-99.00	-99.00	-99.00	-99.00
35	-99.00	-99.00	-99.00	-99.00	-99.00	-99.00
36	8.00	3.00	16.00	3.00	2.00	3.00
37	11.00	15.00	13.00	6.00	4.00	12.00
38	4.00	2.00	8.00	4.00	6.00	10.00

FIGURE 1.4. Modified data file with new missing value code –99.

*KFT.sav [DataSet1] - IBM SPSS Statistics Data Editor

File Edit View Data Transform Analyze Graphs Utilities Add-ons Window Help

	Name	Type	Width	Decimals	Label	Values	Missing
1	kft_v1	Numeric	8	2	Sum score KFT...	None	None
2	kft_v3	Numeric	8	2	Sum score KFT...	None	None
3	kft_q1	Numeric	8	2	Sum score KFT...	None	None
4	kft_q3	Numeric	8	2	Sum score KFT...	None	None
5	kft_n1	Numeric	8	2	Sum score KFT...	None	None
6	kft_n3	Numeric	8	2	Sum score KFT...	None	None
7							

Data View Variable View

IBM SPSS Statistics Processor is ready

FIGURE 1.5. SPSS does not automatically recognize the new missing value code as "missing." This code has to be manually assigned under "Missing" in the SPSS variable view.

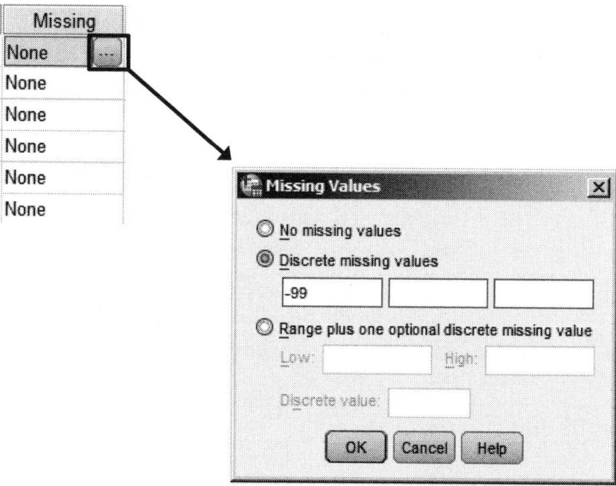

FIGURE 1.6. Entering the value –99 as a user-defined missing value in the SPSS variable view.

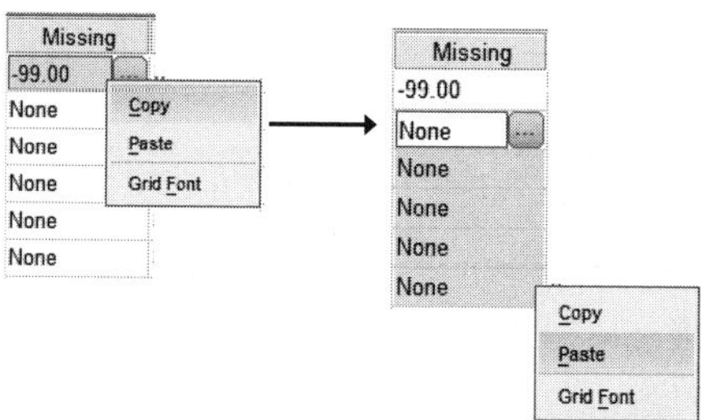

FIGURE 1.7. Using the copy-and-paste function to assign the value –99 as missing value to each of the six variables in the data set.

*KFT.sav [DataSet1] - IBM SPSS Statistics Data Editor

File Edit View Data Transform Analyze Graphs Utilities Add-ons Window Help

	Name	Type	Width	Decimals	Label	Values	Missing
1	kft_v1	Numeric	8	2	Sum score KFT...	None	-99.00
2	kft_v3	Numeric	8	2	Sum score KFT...	None	-99.00
3	kft_q1	Numeric	8	2	Sum score KFT...	None	-99.00
4	kft_q3	Numeric	8	2	Sum score KFT...	None	-99.00
5	kft_n1	Numeric	8	2	Sum score KFT...	None	-99.00
6	kft_n3	Numeric	8	2	Sum score KFT...	None	-99.00
7							

Data View | Variable View

IBM SPSS Statistics Processor is ready

FIGURE 1.8. The SPSS variable view with correctly assigned missing value code for all six variables.

1.2 EXPORTING AN ASCII DATA FILE FOR Mplus

After defining missing values appropriately, one can export the data file into an ASCII format that is acceptable for Mplus. When using the point-and-click interface in SPSS, one can simply use the option **File → Save as** (as shown in Figures 1.9–1.10). Alternatively, the syntax command SAVE TRANSLATE (see companion website) can be used for the same purpose. The resulting tab-delimited text data file that can be processed by Mplus is shown in Figure 1.11.

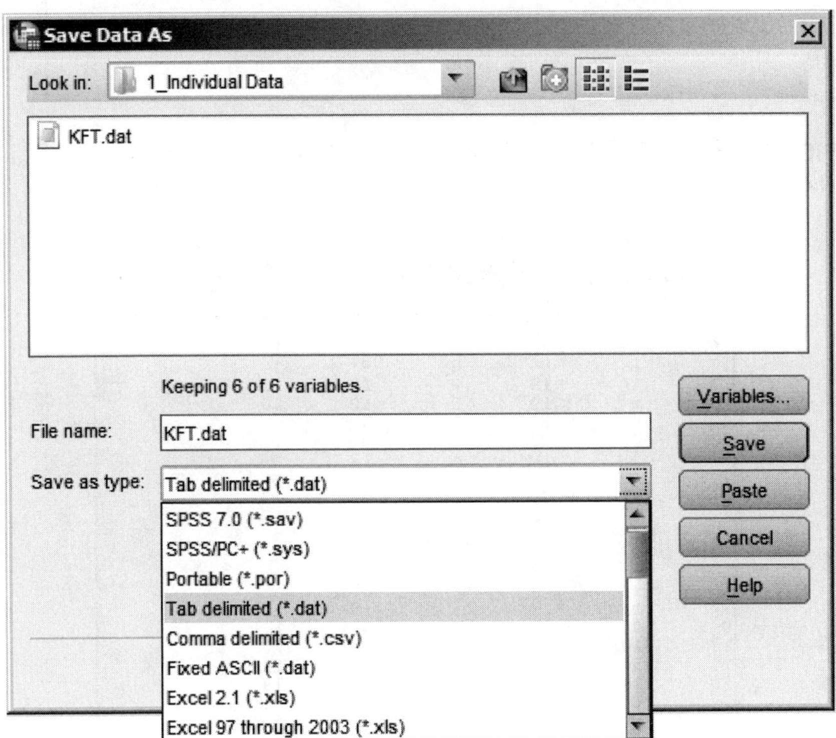

FIGURE 1.9. Exporting an SPSS data file to ASCII format (*.dat).

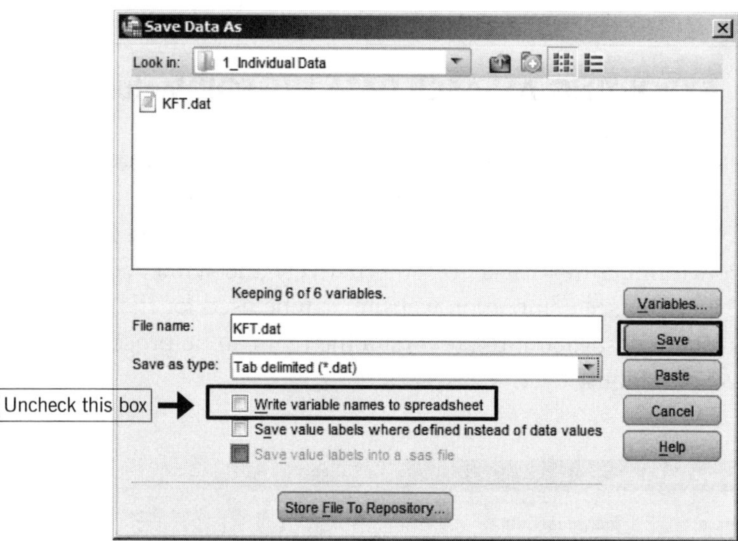

FIGURE 1.10. Deactivating the SPSS option **Write Variable Names to Spreadsheet**.

KFT.dat - Notepad

File Edit Format View Help

```
18	13	14	7	9	5
16	7	4	2	12	10
17	13	8	8	9	10
20	17	13	9	20	12
13	6	19	9	10	10
6	5	8	6	3	5
16	7	19	9	9	10
12	5	10	4	13	9
7	10	9	7	9	9
6	9	9	3	7	12
13	16	12	6	7	10
7	7	7	4	7	5
10	5	7	2	5	4
5	5	10	4	5	4
8	9	7	2	6	5
17	13	12	5	16	12
9	9	10	6	9	14
12	10	8	5	5	7
16	5	12	12	21	11
20	14	15	10	15	13
20	10	14	13	22	11
7	6	9	8	6	5
2	4	10	5	6	5
17	14	16	9	20	9
12	6	12	6	8	9
14	5	8	7	9	9
11	5	7	4	6	11
7	4	10	4	5	8
14	6	9	8	9	7
9	10	12	6	10	7
20	4	16	9	5	4
14	3	15	8	7	8
-99	-99	-99	-99	-99	-99
-99	-99	-99	-99	-99	-99
-99	-99	-99	-99	-99	-99
8	3	16	3	2	3
```

FIGURE 1.11. Excerpt from the newly created text file that contains the variables in tab-delimited format. This file can be processed by Mplus.

2

Reading Data into Mplus

Mplus can process data in different formats. The two most relevant formats are discussed here: individual data and summary data. The *individual data* format is probably the most commonly used format in practice. Individual data are raw data in which the scores of all individuals on all variables are preserved. This is the case, for example, in our KFT data file (see Figure 1.11). The *summary data* format is used when one wants to analyze data in summary format, for example, a covariance or a correlation matrix (and potentially the means and standard deviations of the variables). The possibility to analyze summary data can be useful, for example, when a researcher wants to reanalyze data reported in a research report (e.g., a journal article, grant proposal). Many scholarly publications provide the covariance or correlation matrices that served as the basis for the analyses (e.g., path or structural equation models [SEMs]), whereas raw data are only rarely made available in publications. For many types of structural equation analyses, it is not necessary to analyze individual data (although using individual data may often be advantageous, e.g., when the user wants to take missing data into account or use specific estimation procedures, e.g., for clustered data). For many models, the covariance matrix (sometimes in combination with the mean vector) of the variables is sufficient as input for estimating the model. Let us first consider the case of reading individual data, using the data example from Chapter 1.

2.1 IMPORTING AND ANALYZING INDIVIDUAL DATA (RAW DATA)

Importing individual data into Mplus is usually unproblematic if the procedure described in Chapter 1 is followed. Nevertheless, it is recommended to check the proper import of the data into Mplus by first performing only basic statistical analyses (e.g., running descriptive statistics for all variables in the data set) and making sure that these statistics match the corresponding statistics calculated in at least one other program (e.g., SPSS). This approach can be used to check whether Mplus is reading the data correctly. This point cannot be emphasized enough. In practice, users often skip this step and then realize too late that Mplus has not processed the data correctly—leading to incorrect model estimates. For this reason users should take the time to first run a so-called `basic` analysis in Mplus to ensure the correct processing of the data before carrying out actual analyses in Mplus.

2.1.1 Basic Structure of the Mplus Syntax and `BASIC` Analysis

Mplus is an almost entirely syntax-based program. This means that the estimation of statistical models and many of the other functions in Mplus are executed via syntax commands and are not available through a point-and-click interface as, for example, in SPSS. Nonetheless, for the construction of the basic Mplus syntax, a point-and-click interface (the so-called *Mplus language generator*) is available. This option allows users to generate the most important basic syntax commands. Here I do not discuss the use of the Mplus language generator in detail, because users usually do not refer to this option any more after having learned the basic syntax rules in Mplus—which, fortunately, are not very difficult.

In the following material I demonstrate a useful strategy for reading data into Mplus and to check the correct processing of the data using the Mplus `basic` option. For this purpose we again refer to the sample data set **KFT.dat**. In the first step, the Mplus editor has to be opened (in MS Windows: **Start → Programs → Mplus → Mplus Editor**). An empty window becomes visible, into which one can either type the required syntax commands manually or use the Mplus language generator to get started. The syntax commands needed to run a `basic` analysis in Mplus on the KFT variables are shown in Figure 2.1.

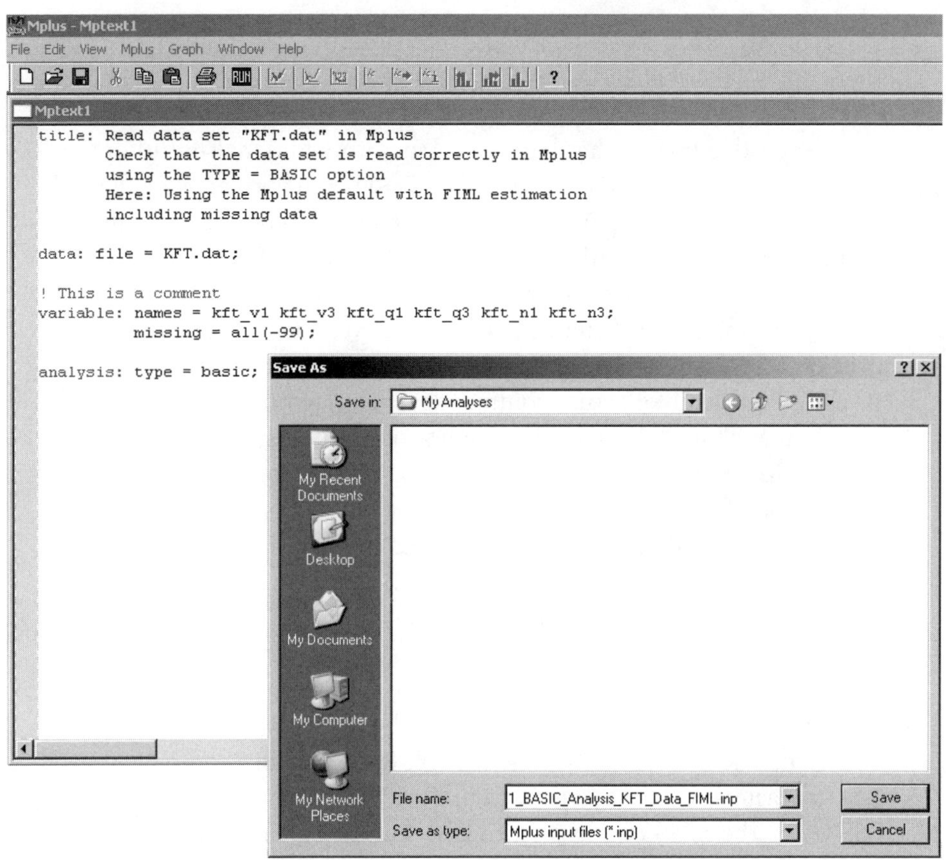

FIGURE 2.1. Mplus syntax file for checking the correct data import using the option `type = basic`. The menu option **File → Save as** is used here to save the input as a *.inp file. It is most convenient to save the input file to the same directory that also contains the data file to be analyzed. That way, no specific path has to be included under `data: file =`.

A new syntax file should immediately be saved as an Mplus input file (see Figure 2.1). In addition, when writing or editing a syntax file, one should not forget to save changes regularly, by either using the save symbol in the menu or hitting the combination CTRL + S so that work is not lost if the computer crashes, etc. Mplus input files contain the file ending *.inp. Unlike, for example, SPSS syntax, Mplus requires that a separate input file be specified for each statistical model.

The `title` command is used to label the analysis that is performed and to provide explanations on what statistical analysis is carried out (and potentially in which way the specific model or analysis is different from others in a series of analyses). Although this command is not required, it is recommended to include a meaningful and informative title section so as to clearly document what has been done. An additional useful option is the use of comments. Each comment has to begin with an exclamation mark (!). No specific ending of the line is required, but every new line of comment has to begin with an exclamation mark again. Comments will appear in green font. Lines of comment that exceed 80 characters (in older versions of Mplus) or 90 characters (in newer versions) will be truncated at the end, so that comments may be incompletely shown in the output. For comments (unlike actual commands) this may not be critical; however, comments would also be incomplete on printouts, etc.

The `data` command is used to inform Mplus about the name, type, and location of the data file to be used. If the data set is saved in the same folder as the Mplus input file, no specific path to the data set needs to be specified in the Mplus input. The `variable` command is used to define the names of the variables in the data set as well as to define the missing value code (see also Section 1.1). Using the subcommand `names =,` the variable names are defined. It is important to list the variable names in the correct order in which they appear in the data set. Furthermore, it is important to know that in Mplus, variable names cannot be longer than eight characters. It is convenient to import variable names directly from SPSS using the SPSS option **Utilities → Variables**. This option is illustrated in Figures 2.2 and 2.3.

Another advantage of this procedure is that the variable names will be identical in both programs. Of course, this requires that variable names be defined that are fewer or equal to eight characters in SPSS as well. It is also important to check whether SPSS provides the variable names in the correct order when using the **Utilities → Variables** option. Furthermore, it is important to know that each subcommand in Mplus has to end with a semicolon (`;`). Missing semicolons are probably the most common cause of error messages in Mplus. Using the `missing` subcommand, we tell Mplus how missing values are coded. In our example, we coded missing values as –99 (cf. Section 1.1). We add the following additional subcommand under `variable`: `missing = all (-99);.` Using the command `analyses: type = basic;` we request descriptive statistics that we can then compare to the descriptive statistics in SPSS. By clicking on *run* (or hitting the combination CTRL + R), the basic analysis is executed. Box 2.1 gives an overview of some basic rules of Mplus syntax. Subsequently, we discuss the results of the `BASIC` analysis.

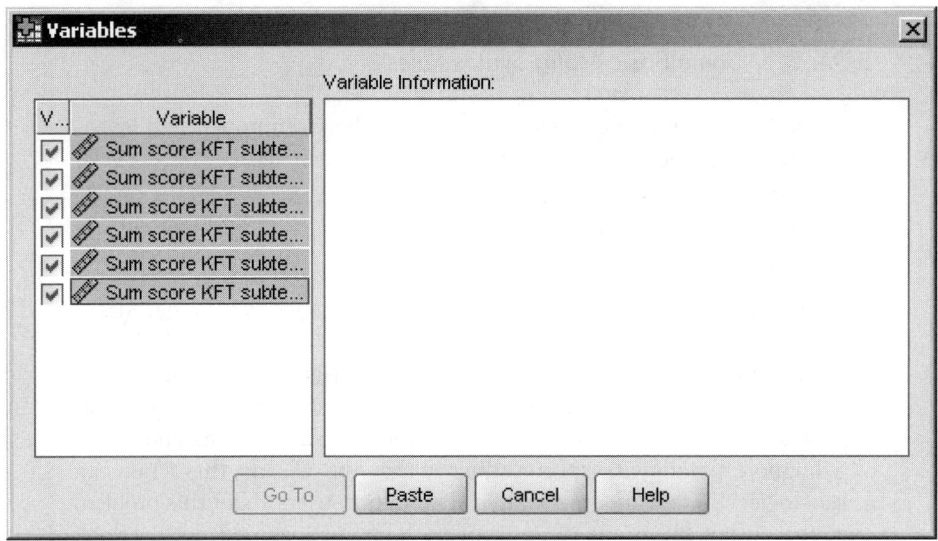

FIGURE 2.2. Exporting variable names from SPSS via the menu option **Utilities → Variables** in SPSS. On the left-hand side, all variable names are highlighted. By clicking on **Paste**, the variable names are added to an SPSS syntax window (see Figure 2.3).

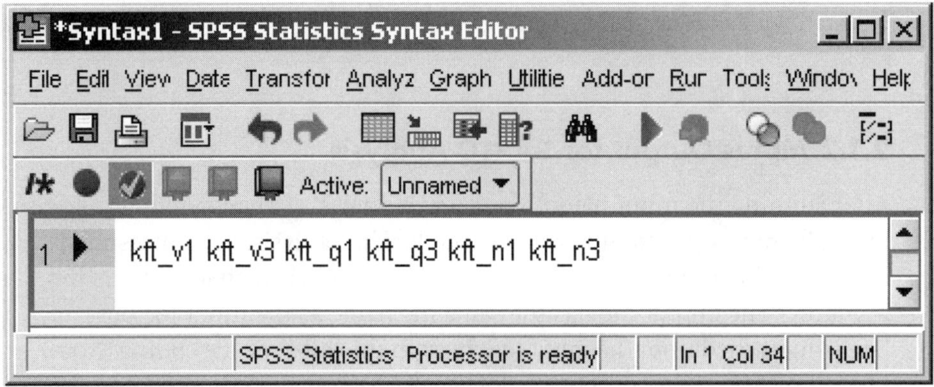

FIGURE 2.3. Variable names in the SPSS syntax window. The names can now be copied and pasted into an Mplus syntax under `variable: names =`. Note that the correct order of the variable names in the SPSS syntax file should be checked before transferring the names to Mplus.

BOX 2.1. *Some Basic Mplus Syntax Rules*

- In the Mplus syntax no differences are made between upper- and lower-case letters. (In other words, Mplus is not case sensitive.)
- In addition, the order in which different commands are listed is largely arbitrary.
- Every command line has to end with a semicolon (`;`).
- A single command line should not exceed 90 characters (in older Mplus versions, only 80 characters were allowed per line). Longer lines can occur, for example, when there is a long list of variables to read into Mplus or when a long file path has to be specified. Lines that are too long will be cut after 80/90 characters (depending on the program version), and Mplus will ignore all following specifications in that line. Clearly, this action can lead to very significant errors. Mplus will inform users about this problem in the output by means of an error message. One should not overlook or ignore this error message. A simple way to deal with the problem of overly long lines is to simply break the lines using the ENTER key on the keyboard.
- Variable names cannot be longer than eight characters.
- Each line of comment has to start with an exclamation mark. Comments appear in green font in the input and output. Comments do not have to end with a specific symbol; however, every new line of comment has to start with an exclamation mark again.

2.1.2 Mplus Output for `BASIC` Analysis

After running the input file for the `basic` analysis, a new window automatically pops up containing the output for the analysis. The corresponding output file is automatically saved to the same folder that contains the input file. The output file has the same file name as the input file but can be distinguished from the input file through the different file ending (*.out instead of *.inp). The output file for our `BASIC` analysis is shown in the following. First of all, the commands used to specify the analysis are reproduced in the output. This is useful because it allows us to review the input specifications to check if everything is set up correctly. In addition, that way, the input specifications will be included in any printout of the results.

```
Mplus VERSION 6.1
MUTHEN & MUTHEN
11/10/2011   4:36 PM
```

```
INPUT INSTRUCTIONS

  title: Read data set "KFT.dat" in Mplus
         Check that the data set is read correctly in Mplus
         using the TYPE = BASIC option
         Here: Using the Mplus default with FIML estimation
         including missing data

  data: file = KFT.dat;

  ! This is a comment
  variable: names = kft_v1 kft_v3 kft_q1 kft_q3 kft_n1 kft_n3;
            missing = all(-99);

  analysis: type = basic;
```

Next, we receive the following warning message, which is caused by the fact that in our data set, 131 students had missing values on *all six* variables:

```
*** WARNING
  Data set contains cases with missing on all variables.
  These cases were not included in the analysis.
  Number of cases with missing on all variables:  131
   1 WARNING(S) FOUND IN THE INPUT INSTRUCTIONS
```

This message appears because Mplus, by default, uses FIML estimation with missing data (e.g., see Enders, 2010). This procedure cannot be used for participants who have no valid scores on any of the variables, because these individuals do not provide any information about the variables.

Following is the title and some technical information about the analysis with regard to, for example, the sample size, the variables used in the analysis, and the data structure in general:

```
Read data set "KFT.dat" in Mplus
Check that the data set is read correctly in Mplus
using the TYPE = BASIC option
Here: Using the Mplus default with FIML estimation
including missing data

SUMMARY OF ANALYSIS

Number of groups                                                 1
Number of observations                                         456

Number of dependent variables                                    6
Number of independent variables                                  0
Number of continuous latent variables                            0
```

```
Observed dependent variables

  Continuous
   KFT_V1      KFT_V3      KFT_Q1      KFT_Q3      KFT_N1      KFT_N3

Estimator                                                        ML
Information matrix                                         OBSERVED
Maximum number of iterations                                   1000
Convergence criterion                                     0.500D-04
Maximum number of steepest descent iterations                    20
Maximum number of iterations for H1                            2000
Convergence criterion for H1                              0.100D-03

Input data file(s)
  KFT.dat

Input data format  FREE
```

This information is useful to check, among other things, that the correct data set was used as well as the intended variables. For `Number of observations` we can see that 456 students contributed one or more values (here, those cases that have missing data on all six variables are already excluded). Next is a summary of the missing data patterns that occurred in the present application:

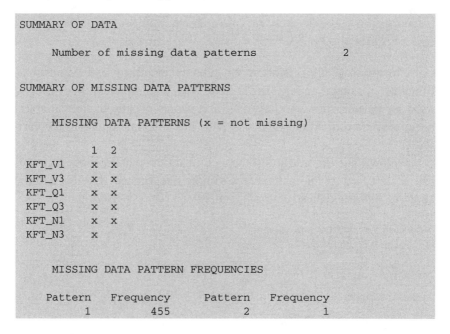

```
SUMMARY OF DATA

     Number of missing data patterns             2


SUMMARY OF MISSING DATA PATTERNS


     MISSING DATA PATTERNS (x = not missing)

           1  2
 KFT_V1    x  x
 KFT_V3    x  x
 KFT_Q1    x  x
 KFT_Q3    x  x
 KFT_N1    x  x
 KFT_N3    x


     MISSING DATA PATTERN FREQUENCIES

    Pattern   Frequency     Pattern   Frequency
          1         455           2           1
```

Under `SUMMARY OF DATA` we see that two distinct missing data patterns occurred in this example. Under `SUMMARY OF MISSING DATA PATTERNS` Mplus shows what those patterns were. Each missing data pattern is represented by a separate column (with the exception of the pattern in which all values are missing, which is not shown). Column 1 (missing data pattern 1) contains only "x's," indicating that this is the pattern in which *no* missing data occurred. The second column contains "x's" except for the last variable KFT_N3. This means that individuals with pattern 2 have valid scores on all variables except for the variable KFT_N3.

The section on MISSING DATA PATTERN FREQUENCIES shows that of the 456 students, all but one student contributed complete data (values on all six variables): 455 students showed missing data pattern 1 (frequency = 455), whereas only one student showed missing data pattern 2 (frequency = 1), that is, a missing value on KFT_N3.

The covariance coverage shows us the proportion of cases that contributes values for the calculation of each variance or covariance. In our case, for the variances and covariances, those are 100% of cases, with the exception of the variance and covariances that are associated with variable KFT_N3 (only 99.8% of cases contribute to this variable because of the one student who has a missing value on this variable). The minimum acceptable value for the covariance coverage is 10% according to the Mplus default ("Minimum covariance coverage value 0.100"). If the covariance coverage fell below this value, Mplus would no longer estimate a model by default because the coverage would be seen as too weak.

```
COVARIANCE COVERAGE OF DATA

Minimum covariance coverage value   0.100

     PROPORTION OF DATA PRESENT

           Covariance Coverage
              KFT_V1        KFT_V3        KFT_Q1        KFT_Q3        KFT_N1
              ________      ________      ________      ________      ________
 KFT_V1         1.000
 KFT_V3         1.000         1.000
 KFT_Q1         1.000         1.000         1.000
 KFT_Q3         1.000         1.000         1.000         1.000
 KFT_N1         1.000         1.000         1.000         1.000         1.000
 KFT_N3         0.998         0.998         0.998         0.998         0.998

           Covariance Coverage
              KFT_N3
              ________
 KFT_N3         0.998
```

Note that the covariance coverage does not refer to the actual variances and covariances of the variables, but instead simply informs us about the "completeness" of the data (the amount of data available to calculate those statistics). The actual estimated sample variances and covariances are obtained next, under the header RESULTS FOR BASIC ANALYSIS/ESTIMATED SAMPLE STATISTICS:

```
RESULTS FOR BASIC ANALYSIS

ESTIMATED SAMPLE STATISTICS

Means
KFT_V1        KFT_V3        KFT_Q1        KFT_Q3        KFT_N1        KFT_N3
________      ________      ________      ________      ________      ________
11.904         8.978        12.377         7.730        11.088         8.277


           Covariances
              KFT_V1        KFT_V3        KFT_Q1        KFT_Q3        KFT_N1
              ________      ________      ________      ________      ________
 KFT_V1        21.592
 KFT_V3        10.761        17.938
 KFT_Q1         6.010         5.267        11.235
 KFT_Q3         4.645         4.406         4.027         6.754
 KFT_N1        11.072        11.644         6.870         6.111        29.826
 KFT_N3         6.347         7.190         4.415         3.986         9.298


           Covariances
              KFT_N3
              ________
 KFT_N3        11.782


           Correlations
              KFT_V1        KFT_V3        KFT_Q1        KFT_Q3        KFT_N1
              ________      ________      ________      ________      ________
 KFT_V1         1.000
 KFT_V3         0.547         1.000
 KFT_Q1         0.386         0.371         1.000
 KFT_Q3         0.385         0.400         0.462         1.000
 KFT_N1         0.436         0.503         0.375         0.431         1.000
 KFT_N3         0.398         0.495         0.384         0.447         0.496


           Correlations
              KFT_N3
              ________
 KFT_N3         1.000

MAXIMUM LOG-LIKELIHOOD VALUE FOR THE UNRESTRICTED (H1) MODEL IS -7152.289

     Beginning Time:  16:36:14
        Ending Time:  16:36:15
       Elapsed Time:  00:00:01


MUTHEN & MUTHEN
3463 Stoner Ave.
Los Angeles, CA  90066

Tel: (310) 391-9971
Fax: (310) 391-8971
Web: www.StatModel.com
Support: Support@StatModel.com

Copyright (c) 1998-2010 Muthen & Muthen
```

The descriptive statistics obtained for each of the six observed KFT variables (i.e., the estimated means, variances, covariances, and product–moment correlations of the variables) were estimated using the FIML procedure. Therefore, the statistics in this form are not directly comparable to the corresponding statistics calculated in SPSS. The reason is that SPSS statistics are based either on pairwise or listwise deletion of cases rather than on FIML estimation.

In order to directly compare Mplus and SPSS descriptive statistics, one can request the use of listwise deletion in Mplus rather than the default (FIML). Note that we discourage the use of listwise deletion in later analysis steps that involve actual model fitting. The procedure is used here for technical reasons only, in order to facilitate the process of checking the proper data entry into Mplus. In later analysis steps, researchers should consider using more advanced missing data analytic techniques, such as FIML, as described by Enders (2010) or by Schafer and Graham (2002), because these techniques are usually more reasonable than listwise deletion.

Listwise deletion of cases is obtained in Mplus by adding the subcommand `listwise = on;` under the `data` command. The `listwise = on;` subcommand deactivates the FIML procedure and excludes all cases that have missing data on at least one of the variables included in the analysis. Note that FIML has been the default since Mplus version 5. In previous versions of the program through Mplus version 4, listwise deletion was the default.

The extended Mplus syntax using listwise deletion is shown in Figure 2.4. The resulting descriptive statistics are shown below. For comparison, the corresponding SPSS statistics (with listwise deletion) are shown in Figure 2.5. The SPSS statistics were generated using the SPSS option **Analyze → Scale → Reliability Analysis → Statistics → Descriptives for Item/Inter-Item Covariances/Correlations**. The results are identical to the Mplus results, rounded to three decimals, which shows us that the data set **KFT.dat** was apparently correctly read by Mplus. In addition, SPSS returns the same sample size (N = 455 listwise cases). After this check, we can start the first actual model in Mplus (see Chapter 3).

```
SAMPLE STATISTICS [Now based on listwise deletion of cases]

Means
KFT_V1       KFT_V3       KFT_Q1       KFT_Q3       KFT_N1       KFT_N3
________     ________     ________     ________     ________     ________
11.899        8.974       12.387        7.732       11.112        8.281
```

```
           Covariances
              KFT_V1        KFT_V3        KFT_Q1        KFT_Q3        KFT_N1
              ________      ________      ________      ________      ________
 KFT_V1        21.677
 KFT_V3        10.799        18.008
 KFT_Q1         6.057         5.310        11.242
 KFT_Q3         4.669         4.429         4.038         6.783
 KFT_N1        11.172        11.745         6.794         6.120        29.686
 KFT_N3         6.383         7.230         4.417         4.001         9.294


           Covariances
              KFT_N3
              ________
 KFT_N3        11.811


           Correlations
              KFT_V1        KFT_V3        KFT_Q1        KFT_Q3        KFT_N1
              ________      ________      ________      ________      ________
 KFT_V1         1.000
 KFT_V3         0.547         1.000
 KFT_Q1         0.388         0.373         1.000
 KFT_Q3         0.385         0.401         0.462         1.000
 KFT_N1         0.440         0.508         0.372         0.431         1.000
 KFT_N3         0.399         0.496         0.383         0.447         0.496


           Correlations
              KFT_N3
              ________
 KFT_N3         1.000
```

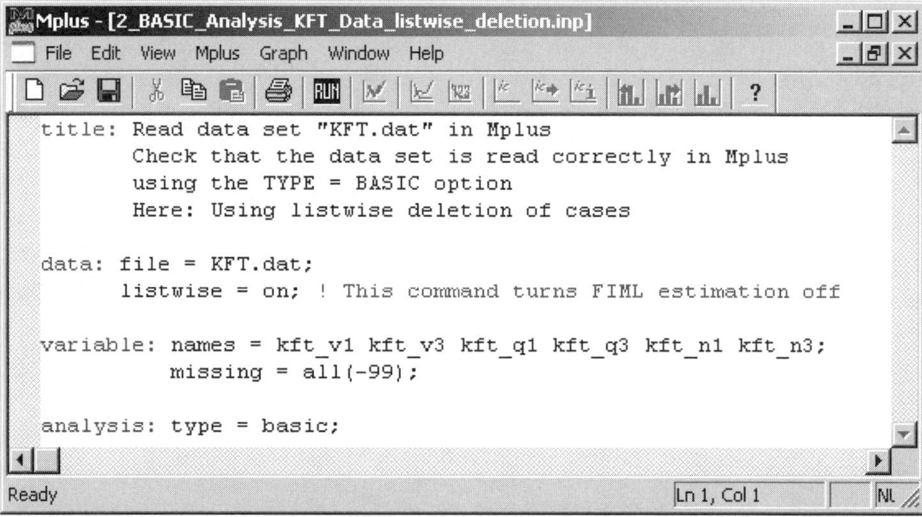


```
title: Read data set "KFT.dat" in Mplus
       Check that the data set is read correctly in Mplus
       using the TYPE = BASIC option
       Here: Using listwise deletion of cases

data: file = KFT.dat;
      listwise = on; ! This command turns FIML estimation off

variable: names = kft_v1 kft_v3 kft_q1 kft_q3 kft_n1 kft_n3;
          missing = all(-99);

analysis: type = basic;
```

FIGURE 2.4. Modified Mplus input file for the `basic` analysis, now with FIML estimation turned off. This file generates descriptive statistics based on a listwise deletion of cases that can be more easily compared to results in SPSS.

Item Statistics

	Mean	Std. Deviation	N
Sum score KFT subtest kft_v1	11.8989	4.65585	455
Sum score KFT subtest kft_v3	8.9736	4.24360	455
Sum score KFT subtest kft_q1	12.3868	3.35293	455
Sum score KFT subtest kft_q3	7.7319	2.60434	455
Sum score KFT subtest kft_n1	11.1121	5.44845	455
Sum score KFT subtest kft_n3	8.2813	3.43665	455

Inter-Item Covariance Matrix

	Sum score KFT subtest kft_v1	Sum score KFT subtest kft_v3	Sum score KFT subtest kft_q1	Sum score KFT subtest kft_q3	Sum score KFT subtest kft_n1	Sum score KFT subtest kft_n3
Sum score KFT subtest kft_v1	21.677	10.799	6.057	4.669	11.172	6.383
Sum score KFT subtest kft_v3	10.799	18.008	5.310	4.429	11.745	7.230
Sum score KFT subtest kft_q1	6.057	5.310	11.242	4.038	6.794	4.417
Sum score KFT subtest kft_q3	4.669	4.429	4.038	6.783	6.120	4.001
Sum score KFT subtest kft_n1	11.172	11.745	6.794	6.120	29.686	9.294
Sum score KFT subtest kft_n3	6.383	7.230	4.417	4.001	9.294	11.811

Inter-Item Correlation Matrix

	Sum score KFT subtest kft_v1	Sum score KFT subtest kft_v3	Sum score KFT subtest kft_q1	Sum score KFT subtest kft_q3	Sum score KFT subtest kft_n1	Sum score KFT subtest kft_n3
Sum score KFT subtest kft_v1	1.000	.547	.388	.385	.440	.399
Sum score KFT subtest kft_v3	.547	1.000	.373	.401	.508	.496
Sum score KFT subtest kft_q1	.388	.373	1.000	.462	.372	.383
Sum score KFT subtest kft_q3	.385	.401	.462	1.000	.431	.447
Sum score KFT subtest kft_n1	.440	.508	.372	.431	1.000	.496
Sum score KFT subtest kft_n3	.399	.496	.383	.447	.496	1.000

FIGURE 2.5. Descriptive statistics for the six KFT variables produced in SPSS through the option **Analyze → Scale → Reliability → Statistics → Descriptive Statistics for Items/Inter-Items → Covariances/Correlations**. The values match the Mplus estimates obtained under the `listwise = on;` option.

2.2 IMPORTING AND ANALYZING SUMMARY DATA (COVARIANCE OR CORRELATION MATRICES)

As already mentioned at the beginning of this chapter, it is sometimes practical to use summary data rather than individual data for an analysis. Summary data are, for example, covariance or correlation matrices, sometimes supplemented by the means and/or standard deviations of all variables. We now show the procedure of reading summary data into Mplus using the six KFT variables as an example. The simplest way to enter summary data is to copy and paste the covariance or correlation matrix into a simple text file. For this purpose one can use, for example, the simple Editor program in Windows (**Start → Programs → Accessories**) or WordPad.

Figure 2.6 shows an example of a text file that contains the means (first row), standard deviations (second row), and product moment correlation matrix of the six observed KFT variables (the file is located on the companion website and is named **KFT_summary-data.txt**). The data shown in this text file can easily be used by Mplus to estimate, for example, an SEM. The Mplus syntax to read the data from the file **KFT_summary-data.txt** is shown in Figure 2.7. The `data` command is again used to define the name of the data set. In addition, it has to be specified what *type* of summary statistics are being read from this file. In our case the subcommand `type = means std corr;` means that the data set **KFT_summary-data.txt** contains the means (`means`) followed by the standard deviations (`std`) and correlations (`corr`) of the variables. Note that the order of the subcommands is important. (They have to be in line with the order in which the summary statistics appear in the data file.) To read a covariance matrix, one would use the subcommand `cova` instead of `corr`.

The additional subcommand `nobservations = 455;` is used to specify the sample size (number of individuals on which the summary data set is based). In this case, the data are based on $N = 455$ listwise

KFT_summary-data.txt - Notepad

File Edit Format View Help

```
11.899  8.974  12.387  7.732  11.112  8.281
 4.656  4.244   3.353  2.604   5.448  3.437

1.000
 .547  1.000
 .388   .373  1.000
 .385   .401   .462  1.000
 .440   .508   .372   .431  1.000
 .399   .496   .383   .447   .496  1.000
```

FIGURE 2.6. Text file with summary data for the six KFT variables. The first line contains the means of the variables. The second line contains their standard deviations. The matrix contains the product–moment correlations of the variables. Figure 2.7 shows how these data can be properly processed in Mplus.

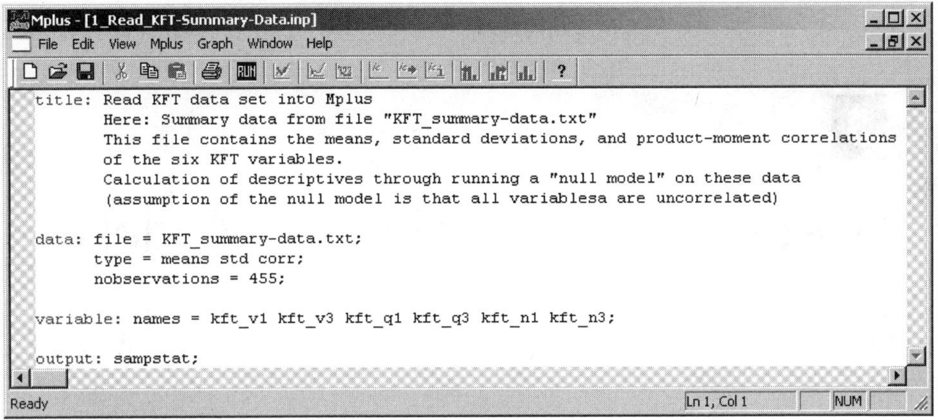

FIGURE 2.7. Mplus input file for reading the summary data shown in Figure 2.6. The `basic` option is not available for summary data. Therefore, descriptive statistics for data checking are requested via the `output: sampstat;` option. Given that we do not explicitly specify a model for the data, by default Mplus estimates a so-called *null model* for all variables listed under `variable: names =`.

cases. This information has to be provided, because it is not possible for Mplus to infer the number of observations from the summary data set (whereas this is possible for individual data). The option `variable: names =` is again used to define variable names—which also are not given in the data file.

The `BASIC` option is not available for summary data in Mplus. For this reason, descriptive statistics for data checking are now requested using the option `output: sampstat;`. The abbreviation `sampstat` stands for *sample statistics* and provides us with descriptive statistics for the six variables (in this case, the observed means and the covariance matrix will be provided). Given that no model is explicitly specified, by default Mplus estimates a so-called *null model* (sometimes referred to as an *independence model*). The null model assumes that there are no relationships among any of the six variables. The only model parameters to be estimated in this model are the means and variances of the observed variables. The output for this analysis is not shown here but can be found on the companion website.

The next chapter provides an introduction to the basics of model specification in Mplus using linear SEMs as an example. I first consider simple linear regression models and subsequently more complex SEMs such as confirmatory factor analysis and latent path analysis.

3

Linear Structural Equation Models

3.1 WHAT ARE LINEAR SEMs?

Linear SEMs with latent variables (often called *covariance structure models*) are used to model complex relationships between continuous variables at the latent level, that is, at the levels of variables that are corrected for measurement error. Linear SEMs can also be viewed as multivariate regression models. In these models, structural relationships between multiple dependent variables and multiple independent variables can be analyzed simultaneously. Variables that serve exclusively as independent variables are referred to as *exogenous variables*, because variability in these variables is not explained by other variables in the model. For exogenous variables, only nondirectional relationships (e.g., covariances or correlations) are analyzed.

Variables that are regressed on one or more other variables in the model are called *endogenous variables*. Endogenous variables that serve as independent and dependent variables at the same time are called *intervening variables* or *mediator variables*, because those variables mediate the relationship between other variables. Mediated effects are frequently of interest and often examined using manifest or latent path analysis, as discussed in detail in Section 3.5.

Linear SEMs with latent variables can be described as consisting of two parts (see Figure 3.1): a *measurement model* and a *structural* (or *latent variable*) *model*. The parameters pertaining to both parts are estimated

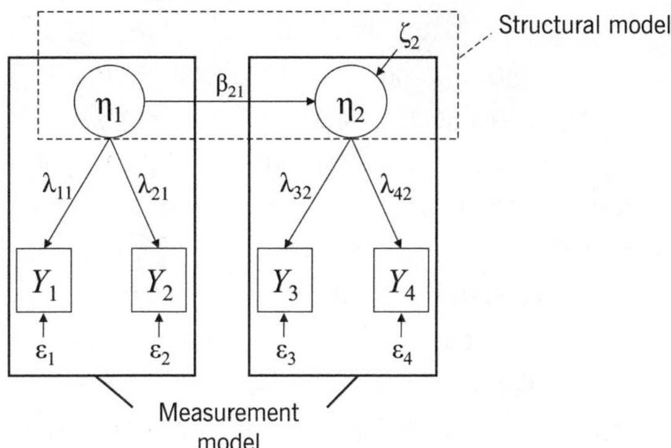

FIGURE 3.1. Path diagram of a simple structural equation model with two latent variables (η_1 and η_2), each of which is measured by two indicators (Y_1 and Y_2 are indicators of η_1, whereas Y_3 and Y_4 are indicators of η_2). The parameters λ_{11}–λ_{42} denote factor loadings. The variables ε_1–ε_4 are residual (error) variables. In the structural model, the latent regression of the factor η_2 on η_1 is estimated. In this latent regression, β_{21} denotes the regression slope coefficient and ζ_2 denotes a latent residual variable.

simultaneously. In the measurement model, the researcher specifies how the latent variables (or *factors*; here indicated as η_j) are measured using observed (manifest) variables (Y_i) as indicators. It is often assumed that the latent variables are responsible for the covariance between different indicators of the same construct (so-called *reflective* measurement model). This means that variation in the latent variable is assumed to cause variation in the indicators and to explain relationships between different indicators.

The manifest and latent variables are connected via linear regressions in the measurement model. In reflective measurement models the indicators serve as dependent variables, whereas the latent variables are independent variables (in so-called *formative measurement models* this is reversed; however, formative measurement models are not discussed in this book). The regression coefficients λ_{ij} of these regressions are often referred to as *factor loadings*. In the structural (latent variable) model, relationships between the latent variables are specified, either through covariances, latent regressions, or path analyses. If the structural model consists only of covariances between latent variables (i.e., nondirectional relationships), the analysis is often referred to as a *confirmatory factor analysis* (CFA; see Section 3.4). If the structural model includes directional paths (regressions) between latent variables, the model could be referred to as a *latent regression analysis* (see Figure 3.1 as well as Section 3.3 for an example). If multiple latent endogenous variables are considered, the model is often referred to as a *latent path analysis* (see Section 3.5).

An important advantage of linear SEMs with latent variables is that the use of latent variables allows researchers to explicitly account for measurement error in the analysis. As a consequence, the relationships between variables in the structural model can be more accurately estimated compared to conventional correlation, regression, or path analyses at the level of manifest variables. In addition, SEMs allow researchers to test complex relationships between variables through formal model tests. It is also possible to compare competing models statistically against each other.

SEMs are very flexible and can be used to analyze a variety of complex research questions. For example, SEMs can be used to analyze variability and change in longitudinal studies, to separate stable from time-specific influences on psychological measurements (see Section 4.2 as well as Steyer, Ferring, & Schmitt, 1992; Steyer, Schmitt, & Eid, 1999), to test for measurement variance (Section 4.1.4), and to analyze latent change (Sections 4.3–4.5) and latent growth curves (Section 4.5; see also Bollen & Curran, 2006; Duncan, Duncan, & Strycker, 2006; Steyer, Eid, & Schwenkmezger, 1997). In addition, SEMs are often used to analyze complex data observed from multiple sources of information (so-called *multimethod data*; see Eid et al., 2008; Eid, Lischetzke, & Nussbeck, 2006; Geiser, 2009).

In order to graphically illustrate SEMs, path diagrams like the one shown in Figure 3.1 are often used. In this book, I frequently use path diagrams (instead of mathematical equations) to illustrate the models analyzed in Mplus. In path diagrams, observed variables (manifest variables, indicators) are typically shown in boxes, whereas not directly observed variables (latent variables, latent factors) are typically shown in circles or ellipses. Directional relationships (regressions) are symbolized through single-headed arrows (→). The variable that emits the arrow is the independent variable (predictor, regressor) with respect to the variable to which the arrow points. All variables that "receive" an arrow are considered endogenous (dependent) variables. Variables that only emit paths but do not receive unidirectional paths are referred to as exogenous variables.

Straight or curved double-headed arrows (↔) indicate nondirectional relationships (i.e., covariances or correlations). In this book, manifest variables are indicated by the letter Y or with the actual variable name. Latent variables are indicated by η or receive a substantive label that characterizes their meaning. Error variables (residual variables) associated with manifest variables are indicated by ε, and latent variable residuals are indicated by ζ.

Useful introductory textbooks on the theory of linear SEMs are, for example, books by Bollen (1989), Kaplan (2009), Kline (2011), Loehlin (1998), Raykov and Marcoulides (2006), as well as Schumacker and Lomax (1996).

BOX 3.1. *Overview of the Most Important Parameters That Are Estimated in SEMs with Latent Variables and Common Notation*

Parameters of the measurement model:

- Factor loading (regression slope coefficients) λ_{ij} of the ith observed variable Y_i on the jth latent variables η_j
- Intercept α_i of the observed variable Y_i
- Residual (error) variance $Var(\varepsilon_i)$ of the observed variable Y_i
- Residual covariance $Cov(\varepsilon_i, \varepsilon_{i'})$ or correlation $Corr(\varepsilon_i, \varepsilon_{i'})$

Parameters of the structural model (model at the level of the η_j variables/factors):

- Factor variance $Var(\eta_j)$ (for exogenous factors)
- Factor mean $E(\eta_j)$ (for exogenous factors)
- Factor covariances $Cov(\eta_j, \eta_{j'})$ or correlations $Corr(\eta_j, \eta_{j'})$ (for exogenous factors)
- Latent path coefficients/regression coefficients $\beta_{jj'}$ for the regression of an endogenous factor η_j on another factor $\eta_{j'}$. In a higher-order factor model, we denote the factor loading of a lower-order factor η_j on a higher-order factor with γ_j.
- Latent intercepts for endogenous factors η_j are denoted as β_{0j} in regression or path analyses and as γ_{0j} in higher-order factor analyses.
- Latent residual variances $Var(\zeta_j)$ (for endogenous factors)
- Latent residual covariances $Cov(\zeta_j, \zeta_{j'})$ or correlations $Corr(\zeta_j, \zeta_{j'})$ (for endogenous factors)

Correlations are also denoted by r in the present book.

3.2 SIMPLE LINEAR REGRESSION ANALYSIS WITH MANIFEST VARIABLES

We introduce the basic principles of the Mplus model specification based on linear regression analysis with manifest variables, which can be seen as a special case of more complex SEMs. Our first model is a simple (bivariate) linear regression model with one manifest independent variable (IV) and one manifest dependent variable (DV).

Formally, the simple linear regression model can be written as follows (e.g., see Cohen, Cohen, West, & Aiken, 2003):

$$Y = \beta_0 + \beta_1 X + \varepsilon$$

where β_0 indicates the intercept (the expected value of Y when X is zero), β_1 indicates the slope (the expected increase in Y for a 1-unit increase in X) for the regression of the dependent variable (criterion Y) on the independent variable (predictor variable X), and ε indicates a residual variable [the difference between Y and the expected value of Y given X: $\varepsilon = Y - E(Y|X)$].

A simple way to specify and run the first model on a newly imported data set in Mplus is to use the Mplus input file for the `BASIC` analysis as a template by first saving it under a new name (so as not to overwrite the original `BASIC` analysis). The new name could be, for example, **1_simple_regression.inp** (see Figure 3.3). In the next step, one can change the syntax commands in the newly saved file in order to estimate the model shown in Figure 3.2.

For simplicity, we use listwise deletion in the following when specifying models in Mplus rather than the default FIML procedure. As noted previously, in actual analyses, users should consider using FIML when missing data are present (e.g., see Enders, 2010; Geiser et al., 2012; as well as Schafer & Graham, 2002).

BOX 3.2. *Example of Simple Linear Regression*

As a concrete example imagine that a researcher is interested in predicting numerical ability from figural ability. For simplicity we use only the variables kft_q1 (as a measure of quantitative ability; this represents the dependent variable = Y in our model) and kft_n1 (as a measure of figural ability; this is the independent variable = X). The corresponding simple linear regression model is depicted as a path diagram in Figure 3.2. This path diagram already contains the estimated Mplus model parameters in unstandardized form.

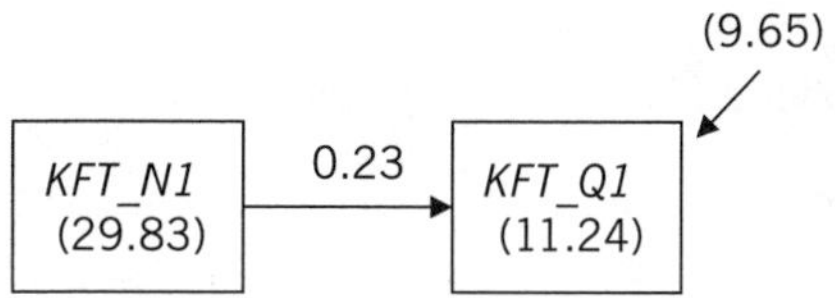

FIGURE 3.2. Path diagram of the estimated bivariate regression model for predicting the observed variable kft_q1 (quantitative ability) from kft_n1 (nonverbal/figural ability). The numbers indicate the estimated unstandardized regression coefficient (0.23) as well as the estimated variances of the variables (29.83 and 11.24) and the estimated residual variance for kft_q1 (9.65).

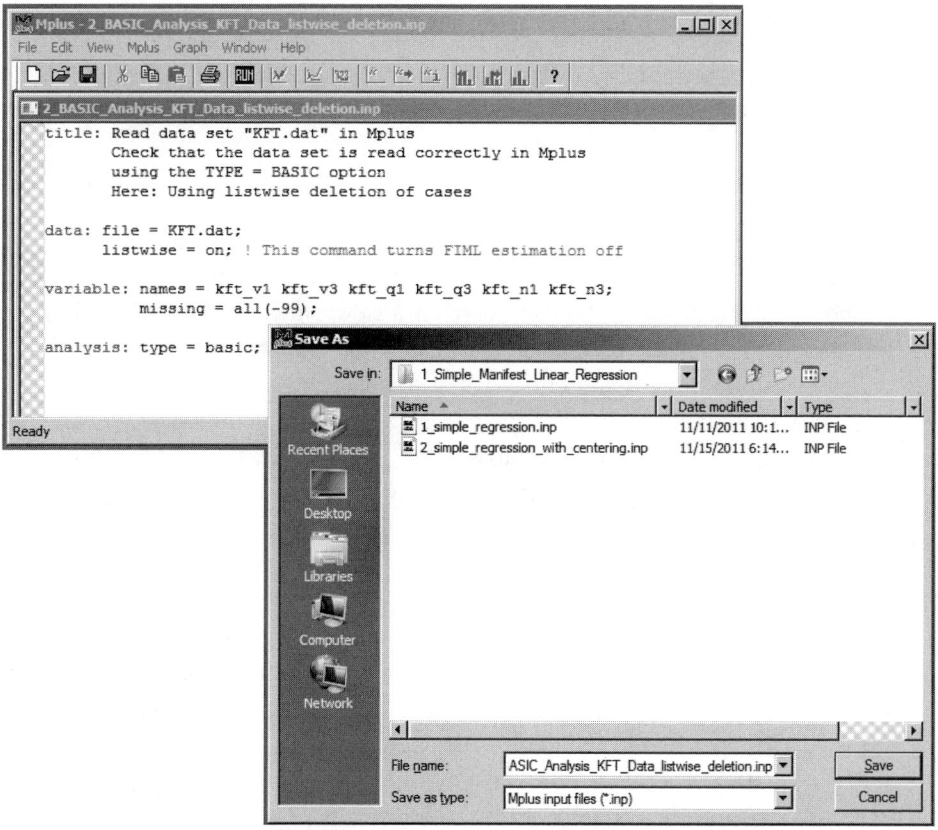

Mplus - 2_BASIC_Analysis_KFT_Data_listwise_deletion.inp

File Edit View Mplus Graph Window Help

2_BASIC_Analysis_KFT_Data_listwise_deletion.inp

```
title: Read data set "KFT.dat" in Mplus
       Check that the data set is read correctly in Mplus
       using the TYPE = BASIC option
       Here: Using listwise deletion of cases

data: file = KFT.dat;
      listwise = on; ! This command turns FIML estimation off

variable: names = kft_v1 kft_v3 kft_q1 kft_q3 kft_n1 kft_n3;
          missing = all(-99);

analysis: type = basic;
```

Ready

Save As

Save in: 1_Simple_Manifest_Linear_Regression

Recent Places
Desktop
Libraries
Computer
Network

Name	Date modified	Type
1_simple_regression.inp	11/11/2011 10:1...	INP File
2_simple_regression_with_centering.inp	11/15/2011 6:14...	INP File

File name: ASIC_Analysis_KFT_Data_listwise_deletion.inp

Save as type: Mplus input files (*.inp)

Save
Cancel

FIGURE 3.3. Saving the Mplus input file from Figure 2.1 under a new name to generate a new input file for the bivariate regression model.

BOX 3.3. *Tips for the First Model Specification*

After checking the correct data import into Mplus using the `BASIC` option (see Chapter 2), one can begin with the specification of the first actual model. In general, it is useful to start with a simple model that may represent one part of a more complex model with many variables. This approach has the advantage that possible errors or technical problems that may arise in a complex model are easier to detect in a small submodel than in a larger model. For example, if one wants to analyze a complex model with many variables, it is useful to build up the model in a step-by-step fashion (Mulaik & Millsap, 2000). This means starting with only some of the manifest variables and/or latent factors instead of including all of the variables at once. Then one can slowly increase the complexity of the model. In this way, possible errors and problems can be more easily traced back to a specific part of the model or constellation of variables. As a consequence, troubleshooting will be easier than for a complex model that already contains many variables and parameters. It can also be useful to first estimate the measurement model before placing restrictions on the structural part of the model (Mulaik & Millsap, 2000).

The Mplus specification for the bivariate linear regression model is shown in Figure 3.4. We can see that a new subcommand has been added to the variable command. The relevant command is the so-called `usevar` subcommand, which allows us to specify which variables in the data set will actually be used in the model. In our simple manifest regression model we only use the variables `kft_q1` and `kft_n1`. Therefore, the `usevar` command is specified as follows in our example:

```
usevar = kft_q1 kft_n1;
```

It is important to note that only variables that are actually used in the model should be listed under `usevar`, because Mplus assumes that all variables listed under `usevar` are part of the model. If variables listed under `usevar` are not included in the actual model specification, Mplus will automatically assume that those variables are uncorrelated with all other variables in the model (see discussion below as well as Appendix B), resulting in the following error message:

```
*** WARNING in Model command
 Variable is uncorrelated with all other variables:  KFT_N3
```

```
*** WARNING in Model command
  All least one variable is uncorrelated with all other
variables in the model.
  Check that this is what is intended.
   2 WARNING(S) FOUND IN THE INPUT INSTRUCTIONS
```

In this example, the variable kft_n3 is erroneously listed under usevar, but is not used in the actual model specification. Similar problems occur when a usevar command is entirely omitted, in which case Mplus assumes that *all* variables listed under names = are part of the model. Whenever a message like the above one appears in the output, the user should go back to the input file and add or correct the usevar subcommand and then reestimate the model based on the corrected input. Failure to do so can result in serious model misspecification and biased parameter estimates.

Note that in the analysis command the type of the analysis changes from type = basic to a type = general because Mplus does not estimate an actual model under the BASIC option. The BASIC option provides only descriptive statistics, but no actual model parameters can

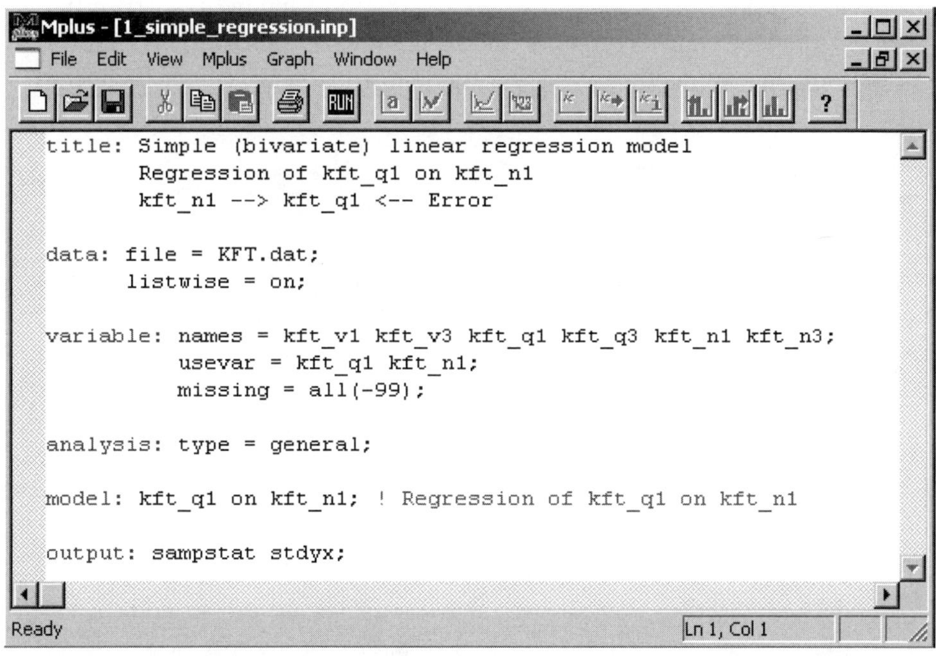

FIGURE 3.4. Mplus input file for the bivariate linear regression model from Figure 3.2.

be obtained. Two new commands have been added to this input file. The first one is the model command, which is used to specify the desired model. The second one is the output command that is used to request additional output that is not part of the Mplus default output:

```
model: kft_q1 on kft_n1;
output: sampstat stdyx;
```

The model command specifies the simple regression analysis in which kft_q1 is regressed on kft_n1. The key word on thus stands for "regressed on." Note that different types of regression analyses (e.g., logistic regression) could be requested by specifying a dependent variable as categorical (using the subcommand categorical =) and requesting a specific method of estimation (see Geiser et al., 2012, as well as Muthén & Muthén, 1998–2012).

In the output command, we request the output of descriptive statistics (the means, covariances, and correlations) for the manifest variables (keyword sampstat for "sample statistics") as well as the completely standardized solution (keyword stdyx), in addition to the Mplus default output. In the following section, the most important part of the output for the simple regression model is shown. First of all, it is important for the user to check whether the following message appears in the output:

```
INPUT READING TERMINATED NORMALLY
```

This message means that Mplus has not found any kind of fatal syntax errors that prevented the program from running the input file. For example, this message indicates that Mplus had no difficulties finding and reading the data set for the analysis. It is important to note that this message is not a guarantee that Mplus read the data correctly or that the model was correctly specified. It is still important to check the accuracy of the calculated sample size and the descriptive statistics, as well as the plausibility of the estimated model parameter estimates, even when the user has already carried out a BASIC analysis (see Section 2.1.1). In addition, this message is not a guarantee that the actual estimated statistical model converged or that all parameter estimates are proper and meaningful. Problems related to the actual *estimation* of the specific statistical model would appear further below in the Mplus output (below the sample statistics).

If the above message (INPUT READING TERMINATED NORMALLY) does *not* appear in the output, error messages will appear in its place. These messages will point to errors in the input (e.g., model) specification and/or to errors that occurred during attempts by the program to locate and read the data set. Appendix B provides an overview of typical problems with the input specification and related troubleshooting.

Under SUMMARY OF ANALYSIS Mplus reports technical details about the analysis (number of groups—here just one because it is not a multigroup analysis, number of observations, number and name of the dependent and independent manifest and latent variables in the model, name and format of the data file).

```
SUMMARY OF ANALYSIS

Number of groups                                                 1
Number of observations                                         456

Number of dependent variables                                    1
Number of independent variables                                  1
Number of continuous latent variables                            0

Observed dependent variables

  Continuous
   KFT_Q1

Observed independent variables
   KFT_N1


Estimator                                                       ML
Information matrix                                        OBSERVED
Maximum number of iterations                                  1000
Convergence criterion                                    0.500D-04
Maximum number of steepest descent iterations                   20

Input data file(s)
  KFT.dat

Input data format  FREE
```

This information is useful to check whether the analysis has been done correctly, as intended by the user. In the following box, descriptive statistics (called *sample statistics* in Mplus) for the variables used in the model are shown. These values should once again be thoroughly checked for accuracy, in case anything went wrong while reading the data into

Mplus. In addition, these statistics are often useful for the interpretation of the model results. In our case, we can see that the correlation between `kft_q1` and `kft_n1` is moderately large ($r = .375$) as shown in the subsection `Correlations`.

```
SAMPLE STATISTICS


     SAMPLE STATISTICS


           Means
              KFT_Q1        KFT_N1
              ________      ________
      1        12.377        11.088


           Covariances
              KFT_Q1        KFT_N1
              ________      ________
 KFT_Q1        11.235
 KFT_N1         6.870        29.826


           Correlations
              KFT_Q1        KFT_N1
              ________      ________
 KFT_Q1         1.000
 KFT_N1         0.375         1.000
```

Following the descriptive statistics, the user should check once again for possible error messages. As mentioned above, Mplus would output additional error messages at this point if there were any kinds of specific problems related to the actual estimation of the model. Possible reasons for such types of error messages include (1) the model is not identified, (2) inadmissible estimation results are encountered (e.g., negative variance or residual variance estimates or correlations > | 1 |), or (3) when the estimation procedure failed to converge on a final optimal set of parameter estimates. In our example, no error messages appear. The model estimation terminated without problems, as is expected for a simple linear regression model with manifest variables. Therefore, we just obtain the message

```
THE MODEL ESTIMATION TERMINATED NORMALLY
```

It is important to note than the user should be cautious whenever additional messages appear at this point in the output. In this case, all following results (including the fit indices and model parameter estimates)

should be interpreted only with great caution or not at all, because severe estimation problems may have occurred.

Subsequently, a number of statistical measures are reported that can be used to evaluate the overall goodness of fit of the model under `MODEL FIT INFORMATION` (formerly referred to as `TESTS OF MODEL FIT` in older versions of Mplus). A description of these indices can be found in Box 3.7 on page 45 (for more detailed discussions, see Bollen & Long, 1993, or Schermelleh-Engel, Moosbrugger, & Müller, 2003). In our case we are analyzing just a simple linear regression model with only manifest variables. The simple regression model uses the entire information in the data to estimate model parameters. Such a model is saturated so that most of the global indices of model fit are not of great interest to us here. Saturated models always show a perfect fit with the observed data. Only the chi-square test for the baseline model (the so-called *independence model*) is relevant. The independence model assumes that all variables used in the model are uncorrelated. In our case, this means that `kft_q1` and `kft_n1` are assumed to be uncorrelated. The chi-square test for the independence model is significant in our example, $\chi^2 = 69.235$, $df = 1$, $p < .0001$, which indicates that the independence model has to be rejected. This shows us that the correlation between `kft_q1` and `kft_n1` is significantly different from zero and that the estimation of a regression model is this meaningful.

```
MODEL FIT INFORMATION

Number of Free Parameters                        3

Loglikelihood

          H0 Value                       -1163.957
          H1 Value                       -1163.957

Information Criteria

          Akaike (AIC)                    2333.913
          Bayesian (BIC)                  2346.281
          Sample-Size Adjusted BIC        2336.760
            (n* = (n + 2) / 24)

Chi-Square Test of Model Fit

          Value                              0.000
          Degrees of Freedom                     0
          P-Value                           0.0000
```

```
RMSEA (Root Mean Square Error Of Approximation)

          Estimate                                    0.000
          90 Percent C.I.                             0.000  0.000
          Probability RMSEA <- .05                    0.000

CFI/TLI

          CFI                                         1.000
          TLI                                         1.000

Chi-Square Test of Model Fit for the Baseline Model

          Value                                      69.235
          Degrees of Freedom                              1
          P-Value                                    0.0000

SRMR (Standardized Root Mean Square Residual)

          Value                                       0.000
```

Following are the parameter estimates for the model, first of all in unstandardized form (under `MODEL RESULTS`).

```
MODEL RESULTS

                                                       Two-Tailed
                    Estimate       S.E.  Est./S.E.      P-Value

 KFT_Q1    ON
    KFT_N1             0.230      0.027      8.647        0.000

 Intercepts
    KFT_Q1             9.823      0.329     29.833        0.000

 Residual Variances
    KFT_Q1             9.652      0.639     15.100        0.000
```

The first number in the column `Estimate` (0.23) is the estimated unstandardized regression slope coefficient $\hat{\beta}_1$ for the regression of `kft_q1` on `kft_n1`. In the second column, the estimated standard error (*SE*) for $\hat{\beta}_1$ is given, which is estimated to be $\hat{\sigma}_{\beta_1}$ = 0.027. The ratio estimate/*SE* (given in the third column) yields a test statistic that is equivalent to a *z*-score in large samples and that can be used for significance testing. In our example, the resulting *z*-score is 8.647. The fourth column (two-tailed *p*-value) gives the probability of the observed estimate of $\hat{\beta}_1$ under the null hypothesis that the coefficient is zero in the population for a two-tailed test. Here the *p*-value is smaller than .0001, which tells us that the slope coefficient is significantly different from zero at an α-level of .0001. This means that kft_n1 significantly predicts kft_q1 (or equivalently, that the two variables are significantly correlated).

The next row gives the estimated intercept parameter, which is $\hat{\beta}_0$ = 9.823. The intercept is also statistically significant (z = 29.833). Using the estimates for $\hat{\beta}_1$ and $\hat{\beta}_0$ we can formulate the regression equation for our example:

$$\texttt{kft\_q1} = 9.823 + 0.23\ \texttt{kft\_n1} + \varepsilon$$

This means that for individuals with a kft_n1 score of zero (none of the items solved correctly), a score of 9.823 on kft_q1 is predicted. Furthermore, according to this equation, the expected increase in the kft_q1 score for a one-unit increase in the kft_n1 score is 0.23 points.

The third row of the MODEL RESULTS table (p. 36) provides us with the unstandardized residual variance (estimated variance of the error variable ε). Here the error of variance equals $\hat{\sigma}_\varepsilon^2$ = 9.652. The value of the error variance becomes meaningful when we relate it to the total variance of the dependent variable ($\hat{\sigma}_Y^2$). The total variance of the dependent variable can be found under SAMPLE STATISTICS in the upper part of the output (in the main diagonal of the covariance matrix). The estimated variance of kft_q1 is 11.235 in our example. This shows us that the residual variance (i.e., that part of the variance that is not explained in the regression analysis) is relatively large compared to the total variance of the dependent variable. In other words, only a small portion of individual differences in kft_q1 scores can be explained by individual differences in the kft_n1 scores. By calculating the so-called *coefficient of determination* (R^2), we can see that only about 14.1% of the variability in kft_q1 scores can be explained by this simple regression model:

$$\hat{R}^2 = 1 - \frac{\hat{\sigma}_\varepsilon^2}{\hat{\sigma}_Y^2} = 1 - \frac{9.652}{11.235} = .141$$

Below the unstandardized model parameter estimates, we obtain the so-called STANDARDIZED MODEL RESULTS in Mplus (here: the fully standardized or STDYX solution). This solution contains the fully standardized parameter estimates as well as the estimated R^2 value that we have just calculated by hand, using the ratio of the unstandardized residual variance to the total variance.

BOX 3.4. *Centering Independent Variables*

The intercept term β_0 in the linear regression analysis can be meaningfully interpreted only when all independent variables in the equation have a meaningful zero point. Many social science variables, however, do not have a meaningful zero point, because, for instance, zero age, zero intelligence, zero extraversion, or zero success in school are often not expected for any individual, and/or psychological scales to measure these constructs are designed in a way that scores of zero are not possible or meaningful. One way to make zero a meaningful score for such variables is to center them. *Centering* refers to the subtraction of some type of meaningful constant from each raw score. Often the arithmetic average (mean) is used for this purpose. Centering scores at the mean causes the zero point of a variable to shift to the observed mean of the variable. This results in a meaningful zero point (even if the original zero point was not meaningful), because the value of zero after centering refers to the typical (average) case in the sample (Cohen et al., 2003).

The intercept term for centered variables therefore represents the expected value on the criterion variable for individuals with an *average* value on the predictor variable, which is typically a meaningful score. Centering plays an especially important role in moderated regression (i.e., regression analysis with interaction terms; see Aiken & West, 1991) as well as in multilevel regression analysis (see Chapter 5).

In Mplus, centering is easily done through adding the subcommand `centering` to the `variable` command. In our case we add the following line to the Mplus input to center the predictor variable `kft_n1` prior to running the regression analysis (the full input/output files with the centered independent variable can be found on the companion website):

```
variable: centering = grandmean(kft_n1);
```

The `centering` subcommand causes Mplus to center the predictor variable `kft_n1` before running the regression analysis. In this case Mplus uses so-called *grand-mean centering*, which means that the overall mean of `kft_n1` is subtracted from each individual `kft_n1` score. After centering, our regression equation reads as

`kft_q1` = 12.377 + 0.23 `kft_n1` + ε

It can be seen that in a simple linear regression analysis, centering only changes the estimated intercept $\hat{\beta}_0$ (which is now 12.377 instead of 9.823 for uncentered scores), but not the estimated regression $\hat{\beta}_1$. The new intercept of 12.377 represents the expected `kft_q1` score for individuals with an average `kft_n1` score (this score is exactly identical to the `kft_q1` mean).

The estimated standardized regression slope coefficient equals 0.375 and hence is exactly identical to the bivariate correlation between kft_n1 and kft_q1 (in a bivariate regression analysis the standardized regression slope coefficient is always identical to the bivariate correlation between the predictor and the criterion variable).

```
STANDARDIZED MODEL RESULTS (STDYX Standardization)

                                                    Two-Tailed
                    Estimate       S.E.  Est./S.E.    P-Value

 KFT_Q1    ON
    KFT_N1             0.375      0.040      9.329      0.000

 Intercepts
    KFT_Q1             2.931      0.166     17.678      0.000

 Residual Variances
    KFT_Q1             0.859      0.030     28.448      0.000

R-SQUARE

    Observed                                        Two-Tailed
    Variable        Estimate       S.E.  Est./S.E.    P-Value

    KFT_Q1             0.141      0.030      4.664      0.000
```

The standardized intercept term (here, the solution with uncentered independent variable) is calculated by dividing the unstandardized intercept estimate (9.823) by the model-implied standard deviation of the dependent variable. This standard deviation is not reported directly by Mplus; however, it can be calculated as the square root of the variance $\hat{\sigma}_Y^2$ of kft_q1 ($\hat{\sigma}_Y = \sqrt{\hat{\sigma}_Y^2} = \sqrt{11.235} = 3.352$), which can be found in the sample statistics output (see above). The standardized intercept term is therefore given by 9.823/3.352 = 2.931. The standardized residual variance of 0.859 equals $1 - \hat{R}^2$ (1 – .141 = .859). This value indicates the proportion of variability in kft_q1 scores that *cannot* be explained by kft_n1 (here, approximately 85.9%).

3.3 LATENT REGRESSION ANALYSIS

The simple linear regression model described in Section 3.2 considered the relationship between quantitative and figural intelligence scores at the level of manifest variables. One important disadvantage of regression analyses with manifest variables is that these analyses make the (unrealistic) assumption that the manifest independent variables are perfectly reliable (i.e., free of measurement error). However, manifest scores typically contain random measurement error, and the results of the regression analyses (e.g., the estimated regression coefficients) may therefore be biased. (Although measurement error variance in the dependent variable is accounted for in these analyses through the residual variance, it is confounded with systematic unexplained variance, which is typically also undesirable.)

SEMs with latent variables allow us to specify regression analyses at the latent level, that is, at the level of latent variables (factors) that are corrected for measurement error. This procedure has the advantage that errors of measurement can be taken into account explicitly for both the independent and the dependent variable(s). Furthermore, SEMs with latent variables allow us to obtain estimates of the reliabilities of the manifest variables. The explicit consideration of measurement error leads to a more precise estimation of the parameters of the regression model (as parameters of a latent structural model) compared to manifest regression analyses with observed variables that are not adjusted for measurement error.

For each latent variable in a latent regression model, multiple indicators are required (at least two manifest variables for each latent variable; for reasons of identification and estimation it is better, however, to use at least three indicators per factor if possible). In this section, we show how the relationship between quantitative and figural KFT scores can be measured at the latent rather than the observed level.

BOX 3.5. *Example of Latent Regression Analysis*

In the data set KFT.dat there are two indicators for each ability facet (i.e., verbal, quantitative, and nonverbal). Therefore, we can model both quantitative and nonverbal ability through a latent factor. The manifest variables `kft_q1` and `kft_q3` are used as indicators of a quantitative ability factor (KFT_Q). The variables `kft_n1` and `kft_n3` are used as indicators of a latent variable representing nonverbal abilities (KFT_N). The regression of quantitative abilities on nonverbal abilities is modeled at the level of latent variables (i.e., in the structural model). The resulting model can be referred to as a *latent regression analysis*. It is shown as a path diagram in Figure 3.5.

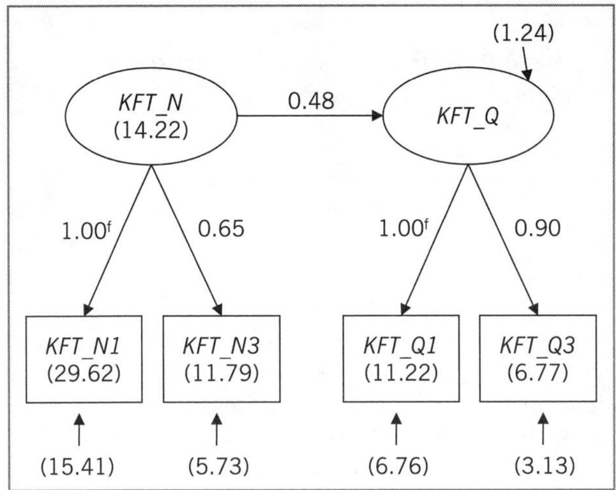

FIGURE 3.5. Latent regression model for predicting quantitative ability (factor KFT_Q) versus nonverbal ability (factor KFT_N). Each factor is measured by two indicators (manifest variables = KFT subscale scores). The values indicate the unstandardized Mplus parameter estimates (the loadings, path coefficients, and variances/residual variances). The superscript f indicates factor loadings that were fixed to 1 to identify the metric of the latent variables.

The Mplus syntax command for specifying the model shown in Figure 3.5 is depicted in Figure 3.6. First of all, note that all manifest variables that are used in the model (and only those) have to be listed under `usevariables`. The measurement models are specified in the `model` command using `by` statements. These `by` statements serve to indicate which manifest variables load onto which latent factor. The word `by` here stands for "measured by." In our example, the latent factor KFT_Q is measured by the manifest variables `kft_q1` and `kft_q3`, whereas the factor KFT_N is measured by the variables `kft_n1` and `kft_n3`.

The factor loading of the first indicator listed in each `by` statement will be fixed to 1 by default in Mplus (here the loadings of `kft_q1` and `kft_n1`). Fixing one loading per factor is necessary to assign a metric to each factor (see also Box 3.6). The loadings of all remaining indicators are freely estimated as the default.

The command `KFT_Q on KFT_N;` is used in the same way as the `on` command is used in the manifest regression analysis in Section 3.2. Here this command refers to the regression of the latent factor `KFT_Q` on the factor `KFT_N`. It therefore defines the structural part of this simple structural equation model. Residual variances for the manifest variables

BOX 3.6. Alternative Strategies for Assigning a Metric to a Latent Factor

The metric of a latent variable is arbitrary and therefore has to be defined by the user (for details see Bollen, 1989). The default setting in Mplus is that the factor loading of the first indicator listed in the `by` statement is fixed to 1 so that the metric of the factor is defined through the metric of this reference (or marker) variable. As an alternative to the fixation of one loading per factor, one can freely estimate *all* loadings and define the factor metric by fixing the factor variance (or, for endogenous variables, the residual variance) to a positive value (usually to 1). Fixing the factor variances to 1 (instead of fixing factor loadings) is sometimes useful for technical reasons in practical applications. This is the case, for example, when indicators of the same factor differ strongly in their metrics (e.g., when they have very different variances) so that the specification with one fixed loading leads to convergence problems. Another case in which one may prefer fixing the factor variances rather than the loadings is when certain parameters of the structural model (e.g., factor correlations) are supposed to be fixed to a priori hypothesized values. For example, researchers are sometimes interested in fixing factor correlations to certain values based on theory. If the factors are assigned variances of 1, fixing their correlations to a certain hypothesized value is much easier than when their variances are freely estimated. Fixing the factor variances to 1 puts the factors into a standardized metric, in which the covariance is identical to the correlation.

On the other hand, fixations of factor variances can sometimes be undesirable. This is the case, for example, in longitudinal SEMs when changes in the factor variances across time are expected or subject to a researcher's hypotheses.

As an example of how to override the Mplus default, we consider the factor `KFT_N`. To set the loading of the first indicator free, we add an asterisk (*) after the first indicator:

```
KFT_N by kft_n1* kft_n3;
```

This causes Mplus to set the first loading free. The variance of factor `KFT_N` can be fixed to 1 by adding an additional command that lists the name of the factor and adds "`@1`" after the name of the factor:

```
KFT_N@1;
```

Neither the model fit nor the standardized parameter estimates are affected by fixing the factor variance rather than the loading in this example (see output on the companion website).

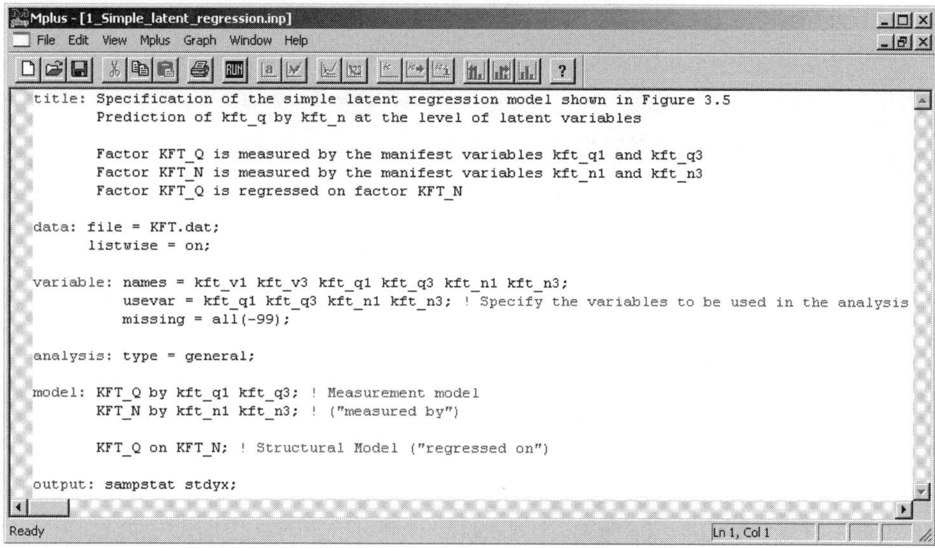

```
title: Specification of the simple latent regression model shown in Figure 3.5
       Prediction of kft_q by kft_n at the level of latent variables

       Factor KFT_Q is measured by the manifest variables kft_q1 and kft_q3
       Factor KFT_N is measured by the manifest variables kft_n1 and kft_n3
       Factor KFT_Q is regressed on factor KFT_N

data: file = KFT.dat;
      listwise = on;

variable: names = kft_v1 kft_v3 kft_q1 kft_q3 kft_n1 kft_n3;
          usevar = kft_q1 kft_q3 kft_n1 kft_n3; ! Specify the variables to be used in the analysis
          missing = all(-99);

analysis: type = general;

model: KFT_Q by kft_q1 kft_q3; ! Measurement model
       KFT_N by kft_n1 kft_n3; ! ("measured by")

       KFT_Q on KFT_N; ! Structural Model ("regressed on")

output: sampstat stdyx;
```

FIGURE 3.6. Mplus input file for the latent regression model from Figure 3.5.

and the latent dependent variable KFT_Q are estimated by Mplus as the default. All other commands shown in this input have already been discussed. By clicking on *run*, we obtain the model results (maximum likelihood estimates are the default), which are shown, in part, below:

```
MODEL FIT INFORMATION

Number of Free Parameters                         13

Loglikelihood

         H0 Value                          -4696.080
         H1 Value                          -4696.079

Information Criteria

         Akaike (AIC)                       9418.160
         Bayesian (BIC)                     9471.724
         Sample-Size Adjusted BIC           9430.466
           (n* = (n + 2) / 24)

Chi-Square Test of Model Fit

         Value                                 0.002
         Degrees of Freedom                        1
         P-Value                              0.9653
```

```
RMSEA (Root Mean Square Error Of Approximation)

          Estimate                          0.000
          90 Percent C.I.                   0.000  0.000
          Probability RMSEA <= .05          0.980

CFI/TLI

          CFI                               1.000
          TLI                               1.015

Chi-Square Test of Model Fit for the Baseline Model

          Value                           406.899
          Degrees of Freedom                    6
          P-Value                          0.0000

SRMR (Standardized Root Mean Square Residual)

          Value                             0.000
```

The model fit information shows that the model fits the data very well. The chi-square value for the target model shows that the model-implied covariance matrix and mean vector do not differ significantly from the corresponding observed values, $\chi^2 = 0.002$, $df = 1$, $p = .9635$. The chi-square value for the baseline model is very large and highly statistically significant, $\chi^2 = 406.899$, $df = 6$, $p < .0001$, which shows us that the assumption that all four observed KFT variables are unrelated is not tenable. The remaining fit statistics also indicate a good model fit, given that they all show values better than the recommended cutoff scores (see Box 3.7 for details). According to these cutoff scores, *CFI* and *TLI* should be larger than 0.95 or 0.97, and *RMSEA* and *SRMR* should both be smaller than 0.05 (Schermelleh-Engel et al., 2003). In the present example, *CFI* and *TLI* are both larger than 0.97, and *RMSEA* and *SRMR* are both smaller than 0.05. The test of close fit also leads to a positive outcome for the model. This test can be used to test the hypothesis that *RMSEA* is smaller than or equal to .05 in the population. This hypothesis is not rejected at the .05 level in the present case given that $p = .980$.

In the following (beginning on page 47), the unstandardized Mplus parameter estimates for the latent regression model from Figure 3.5 are shown. The unstandardized parameter estimates appear under the header `MODEL RESULTS`. The most important estimates are also shown in Figure 3.5.

BOX 3.7. *Criteria for Assessing Goodness of Fit in Structural Equation Modeling*

This box provides an overview of the most important tests and indices available in Mplus to assess model fit of SEM as well as common cutoff values for acceptable fit (Hu & Bentler, 1999; Schermelleh-Engel et al., 2003).

Chi-Square Test. This tests the null hypothesis that the covariance matrix and mean vector in the population are equal to the model-implied covariance matrix and mean vector (test of exact model fit). A significant chi-square value leads to the rejection of the null hypothesis that the model fits exactly in the population. The degrees of freedom of this test are calculated as the difference between the number of pieces of available information (variances, covariances, and means of the manifest variables) minus the number of estimated model parameters. In Mplus, the chi-square value, the corresponding degrees of freedom, and the *p*-value are reported as the default.

Chi-Square Difference Test. This test can be used to statistically compare two nested SEMs against each other. *Nested* means that one model is a special case of another, more general model (i.e., that it can be derived directly from this model by means of parameter constraints). Important assumptions of the test are that (1) the more general model fits the data, and (2) the additional restrictions that lead to the more restricted model do not cause parameters to be fixed to boundary values of the admissible parameter space (e.g., a variance fixed to 0 or a correlation set to 1). To conduct a chi-square difference test the difference between the chi-square values of two nested models as well as the difference in the degrees of freedom are calculated. The chi-square difference value is then tested for significance based on the difference in degrees of freedom. If the chi-square difference value is significant, this means that the more restricted model fits the data significantly worse than the more general model. Chi-square difference tests are frequently used in longitudinal modeling when the assessment of measurement invariance is of interest. Researchers can use Crayen's (2010) software, which allows calculating chi-square difference tests on the basis of Mplus outputs. This program is presented in Section 4.1.4 (Box 4.4) and is included on the companion website.

Comparative Fit Index (*CFI*). The *CFI* belongs to the family of so-called *incremental fit indices* that compare the fit of the target model to the fit of a baseline model. In Mplus, the baseline model currently is the so-called *independence model*, which assumes that the population covariance matrix of the observed variables is a diagonal matrix. This means that the observed variables are allowed to have different variances, but are assumed to have zero covariances. In other words, it is assumed that there are no relationships between any of the variables. The *CFI* indicates by how much the target model fits better than the more parsimonious independence model. For a good model, the *CFI* should be larger than 0.95 (better: larger than 0.97). The *CFI* is reported as part of the Mplus standard output.

Tucker–Lewis Index (*TLI*). The *TLI* also belongs to the family of incremental fit indices and compares the fit of the target model to the fit of the independence model. The same cutoff values as for the *CFI* apply. The *TLI* is also part of the Mplus standard output.

Root Mean Square Error of Approximation (*RMSEA*). The *RMSEA* coefficient is a measure of approximate model fit. A good model should have an *RMSEA* value smaller than 0.05. Mplus reports the point estimate of *RMSEA* as well as a 90% confidence interval around this estimate. Furthermore, a *p*-value is provided that can be used to test the null hypothesis that the population *RMSEA* is ≤ .05.

Standardized Root Mean Square Residual (*SRMR*). The *SRMR* coefficient is a standardized measure for the evaluation of the model residuals (sample minus model-implied covariances and means). Small *SRMR* values indicate that the observed variances, covariances, and means are well reproduced by the model on average. Values below .05 are usually seen as indicative of a good fit. *SRMR* is output by default in Mplus.

Information Criteria (*AIC*, *BIC*, Sample-Size Adjusted *BIC*). Information criteria can be used to compare different models on a descriptive basis. In contrast to the chi-square difference test, these indices can also be used to compare models that are not nested. As a rule, the model with the smallest value of the relevant information criterion is preferred. Information criteria are part of the Mplus standard output.

Residuals. Covariance and mean residuals can be used as measures of local (as opposed to global or omnibus) model fit. Residuals represent the difference between the observed (sample) variances, covariances, and means and the corresponding model-implied values. For each observed variance, covariance, and mean, residuals indicate how well these statistics were reproduced by the model. Residuals are therefore an important diagnostic tool to detect possible causes of global model misfit. Unstandardized covariance residuals are often hard to interpret, because they depend on the metric of the observed variables. Researchers, therefore, often study *standardized* residuals (provided as *z*-scores in Mplus) to evaluate model fit. Standardized residuals can be more easily compared across different variables, and the *z*-score metric allows us to test whether a residual is significantly different from zero. Both unstandardized and standardized residuals are available in Mplus as of version 5. They are not part of the standard output, but can be requested by the user by adding the command

```
output: residual;
```

Model Modification Indices. Using model modification indices, a researcher can examine which restrictions may be relaxed to obtain a significant improvement of the global model fit. A modification index for the single modification (a single additional parameter) is approximately equivalent to a chi-square value with 1 degree of freedom. It is therefore roughly equivalent to a chi-square difference test between the estimated model and the less restrictive model in which the corresponding restriction is relaxed. Large modification indices may indicate that a specific restriction is related to global misfit. In Mplus, modification indices can be obtained using the command

```
output: modindices;
```

Mplus also outputs the expected parameter change, that is, the actual value that is expected for the additional parameter to be estimated in a less restrictive version of the model.

Similar to residuals, modification indices often provide useful hints as to the cause of an insufficient global model fit. However, they can also sometimes lead to confusing results and often are not directly related to the true cause of a bad fit. Therefore, model modification indices should never be used in a purely data-driven way. In addition, users should always implement just one (theoretically meaningful) modification at a time. Model modifications should be theoretically justified rather than purely data-driven, and they should be validated with independent data.

```
MODEL RESULTS

                                                        Two-Tailed
                       Estimate       S.E.  Est./S.E.    P-Value

 KFT_Q    BY
    KFT_Q1                1.000      0.000    999.000    999.000
    KFT_Q3                0.903      0.094      9.588      0.000

 KFT_N    BY
    KFT_N1                1.000      0.000    999.000    999.000
    KFT_N3                0.652      0.064     10.222      0.000
```

```
KFT_Q      ON
   KFT_N                 0.476        0.056        8.467        0.000

Intercepts
   KFT_Q1               12.387        0.157       78.890        0.000
   KFT_Q3                7.732        0.122       63.398        0.000
   KFT_N1               11.112        0.255       43.552        0.000
   KFT_N3                8.281        0.161       51.457        0.000

Variances
   KFT_N                14.215        2.074        6.854        0.000

Residual Variances
   KFT_Q1                6.758        0.608       11.107        0.000
   KFT_Q3                3.128        0.395        7.921        0.000
   KFT_N1               15.406        1.591        9.683        0.000
   KFT_N3                5.734        0.644        8.911        0.000
   KFT_Q                 1.238        0.425        2.916        0.004
```

Under `KFT_Q BY KFT_Q1 KFT_Q3` and `KFT_N BY KFT_N1 KFT_N3` we obtain estimates of the unstandardized factor loadings (column `Estimate`), as well as their standard errors (`S.E.`), test statistics (`Est./S.E.`), and two-tailed *p*-values. As explained above, the first factor loading has been fixed to 1 by Mplus as the default so that the metric of each of the two latent factors is identified. For this reason, the loadings of the indicators `KFT_Q1` and `KFT_N1` do not have a standard error. The value of 999.000 in the columns `Est./S.E.` and `Two-Tailed P-Value` indicates that a significance test is not available for these parameters because they are fixed.

The loadings of the two remaining indicators (KFT_Q3 and KFT_N3) were estimated to 0.903 and 0.652, respectively, and are statistically significantly different from zero (two-tailed *p*-values < .0001). The unstandardized regression coefficient for the regression of the latent factor KFT_Q on the factor KFT_N equals 0.476 and is also statistically significantly different from zero ($z = 8.467$, $p < .0001$). This shows that the factor KFT_N is a significant predictor of the factor KFT_Q.

In addition, Mplus outputs the unstandardized intercepts and residual variances of the observed variables as well as the latent variance of the exogenous factor KFT_N and the residual variances of the endogenous factor KFT_Q. (For all latent exogenous variables, Mplus estimates the variance of these variables as a model parameter. For all latent endogenous variables, the corresponding *residual* variance is estimated.)

The standardized solution `STANDARDIZED MODEL RESULTS (STDYX Standardization)` contains fully standardized versions of the model parameters. The fully standardized factor loadings in this model can be interpreted as correlations between the observed variables and the factor on which they load (this is possible here because each variable loads only onto one factor). For example, 0.631 is the estimated correlation between the observed variable KFT_Q1 and the latent factor KFT_Q.

Under `KFT_Q ON KFT_N` the standardized regression coefficient for the latent regression of KFT_Q on KFT_N is 0.85. In the present example, this value can be interpreted as the correlation between the two latent factors, because KFT_N is the only predictor in the latent regression (this would not be true for multiple regression analyses with several correlated predictor variables). Hence, the estimated latent correlation between KFT_Q and KFT_N equals .85, indicating a very strong relationship between numeric and nonverbal abilities as measured by the KFT at the latent level.

```
STANDARDIZED MODEL RESULTS (STDYX Standardization)

                                                    Two-Tailed
                    Estimate       S.E.  Est./S.E.    P-Value

 KFT_Q    BY
    KFT_Q1             0.631      0.041     15.548      0.000
    KFT_Q3             0.733      0.040     18.247      0.000

 KFT_N    BY
    KFT_N1             0.693      0.038     18.019      0.000
    KFT_N3             0.717      0.038     18.717      0.000

 KFT_Q    ON
    KFT_N              0.850      0.049     17.245      0.000

 Intercepts
    KFT_Q1             3.698      0.131     28.177      0.000
    KFT_Q3             2.972      0.109     27.240      0.000
    KFT_N1             2.042      0.082     24.798      0.000
    KFT_N3             2.412      0.093     26.024      0.000

 Variances
    KFT_N              1.000      0.000    999.000    999.000

 Residual Variances
    KFT_Q1             0.602      0.051     11.781      0.000
    KFT_Q3             0.462      0.059      7.840      0.000
    KFT_N1             0.520      0.053      9.765      0.000
    KFT_N3             0.487      0.055      8.869      0.000
    KFT_Q              0.278      0.084      3.315      0.001
```

```
R-SQUARE

   Observed                                                Two-Tailed
   Variable           Estimate        S.E.  Est./S.E.        P-Value
   KFT_Q1                0.398       0.051      7.774          0.000
   KFT_Q3                0.538       0.059      9.124          0.000
   KFT_N1                0.480       0.053      9.010          0.000
   KFT_N3                0.513       0.055      9.359          0.000

    Latent                                                 Two-Tailed
   Variable           Estimate        S.E.  Est./S.E.        P-Value

   KFT_Q                 0.722       0.084      8.622          0.000
```

The standardized residual variances for the observed variables give the proportion of variability in each manifest variable that is *not* accounted for by the corresponding latent factor. Likewise, the latent standardized residual variance of KFT_Q (0.278) indicates that 27.8% of the variability in latent (error-free) KFT_Q scores are *not* accounted for by KFT_N.

In contrast, the estimated R^2 values indicate the proportion of variability in each endogenous variable that is explained in the model. In this example, the R^2 values equal the squared standardized factor loading of each indicator because each variable loads only onto one factor. The estimated R^2 values for the observed variables can be seen as a lower bound estimate of the reliabilities of these indicators. The values represent a lower bound because indicator- or scale-specific variance cannot be separated from random measurement error in this model. Here, the values indicate rather low reliabilities of the observed variables. Another interpretation of the rather small R^2 values is that the scales are rather heterogeneous. This implies that a relatively large part of their true score (i.e., reliable) variance is scale-specific and thus becomes confounded with measurement error in this model—leading to an underestimation of the reliabilities.

Under `R-SQUARE—Latent Variable` we can see that about 72.2% of the variability in the KFT_Q factor can be explained by the KFT_N factor, which is a pretty substantial amount. In comparison to the manifest regression analysis (see Section 3.2), in which only the two observed variables, KFT_Q1 and KFT_N1, were used and no correction for measurement error was implemented, the amount of explained variance is much higher in the latent model. This can partly be explained by the fact that the manifest model did not take measurement error into account, so that the actual strength of the relationship between the two variables was underestimated owing to the influences of random measurement error. In addition, the latent regression model used multiple indicators so that indicator-specific variance was separated out and became part of the error variance. This likely contributed to the fairly large difference in the amount of explained variance between the manifest and the latent model.

3.4 CONFIRMATORY FACTOR ANALYSIS

In this section, we discuss confirmatory factor analysis (CFA) in Mplus. An SEM is commonly referred to as a CFA when only nondirectional relationships (covariances, correlations) are assumed between the latent variables in the structural model (rather than directional paths such as latent regressions) or when the factors are assumed to be orthogonal (uncorrelated). CFA is often used to test whether a set of measures has a specific hypothesized dimensionality, for example, one-factorial, two-factorial, three-factorial, and so forth.

3.4.1 First-Order CFA

The first model tested here is a one-factor model (so-called *general factor* or *g*-factor model; see Figure 3.7), in which all six KFT scale scores load onto a single common factor. This model suggests that all six KFT scales assess a single latent ability dimension and, in addition, include only random measurement error and indicator-specific variance. If the *g*-factor model fits the data well, one would have to assume that it may be unnecessary to distinguish between verbal, numerical, and figural abilities or at least that such a distinction is not possible based on the measures used here. In more technical terms, the scales would show a lack of discriminant validity.

BOX 3.8. *Example of CFA*

As an example, consider the six KFT variables in the data set **KFT.dat**. The following research question may be of interest: Do the six KFT scales **kft_v1**, **kft_v2**, **kft_q1**, **kft_q3**, **kft_n1**, and **kft_n3** measure three distinct dimensions (verbal, quantitative, and nonverbal/figural abilities) or are they merely indicators of the single latent ability dimension, for example, a general factor of intelligence? We examine this question by means of two different first-order CFA models in Mplus. Subsequently, we also discuss the specification of a second-order CFA model.

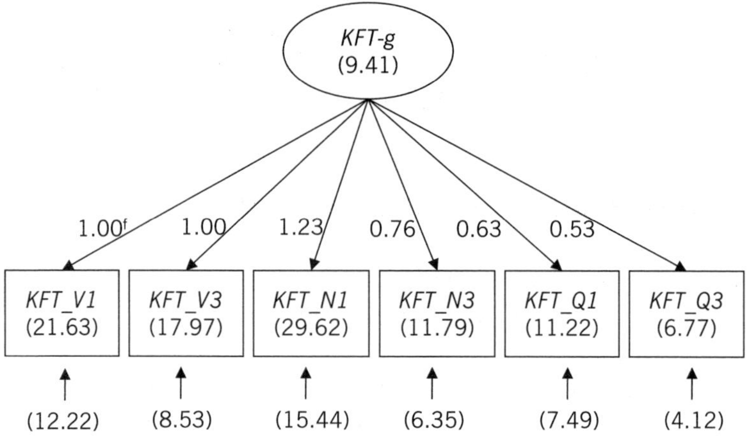

FIGURE 3.7. Single-factor (g-factor) model for the six KFT variables with unstandardized Mplus parameter estimates. The superscript f indicates that the factor loading of the first indicator (KFT_V1) was fixed to 1 to identify the metric of the latent variable.

The second model (see Figure 3.8) contains three latent factors suggesting that the six KFT scales measure three distinct dimensions of mental ability (**kft_v1** and **kft_v3** as indicators of a verbal ability factor, **kft_q1** and **kft_q3** as indicators of a quantitative/numerical ability factor, and **kft_n1** and **kft_n3** as indicators of a nonverbal/figural ability factor). A statistical comparison of the two models allows us to find out whether a one- or a three-factor model is more appropriate to represent what is measured by the KFT scales.

The Mplus input files for the one- and three-factor models are shown in Figure 3.9 and Figure 3.10, respectively. Note that as an exception, the `usevariables` command is not needed in this example, because all variables in the data set (all variables that are listed under `names =`) are actually used in the `model` statement. In all other cases, the `usevariables` command needs to be included (compare Section 3.2).

Further note that the covariances between the three latent variables in the three-factor model do not have to be explicitly specified in the Mplus input file. By default Mplus estimates all covariances between exogenous factors automatically (because none of the three factors is predicted by another variable in the model, they are all considered exogenous variables).

Sometimes a user may be interested in explicitly setting the covariance/correlation between two factors to zero (e.g., see Section 4.1.3). This

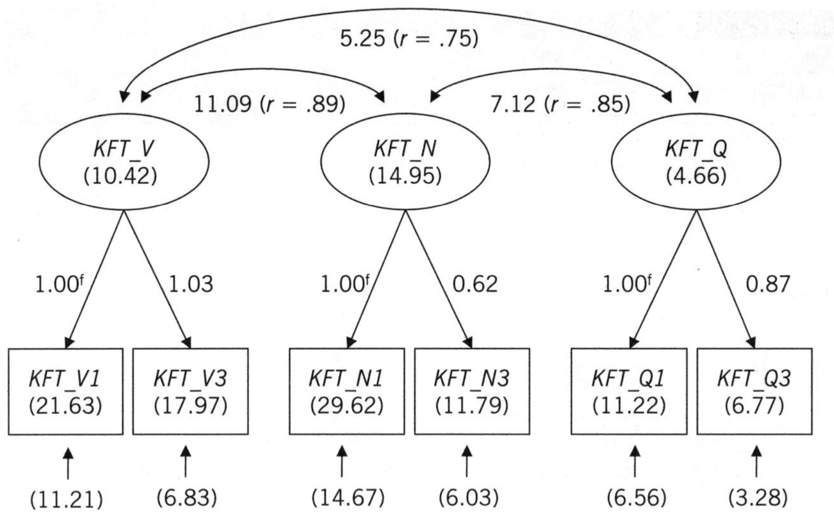

FIGURE 3.8. Three-factor model for the six KFT variables with unstandardized Mplus parameter estimates (latent correlations are given in parentheses). The superscript f indicates factor loadings that were fixed to 1 to identify the metric of the latent variables.

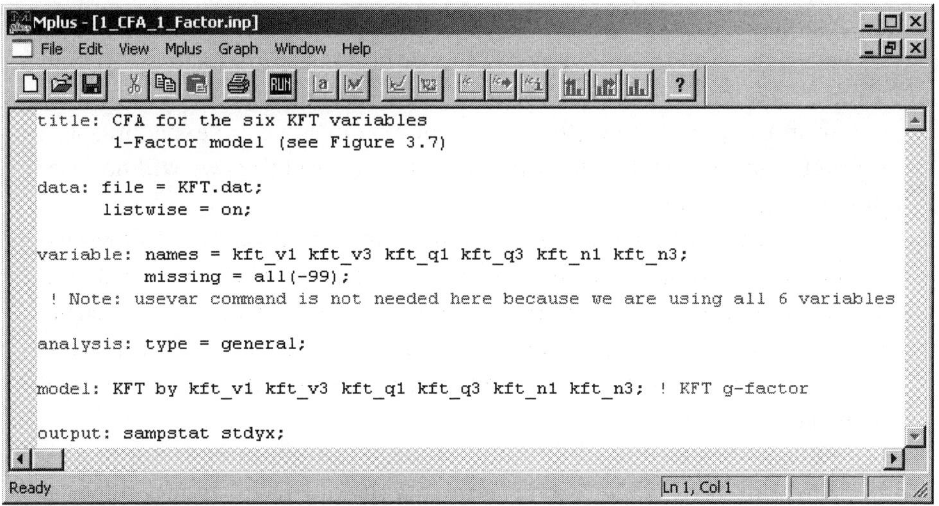

FIGURE 3.9. Mplus input file for the single-factor model from Figure 3.7.

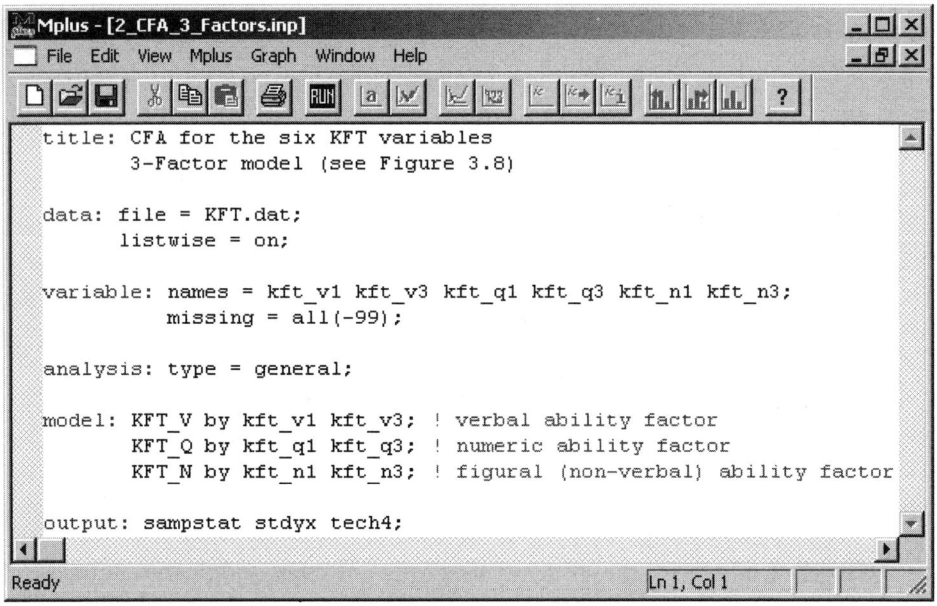

```
title: CFA for the six KFT variables
       3-Factor model (see Figure 3.8)

data: file = KFT.dat;
      listwise = on;

variable: names = kft_v1 kft_v3 kft_q1 kft_q3 kft_n1 kft_n3;
          missing = all(-99);

analysis: type = general;

model: KFT_V by kft_v1 kft_v3; ! verbal ability factor
       KFT_Q by kft_q1 kft_q3; ! numeric ability factor
       KFT_N by kft_n1 kft_n3; ! figural (non-verbal) ability factor

output: sampstat stdyx tech4;
```

FIGURE 3.10. Mplus input file for the three-factor model from Figure 3.8.

can be done by specifying, for example, `F1 with F2@0;` in the model command. In this case, the correlation between the two factors F1 and F2 would be fixed to zero, which could be of interest, for example, if one wanted to test the hypothesis that the correlation between these factors is zero in the population. (In the present example, we are expecting significant positive correlations between all factors, and thus we will not use this command here.)

Using the additional `tech4` option in the output command allows us to output the estimated covariance and correlation matrices for the latent factors in matrix form (in addition to the output of these parameters in the regular Mplus model results table). Obtaining these estimates in matrix form can be practical and is sometimes clearer, especially when there are many latent factors.

Fit statistics estimated for both the one- and the three-factor model are shown in Table 3.1. It can be seen that the one-factor model shows a significant chi-square value, whereas the chi-square value for the three-factor model is not significant. According to this criterion, the one-factor model would have to be rejected, whereas the three-factor model fits the data well. In addition, the *RMSEA* value for the one-factor model is larger than the commonly recommended cutoff value of 0.05. According to the

TABLE 3.1. Model Fit Statistics for the One- and Three-Factor Models for the Six KFT Variables

	One factor	Three factors
χ^2 (*df*)	33.939 (9)	7.093 (6)
$p(\chi^2)$	0.0001	0.3123
CFI/TLI	0.969/0.948	0.999/0.997
RMSEA (90% confidence interval)	0.078 (0.051, 0.107)	0.020 (0.000, 0.066)
$p(RMSEA \leq 0.05)$	0.043	0.820
SRMR	0.031	0.014
AIC	14343.362	14322.516

Note. A detailed description of these fit indices is provided in Box 3.7.

CFI, *TLI*, and *SRMR* values, both the one- and the three-factor model would be acceptable. The *AIC* value for the one-factor model is somewhat higher than the *AIC* value for the three-factor model, so that according to this criterion, the three-factor model would again be preferred. In summary, the fit statistics seem to point more to the three-factor solution than to the one-factor solution.

The Mplus parameter estimates for the three-factor model are shown in the following. We again begin with the `MODEL RESULTS` table, which provides the unstandardized solution. It turns out that all loadings (listed under `BY`) that were freely estimated are significantly different from zero (the first loadings of the first indicator is again set to 1 for each factor to identify the metric of each factor). All three estimated factor covariances (shown under `WITH`) are also statistically significant. The size of the relationship between the three factors is difficult to evaluate based on the covariances, however, because covariances are unstandardized measures of association. Standardized covariances (correlations r) are easier to interpret because they are restricted to a standardized range ($-1 \leq r \leq 1$). The correlations of the latent factors are provided in the standardized solution and are discussed below.

The unstandardized solution furthermore contains the unstandardized intercepts of the manifest variables. In this case, the intercepts are identical to the observed means of the manifest variables because there are no restrictions on the mean structure in this model. Also given are the estimated factor variances and the residual variances for the manifest variables.

```
MODEL RESULTS

                                                    Two-Tailed
                    Estimate       S.E.  Est./S.E.    P-Value

 KFT_V    BY
    KFT_V1             1.000      0.000    999.000    999.000
    KFT_V3             1.034      0.083     12.434      0.000

 KFT_Q    BY
    KFT_Q1             1.000      0.000    999.000    999.000
    KFT_Q3             0.865      0.084     10.337      0.000

 KFT_N    BY
    KFT_N1             1.000      0.000    999.000    999.000
    KFT_N3             0.620      0.050     12.394      0.000

 KFT_Q    WITH
    KFT_V              5.247      0.697      7.533      0.000

 KFT_N    WITH
    KFT_V             11.088      1.222      9.074      0.000
    KFT_Q              7.123      0.839      8.488      0.000

 Intercepts
    KFT_V1            11.899      0.218     54.574      0.000
    KFT_V3             8.974      0.199     45.155      0.000
    KFT_Q1            12.387      0.157     78.888      0.000
    KFT_Q3             7.732      0.122     63.396      0.000
    KFT_N1            11.112      0.255     43.552      0.000
    KFT_N3             8.281      0.161     51.457      0.000

 Variances
    KFT_V             10.424      1.401      7.442      0.000
    KFT_Q              4.659      0.720      6.471      0.000
    KFT_N             14.953      1.968      7.596      0.000

 Residual Variances
    KFT_V1            11.205      1.004     11.156      0.000
    KFT_V3             6.830      0.853      8.011      0.000
    KFT_Q1             6.559      0.586     11.192      0.000
    KFT_Q3             3.283      0.366      8.980      0.000
    KFT_N1            14.667      1.382     10.615      0.000
    KFT_N3             6.033      0.550     10.967      0.000
```

Under STANDARDIZED MODEL RESULTS (STDYX Standardization) Mplus provides the fully standardized solution. The standardized factor loadings again appear under BY, the latent factor correlations under WITH. It can be seen that all three KFT factors are strongly positively correlated (.75 ≤ r ≤ .89), which shows that there is rather little discriminant validity among the three KFT subscales.

Despite the rather large correlations among the three factors, the fit statistics indicated that more than one factor is needed to sufficiently account for the observed variances and covariances of the six KFT subscales and that a *g*-factor solution (which implies perfectly correlated factors) had to be rejected for the present data. Therefore, we can conclude that even though the three subscales appear to share a substantial amount of common variance, there also is a nontrivial portion of systematic domain-specific (verbal, numerical, and figural) ability variance that needs to be taken into account and that explains why the correlations among the three factors differ from 1.

```
STANDARDIZED MODEL RESULTS (STDYX Standardization)

                                                        Two-Tailed
                    Estimate       S.E.  Est./S.E.        P-Value

 KFT_V    BY
    KFT_V1             0.694      0.033     20.963          0.000
    KFT_V3             0.787      0.031     25.290          0.000

 KFT_Q    BY
    KFT_Q1             0.644      0.039     16.698          0.000
    KFT_Q3             0.718      0.038     18.959          0.000

 KFT_N    BY
    KFT_N1             0.711      0.033     21.591          0.000
    KFT_N3             0.699      0.033     21.046          0.000

 KFT_Q    WITH
    KFT_V              0.753      0.051     14.764          0.000

 KFT_N    WITH
    KFT_V              0.888      0.041     21.589          0.000
    KFT_Q              0.853      0.049     17.458          0.000

 Intercepts
    KFT_V1             2.558      0.097     26.401          0.000
    KFT_V3             2.117      0.084     25.083          0.000
    KFT_Q1             3.698      0.131     28.176          0.000
    KFT_Q3             2.972      0.109     27.239          0.000
    KFT_N1             2.042      0.082     24.798          0.000
    KFT_N3             2.412      0.093     26.024          0.000
```

```
 Variances
    KFT_V              1.000       0.000    999.000    999.000
    KFT_Q              1.000       0.000    999.000    999.000
    KFT_N              1.000       0.000    999.000    999.000

 Residual Variances
    KFT_V1             0.518       0.046     11.267      0.000
    KFT_V3             0.380       0.049      7.753      0.000
    KFT_Q1             0.585       0.050     11.753      0.000
    KFT_Q3             0.485       0.054      8.933      0.000
    KFT_N1             0.495       0.047     10.589      0.000
    KFT_N3             0.512       0.046     11.037      0.000

R-SQUARE

    Observed                                           Two-Tailed
    Variable        Estimate       S.E.  Est./S.E.    P-Value

    KFT_V1             0.482       0.046     10.482      0.000
    KFT_V3             0.620       0.049     12.645      0.000
    KFT_Q1             0.415       0.050      8.349      0.000
    KFT_Q3             0.515       0.054      9.479      0.000
    KFT_N1             0.505       0.047     10.796      0.000
    KFT_N3             0.488       0.046     10.523      0.000
```

3.4.2 Second-Order CFA

The high (albeit imperfect) correlations among the three KFT factors in the three-factor CFA model made us speculate about whether there might be a common ability factor that underlies all three ability domains (a g-factor of intelligence?). Given the high correlations, there appeared to be a large amount of shared variance and only a relatively minor amount of specific verbal, numerical, and figural ability variance. A model that is in line with the idea of a g-factor, while still allowing for domain-specific (residual) variability, is the second-order factor model shown in Figure 3.11. In this model, the three first-order KFT factors (KFT_V, KFT_Q, and KFT_N) themselves load onto a factor, a so-called *second-order factor* (KFT_g).

The Mplus model specification for the second-order CFA model shown in Figure 3.11 is provided in Figure 3.12. Note that in this example, even though a second-order factor model can be specified, the model is statistically equivalent to the correlated three-factor model discussed previously. At least four first-order factors are required for the second-order factor structure to be overidentified and more restrictive than a model with correlated first-order factors. This means that the second-order factor model

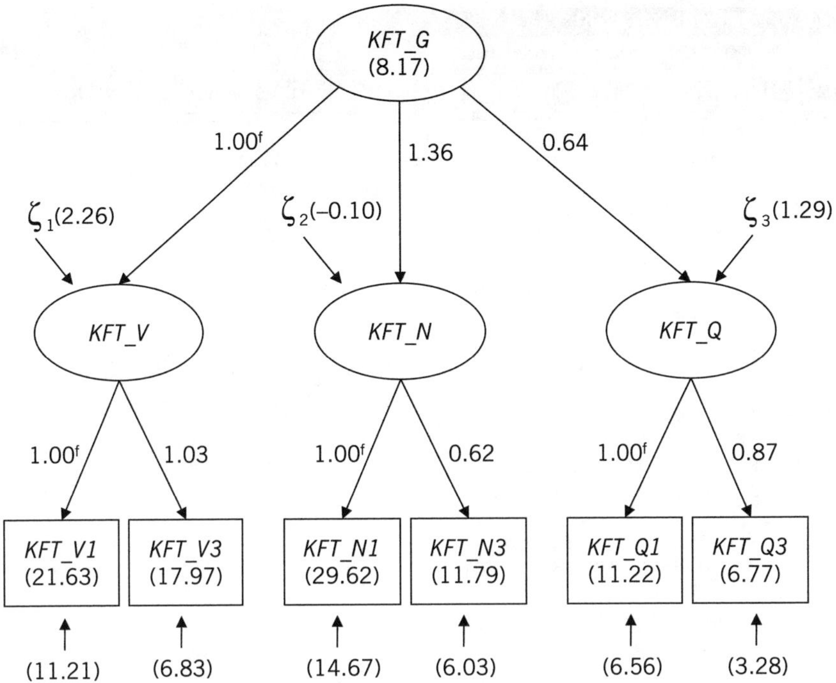

FIGURE 3.11. Second-order factor model for the six KFT variables with unstandardized Mplus parameter estimates. In this model, the three first-order KFT factors KFT_V, KFT_N, and KFT_Q load onto a second-order factor (KFT_G). The superscript ^{f} indicates factor loadings that were fixed to 1 to identify the metric of the latent variables. Variances and residual variances are given in parentheses. Note the estimated negative residual variance ("Heywood case") for the factor KFT_N (–0.10).

cannot be statistically distinguished from the correlated three-factor model based on model fit in this example. Another possibility to obtain an overidentified structural model would be to impose restrictions on the loadings of the first-order factors on the second-order factor (e.g., the restriction of equal loadings).

In this example, even though the fit of the second-order model is identical to the fit of the correlated three-factor model, there is still some doubt as to whether the second-order factor model should be used. The reason is that this model results in an inadmissible parameter estimate (so-called *Heywood case*; Chen, Bollen, Paxton, Curran, & Kirby, 2001; see also Box 3.9). In this case, the residual variance of the factor KFT_N is estimated to a negative value (–0.099), which represents a nonadmissible

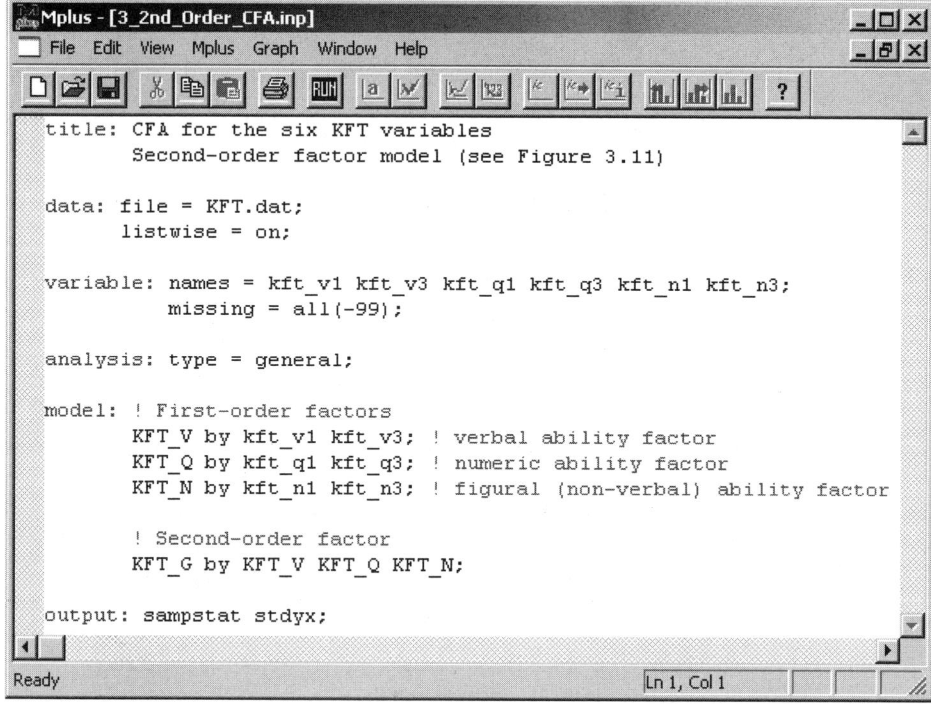

FIGURE 3.12. Mplus input file for the second-order factor model from Figure 3.11.

parameter estimate because variances, by definition, cannot be negative. Mplus indicates this problem with the following warning message:

```
WARNING:  THE LATENT VARIABLE COVARIANCE MATRIX (PSI) IS NOT POSITIVE
DEFINITE.  THIS COULD INDICATE A NEGATIVE VARIANCE/RESIDUAL VARIANCE
FOR A LATENT VARIABLE, A CORRELATION GREATER OR EQUAL TO ONE BETWEEN
TWO LATENT VARIABLES, OR A LINEAR DEPENDENCY AMONG MORE THAN TWO LATENT
VARIABLES.  CHECK THE TECH4 OUTPUT FOR MORE INFORMATION.  PROBLEM
INVOLVING VARIABLE KFT_N.
```

The estimated negative residual variance could be an indication that the first-order factors show a heterogeneous correlation pattern that is not in line with the idea of a common second-order factor. In this case, it seems best to work with the less problematic model of three correlated first-order factors instead of the second-order factor model and to interpret the parameters of the second-order model only with great caution.

In the following, the Mplus estimates for the residual variances of the model from Figure 3.11 are shown. Note the negative residual variance for the factor KFT_N (–0.099).

BOX 3.9. *Inadmissible Parameter Estimates (Heywood Cases) in Structural Equation Modeling*

A solution is commonly referred to as a *Heywood case* if it contains inadmissible (out-of-range) parameter estimates such as negative (residual) variances or correlations larger than 1. These kinds of inadmissible estimates can have multiple causes, which can also occur in combination with each other. The most typical causes are:

- Model misspecification, for example, because of heterogeneous indicators in the measurement model or the specification of too many or too few factors
- Use of too small a sample size
- Use of too few indicators per factor
- Sampling error
- Outliers or extreme cases

In my experience, the most common cause of inadmissible parameter estimates are model misspecifications. For this reason, inadmissible estimates should not simply be eliminated through parameter fixations (e.g., set a negative variance to zero) or other cosmetic actions. Instead, the possible causes of these problems should be examined carefully. Often, a model can be respecified in a more meaningful way that does not produce offending parameter estimates. A more detailed discussion of the issue of Heywood cases can be found in Chen et al. (2001).

```
MODEL RESULTS
Residual Variances
   KFT_V1          11.206      1.004     11.156      0.000
   KFT_V3           6.829      0.853      8.010      0.000
   KFT_Q1           6.559      0.586     11.192      0.000
   KFT_Q3           3.283      0.366      8.979      0.000
   KFT_N1          14.667      1.382     10.614      0.000
   KFT_N3           6.033      0.550     10.967      0.000
   KFT_V            2.256      0.754      2.992      0.003
   KFT_Q            1.289      0.402      3.209      0.001
   KFT_N           -0.099      1.206     -0.082      0.935
```

Negative residual variance ("Heywood case")!

3.5 PATH MODELS AND MEDIATOR ANALYSIS

3.5.1 Introduction and Manifest Path Analysis

Path analyses, like CFAs, are among the most frequently used models that are estimated in the SEM framework. In general, path analysis can be seen as a multivariate regression model—that is, a regression analysis that simultaneously considers multiple dependent (and often also multiple independent) variables, in contrast to conventional regression analyses that are restricted to a single dependent variable (see Section 3.2). In a path analysis, exogenous variables are typically allowed to be correlated.

Path analyses can be carried out at either the level of manifest variables (an example is shown in Figure 3.13) or at the level of latent variables (latent path analysis; see Section 3.5.3). Here, we first discuss the simpler case of a manifest path analysis.

Figure 3.13 shows the path model proposed by Whitelaw and Liang (1991) using three manifest variables. In this model, it is assumed that the exogenous variable, physical health (X; here measured as the number of diseases in the last 12 months; variable `SICK`), predicts the endogenous variable, functional health (Y_1; the sum score of the SF-36 questionnaire for measuring functional health; variable `FH`), which itself predicts the second endogenous variable, subjective health (Y_2; measured through the self-report of subjective health in the present; variable `SHP`). In addition, it is assumed that the construct physical health also has a direct effect on subjective health. The coefficients β_1, β_2, and β_3 denote regression or path coefficients that characterize the strength of the influence of one variable on another. These coefficients are equivalent to slope coefficients in linear regression analysis.

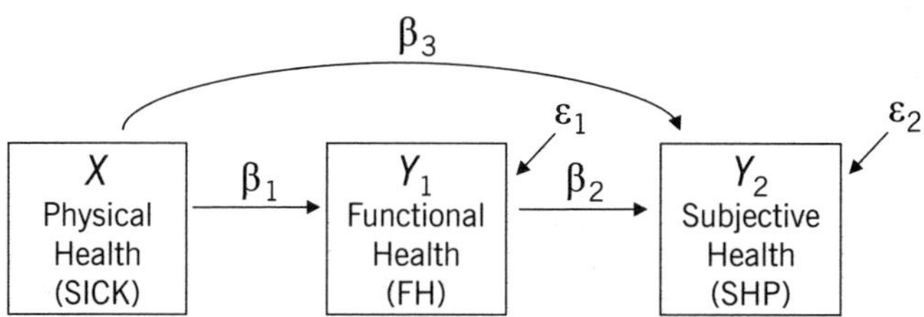

FIGURE 3.13. Manifest path model for the relationship between physical health (X), functional health (Y_1), and subjective health (Y_2) proposed by Whitelaw and Liang (1991). The constants β_1, β_2, and β_3 indicate regression (path) coefficients. The variables ε_1 and ε_2 are residual variables. The model contains one indirect effect, which can be expressed as the product $\beta_1 \cdot \beta_2$. The variable names used in the Mplus analyses are given in parentheses.

BOX 3.10. *Example Path Analysis*

As an example, we consider the theoretical model proposed by Whitelaw and Liang (1991) that is used in health psychology. This model deals with the relationship between three constructs: physical health, functional health, and subjective health. *Physical health* refers to the actual objective physiological health status (e.g., presence or absence of trouble or disease). *Functional health* refers to the ability to carry out everyday activities and actions (e.g., walking, climbing stairs). *Subjective health* refers to the individual, global subjective judgment of one's own health (a more detailed description of these three constructs can be found in Pinquart, 2001).

The data considered here are taken from the age survey sample of the German center of gerontology (Deutsches Zentrum für Altersfragen, DZA)* and are located in the file **health.dat**. This data set contains individual data for six variables: the number of diseases or health problems (variable `SICK`) as well as the number of consultations of medical doctors in the last 12 months (variable `CONSULT`) as indicators of physical health, the subscale for the assessment of functional health taken from the SF-36 Health Survey questionnaire (Ware & Sherborne, 1992). This scale is represented in terms of both a global sum score (variable `FH`) and also in terms of two scale scores (so-called *item parcels*) as represented by the variables `FH1` and `FH2`. Finally, two items are included to assess subjective health: (1) subjective health in the present (variable `SHP`) and (2) changes in subjective health across the last 6 years (variable `SHC`).

*I would like to thank Susanne Wurm from the DZA for providing the data for this example as well as Christopher Marx for running some of the analyses.

One reason why path analysis is very popular in the social sciences is that many social science theories include hypotheses with regard to direct and indirect effects of variables on each other (e.g., see MacKinnon, 2008). *Indirect effects* are effects that are mediated through other variables and are therefore also referred to as *mediated effects* (Baron & Kenny, 1986). Mediated effects are present in a path model when the model contains one or more variables that are dependent and independent variables at the same time. Those types of variables are often referred to as *intermittent* or *mediator variables*. Mediated effects can be analyzed by means of either manifest or latent path analyses.

In the model in Figure 3.13, the variable Y_1 (functional health, `FH`) is a mediator variable, because this variable is a dependent variable with regard to the variable X (physical health, `SICK`) but an independent variable with regard to the variable Y_2 (subjective health, `SHP`). In other words, Y_1 receives an effect from X (path β_1) while at the same time sending an effect out to Y_2 (path β_2). Hence, Y_1 partly mediates the effect of X on Y_2, which explains the term *mediator variable*. Formally, the indirect (or mediated) effect of X on Y_2 can be quantified as the product of β_1 times β_2 (MacKinnon, 2008). Variable X, in this example, also has a direct effect on Y_2, which is expressed through the path coefficient β_3.

In substantive terms, all this means that, in this model, it is assumed that the objective health status (physical health) of a person has both a direct (nonmediated) and an indirect (mediated) effect (via functional health) on subjective health. The mediated effect is caused by the fact that objective physical problems often result in a loss of functional competencies that, in turn, cause a decrease in subjective health. By fitting the path model to our data, we can test whether physical health indeed has both a direct and an indirect effect on subjective health, or whether the effect of physical health on subjective health is fully mediated through functional health.

In path analyses that contain one or more indirect effects, an effect decomposition is often of interest. In this decomposition, the total effect is split up into the sum of all indirect effects plus the direct effect (if a direct effect is assumed). In other words, the total effect is equal to the sum of the direct effect plus all indirect effects. In our example, the direct effect of X on Y_2 is measured by the coefficient β_3, whereas the indirect effect is measured by the product $\beta_1 \cdot \beta_2$. Therefore, the total effect can be calculated as the sum $\beta_3 + (\beta_1 \cdot \beta_2)$.

BOX 3.11. *Mediated versus Moderated Effects*

Mediator effects should not be confused with moderator effects (see also Baron & Kenny, 1986). In contrast to a mediator effect, a moderator effect is present when there is an *interaction* between two variables. A variable is referred to as a *moderator variable* when the strength of the direct influence of one variable (say, X) on another variable (say, Y) depends on the values of a third variable (say, Z). If, for example, the regression coefficient β_3 (which characterizes the direct effect of X on Y_2 in Figure 3.13) varied across different levels of Y_1 (i.e., if the direct influence of X on Y_2 was moderated by Y_1), then Y_1 could be seen as a moderator variable. The analysis of moderator (interaction) effects is not discussed in this book. Aiken and West (1991; as well as Cohen et al., 2003, their Chapters 7–9) discuss the analysis of moderated effects in detail in the context of manifest regression models (so-called *moderated regression*). Latent moderator models (SEMs with interaction effects) are discussed, for example, in Marsh, Wen, and Hau (2006).

BOX 3.12. *Significance Testing of Indirect Effects*

Often, the statistical significance of indirect effects is of interest when mediated effects are the subject of the study. One difficulty for statistical inference with mediated effects is that the indirect effect is the product of two or more regression coefficients (in our example, the product $\beta_1 \cdot \beta_2$). The assumption of a normal distribution of this product term in the population is often violated. For this reason, conventional methods of significance testing for indirect effects may lead to biased results (MacKinnon, Lockwood, & Williams, 2004). MacKinnon and his colleagues have studied different methods for testing indirect effect in detail (MacKinnon, 2008; MacKinnon et al., 2004; MacKinnon, Lockwood, Hoffman, West, & Sheets, 2002). Among other methods, these authors recommend testing mediated effects via asymmetric confidence intervals derived from bootstrapping. The theoretical background of these methods is discussed in detail in MacKinnon (2008). An indirect effect is significant at the .05 level, according to this method, if the value of 0 is not part of the 95% bootstrap confidence interval around the indirect effect. MacKinnon et al. (2004) recommend, among others, the so-called *bias-corrected bootstrap* as a method for statistical inference in statistical mediation analysis using confidence intervals. Bootstrap methods as well as confidence intervals are implemented in Mplus and are easy to obtain. An application of these methods to testing mediated effects is shown in Section 3.5.2.

3.5.2 Manifest Path Analysis in Mplus

Figure 3.14 shows the Mplus input file for the specification of manifest path model in Figure 3.13. In this model, the variable `SICK` is used for the operationalization of the construct physical health. Functional health is operationalized by the total score of the SF-36 subscale for measuring functional health (variable `FH`). Subjective health is represented by the item referring to subjective health in the present (variable `SHP`).

In contrast to the regression analysis discussed in Section 3.2, we now use more than one `on` statement in the `model` command, because we simultaneously consider two linear regression analyses. In our model, there are two dependent variables (`FH` and `SHP`). Therefore, two `on` statements are required: one for the (multiple) regression of `SHP` on `FH` and `SICK`, and one for the (simple) regression of `FH` on `SICK`.

```
FH on SICK;
SHP on SICK FH;
```

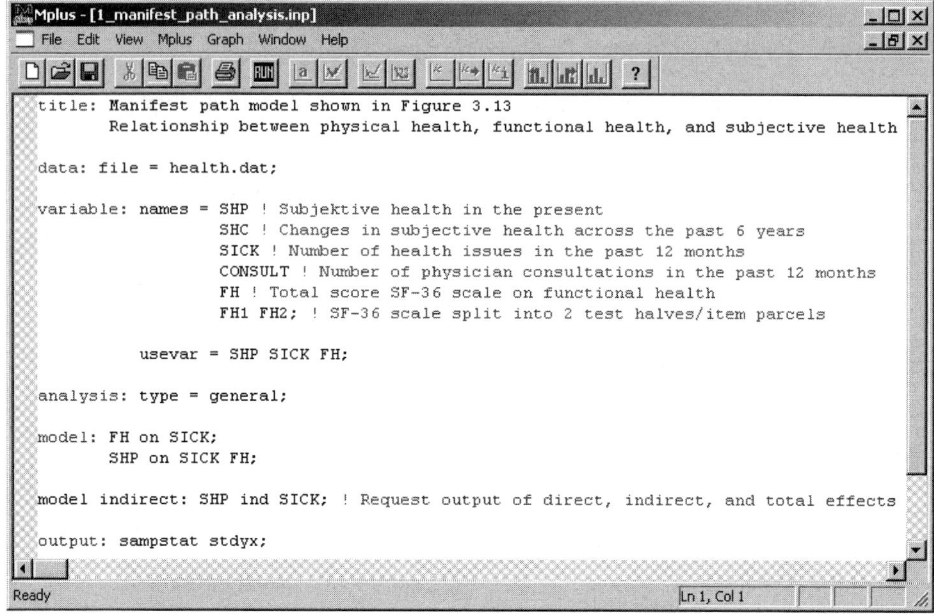

FIGURE 3.14. Mplus input file for the manifest path model from Figure 3.13.

By using the additional `model indirect` subcommand, we request that in addition to the standard output, we obtain a separate listing of all direct, indirect, and total effects on the outcome variable `SHP` (note that the `model indirect` subcommand can be used in both manifest and latent path analyses):

```
model indirect: SHP ind SICK;
```

The keyword `ind` between the two variable names causes Mplus to output all indirect effects that the variable `SICK` has on the variable `SHP` (in this case, there is only one indirect effect via `FH`), along with the relevant standard errors and tests of significance. The `model indirect` subcommand is particularly useful when a researcher wants to test specific indirect effects for significance (see below).

In the Mplus output, we obtain sample statistics with the means, covariances, and correlations of the three manifest variables (only the correlation table is shown here). As expected, subjective health correlates positively with functional health and negatively with the number of health problems in the last 12 months. In addition, the frequency of health problems is negatively correlated with functional health.

```
Correlations
              SHP           FH            SICK
              ________      ________      ________
 SHP            1.000
 FH             0.594         1.000
 SICK          -0.458        -0.447         1.000
```

Under the rubric `MODEL FIT INFORMATION` we can see that the estimated manifest path model in our example has zero degrees of freedom. The reason is that all means, variances, and covariances of the three manifest variables are used up in the model to estimate model parameters. One therefore speaks of a so-called *saturated* or *just identified model* in this case (this was the same issue for the manifest regression model discussed in Section 3.2). One consequence is that the model does not contain any testable restrictions with respect to the mean and covariance structure of the observed variables and therefore fits perfectly (for details see Bollen, 1989). This can be seen from the chi-square model test:

```
MODEL FIT INFORMATION

Chi-Square Test of Model Fit

          Value                              0.000
          Degrees of Freedom                     0
          P-Value                           0.0000
```

The chi-square value is zero with zero degrees of freedom. The test is therefore not useful to evaluate the model fit in this case (the p-value is erroneously reported to be 0 by Mplus; it should in fact be printed as p = 1 in this case, given that the model has a perfect fit to the data). In general, the judgment of the model fit of a saturated model focuses more on the estimated model parameters (in particular, the estimated path coefficients) and the obtained proportion of the explained variability in the endogenous variables (as measured by the R^2 value) rather than the global fit statistics output by Mplus.

The Mplus `MODEL RESULTS` table provides us with the estimates of the unstandardized path coefficients (here for the saturated path model that includes the direct effect from `SICK` to `SHP`). Fully standardized path coefficients can again be found under `STANDARDIZED MODEL RESULTS (STDYX Standardization)`. It can be seen that there is a significant negative direct effect of the frequency of health issues on subjective health (direct effect from `SICK` to `SHP`, $\hat{\beta}_3 = -0.094$, $z = -11.258$, $p < .001$, $\hat{\beta}_3^{\text{standardized}} = -0.24$). For every additional health issue encountered in the last 12 months, the expected *decrease* in subjective health is

BOX 3.13. *Saturated versus Nonsaturated Path Models*

Note that not every manifest path model is necessarily saturated. If, for example, in the present model one deletes the direct path from SICK to SHP (which is equivalent to fixing the corresponding path coefficient β_3 to zero), the model would no longer be saturated. Instead, it would have one degree of freedom, implying one testable restriction. Using tests or indices of model fit, the assumption that the effect of physical health on subjective health is fully mediated by functional health could then be tested. In other words, this restricted model would be in line with the idea that physical health only indirectly affects subjective health.

The Mplus model specification would have to be changed, as follows, to obtain a nonsaturated model as described above (the full input for this alternative model can be found on the companion website):

```
FH on SICK;
SHP on FH;
```

The resulting more restricted model, without the direct effect from SICK to SHP, shows a highly significant chi-square value of 122.11 with one degree of freedom ($p < .0001$). The remaining fit indices (especially the *RMSEA* index) also point to a rather bad fit of this model (*RMSEA* = .27, *CFI* = .90, *SRMR* = .06). Therefore, the hypothesis of complete mediation has to be rejected (there is also a significant direct effect from physical health to subjective health).

–0.094, controlling for functional health. Functional health is positively related to subjective health (direct effect $\hat{\beta}_2 = 0.885$, $z = 22.765$, $p < .001$, $\hat{\beta}_2^{\text{standardized}} = 0.486$): For every one-unit increase in functional health as measured by the SF-36 questionnaire, the expected increase in subjective health is 0.885, controlling for the number of health problems reported for the last 12 months. Physical health problems are significantly negatively related to functional health ($\hat{\beta}_1 = -0.096$, $z = -20.273$, $p < .001$, $\hat{\beta}_1^{\text{standardized}} = -0.447$): For every additional health issue in the last 12 months, the expected decrease in the functional health score is –0.096 units. The indirect effect from physical health to subjective health is discussed in detail below.

The estimated R^2 values for the two endogenous variables appear under the standardized parameter estimates. With the present model, approximately 39.9% of the variability in subjective health ($\hat{R}^2 = .399$) and approximately 20% of the variability in functional health ($\hat{R}^2 = .20$) can be explained.

```
MODEL RESULTS

                                                    Two-Tailed
                    Estimate       S.E.  Est./S.E.    P-Value

 FH         ON
    SICK              -0.096      0.005    -20.273      0.000

 SHP        ON
    SICK              -0.094      0.008    -11.258      0.000
    FH                 0.885      0.039     22.765      0.000

 Intercepts
    SHP                1.408      0.117     12.034      0.000
    FH                 2.936      0.016    179.357      0.000

 Residual Variances
    SHP                0.432      0.015     28.705      0.000
    FH                 0.174      0.006     28.705      0.000

STANDARDIZED MODEL RESULTS

STDYX Standardization

                                                    Two-Tailed
                    Estimate       S.E.  Est./S.E.    P-Value

 FH         ON
    SICK              -0.447      0.020    -22.661      0.000

 SHP        ON
    SICK              -0.240      0.021    -11.441      0.000
    FH                 0.486      0.019     25.057      0.000

 Intercepts
    SHP                1.661      0.151     10.973      0.000
    FH                 6.304      0.099     63.378      0.000

 Residual Variances
    SHP                0.601      0.019     32.153      0.000
    FH                 0.800      0.018     45.431      0.000

R-SQUARE

    Observed                                        Two-Tailed
    Variable        Estimate       S.E.  Est./S.E.    P-Value

    SHP                0.399      0.019     21.304      0.000
    FH                 0.200      0.018     11.330      0.000
```

The additional output that we requested through the `model indirect` command provides information about the size and statistical significance of the indirect effect from physical health to subjective health that is estimated in the model (reminder: formally, the indirect effect is the product of the path coefficients $\beta_1 \cdot \beta_2$). In the first part of the additional output (labeled `TOTAL, TOTAL INDIRECT, SPECIFIC INDIRECT, AND DIRECT EFFECTS`), the effects are reported in unstandardized form together with their respective standard errors and tests of significance:

```
TOTAL, TOTAL INDIRECT, SPECIFIC INDIRECT, AND DIRECT EFFECTS

                                                          Two-Tailed
                    Estimate       S.E.  Est./S.E.         P-Value

Effects from SICK to SHP

  Total               -0.178      0.009    -20.892          0.000
  Total indirect      -0.085      0.006    -15.140          0.000

  Specific indirect

    SHP
    FH
    SICK              -0.085      0.006    -15.140          0.000

  Direct
    SHP
    SICK              -0.094      0.008    -11.258          0.000
```

The estimated total effect is the sum of the estimated direct effect $\hat{\beta}_3$ and the estimated indirect effect $\hat{\beta}_1 \cdot \hat{\beta}_2$:

$$\hat{\beta}_3 + (\hat{\beta}_1 \cdot \hat{\beta}_2) = -0.094 + (-0.096 \cdot 0.885) = -0.178$$

The total indirect effect is given by

$$\hat{\beta}_1 \cdot \hat{\beta}_2 = -0.096 \cdot 0.885 = -0.085$$

In this example, we have to deal with only one indirect effect from physical health to subjective health (mediated by functional health), such that the total indirect effect is equal to the specific indirect effect (given under `Specific indirect`). The default test used by Mplus to test the indirect effect for significance is the so-called *Sobel test* (Sobel, 1982).

The standard error for the indirect effect provided by Mplus is 0.006 ($z = -15.14$). Therefore, the indirect effect is significant ($p < .001$) according to this test.

Mplus also outputs the estimated direct effect $\hat{\beta}_3$ again, which equals –0.094. The standardized solution lists the same effects again now in fully standardized form:

```
STANDARDIZED TOTAL, TOTAL INDIRECT, SPECIFIC INDIRECT, AND
DIRECT EFFECTS (STDYX Standardization)

                                                    Two-Tailed
                        Estimate       S.E.  Est./S.E.    P-Value

Effects from SICK to SHP

  Total                   -0.458      0.019    -23.496      0.000
  Total indirect          -0.217      0.013    -16.600      0.000

  Specific indirect

    SHP
    FH
    SICK                  -0.217      0.013    -16.600      0.000

  Direct
    SHP
    SICK                  -0.240      0.021    -11.441      0.000
```

The use of conventional tests of significance for testing indirect effects can be problematic in practice, because the product of two or more regression coefficients is tested. This product often is not normally distributed, which can make conventional tests of significance unreliable (MacKinnon, 2008; see Box 3.12). MacKinnon and his colleagues (MacKinnon, 2008; MacKinnon et al., 2004) therefore recommend the use of asymmetric confidence intervals based on bootstrap methods for significance testing of indirect effects as a more appropriate alternative. In Mplus, confidence intervals around model parameter estimates can generally (i.e., with or without bootstrap methods) be obtained via the following command:

```
output: cinterval;
```

If one wants to estimate confidence intervals based on bias-corrected bootstrap methods, the following additional specification is required in the `analysis` statement:

```
analysis: bootstrap = <number of bootstrap samples>;
output: cinterval (bcbootstrap);
```

The subcommand `bootstrap =` is used to choose the number of bootstrap samples. For a high precision, a large number of bootstrap samples should be chosen (e.g., 10,000). The type of bootstrap method used is chosen in the `output` command (in parentheses behind `cinterval`). The keyword `bcbootstrap` refers to the bias-corrected version of the bootstrap recommended by MacKinnon et al. (2004). Conventional bootstrap confidence intervals can be obtained using the command `output: cinterval (bootstrap);`

The complete input and output files for the estimation of the path model with bias-corrected bootstrap confidence intervals can be found on the companion website. In the following we show only the part of the Mplus output that contains the bias-corrected bootstrap confidence intervals estimated based on 10,000 bootstrap draws for both the unstandardized and the standardized parameter estimates. Under the columns `Lower .5%` and `Upper .5%` we find the lower and upper limits of 99% confidence intervals around each parameter estimate, respectively. The columns labeled `Lower 2.5%` and `Upper 2.5%` contain the lower and upper bounds of 95% confidence intervals, respectively.

```
CONFIDENCE INTERVALS OF TOTAL, TOTAL INDIRECT, SPECIFIC INDIRECT,
AND DIRECT EFFECTS

                    Lower .5%  Lower 2.5%  Estimate  Upper 2.5%  Upper .5%

Effects from SICK to SHP
  Total              -0.203     -0.197     -0.178     -0.159     -0.153
  Total indirect     -0.102     -0.098     -0.085     -0.072     -0.068

  Specific indirect
    SHP
    FH
    SICK             -0.102     -0.098     -0.085     -0.072     -0.068
  Direct
    SHP
    SICK             -0.117     -0.111     -0.094     -0.076     -0.071
```

It turns out that also according to the bias-corrected bootstrap confidence interval, the indirect effect is significant at the 1% level. This can be seen from the fact that neither the 95% confidence interval (–0.098, –0.072) nor the 99% confidence interval (–0.102, –0.068) around the indirect effect includes the value of zero. The same is true for the standardized indirect effect. The relevant output lines are shown in boldface, respectively:

```
CONFIDENCE INTERVALS OF STANDARDIZED TOTAL, TOTAL INDIRECT, SPECIFIC INDIRECT,
AND DIRECT EFFECTS (STDYX Standardization)

                      Lower .5%  Lower 2.5%   Estimate  Upper 2.5%  Upper .5%

Effects from SICK to SHP
  Total                 -0.513      -0.500     -0.458      -0.415     -0.402
  Total indirect        -0.257      -0.247     -0.217      -0.187     -0.178

  Specific indirect
    SHP
    FH
    SICK                -0.257      -0.247     -0.217      -0.187     -0.178

  Direct
    SHP
    SICK                -0.299      -0.285     -0.240      -0.196     -0.182
```

The results therefore indicate that physical health has a significant direct, as well as a significant indirect effect on subjective health.

3.5.3 Latent Path Analysis

In latent path analysis, the idea of CFA is combined with the idea of a manifest path analysis. This means that, as in CFA, a measurement model with multiple indicators for each construct of interest is added to the model. Each construct of interest is represented by a latent factor, and the latent factors are connected via directional regression paths in the same way as in a manifest path analysis. (This is in contrast to CFA in which only nondirectional relationships between factors are assumed, with the exception of higher-order factor models; see Section 3.4.2.)

Figure 3.15 shows a path diagram of a latent path analysis with three latent variables (η_1, η_2, and η_3), each of which is measured with two indicators (Y_{11}–Y_{23}), respectively. Substantively, the path model again corresponds to the theoretical model of Whitelaw and Liang (1991); however, this time, the mediator model is specified at the level of latent variables (i.e., at the level of the η-variables). A latent path analysis has the advantage over manifest path analysis in that it takes random measurement error in the observed variables into account when estimating direct, indirect, and total effects between the constructs of interest.

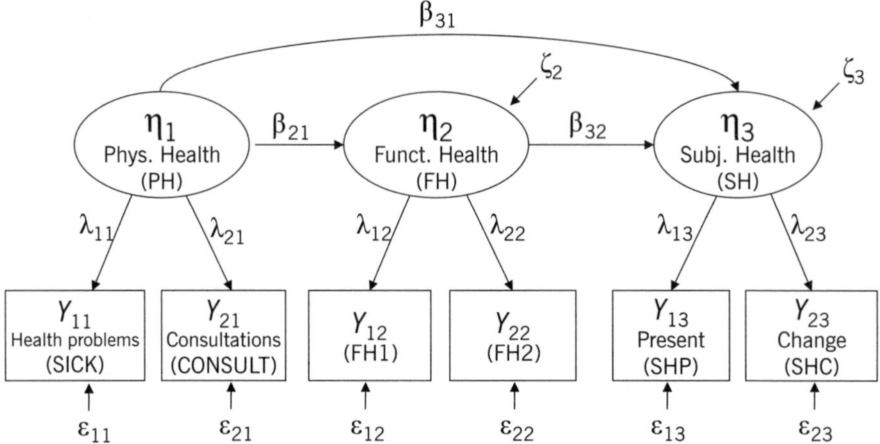

FIGURE 3.15. Latent path model with three latent variables η_1, η_2, and η_3, each of which is measured with two manifest variables Y_{ij}. The variable names used in the Mplus analyses appear in parentheses. The constants λ_{ij} indicate factor loadings. The variables ε_{ij} are measurement error variables. The constants $\beta_{jj'}$ indicate latent regression (path) coefficients. The ζ_j variables are latent residual variables. At the level of the latent variables, the model contains the indirect effect $\beta_{21} \cdot \beta_{32}$.

3.5.4 Latent Path Analysis in Mplus

Each of the three constructs in our example is measured by two indicators (manifest variables): physical health is measured by the number of diseases (variable SICK) as well as the number of consultations of doctors in the last 12 months (variable CONSULT); functional health is measured by the two test halves created for the SF-36 questionnaire (variables FH1 and FH2); and subjective health is measured by two single items, one of which refers to the subjective health in the present (SHP), whereas the second item refers to changes in subjective health across the last 6 years (variables SHC).

The three η-variables represent the latent scores with regard to the three constructs of physical health, functional health, and subjective health, which are corrected for random measurement error as well as for item- and scale-specific influences. The theoretical model by Whitelaw and Liang (1991) can therefore now be examined at the level of latent variables, which are corrected for measurement error and indicator-specific influences. Figure 3.16 shows the Mplus input file for the estimation of the parameters of the latent path analysis represented in Figure 3.15.

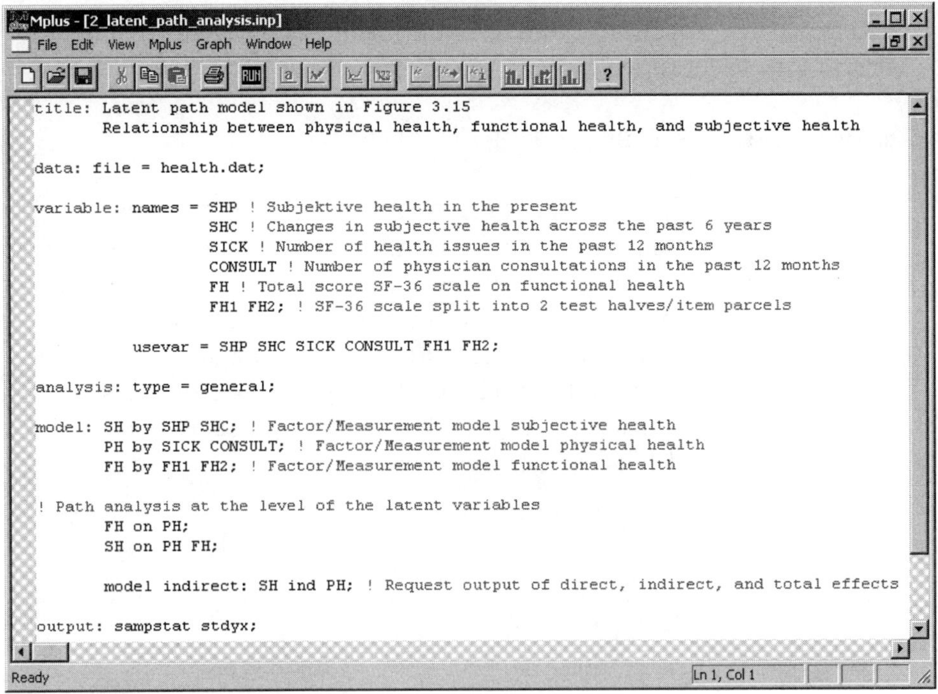

```
title: Latent path model shown in Figure 3.15
       Relationship between physical health, functional health, and subjective health

data: file = health.dat;

variable: names = SHP ! Subjektive health in the present
                  SHC ! Changes in subjective health across the past 6 years
                  SICK ! Number of health issues in the past 12 months
                  CONSULT ! Number of physician consultations in the past 12 months
                  FH ! Total score SF-36 scale on functional health
                  FH1 FH2; ! SF-36 scale split into 2 test halves/item parcels

          usevar = SHP SHC SICK CONSULT FH1 FH2;

analysis: type = general;

model: SH by SHP SHC; ! Factor/Measurement model subjective health
       PH by SICK CONSULT; ! Factor/Measurement model physical health
       FH by FH1 FH2; ! Factor/Measurement model functional health

! Path analysis at the level of the latent variables
       FH on PH;
       SH on PH FH;

       model indirect: SH ind PH; ! Request output of direct, indirect, and total effects

output: sampstat stdyx;
```

FIGURE 3.16. Mplus input file for the latent path model from Figure 3.15.

In the latent path model, we first specify the measurement model for the latent factors as in a CFA:

```
SH by SHP SHC;
PH by SICK CONSULT;
FH by FH1 FH2;
```

The latent factor `SH` represents subjective health, the factor `PH` refers to physical health, and the factor `FH` represents functional health. In the next step, the structural model is specified—which, in our case, is the path analysis at the latent level:

```
FH on PH;
SH on PH FH;
```

Note that `SH`, `PH`, and `FH` are now latent variables that are not part of our data set and that therefore do not have to be listed under `variable: names`. The subcommand for obtaining a summary of all direct, indirect, and total effect remains the same as in the manifest path model (but now refers to the latent variables):

```
model indirect: SH ind PH;
```

In the output, we see under MODEL FIT INFORMATION that the latent path model—in contrast to the manifest model—is not saturated, but has 6 degrees of freedom. In this case, all 6 degrees of freedom are coming out of the measurement model (due to using more than one indicator for each construct). The structural model (the path analysis at the latent level) is saturated in this model as well. That is, no testable restrictions arise from the structural model. The model fit indices indicate that the latent path model fits the data well.

```
MODEL FIT INFORMATION

Chi-Square Test of Model Fit

          Value                                  5.509
          Degrees of Freedom                         6
          P-Value                               0.4804

CFI/TLI

          CFI                                    1.000
          TLI                                    1.000

RMSEA (Root Mean Square Error Of Approximation)

          Estimate                               0.000
          90 Percent C.I.                        0.000  0.031
          Probability RMSEA <= .05               1.000

SRMR (Standardized Root Mean Square Residual)

          Value                                  0.007
```

With regard to the parameter estimates (see table MODEL RESULTS), we can first of all see that all freely estimated factor loadings are significantly different from zero (the first unstandardized loading is fixed to one for each factor, respectively, to identify the metric of the latent variables as the default in Mplus). In addition, all standardized loadings (see STANDARDIZED MODEL RESULTS [STDYX Standardization]) are substantial (range: 0.494–0.972). The indicators of the FH (functional health) factor show particularly high standardized loadings

($\hat{\lambda}_{12}^{\text{standardized}}$ = 0.972; $\hat{\lambda}_{22}^{\text{standardized}}$ = 0.955). This finding shows that the indicators of this factor are very homogeneous (the two test halves seem to measure very similar aspects of functional health) and are highly reliable.

The factor for physical health (PH) has the smallest standardized loadings ($\hat{\lambda}_{11}^{\text{standardized}}$ = 0.623, $\hat{\lambda}_{21}^{\text{standardized}}$ = 0.494). This finding can be explained by the fact that even though the frequency of health problems is positively correlated with the number of physician consultations, this correlation is rather moderate in size in the present data set (r = .308, p < .001; see full output on the companion website). Therefore, the two indicators of physical health can be seen as rather heterogeneous (they measure different facets of the construct physical health). The variable SICK shows a somewhat larger standardized loading on the factor than the number of physician consultations and might therefore be seen as the marker variable for this factor. (*Marker variables* are indicators that show high loadings on the intended factor and are therefore seen as most relevant for the interpretation of this factor.)

With regard to the structural model, the relationships between the three constructs go in the same direction: physical health problems negatively impact both functional health ($\hat{\beta}_{21}$ = –0.246, z = –13.189, p < .001, $\hat{\beta}_{21}^{\text{standardized}}$ = –0.722) and subjective health ($\hat{\beta}_{31}$ = –0.379, z = –6.944, p < .001, $\hat{\beta}_{31}^{\text{standardized}}$ = –0.709), whereas functional health is positively related to subjective health ($\hat{\beta}_{32}$ = 0.314, z = 2.631, p = .009, $\hat{\beta}_{32}^{\text{standardized}}$ = –0.200).

```
MODEL RESULTS

                                                   Two-Tailed
                    Estimate       S.E.  Est./S.E.    P-Value

 SH       BY
    SHP                1.000      0.000    999.000    999.000
    SHC                0.710      0.031     23.145      0.000

 PH       BY
    SICK               1.000      0.000    999.000    999.000
    CONSULT            5.547      0.363     15.265      0.000

 FH       BY
    FH1                1.000      0.000    999.000    999.000
    FH2                0.981      0.014     68.107      0.000

 FH       ON
    PH                -0.246      0.019    -13.190      0.000
```

```
 SH       ON
    PH                -0.379      0.055     -6.945      0.000
    FH                 0.314      0.119      2.632      0.008

 Intercepts
    SHP                3.525      0.021    168.751      0.000
    SHC                2.521      0.020    128.763      0.000
    SICK               2.706      0.054     50.435      0.000
    CONSULT           13.082      0.375     34.892      0.000
    FH1                2.646      0.012    226.225      0.000
    FH2                2.709      0.012    232.059      0.000

 Variances
    PH                 1.839      0.179     10.277      0.000

 Residual Variances
    SHP                0.194      0.019     10.359      0.000
    SHC                0.367      0.016     23.627      0.000
    SICK               2.906      0.159     18.304      0.000
    CONSULT          175.061      7.166     24.429      0.000
    FH1                0.012      0.002      5.135      0.000
    FH2                0.020      0.002      8.231      0.000
    SH                 0.132      0.026      5.115      0.000
    FH                 0.102      0.009     11.015      0.000

STANDARDIZED MODEL RESULTS (STDYX Standardization)

                                                    Two-Tailed
                    Estimate       S.E.  Est./S.E.    P-Value

 SH       BY
    SHP                0.854      0.016     54.333      0.000
    SHC                0.647      0.018     36.103      0.000

 PH       BY
    SICK               0.623      0.026     24.309      0.000
    CONSULT            0.494      0.025     19.907      0.000

 FH       BY
    FH1                0.972      0.006    173.398      0.000
    FH2                0.955      0.006    165.700      0.000

 FH       ON
    PH                -0.722      0.030    -24.379      0.000

 SH       ON
    PH                -0.709      0.080     -8.836      0.000
    FH                 0.200      0.076      2.631      0.009

 Intercepts
    SHP                4.157      0.076     54.352      0.000
```

```
    SHC                 3.172      0.060     52.435      0.000
    SICK                1.242      0.033     37.891      0.000
    CONSULT             0.860      0.029     29.817      0.000
    FH1                 5.573      0.100     55.647      0.000
    FH2                 5.716      0.103     55.731      0.000

 Variances
    PH                  1.000      0.000    999.000    999.000

 Residual Variances
    SHP                 0.270      0.027     10.062      0.000
    SHC                 0.581      0.023     25.043      0.000
    SICK                0.612      0.032     19.203      0.000
    CONSULT             0.756      0.025     30.786      0.000
    FH1                 0.055      0.011      5.063      0.000
    FH2                 0.088      0.011      7.966      0.000
    SH                  0.251      0.045      5.549      0.000
    FH                  0.479      0.043     11.219      0.000


R-SQUARE

    Observed                                            Two-Tailed
    Variable        Estimate       S.E.  Est./S.E.    P-Value

    SHP                 0.730      0.027     27.166      0.000
    SHC                 0.419      0.023     18.052      0.000
    SICK                0.388      0.032     12.155      0.000
    CONSULT             0.244      0.025      9.953      0.000
    FH1                 0.945      0.011     86.699      0.000
    FH2                 0.912      0.011     82.850      0.000

     Latent                                             Two-Tailed
    Variable        Estimate       S.E.  Est./S.E.    P-Value

    SH                  0.749      0.045     16.517      0.000
    FH                  0.521      0.043     12.189      0.000
```

It is noteworthy that, in the latent model, the relationships between the constructs are much stronger than in the manifest model. This can be seen, in particular, from the latent variable R^2 values. According to these values, the latent model allows us to account for approximately 74.9% of the variability in subjective health and about 52.1% of the variability in functional health. In the manifest model, the corresponding proportions of variability accounted for were only 39.9% and 20%, respectively. There are two explanations for this rather large discrepancy. First, the latent analysis takes measurement error into account, which is not the case in the manifest model. The correction for measurement error leads to a disattenuation of the relationships at the latent level. Second, specific variance in the indicators (due to indicator heterogeneity) also contributes to the different estimates in the manifest and latent models. As seen above, the indicators of physical health are rather heterogeneous, as shown by the rather modest correlation between those indicators. In addition, the items used as indicators of subjective health are only moderately correlated (r = .553). These indicators therefore also show relatively large specific variance components that are treated as part of the error variables in the latent model.

In the manifest path model we did not use the variable `SHC` as indicator of subjective health, and we did not use the variable `CONSULT` as indicator of physical health. Therefore, the constructs of subjective health and physical health were defined in a narrower way in the manifest than in the latent model, and specific variance not shared with the other indicators used in the latent model could not be separated from variance that is shared with these indicators. This issue is probably not relevant for the indicators of functional health, because `FH1` and `FH2` are test halves created from the same subscale and are strongly correlated (r = .928), indicating that there is little specific variance in each test half.

In summary, in the present example there is a substantial amount of indicator specificity related to the indicators of subjective health and physical health. Removal of specific variance is partly responsible for the stronger relationships seen in the latent model compared to the manifest model because indicator-specific variance is separated from common variance and treated as part of the error. This means that the results should be interpreted with great caution in this case because the large amounts of specific variance may have inflated the relationships between the constructs. Hence, one should think carefully about whether the present operationalization of the latent variables for subjective and physical health is appropriate. This is a theoretical rather than a statistical problem that the user needs to solve based on substantive considerations.

The additional output obtained based on the `model indirect` command is not shown here in detail, but is available on the companion website. This output again provides us with detailed information on the size and statistical significance of the indirect effect in our model. In addition—and analogous to the manifest path model—we may again request bootstrap confidence intervals for testing the indirect effect. The principle is the same as for the manifest path model and is therefore not shown here in detail. The relevant input and output files can be found on the companion website.

4

Structural Equation Models for Measuring Variability and Change

Because of their high flexibility in modeling complex relationships between a large number of variables, and because of their ability to explicitly account for measurement error, linear SEMs are also very useful for analyzing longitudinal data (data obtained from repeated-measures designs). In the following sections we discuss the specification and analysis of five different types of longitudinal SEMs in Mplus. We distinguish between models for analyzing variability (variability models) and models for analyzing change (change models; Eid, Courvoisier, & Lischetzke, 2011). *Variability models* are used to model situation-specific fluctuations in scores around a stable set point or trait value. In contrast, *change models* are often used when the goal is to measure more long-lasting and potentially irreversible changes of psychological constructs over time.

With regard to variability models, we discuss latent state (LS) and latent state–trait (LST) models (Steyer et al., 1992, 1999) in Sections 4.1 and 4.2. In Section 4.1, we also discuss general issues relevant to longitudinal data analysis using SEMs; for example, the modeling of indicator-specific effects in multiple-indicator models and the issue of testing measurement invariance across time. Subsequently, we discuss three types of change models commonly used in the literature: (1) manifest and latent autoregressive models (Hertzog & Nesselroade, 1987; Jöreskog, 1979a, 1979b; see Section 4.3), (2) latent change (LC) models (McArdle, 1988; Raykov, 1993; Steyer et al., 1997; Steyer, Partchev, & Shanahan, 2000; see Section 4.4), and (3) latent growth curve models (LGCMs; Bollen & Curran, 2006; Duncan et al., 2006; see Section 4.5).

The main goal of the analysis of variability models is to determine the degree to which individual differences on an attribute or construct depend on situation- or occasion-specific effects versus stable person-specific effects. Following Steyer and colleagues (Steyer et al., 1992, 1999), we distinguish between a trait component (a component that characterizes stable person-specific effects), a state residual component (a component that characterizes effects of the situation and/or person × situation interactions), and a random measurement error component. We therefore speak of LST models (Steyer et al., 1992, 1999; see Section 4.2). For example, it is often of interest to which degree measurements (e.g., questionnaire or test scores) measure aspects of the situation or occasion of measurement (e.g., anxiety in a specific situation) versus stable personality dispositions (traits; e.g., trait anxiety = general anxiety of a person across situations) and random measurement error. These questions concern the temporal stability, reliability, and validity of the measurement of individual differences. LST models allow us to determine the degree of occasion specificity, consistency, and reliability through the calculation of variance components (Steyer et al., 1992, 1999).

4.1 LS ANALYSIS

In our introduction to longitudinal SEMs, we first consider different versions of the less complex LS models (see Figure 4.1 as well as Steyer et al., 1992). LS models can be seen as "precursors" of LST models and represent general CFA models for the analysis of longitudinal data (CFA models for cross-sectional data were discussed in Section 3.4). In LS models, no separation of stable from occasion-specific variance components is possible. Nonetheless, LS models are frequently used in practice for analyzing longitudinal data, partly because they are rather simple and unrestrictive.

The analysis of an LS model requires that multiple (and preferably the same) indicators are available at each time point to measure the construct of interest (e.g., depression). In an LS model, each observed variable Y_{ik} (i = indicator, k = occasion of measurement) is decomposed into a constant

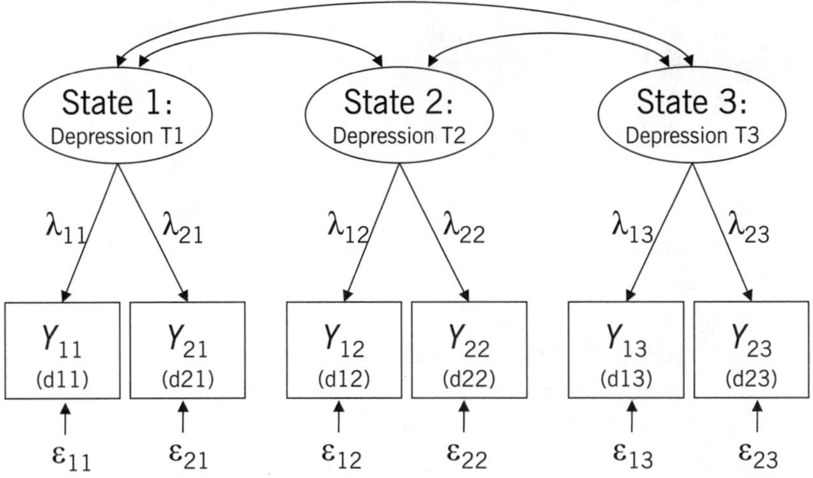

FIGURE 4.1. Latent state (LS) model for depression measured on three occasions of measurement (T1–T3). Y_{ik} = observed variable i measured at time point k; ε_{ik} = measurement error variable; λ_{ik} = factor loading. The variable names of the indicators used in Mplus appear in parentheses.

BOX 4.1. *Example of LS Analysis*

We use data from *Proyecto: La Familia* (The Family Project; Roosa et al., 2008), which assessed the health and adjustment of Mexican American children and their parents every 2 years, beginning in the fifth grade for the target children.* In the applications presented in this chapter, we fit longitudinal SEMs to three waves of fathers' (N = 323 complete cases) ratings of their own depressive symptoms, using the 20-item Center for Epidemiological Studies Depression scale (CES-D; Radloff, 1977). Sample items include "You felt depressed" and "You felt that everything you did was an effort." Items were answered on a 4-point scale ranging from "Rarely or none of the time" to "Most or all of the time." For the purpose of the present illustration, the items of this questionnaire were aggregated to two test halves, so that there would be two indicators of depression at each time point. The data set **depression.dat** contains the summary data (means, standard deviations, and correlations) for the two test halves measured on three occasions of measurement (variables **d11**, **d21**, **d12**, **d22**, **d13**, and **d23**).

*I would like to thank Mark Roosa for providing the data set for the analyses.

intercept term α_{ik}, an occasion-specific latent state variable (*State k*), and an occasion-specific measurement error (residual) variable ε_{ik}:

$$Y_{ik} = \alpha_{ik} + \lambda_{ik} \cdot (State\ k) + \varepsilon_{ik}$$

where λ_{ik} denotes a factor loading. Figure 4.1 shows an LS model for depression, measured with two variables Y_{1k} and Y_{2k} on three occasions of measurement (k = 1, 2, 3).

Figure 4.1 shows that all latent state variables can be correlated. These correlations reflect the "true" stability of individual differences across time (i.e., stability corrected for measurement error). The correlations between the state variables allow us to examine whether a construct is better described as a temporally stable disposition ("trait") or as an attribute that is prone to substantial occasion-specific fluctuations (a more state-like construct). Correlations between state factors that approach 1 indicate high stability of individual differences and therefore the construct can be seen as rather trait-like (e.g., intelligence). In contrast, moderate to small correlations between LS factors indicate that a construct depends strongly on the situation (i.e., is more state-like; e.g., anger, mood states, cortisol levels) or that some individuals changed more than others over time.

In addition, the correlations between the state factors also reveal whether an autoregressive process is present in the data. This is the case if the state factor correlations decline with increasing temporal distance between the measurements. Latent autoregressive models, which can be seen as special cases of LS models, are discussed in Section 4.3.

LS analyses typically do not involve any specific assumptions as to the structure of the correlations between the state factors (as is the case, e.g., in LST and latent autoregressive models; see below). This means that all possible correlations between LS variables are usually estimated as free, unconstrained parameters. This implies that the structural model of LS models is typically saturated, meaning that no testable restrictions can be derived from the structural model and therefore no degrees of freedom are obtained from this part of the model. This aspect makes LS models rather unrestrictive, which is one reason why they are often useful as a starting point for a longitudinal statistical analysis. Causes of potential misfit that may occur in more complex longitudinal SEMs are more easily identified in the LS model, because in an LS model misfit can be caused only by a misspecified measurement model (the structural model is saturated and hence does not contribute to any global misfit of the model).

4.1.1 LS versus LST Models

In LS models—in contrast to LST models, which are discussed in Section 4.2—only LS and measurement error variables are modeled. The LS variables in LS models are not further decomposed into trait and state residual components as in LST models (Steyer et al., 1992). Therefore, LS models do not allow for a separation of stable from occasion-specific components of variance.

Despite this limitation, LS models are useful for longitudinal data analysis. They serve as good baseline models not only in an LST analysis, but also in other types of longitudinal analyses. The reason is that many other types of longitudinal models are either reformulations (e.g., as LC models; see Section 4.4) or special cases of the LS model (e.g., as latent autoregressive models and second-order LGCMs; see Sections 4.3 and 4.5, respectively), some of which make more restrictive assumptions than the LS model (e.g., autoregressive models and LGCMs).

LS models allow the testing of basic aspects of longitudinal measurement models (e.g., the question of whether indicators used to measure a construct are homogeneous, whether the factor structure is invariant across time, and whether measurement invariance holds across time) before additional restrictive assumptions with regard to the LS factors are introduced (e.g., regarding a state–trait, autoregressive, or specific growth structure). Different options for modeling indicator-specific effects (situations where indicators are not perfectly homogeneous) are presented in Section 4.1.3. The issue of testing measurement invariance across time is discussed in Section 4.1.4. In Section 4.2, we discuss the extension of an LS model to an LST model.

4.1.2 Analysis of LS Models in Mplus

In the first step of an LS analysis, it is often a good idea to start with a rather unrestrictive model, which, for example, does not make any assumptions about time-invariant factor loadings, etc. An important question that should be clarified at the beginning is whether the basic hypothesized factor structure holds across time and whether indicators are homogeneous (or whether so-called *indicator-specific effects* are present).

Indicator specificity refers to method effects of indicators that become apparent in longitudinal analyses because the same indicators are repeatedly measured (Raffalovich & Bohrnstedt, 1987). An indicator that shares specific variance (i.e., variance that is not shared with the other indicators) with itself over time violates the assumption of uncorrelated residual variables made in the standard LS model. The reason is that, due to the presence of indicator-specific effects, the indicator would be more highly correlated with itself over time than with other indicators—violating the assumption of indicator homogeneity made in an LS model with uncorrelated residual variables. In other words, the standard LS model with uncorrelated residual variables would, in this case, be too restrictive, and the researcher would have to think of possibilities to adequately account for indicator-specific effects.

In the following, I first show the specification of a simple LS model in Mplus that does not account for indicator-specific effects. As we will see, this model shows a somewhat unsatisfactory fit in the present example due to the presence of indicator-specific effects. Subsequently, I demonstrate how the simple LS model can be extended to take indicator-specific effects into account. Figure 4.2 shows the Mplus input file for the estimation of the simple LS model without indicator-specific effects from Figure 4.1, based on the two repeatedly measured depression test halves. Using the subcommands

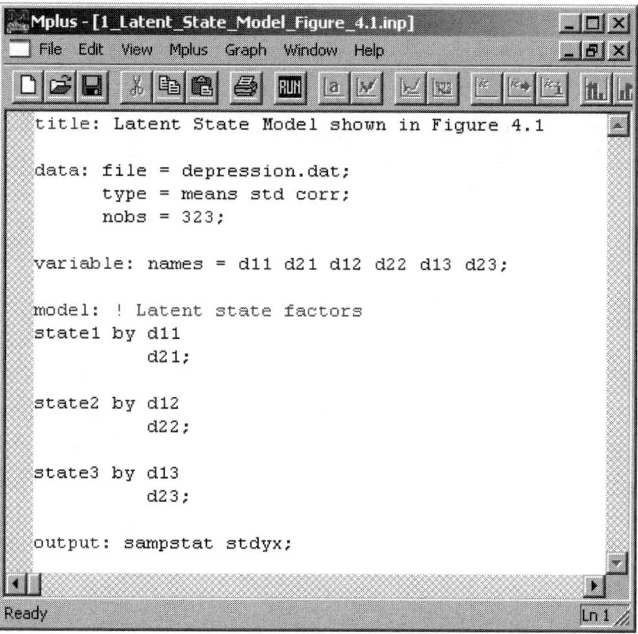

FIGURE 4.2. Mplus input file for the specification of a simple LS model for three measurement occasions without measurement invariance restrictions.

```
state1 by d11
          d21;
state2 by d12
          d22;
state3 by d13
          d23;
```

the indicators are assigned to the relevant LS factors. This command is analogous to the by statements in a conventional cross-sectional CFA model (see Section 3.4).

In the following, the model fit criteria reported in the Mplus output are shown for the simple LS model:

```
MODEL FIT INFORMATION

Chi-Square Test of Model Fit

        Value                              18.474
        Degrees of Freedom                      6
        P-Value                            0.0052
```

BOX 4.2. *Mplus Default for the Mean Structure*

In our basic LS model, we do not include latent means for the state factors and instead make use of the Mplus default settings, according to which all latent variable means are set to zero and all observed variable intercepts (α_{ik}) are freely estimated. To the degree that no restrictions are imposed on the intercepts of the observed variables, the intercepts will be identical to the observed variable means [expected values $E(Y_{ik})$]. This follows from the decomposition of the observed variable means in the LS model, because the LS means are set to zero by default in Mplus and the residual variables ε_{ik} have means of zero by definition (see Steyer et al., 1992):

$$\begin{aligned} E(Y_{ik}) &= E(\alpha_{ik}) + E(\lambda_{ik} \cdot State\ k) + E(\varepsilon_{ik}) \\ &= \alpha_{ik} \end{aligned}$$

In Section 4.1.4, I demonstrate how the means of the LS variables (that are often of interest in longitudinal studies) can be identified and estimated in Mplus.

```
Information Criteria

          Number of Free Parameters                    21
          Akaike (AIC)                           1088.313
          Bayesian (BIC)                         1167.643
          Sample-Size Adjusted BIC               1101.034
            (n* = (n + 2) / 24)

RMSEA (Root Mean Square Error Of Approximation)

          Estimate                                  0.080
          90 Percent C.I.                           0.040  0.123
          Probability RMSEA <= .05                  0.098

CFI/TLI

          CFI                                       0.990
          TLI                                       0.976

SRMR (Standardized Root Mean Square Residual)

          Value                                     0.012
```

It can be seen that the model shows a somewhat unsatisfactory fit, which is indicated, in particular, by the significant chi-square test (χ^2 = 18.474, df = 6, p = .0052) and the high *RMSEA* coefficient (.08), whereas the *CFI* (0.99) and *SRMR* (0.012) coefficients show acceptable values, according to commonly used criteria (see Box 3.7). A bad model fit in longitudinal SEMs with multiple indicators can often be explained by the presence of indicator-specific effects, which are not sufficiently accounted for in the simple LS model.

4.1.3 Modeling Indicator-Specific Effects

One possibility for modeling indicator-specific effects is to allow for correlations between the measurement error (residual) variables that pertain to the same indicator over time (e.g., Sörbom, 1975; see Figure 4.3). This is often referred to as an *LS model with autocorrelated error variables* (or—in the context of multitrait–multimethod analysis—as a *correlated uniqueness model*; e.g., see Cole & Maxwell, 2003; Lance, Noble, & Scullen, 2002).

Given that the estimation of error correlations is relatively straightforward, this approach to accounting for indicator-specific effects over time is popular among longitudinal researchers. A disadvantage of this method, however, is that it leaves indicator-specific effects confounded

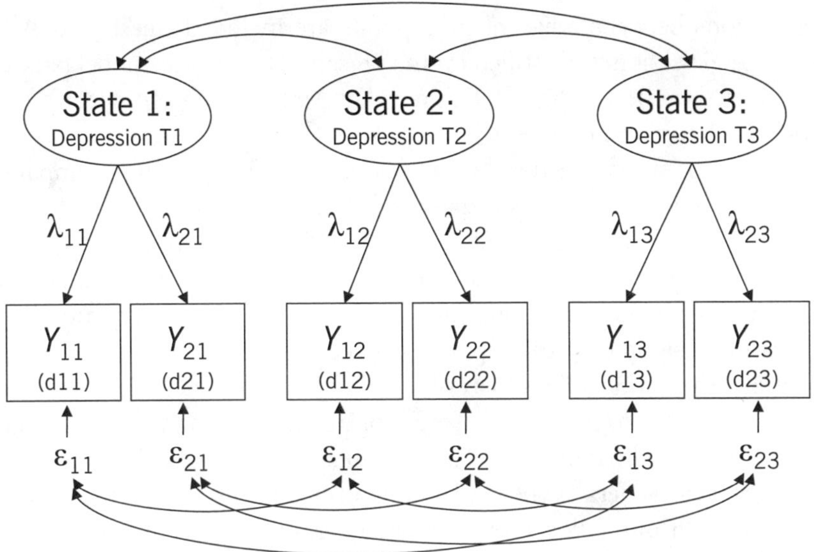

FIGURE 4.3. LS model with autocorrelated error variables for modeling indicator-specific effects. This model is underidentified in the present application because there are only two indicators per time point.

with random measurement error. Therefore, indicator-specific effects as a reliable source of individual differences are confounded with random error variance. As a consequence, the reliabilities of the indicators tend to be underestimated in models with correlated residuals (e.g., Geiser & Lockhart, 2012). An alternative way to account for indicator-specific effects is to include additional latent variables instead of correlated residual variables in the model—so-called *indicator-specific* (or method) factors. I first show the specification of correlated residuals in Mplus and then an alternative model version with an indicator-specific factor.

In our example with only two indicators per LS factor and only three time points, an LS model that allows all possible autocorrelations between residual variables is not identified (due to a lack of information) and therefore cannot be estimated (for a more detailed discussion of the issue of model identification in SEMs, see Bollen, 1989). In order to estimate a model with all possible autocorrelations between error variables, more indicators per time point and/or more than three time points are required.

In order to illustrate the principle of specifying correlated error variables in Mplus, we choose a slightly more restrictive version of the LS model, with autocorrelated error variables in which only the error correlations between adjacent time points are included (see Figure 4.4). This model version is identified for the present data and the model parameters can thus be estimated. The relevant Mplus syntax to specify this model is shown in Figure 4.5.

The model fit statistics for this model are slightly better compared to the LS model without correlated residual variables, χ^2 = 8.536, *df* = 2, *p* = .014; *RMSEA* = .101, *CFI* = 0.995, *SRMR* = 0.008, except for the higher *RMSEA* value. Nonetheless, the model with autocorrelated residuals between adjacent time points also shows a significant chi-square value, indicating a significant discrepancy between the model and the data. In addition, the *RMSEA* value is even higher than for the original model (presumably due to the loss in degrees of freedom through the estimation of four additional parameters). These results might suggest that indicator-specific effects generalize beyond adjacent time points, so that the current model (which only allows for correlated errors of adjacent time points) does not sufficiently account for these effects.

Eid, Schneider, and Schwenkmezger (1999; see also Eid, 2000) proposed an approach for modeling indicator-specific effects that does not require the estimation of correlated error variables and thus allows

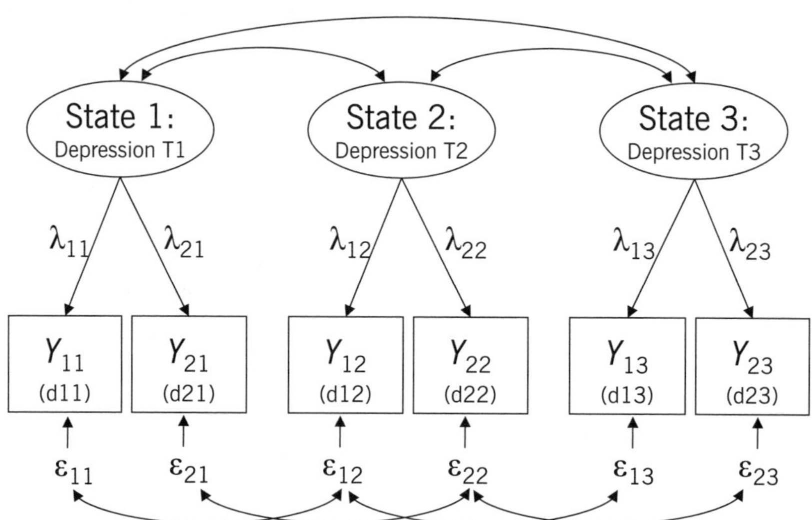

FIGURE 4.4. LS model with autocorrelated error variables for modeling indicator-specific effects. In contrast to the model in Figure 4.3, error correlations are admitted only between adjacent measurement occasions. This model is identified in the present application.

```
model: ! Latent state factors
state1 by d11
          d21;

state2 by d12
          d22;

state3 by d13
          d23;

! Specification of correlated residual variables for adjacent time points
d11 with d12;
d12 with d13;
d21 with d22;
d22 with d23;
```

FIGURE 4.5. Mplus `model` command for the specification of the LS model with autocorrelated error variables between adjacent measurement occasions shown in Figure 4.4.

researchers to avoid the problem of underestimated reliabilities of indicators. In this approach, one indicator is chosen as comparison standard (i.e., a reference indicator). The reference indicator could, for example, be a marker variable that best represents the construct—either theoretically or empirically. For simplicity, we assume in the following that the first indicator (Y_{1k}) is selected as the reference indicator. However, in principle, any other indicator could serve as reference indicator as well.

The reference indicators Y_{1k} load only on the LS factors, whereas the remaining (non-reference) indicators Y_{ik}, $i \neq 1$, have loadings on both the state factors and a so-called *indicator-specific* (or method) factor (IS_2; see Figure 4.6). The indicator-specific factor reflects the specificity of the non-reference indicators Y_{ik}, $i \neq 1$, relative to the reference indicators Y_{1k}. In the present case, we therefore need only *one* indicator-specific factor (i.e., for the second indicator Y_{2k}). In general, if I indicates the total number of indicators, then $I - 1$ indicator-specific factors are needed to account for indicator-specific effects in LS models.

The indicator-specific factors are defined as residual factors with regard to the state variables pertaining to the reference indicator (Eid, 2000; Eid et al., 1999; Geiser, 2009). The indicator-specific factors therefore represent that part of the reliable variance of the non-reference indicators that is not shared with the reference indicators. It follows from this definition that the mean of each indicator-specific factor is zero and that the means are uncorrelated with all LS factors that pertain to the same construct. The latter aspect is particularly relevant for the specification

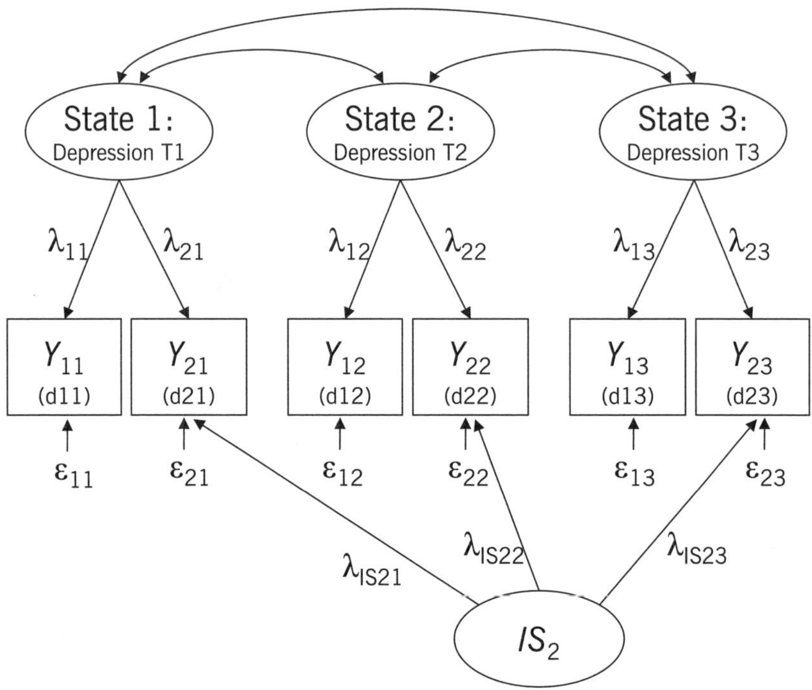

FIGURE 4.6. LS model with an indicator-specific (method) factor (IS_2) for the second indicator. The parameters λ_{IS2k} indicate factor loadings on the indicator-specific factor. The indicator-specific factor is defined as a residual factor with respect to the LS factors and is therefore by definition uncorrelated with all state factors that pertain to the same construct.

in Mplus, because we need to tell Mplus explicitly which factors *cannot* be correlated. (The mean of all factors is assumed to be zero by default in Mplus [see Box 4.2] so that the zero mean of the indicator-specific factor is not a specific issue in Mplus.)

Note that the meaning of the LS factors in Figure 4.6 is now determined by the meaning of the reference indicator (Y_{1k}). In our case, for example, the meaning of *State* 1 depends on the meaning of indicator `d11`. For this reason, as mentioned above, researchers should choose a reference variable that best represents the construct (a so-called *marker variable*). This step is particularly important when a researcher deals with rather heterogeneous indicators that represent different facets of a construct. We return to this issue below when we discuss the model results in detail. Figure 4.7 shows the Mplus syntax for the specification of the LS model with an indicator-specific factor for the second indicator.

The indicator-specific factor (here named `is2`) is introduced analogously to the state factors by using a `by` statement. Of importance, the correlations of the factor `is2` and the state factors `state1–state3` (that Mplus would try to estimate as the default) have to be set to zero explicitly, because `is2` is defined as a residual factor with respect to all three state factors. The following command is used to set these correlations to zero:

```
is2 with state1@0 state2@0 state3@0;
```

In the output, we can see that the LS model with indicator-specific factor shows a better fit than either the simple LS model or the LS model with autocorrelated residual variables between adjacent time points. The chi-square value for the LS model with indicator-specific factors is smaller and statistically nonsignificant, $\chi^2 = 3.569$, $df = 3$, $p = .3119$. Furthermore, *RMSEA* (.024) and *SRMR* (0.008) also indicate an improved fit. In addition, the *AIC* value for the model with indicator-specific factor (1079.408) is lower than the *AIC* values for both the simple LS model (1088.313) and the LS model with autocorrelated residual variables (1086.375) between adjacent time points. We therefore only show the results for the well-fitting model with an indicator-specific factor for the second indicator. The complete outputs for the two previous LS models can be found on the companion website.

As usual, Mplus first outputs the unstandardized model parameter estimates. It can be seen that the unstandardized state factor loadings of the second indicator are slightly lower than the loadings of the first

```
model: ! Latent state factors
state1 by d11
          d21;

state2 by d12
          d22;

state3 by d13
          d23;

! Indicator-specific (residual) factor for the second indicator
is2 by d21 d22 d23;

! Indicator-specific factor is not allowed to correlate with the state factors
is2 with state1@0 state2@0 state3@0;
```

FIGURE 4.7. Mplus `model` command for the specification of the LS model with one indicator-specific factor (`is2`) for the second indicator shown in Figure 4.6.

indicator (the unstandardized loadings of the first indicator have been fixed to 1 for identification as the default). This may indicate that the second indicator does not discriminate as well as the first indicator between individuals with lower versus higher scores on the LS. In other words, a one-unit change in each LS factor score is associated with a slightly smaller expected increase in the score on the second indicator than in the score on the first one.

In addition, we see that the state loadings of the second indicator are estimated to very similar values at each time point. This already indicates that the assumption of time-invariant loadings is probably tenable in this case (a formal test of this assumption is discussed in Section 4.1.4). Furthermore, we can see that the two freely estimated factor loadings on the indicator-specific factor `is2` are not significantly different from zero. This indicates that indicator-specific effects are rather weak in this example, showing that the indicators are rather homogeneous. The standardized loadings (see output `STANDARDIZED MODEL RESULTS [STDYX Standardization]`), however, are significantly different from zero and range between .157 and .278.

In practice, it is very important to closely examine the degree of heterogeneity of the indicators (i.e., strength of indicator-specific effects). If the standardized loadings on the indicator-specific factors are large (e.g., say, .5 or larger), this finding would indicate that 25% or more of observed individual differences are due to indicator specificity (i.e., the squared standardized loadings indicate the proportion of variability in the observed variables that is accounted for by the relevant factor). This would mean that the indicators are rather heterogeneous and mirror at least somewhat different facets of a construct.

In such cases, one should carefully think about which indicator best serves as the reference indicator, because the substantive meaning and interpretation of the LS factors depend on the choice of the reference indicator in the model with $I - 1$ indicator-specific factors. For example, if indicators are rather heterogeneous, correlations of state factors with external variables might vary substantially for different reference indicators. In addition, different indicators may show differential mean changes over time.

If strong indicator-specific effects are present in a study, primarily theoretical/substantive criteria should be used to decide which indicator best represents the construct of interest, and the corresponding indicator should be selected as the reference indicator to ensure that the state factors represent the intended construct (for a more detailed discussion of this issue, see Geiser, Eid, & Nussbeck, 2008). In addition, researchers should carry out careful sensitivity analyses to examine in which way the choice of different reference indicators does, or does not, affect the results obtained for the structural model (e.g., intercorrelation of the state factors, relationships of state factors to external variables, LS factor means and variances).

In our example, indicator-specific effects are minor, as indicated by the small standardized loadings on the `is2` factor, which, as mentioned above, range from .157 to .278. Therefore, at most $.278^2 = 7.7\%$ of the observed variability is due to indicator-specific effects, which can be seen as unproblematic. From a substantive point of view this suggests that the indicators are rather homogeneous (i.e., measure, to a large extent, the same true score) and have only small indicator-specific variance components.

In addition, we see that all covariances between the indicator-specific factor and the three state factors were set to zero as requested. Therefore, the `is2` factor can be interpreted as a residual factor. In contrast, the covariances among the state factors were freely estimated. All state covariances are significantly different from zero ($8.354 \leq z \leq 7.586$). Hence, a significant portion of individual differences with regard to depression remained stable across time. The exact amount of stability, however, is difficult to assess based on the covariances, because covariances are unstandardized measures of association. For this reason, researchers typically report the *correlations* between the state factors as measures of stability because correlations are standardized measures of association that do not depend on the metric of the variables and are therefore easier to interpret (see below).

In the unstandardized solution, we furthermore obtain the estimated intercepts, factor variances, and residual variances. The unstandardized intercepts are, in this case, identical to the observed variable means, because the present model does not impose any restrictions on the mean structure of the variables (cf. Box 4.2).

```
MODEL RESULTS

                                                    Two-Tailed
                    Estimate       S.E.  Est./S.E.    P-Value

 STATE1    BY
    D11                1.000      0.000    999.000    999.000
    D21                0.700      0.049     14.221      0.000
```

```
STATE2   BY
   D12                1.000      0.000    999.000    999.000
   D22                0.749      0.043     17.342      0.000

STATE3   BY
   D13                1.000      0.000    999.000    999.000
   D23                0.755      0.047     16.192      0.000

IS2      BY
   D21                1.000      0.000    999.000    999.000
   D22                0.623      0.378      1.650      0.099
   D23                0.793      0.507      1.564      0.118

IS2      WITH
   STATE1             0.000      0.000    999.000    999.000
   STATE2             0.000      0.000    999.000    999.000
   STATE3             0.000      0.000    999.000    999.000

STATE2   WITH
   STATE1             0.120      0.015      7.917      0.000

STATE3   WITH
   STATE1             0.110      0.014      7.586      0.000
   STATE2             0.128      0.015      8.354      0.000

Intercepts
   D11                1.584      0.027     58.307      0.000
   D21                1.354      0.021     65.148      0.000
   D12                1.642      0.028     58.527      0.000
   D22                1.389      0.023     60.772      0.000
   D13                1.631      0.027     60.284      0.000
   D23                1.402      0.023     62.159      0.000

Variances
   STATE1             0.205      0.022      9.287      0.000
   STATE2             0.230      0.023     10.185      0.000
   STATE3             0.214      0.021     10.012      0.000
   IS2                0.011      0.008      1.402      0.161

Residual Variances
   D11                0.033      0.012      2.717      0.007
   D21                0.028      0.009      3.134      0.002
   D12                0.025      0.011      2.284      0.022
   D22                0.036      0.007      5.326      0.000
   D13                0.022      0.011      2.028      0.043
   D23                0.035      0.008      4.692      0.000
```

Based on the completely standardized solution (STANDARDIZED MODEL RESULTS [STDYX Standardization]), in which all observed and all latent variables are standardized, we can see that the observed variables have rather high loadings on the state factors (≥ .849) and rather small loadings on the indicator-specific factor (largest loading = .278; see discussion above). The standardized loadings can again be interpreted as the estimated correlations between each indicator and the corresponding latent variable, because the state factors are uncorrelated with the indicator-specific factor. Based on the indicators' high standardized loadings on the state factors and the low loadings on the `is2` factor, we can conclude that the indicators are highly reliable and rather homogeneous.

The standardized solution also provides us with the estimated latent correlations between the state factors. In this example, the states show moderately high correlations across time ($.523 \leq r \leq .578$), which indicates a moderate degree of stability of individual differences over time. Note that adjacent state factors (*State* 1 and *State* 2 as well as *State* 2 and *State* 3) are slightly more highly correlated than the more "distant" state factors *State* 1 and *State* 3. This finding indicates the presence of a small autoregressive effect (cf. Section 4.3).

Of interest are also the estimated R^2 values for the observed variables, which are reported at the end of the standardized solution. These values can be used as estimates of the reliabilities of the indicators. As we already saw based on the high standardized loadings, all six variables show high reliabilities (*Rel*), which range between .785 and .907. This shows that the six indicators of depression (here: questionnaire scales) allow for a high precision of measurement (small error).

```
STANDARDIZED MODEL RESULTS (STDYX Standardization)

                                                    Two-Tailed
                    Estimate       S.E.  Est./S.E.    P-Value

 STATE1   BY
    D11                0.928      0.028     32.992      0.000
    D21                0.849      0.029     28.934      0.000

 STATE2   BY
    D12                0.950      0.023     42.147      0.000
    D22                0.874      0.024     36.260      0.000

 STATE3   BY
    D13                0.952      0.024     39.012      0.000
    D23                0.862      0.026     33.195      0.000
```

```
 IS2      BY
    D21                0.278       0.099        2.810        0.005
    D22                0.157       0.062        2.551        0.011
    D23                0.203       0.076        2.687        0.007

 IS2      WITH
    STATE1             0.000       0.000      999.000      999.000
    STATE2             0.000       0.000      999.000      999.000
    STATE3             0.000       0.000      999.000      999.000

 STATE2   WITH
    STATE1             0.552       0.045       12.293        0.000

 STATE3   WITH
    STATE1             0.523       0.047       11.194        0.000
    STATE2             0.578       0.043       13.524        0.000

 Intercepts
    D11                3.244       0.139       23.299        0.000
    D21                3.625       0.153       23.727        0.000
    D12                3.257       0.140       23.313        0.000
    D22                3.381       0.144       23.463        0.000
    D13                3.354       0.143       23.420        0.000
    D23                3.459       0.147       23.556        0.000

 Variances
    STATE1             1.000       0.000      999.000      999.000
    STATE2             1.000       0.000      999.000      999.000
    STATE3             1.000       0.000      999.000      999.000
    IS2                1.000       0.000      999.000      999.000

 Residual Variances
    D11                0.139       0.052        2.673        0.008
    D21                0.202       0.066        3.063        0.002
    D12                0.097       0.043        2.255        0.024
    D22                0.212       0.042        5.063        0.000
    D13                0.093       0.046        2.007        0.045
    D23                0.215       0.048        4.501        0.000

R-SQUARE

    Observed                                                Two-Tailed
    Variable        Estimate       S.E.  Est./S.E.          P-Value

    D11                0.861       0.052       16.496        0.000
    D21                0.798       0.066       12.080        0.000
    D12                0.903       0.043       21.073        0.000
    D22                0.788       0.042       18.865        0.000
    D13                0.907       0.046       19.506        0.000
    D23                0.785       0.048       16.401        0.000
```

The LS model with an indicator-specific factor for the second indicator showed a very good fit to the data and fit better than both a model that did not account for indicator-specific effects and a model with correlated residual variables between adjacent time points. It therefore makes sense to use the model with the indicator-specific factor as the basis for tests of measurement invariance across time (see next section) and other more advanced longitudinal analyses. Had there not been any indicator-specific effects, we would have preferred the simpler model without the indicator-specific factor and would have used this simpler model as the basis for further analysis.

4.1.4 Testing for Measurement Invariance across Time

In most longitudinal investigations the question of measurement invariance or *measurement equivalence* across time is an important concern. Usually, researchers want to make sure that the indicators (e.g., items, scale scores) that they used did not change their relationship to the latent variables in any critical way over the course of the study. The reason is that changes in, for example, the factor loadings of the same indicator over time may result in a different interpretation of an LS factor on different occasions of measurement. This is typically not desirable, because it can make across-time comparisons of latent scores difficult. In particular, we want to make sure that key parameters of our LS measurement model for depression do not change over time so that the latent states are comparable across time. If a sufficient degree of measurement invariance does not hold, comparisons of, for example, LS factor means across time may be uninterpretable. In this case, the LS variables may not represent the same constructs, or the constructs may be measured on different scales with different origins and/or different units of measurement, making it hard to compare them across time.

SEMs for longitudinal data that are based on the same multiple indicators at each time point (such as the LS model) allow us to formally test whether, and to what degree, measurement invariance holds over time, using model tests and fit indices. Specifically, the question of measurement invariance refers to the time invariance of the measurement model parameters—that is, the factor loadings, intercepts, and residual variances. The level of measurement invariance present in the data can be determined by imposing equality constraints on these parameters and checking whether these additional restrictions lead to a significant decrease in model fit. An *equality constraint* is a constraint that forces a parameter to be estimated to an equivalent value as another parameter and is easily implemented in Mplus.

A minimum level of measurement invariance is typically desired in longitudinal studies, because certain across-time comparisons (e.g., examination of latent mean differences) depend on a certain level of measurement invariance. The absence of measurement invariance can render these comparisons impossible or at least difficult to interpret.

The degree of measurement invariance (see Box 4.3) that can be assumed for the data at hand is often determined through statistical model comparisons. In these comparisons, models with different levels of

BOX 4.3. *Different Levels of Measurement Invariance According to Widaman and Reise (1997)*

Widaman and Reise (1997; see also Meredith, 1993; Meredith & Horn, 2001) distinguish between the following levels of measurement invariance:

- *Configural invariance* is the weakest form of measurement invariance. Configural invariance requires only the factor structure (the number of factors and the loading pattern) to be constant across time. No specific *parameters* have to be equal across time to satisfy this criterion.
- The next highest level, *weak factorial invariance*, requires the factor loadings λ_{ik} to be the same over time for all indicators.
- The condition of *strong factorial invariance* is satisfied when, in addition to the loadings, the intercepts α_{ik} of the indicators are also time-invariant.
- *Strict factorial invariance* means that, in addition to loadings and intercepts, indicator residual variances $Var(\varepsilon_{ik})$ are constant across time.

Additional, even stricter, forms of parameter invariance such as, for example, the assumption of equal LS factor variances and/or covariances across time, can also be tested. In addition to the stability of the latent variance/covariance structure, latent mean stability can be tested, which is often of interest in longitudinal studies. A prerequisite for a meaningful interpretation of latent mean change over time is that at least strong factorial invariance can be assumed for the measurement model. Sometimes the assumption of invariance in parameters across time can be made for only a subset of the indicators, whereas other indicators show noninvariant parameters. In this case, one speaks of *partial measurement invariance*. Byrne, Shavelson, and Muthén (1989) discuss issues related to partial measurement invariance in detail.

measurement invariance are estimated and evaluated in terms of their relative fit compared to other more and less restrictive models. For example, a configural invariance model (model without equality restrictions) can be tested against a model in which the loadings are set equal across time (weak factorial invariance model) and/or against a model with equal loadings and equal intercepts (strong factorial invariance model). The most restrictive model that still shows an acceptable fit is selected, because it is most parsimonious while still representing the data adequately.

One strategy to determine the degree of measurement invariance is to specify more and more restrictive versions of the LS model until model fit criteria (e.g., the chi-square test of model fit) indicate that the latest set of restrictions is no longer tenable for the data. The LS model version with the most comprehensive set of restrictions that still shows an acceptable fit is then selected. The most restricted model is chosen, because it typically allows for an easier interpretation and comparability of certain parameters and because it is more parsimonious (uses fewer parameters) than less constrained model versions.

In our application in Section 4.1.3, we already estimated an LS model with configural invariance. We therefore start our analysis of measurement invariance with the next highest level of measurement invariance, which is weak factorial invariance. In this model, only the factor loadings, but not the intercepts and residual variances, are set equal across time.

In general, parameters can be set equal in Mplus by providing the same number or parameter label in parentheses on the same input line after parameters that should be held equal. Which particular number (or label) is chosen is arbitrary. The user only has to make sure that the *same* number is chosen for parameters to be set equal and that *different* numbers are chosen for different groups of parameters that should be set equal, respectively. (This point will become clearer below when we specify a model with time-invariant loadings and intercepts.) In our case, for the weak factorial invariance model, only the loadings of the second indicator have to be set equal, because the loadings of the first indicator are fixed to 1 at each time point to set the scale of the LS factors and are therefore already implicitly set equal across time.

We chose the number `(1)` to set the state factor loadings of the second indicator equal across time:

```
state1 by d11
          d21 (1);
```

```
state2 by d12
          d22 (1);

state3 by d13
          d23 (1);
```

It is important to note that the specification `(1)` does not mean that the parameter is supposed to be estimated to a value that is equal (or even close) to 1. The number `(1)` merely causes Mplus to estimate the *same* value for each of the loadings λ_{21}, λ_{22}, and λ_{23}. This specification does *not* tell Mplus *which* specific value it is. The optimal value in terms of the ML criterion is determined by Mplus when the parameters of the model are estimated. (In order to fix parameters to specific values, the `@` command is used in Mplus.)

For the indicator-specific factor (`is2`), we also specify equal loadings over time. Although equality of indicator-specific factor loadings is not strictly necessary for most purposes, this restriction is often plausible and meaningful (because the indicator remains the same). In addition, it contributes to the parsimony of the model. The equality restrictions for this factor are slightly different, because the parameters that are subject to the equality constraint here are loadings on a time-unspecific factor. Given that the first loading on this factor is again fixed to 1 by default in Mplus (i.e., $\lambda_{IS21} = 1$), we have to *fix* the remaining two indicator-specific factor loadings (λ_{IS22} and λ_{IS23}) to 1 as well to obtain equal loadings on this factor. (This was not necessary for the three state factor loadings of the second indicator because none of the loadings was fixed to any specific value as the default.) The loadings λ_{IS22} and λ_{IS23} are therefore fixed to 1 in the `model` command using the `@` symbol:

```
is2 by d21 d22@1 d23@1;
```

The complete Mplus `model` command for the model with weak factorial invariance is shown in Figure 4.8. The fit indices reported by Mplus show that—similar to the configural invariance model (see Section 4.1.3)—the weak factorial invariance model shows a good fit to the data, $\chi^2 = 5.094$, $df = 7$, $p = .6484$, $RMSEA = .00$, $p(RMSEA \leq .05) = .925$, $SRMR = .012$, $CFI = 1.00$. To test whether the more restrictive model with weak factorial invariance fits the data significantly worse than the configural model with unrestricted factor loadings for the second indicator,

```
model: ! Latent state factors
state1 by d11
          d21 (1);

state2 by d12
          d22 (1);

state3 by d13
          d23 (1);

! Indicator-specific (residual) factor for the second indicator
is2 by d21 d22@1 d23@1;

! Indicator-specific factor is not allowed to correlate with the state factors
is2 with state1@0 state2@0 state3@0;
```

FIGURE 4.8. Mplus `model` command for the specification of the LS model with one indicator-specific factor (`is2`) for the second indicator and time-invariant loadings (model of weak factorial invariance).

a chi-square difference test can be used, because the models are hierarchically nested (cf. Box 3.7). *Nested* means that the model with invariant loadings can be seen as a special case of the baseline model with unrestricted loadings: The model with invariant loadings directly follows from the configural model by constraining certain parameters.

Chi-square difference tests can be easily calculated by hand or using specialized software. In Box 4.4, I provide a description of how chi-square difference tests can be conducted automatically, based on Mplus outputs, using Crayen's (2010) software *Chi-Square Difference Calculator* (CDC). The CDC program (version 3) as well as a manual can be found on the companion website.

In our example, the comparison of the weak factorial invariance model with the configural invariance model yields a chi-square difference value of $\chi^2_\Delta = 5.094 - 3.569 = 1.525$. A chi-square value of 1.525 with $df_\Delta = 7 - 3 = 4$ is not significant at the .05 level ($p = .82$; see also Box 4.4). This means that the more restrictive model with equal loadings across time does not fit significantly worse than the configural model with unrestricted loadings. Hence, the assumption of weak factorial invariance is not rejected for these data. The *AIC* also favors the more restricted model (*AIC* = 1072.933) over the configural model (*AIC* = 1079.408), even though the difference in the values is not very large.

By looking at the unstandardized parameter estimates (rubric MODEL RESULTS; see below), we can see that the desired invariance restrictions on the factor loadings were correctly implemented by Mplus. The

BOX 4.4. Automated Chi-Square Difference Test Using Crayen's (2010) CDC Software

The Chi-Square Difference Calculator (CDC) program allows for an automated comparison of model fit between two nested models based on Mplus output files. In the first step, the two nested models have to be estimated in Mplus. Subsequently, the file CDC.exe (see companion website) is executed.

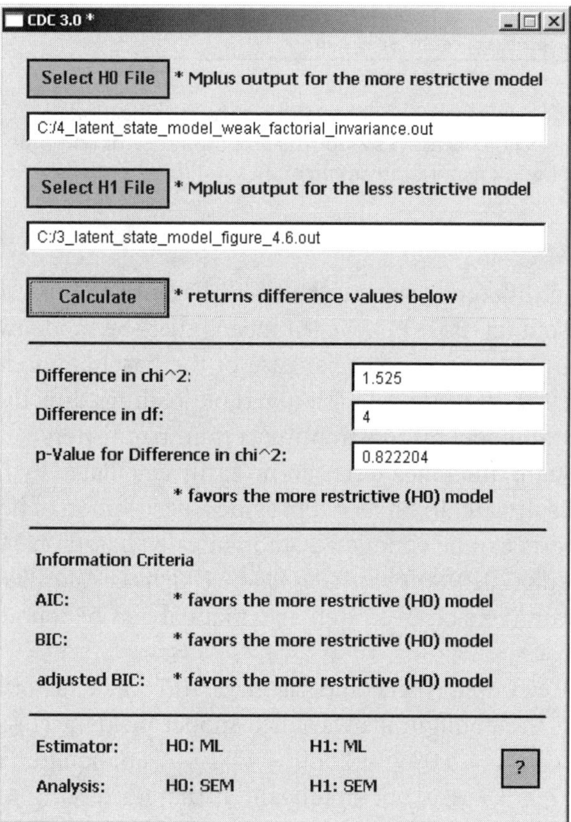

We then have to specify the location of the output file for (1) the more restrictive (**H0**) model and (2) the less restrictive (**H1**) model. Either the corresponding paths can be typed directly into the respective fields or the **Select H0/H1 File** buttons can be used to browse the computer for these files. By clicking on **Calculate**, the program determines the chi-square difference value, the differences in *df*, and the *p*-value for the chi-square difference under the null hypothesis that the more restrictive model fits the data. In addition, the program reports which model would be favored based on *AIC*,

BIC, and sample-size-adjusted *BIC* (see Box 3.7). In this example, the more restrictive model with equal loadings is preferred according to all criteria (see discussion in the text).

It is important to note that the CDC program does not check whether the assumptions required for proper chi-square difference testing (see Box 3.7) are met. Specifically, the program does not check whether the two models chosen by the user are, in fact, nested. This has to be determined by the user *prior* to the analysis. For certain non-nested models, statistical comparisons via the *AIC*, *BIC*, and/or sample-size-adjusted *BIC* may still be meaningful, but chi-square difference testing would not be appropriate for these models.

unstandardized state factor loadings of the second indicator were all estimated to the same value ($\hat{\lambda}_{21} = \hat{\lambda}_{22} = \hat{\lambda}_{23} = 0.737$ as intended). In addition, all three loadings show the same standard error ($SE = 0.03$), test statistic ($z = 24.857$), and *p*-value ($p < .001$). All loadings on the indicator-specific factor `is2` were fixed to 1, as desired. The fact that no standard errors (and consequently no test statistic) were estimated for any of the `is2` factor loadings shows that they are fixed parameters in this model—as was intended.

BOX 4.5. *Checking the Correct Implementation of Constraints*

The Mplus output for all models that include specific equality or other constraints should be carefully screened for correct implementation of the desired restrictions. The reason is that, especially with complex models, errors can easily be made in the input specification. One should therefore always check carefully whether the intended parameters were set equal (or not equal). Sometimes an implausibly bad model fit can be a sign that one or more parameter constraints were incorrectly specified. For example, it can occur that erroneously, the same number is used twice for setting *different* parameter groups equal. This may lead to the implementation of overly restrictive and/or meaningless model constraints (e.g., the constraint that loadings are set equal to intercepts). Such errors can lead to a significant misfit of the model and to incorrect conclusions. Therefore, a careful inspection of the correct implementation of all restrictions should always be carried out before interpreting key model results, conducting statistical model comparisons, etc.

```
MODEL RESULTS

                                                    Two-Tailed
                    Estimate       S.E.  Est./S.E.    P-Value

 STATE1   BY
    D11                1.000      0.000    999.000    999.000
    D21                0.737      0.030     24.857      0.000

 STATE2   BY
    D12                1.000      0.000    999.000    999.000
    D22                0.737      0.030     24.857      0.000

 STATE3   BY
    D13                1.000      0.000    999.000    999.000
    D23                0.737      0.030     24.857      0.000

 IS2      BY
    D21                1.000      0.000    999.000    999.000
    D22                1.000      0.000    999.000    999.000
    D23                1.000      0.000    999.000    999.000

 IS2      WITH
    STATE1             0.000      0.000    999.000    999.000
    STATE2             0.000      0.000    999.000    999.000
    STATE3             0.000      0.000    999.000    999.000

 STATE2   WITH
    STATE1             0.118      0.015      7.963      0.000

 STATE3   WITH
    STATE1             0.108      0.014      7.622      0.000
    STATE2             0.129      0.015      8.419      0.000

 Intercepts
    D11                1.584      0.027     58.666      0.000
    D21                1.354      0.021     64.730      0.000
    D12                1.642      0.028     58.461      0.000
    D22                1.389      0.023     60.797      0.000
    D13                1.631      0.027     60.172      0.000
    D23                1.402      0.022     62.502      0.000

 Variances
    STATE1             0.195      0.019     10.505      0.000
    STATE2             0.233      0.021     11.021      0.000
    STATE3             0.218      0.020     10.982      0.000
    IS2                0.007      0.002      3.456      0.001

 Residual Variances
    D11                0.040      0.009      4.462      0.000
    D21                0.028      0.005      5.422      0.000
```

```
  D12                 0.022        0.009        2.434        0.015
  D22                 0.035        0.006        6.288        0.000
  D13                 0.019        0.009        2.173        0.030
  D23                 0.037        0.006        6.592        0.000
```

Notice that the *standardized* loadings (shown in the following) are *not* invariant, but can vary across time in this model. The reason is that the weak factorial invariance model does not involve invariance constraints on the state factor variances and the residual variances. The standardized loadings would be the same across time only if the state factor variances and the residual variances were also held equal across time.

```
STANDARDIZED MODEL RESULTS (STDYX Standardization)

                                                        Two-Tailed
                    Estimate       S.E.  Est./S.E.     P-Value

 STATE1    BY
    D11                 0.911      0.021     43.928       0.000
    D21                 0.867      0.022     39.796       0.000

 STATE2    BY
    D12                 0.957      0.018     52.262       0.000
    D22                 0.867      0.020     43.413       0.000

 STATE3    BY
    D13                 0.959      0.019     49.979       0.000
    D23                 0.855      0.021     41.265       0.000

 IS2       BY
    D21                 0.221      0.033      6.773       0.000
    D22                 0.202      0.030      6.761       0.000
    D23                 0.206      0.030      6.774       0.000

 IS2       WITH
    STATE1              0.000      0.000    999.000     999.000
    STATE2              0.000      0.000    999.000     999.000
    STATE3              0.000      0.000    999.000     999.000

 STATE2    WITH
    STATE1              0.552      0.045     12.346       0.000

 STATE3    WITH
    STATE1              0.521      0.047     11.179       0.000
    STATE2              0.574      0.043     13.455       0.000

 Intercepts
    D11                 3.264      0.138     23.632       0.000
    D21                 3.602      0.149     24.153       0.000
```

```
    D12                   3.253      0.139     23.399      0.000
    D22                   3.383      0.141     23.959      0.000
    D13                   3.348      0.143     23.490      0.000
    D23                   3.478      0.144     24.194      0.000

 Variances
    STATE1                1.000      0.000    999.000    999.000
    STATE2                1.000      0.000    999.000    999.000
    STATE3                1.000      0.000    999.000    999.000
    IS2                   1.000      0.000    999.000    999.000

 Residual Variances
    D11                   0.171      0.038      4.517      0.000
    D21                   0.200      0.036      5.529      0.000
    D12                   0.085      0.035      2.429      0.015
    D22                   0.207      0.033      6.316      0.000
    D13                   0.080      0.037      2.172      0.030
    D23                   0.227      0.034      6.744      0.000

R-SQUARE

    Observed                                                Two-Tailed
    Variable          Estimate       S.E.  Est./S.E.    P-Value

    D11                   0.829      0.038     21.964      0.000
    D21                   0.800      0.036     22.122      0.000
    D12                   0.915      0.035     26.131      0.000
    D22                   0.793      0.033     24.138      0.000
    D13                   0.920      0.037     24.989      0.000
    D23                   0.773      0.034     22.926      0.000
```

In the next step, we test a model in which strong factorial invariance is assumed. In this model, the intercepts of all indicators are set equal across time in addition to the factor loadings. Given that we want to allow for differences in the LS variable means across time, we have to override the Mplus default according to which all latent variables have means of 0 (cf. Box 4.2). Otherwise, our specification with equal intercepts in conjunction with zero latent means would be very restrictive because it would reflect the assumption of zero mean change across time. (In the weak factorial invariance model, this was not an issue, because all intercepts were freely estimated and hence there were no constraints whatsoever on the observed or latent mean structure.)

We first have to figure out how we can identify the LS factor means. For this purpose, we once again consider the decomposition of the means of the observed variables, $E(Y_{ik})$, in the LS model (cf. Box 4.2):

$$
\begin{aligned}
E(Y_{ik}) &= E(\alpha_{ik}) + E(\lambda_{ik} \cdot State\ k) + E(\varepsilon_{ik}) \\
&= \alpha_{ik} + \lambda_{ik} \cdot E(State\ k)
\end{aligned}
$$

This formula shows that the means of the LS variables, *E(State k)*, can be identified in a relatively straightforward way by setting the intercepts, α_{1k}, pertaining to the marker indicators, Y_{1k}, to zero. If we set $\alpha_{1k} = 0$ for all *k*, then all LS factor means become identified through the means of the marker indicators:

$$
\begin{aligned}
E(Y_{1k}) &= \alpha_{1k} + \lambda_{1k} \cdot E(State\ k) \\
&= 0 + 1 \cdot E(State\ k) \\
&= E(State\ k)
\end{aligned}
$$

In this way, the latent variable means are (1) identified and estimable, and (2) they can potentially take on different values at each time point, reflecting latent mean change over time. Furthermore, this specification ensures that the intercepts of the marker indicators are time-invariant (each one takes on the same value of 0), reflecting measurement invariance across time for these indicators. The intercepts of the remaining (non-marker) indicators are set equal across time, following the same principle as shown for the factor loadings in the weak factorial invariance model.

The full Mplus model specification for the strong factorial invariance model is shown in Figure 4.9. Note that commands related to the mean structure (observed and latent variable means and intercept parameters) involve variable names in brackets []. Depending on whether a variable is exogenous or endogenous in the model (as determined automatically by Mplus, based on the model specification), a variable name in brackets refers to either the mean (for exogenous variables) or the intercept (for endogenous variables) of that variable.

Figure 4.9 shows that the intercepts of the marker indicators (`d11`, `d12`, and `d13`) are set to zero to identify the LS factor means:

```
[d11@0 d12@0 d13@0];
```

Furthermore, the estimation of the LS factor means is explicitly requested using the command `[state1 state2 state3];`. Otherwise, the LS factor means would remain fixed at zero, which is no longer adequate.

```
model: ! Latent state factors
 state1 by d11
           d21 (1);

 state2 by d12
           d22 (1);

 state3 by d13
           d23 (1);

 ! Indicator-specific (residual) factor for the second indicator
 is2 by d21 d22@1 d23@1;

 ! Indicator-specific factor is not allowed to correlate with the state factors
 is2 with state1@0 state2@0 state3@0;

 ! Fix the intercepts of the first indicator to zero
 [d11@0 d12@0 d13@0];

 ! Estimate the means of the latent state factors
 [state1 state2 state3];

 ! Set the intercepts of the second indicator equal across time
 [d21 d22 d23] (2);
```

FIGURE 4.9. Mplus `model` command for the specification of the LS model with one indicator-specific factor (`is2`) for the second indicator, time-invariant loadings, and time-invariant intercepts (model of strong factorial invariance).

Finally, the intercepts of the indicators `d21`, `d22`, and `d23` are set equal across time. Note that we use the number `(2)` to set these parameters equal, which is a different number than the one used to set the loadings equal. [The number `(1)` is still used to set the loadings of the indicators `d21`, `d22`, and `d23` equal across time.] The mean of the indicator-specific factor does not have to be specified, because it is set to zero by default (as is desired in this model).

The Mplus output shows that the model with strong factorial invariance also fits the data well, $\chi^2 = 6.656$, $df = 9$, $p = .6729$, $RMSEA = .00$, $p(RMSEA) \leq .05 = .95$, $SRMR = .014$, $CFI = 1.00$. In addition, the chi-square difference test against the model with weak factorial invariance is not significant, $\chi^2_\Delta = 1.562$, $df_\Delta = 2$, $p = .46$, indicating that the more restrictive, strong factorial invariance model is preferred. A comparison of the *AIC* values also indicates that the more constrained model should be chosen (strong factorial invariance model: $AIC = 1070.494$; weak factorial invariance model: $AIC = 1072.933$). We can conclude that the assumption of strong factorial invariance is not rejected in this example.

Based on the unstandardized parameter estimates (`MODEL RESULTS`, see below), we can see that our equality constraints were correctly implemented by Mplus ($\hat{\lambda}_{21} = \hat{\lambda}_{22} = \hat{\lambda}_{23} = 0.738$; $\hat{\alpha}_{21} = \hat{\alpha}_{22} = \hat{\alpha}_{23} = 0.187$). Mplus also correctly fixed the intercepts pertaining to the first indicator to zero (i.e., $\alpha_{11} = \alpha_{12} = \alpha_{13} = 0$), as can be seen from the fact that no standard error was estimated any more for these intercepts. We now also obtain estimates of the LS variable means in the output (under `Means`). We can see that the latent depression means have slightly increased from time 1 to time 2 ($M_1 = 1.583$ vs. $M_2 = 1.639$), whereas there is almost no change from time 2 to time 3 ($M_3 = 1.634$). A formal test of equality of means is demonstrated in Box 4.6.

```
MODEL RESULTS

                                                       Two-Tailed
                    Estimate       S.E.  Est./S.E.    P-Value

 STATE1   BY
    D11                1.000      0.000    999.000    999.000
    D21                0.738      0.030     24.997      0.000

 STATE2   BY
    D12                1.000      0.000    999.000    999.000
    D22                0.738      0.030     24.997      0.000

 STATE3   BY
    D13                1.000      0.000    999.000    999.000
    D23                0.738      0.030     24.997      0.000

 IS2      BY
    D21                1.000      0.000    999.000    999.000
    D22                1.000      0.000    999.000    999.000
    D23                1.000      0.000    999.000    999.000

 IS2      WITH
    STATE1             0.000      0.000    999.000    999.000
    STATE2             0.000      0.000    999.000    999.000
    STATE3             0.000      0.000    999.000    999.000

 STATE2   WITH
    STATE1             0.118      0.015      7.964      0.000

 STATE3   WITH
    STATE1             0.108      0.014      7.623      0.000
    STATE2             0.129      0.015      8.419      0.000

 Means
    STATE1             1.583      0.026     60.157      0.000
    STATE2             1.639      0.028     58.762      0.000
    STATE3             1.634      0.027     60.652      0.000
```

```
 Intercepts
    D11                0.000        0.000      999.000      999.000
    D21                0.187        0.049        3.861        0.000
    D12                0.000        0.000      999.000      999.000
    D22                0.187        0.049        3.861        0.000
    D13                0.000        0.000      999.000      999.000
    D23                0.187        0.049        3.861        0.000

 Variances
    STATE1             0.195        0.019       10.510        0.000
    STATE2             0.233        0.021       11.023        0.000
    STATE3             0.218        0.020       10.983        0.000
    IS2                0.007        0.002        3.433        0.001

 Residual Variances
    D11                0.040        0.009        4.477        0.000
    D21                0.028        0.005        5.425        0.000
    D12                0.022        0.009        2.453        0.014
    D22                0.035        0.006        6.299        0.000
    D13                0.019        0.009        2.192        0.028
    D23                0.037        0.006        6.608        0.000


STANDARDIZED MODEL RESULTS (STDYX Standardization)

                                                           Two-Tailed
                    Estimate       S.E.  Est./S.E.    P-Value

 STATE1   BY
    D11                0.911        0.021       43.988        0.000
    D21                0.867        0.022       39.895        0.000

 STATE2   BY
    D12                0.956        0.018       52.311        0.000
    D22                0.867        0.020       43.500        0.000

 STATE3   BY
    D13                0.959        0.019       50.014        0.000
    D23                0.854        0.021       41.331        0.000

 IS2      BY
    D21                0.220        0.033        6.732        0.000
    D22                0.202        0.030        6.721        0.000
    D23                0.205        0.031        6.733        0.000

 IS2      WITH
    STATE1             0.000        0.000      999.000      999.000
    STATE2             0.000        0.000      999.000      999.000
    STATE3             0.000        0.000      999.000      999.000

 STATE2   WITH
    STATE1             0.553        0.045       12.350        0.000
```

```
 STATE3   WITH
    STATE1               0.521      0.047     11.184      0.000
    STATE2               0.574      0.043     13.463      0.000

 Means
    STATE1               3.583      0.181     19.792      0.000
    STATE2               3.395      0.164     20.655      0.000
    STATE3               3.499      0.169     20.664      0.000

 Intercepts
    D11                  0.000      0.000    999.000    999.000
    D21                  0.498      0.134      3.707      0.000
    D12                  0.000      0.000    999.000    999.000
    D22                  0.456      0.124      3.677      0.000
    D13                  0.000      0.000    999.000    999.000
    D23                  0.465      0.126      3.686      0.000

 Variances
    STATE1               1.000      0.000    999.000    999.000
    STATE2               1.000      0.000    999.000    999.000
    STATE3               1.000      0.000    999.000    999.000
    IS2                  1.000      0.000    999.000    999.000

 Residual Variances
    D11                  0.171      0.038      4.532      0.000
    D21                  0.200      0.036      5.535      0.000
    D12                  0.086      0.035      2.448      0.014
    D22                  0.208      0.033      6.332      0.000
    D13                  0.081      0.037      2.191      0.028
    D23                  0.228      0.034      6.767      0.000

R-SQUARE

    Observed                                             Two-Tailed
    Variable          Estimate       S.E.  Est./S.E.    P-Value

    D11                  0.829      0.038     21.994      0.000
    D21                  0.800      0.036     22.155      0.000
    D12                  0.914      0.035     26.155      0.000
    D22                  0.792      0.033     24.165      0.000
    D13                  0.919      0.037     25.007      0.000
    D23                  0.772      0.034     22.941      0.000
```

Finally, we test a model of strict factorial invariance. In this model, we also set the residual variances of the indicators [$Var(\varepsilon_{ik})$] equal across time. (We use the model with unequal latent means as the basis here.) We use the number `(3)` to set the error variances of the first indicator equal across time. The number `(4)` is used to set the error variances of the second indicator equal over time. The complete `model` statement for the specification of the model with strict factorial invariance is shown in Figure 4.10.

The model with strict factorial invariance and unequal means also shows a good absolute fit, χ^2 = 11.61, *df* = 13, *p* = .5599, *RMSEA* = .00, *p*(*RMSEA*) ≤ .05 = .95, *SRMR* = .024, *CFI* = 1.00. (The full output for this model can be found on the companion website.) The chi-square difference test against the strong factorial invariance model with unequal means is again nonsignificant, χ^2_Δ = 4.954, df_Δ = 4, *p* = .29, favoring the strict invariance model. A comparison of the *AIC* values leads to the same conclusion (strict factorial invariance model: *AIC* = 1067.448; strong factorial invariance model: *AIC* = 1070.494). We can conclude that the assumption

BOX 4.6. *Test of Equality of Latent Means across Time*

A question of substantive interest is whether the three depression state factor means are significantly different from each other (which would indicate significant mean change between at least two measurement occasions). Formally, the assumption of equality of means can be tested by fitting an additional model to the data in which all three latent state means are set equal across time. If this model fits significantly worse than the strong factorial invariance model without restrictions on the latent means, we can conclude that mean change occurred over time between at least two time points. The following command can be used to set the latent state factor means equal across time in Mplus (the full Mplus input for this model can be found on the companion website):

```
[state1 state2 state3] (mean);
```

Here the label `(mean)` is used to set the state means equal across time. (We could have equally well used a number again.) In our example, the model with equal means does not fit significantly worse than the strong factorial invariance model with unequal means, according to the chi-square difference test, χ^2_Δ = 5.181, df_Δ = 2, *p* = .07, indicating that the observed mean differences are *not* statistically significant at the .05 level. On the other hand, according to the *AIC* index, the less constrained model would be preferred (strong factorial invariance model with equal means: *AIC* = 1071.675; strong factorial invariance model with unequal means: *AIC* = 1070.494), although the difference in *AIC* values is rather small. In practice, a researcher would have to take substantive considerations as well as the actual size of the mean differences into account before making a final decision as to whether the model with equal or unequal means should be preferred.

```
model: ! Latent state factors
 state1 by d11
          d21 (1);

 state2 by d12
          d22 (1);

 state3 by d13
          d23 (1);

 ! Indicator-specific (residual) factor for the second indicator
 is2 by d21 d22@1 d23@1;

 ! Indicator-specific factor is not allowed to correlate with the state factors
 is2 with state1@0 state2@0 state3@0;

 ! Fix the intercepts of the first indicator to zero
 [d11@0 d12@0 d13@0];

 ! Estimate the means of the latent state factors
 [state1 state2 state3];

 ! Set the intercepts of the second indicator equal across time
 [d21 d22 d23] (2);

 ! Set residual variances of the first indicator equal across time
 d11 d12 d13 (3);

 ! Set residual variances of the second indicator equal across time
 d21 d22 d23 (4);
```

FIGURE 4.10. Mplus `model` command for the specification of the LS model with one indicator-specific factor (`is2`) for the second indicator, time-invariant loadings, time-invariant intercepts, and time-invariant error variances (model of strict factorial invariance).

of strict factorial invariance is not rejected in this example. Therefore, the more parsimonious model with equal residual variances should be selected.

We now terminate our series of invariance tests, noting that—depending on the research question—further invariance tests may be of interest, for example, with respect to the LS factor variances and covariances. In summary, our analysis of the LS model yielded a number of interesting findings that can be summarized as follows:

- The indicators used to measure depression show relatively high reliabilities and low indicator-specificity.
- The parameters of the measurement model did not change significantly across time; that is, strict factorial invariance could be assumed for these data.

- True individual differences in depression were moderately stable across time, as indicated by the medium-size correlations among LS factors; in other words, there was a substantial amount of reliable occasion-specific variance that may be examined in more detail using LST analyses (see next section).
- The correlation structure of the LS factors indicates a slight autoregressive effect across time.
- A global test of latent mean differences across time was not statistically significant at the .05 level, indicating that there was no significant mean change over time in depression.

As mentioned above, the LS model is a useful baseline model for the analysis of more complex longitudinal SEMs. In the following material, we discuss its extension to an LST model, using the same data example.

4.2 LST ANALYSIS

One limitation of the LS model is that the degree to which measurements are affected by occasion-specific effects versus stable person-specific effects can only be quantified indirectly in this model by means of the correlations among the state factors. However, a decomposition of the observed variance into stable, occasion-specific, and error components is not available in this model (e.g., Steyer et al., 1992). By extending the LS model to an LST model, we can obtain more detailed information on the amount of state- versus trait-related variance of observed and latent variables.

In an LST model, the observed variables Y_{ik} (i = indicator, k = occasion of measurement) can again be decomposed into a constant intercept term α_{ik}, an occasion-specific LS variable (*State k*), and an occasion-specific measurement error (residual) variable ε_{ik}:

$$Y_{ik} = \alpha_{ik} + \lambda_{ik} \cdot (State\ k) + \varepsilon_{ik}$$

where λ_{ik} again indicates the factor loading of Y_{ik} on the LS factor.

In contrast to the LS model, the LST model further decomposes the LS factors into a latent trait factor (which reflects that part of the LS factors that is due to stable individual differences or trait effects) and an LS residual variable ζ_k that characterizes occasion-specific deviations of the latent state from the latent trait scores (cf. Steyer et al., 1992, 1999):

$$State\ k = \gamma_{0k} + \gamma_k \cdot Trait + \zeta_k$$

where γ_{0k} indicates a constant latent intercept term and γ_k a second-order factor loading of *State k* on the factor *Trait*.

In our analysis of the LS model in Section 4.1.3, we saw that the covariances (or, in the completely standardized solution, the correlations) among the state factors were an indicator of the degree of stability of individual differences across time. In the LST model, the covariance structure of the LS factors is explained by a single underlying latent (trait) factor. The single latent trait factor reflects that part of the variance in the state factors that is stable across time (i.e., their covariance).

Figure 4.11 shows an LST model for two observed variables Y_{1k} and Y_{2k} measured on three measurement occasions (k = 1, 2, 3). It can be seen that the LST model implies a second-order factor model (cf. Section 3.4.2).

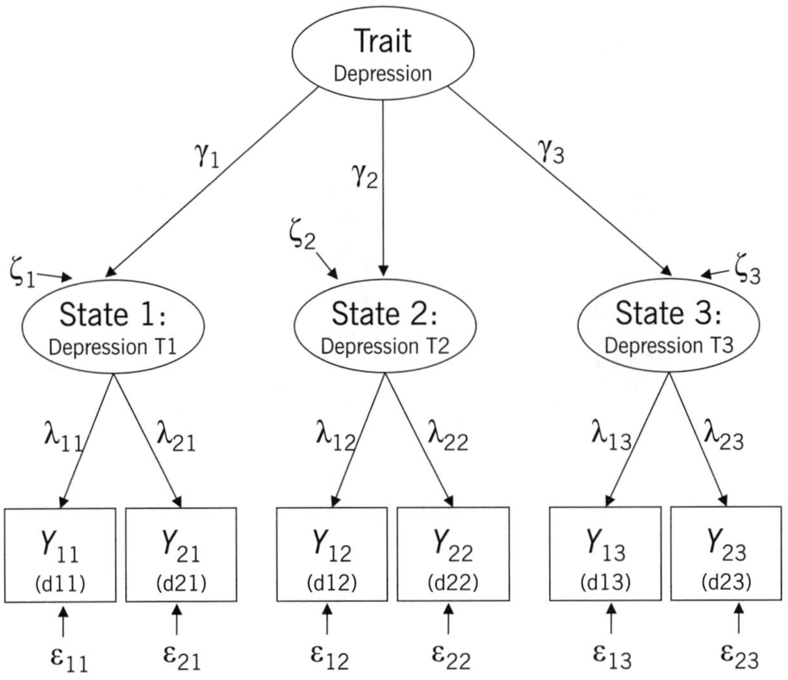

FIGURE 4.11. Latent state–trait (LST) model for depression measured on three occasions of measurement (T1–T3). Y_{ik} = observed variable i measured at time point k; ε_{ik} = measurement error variable; λ_{ik} = first-order factor loading; γ_k = second-order factor loading; ζ_k = LS residual variable. The variable names of the indicators used in Mplus appear in parentheses.

As an example, we specify an LST model for the depression data (data set **depression.dat**), which we have already used to illustrate different analyses based on the LS model in Section 4.1. As a starting point, we use the LS model with an indicator-specific factor and without invariance constraints that showed a good fit (cf. Section 4.1.3). The extension of this model to an LST model is shown in Figure 4.12. A similar LST model with an indicator-specific factor for the second indicator is discussed in detail in Eid et al. (1999).

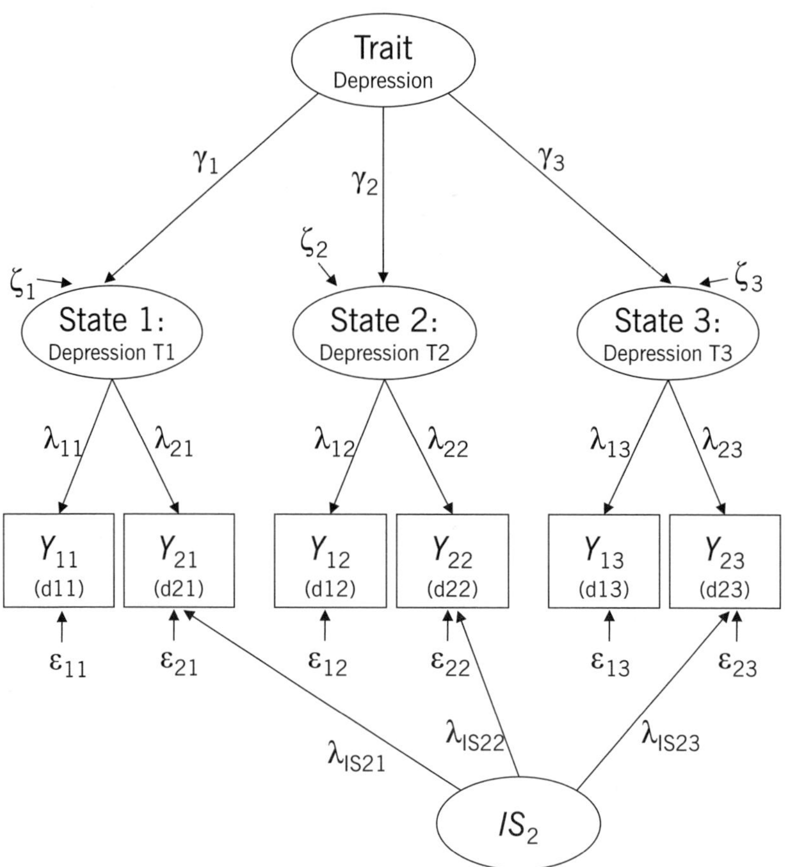

FIGURE 4.12. LST model for depression measured on three occasions of measurement (T1–T3). Y_{ik} = observed variable i measured at time point k; ε_{ik} = measurement error variable; λ_{ik} = first-order factor loading; γ_k = second-order factor loading; ζ_k = LS residual variable. The model additionally contains an indicator-specific (method) factor (IS_2) for the second indicator. The parameters λ_{IS2k} indicate factor loadings on the indicator-specific factor. The variable names of the indicators used in Mplus appear in parentheses.

```
model: ! Latent state factors
state1 by depdad11
          depdad21;

state2 by depdad12
          depdad22;

state3 by depdad13
          depdad23;

trait by state1 state2 state3; ! Latent trait factor as 2nd order factor

! Indicator-specific (residual) factor for the second indicator
is2 by depdad21 depdad22 depdad23;

! Indicator-specific factor is not allowed to correlate with the state factors
is2 with state1@0 state2@0 state3@0 trait@0;

! Identification of the mean structure of the latent variables
[depdad11@0 depdad12@0 depdad13@0]; ! Set intercepts of the marker indicator to zero
[state1@0]; ! Set intercept of the first state factor to zero
[trait]; ! Estimate the mean of the trait factor
[state2 state3]; ! Estimate the intercepts of the remaining state factors
```

FIGURE 4.13. Mplus `model` command for the specification of the LST model with one indicator-specific factor (`is2`) for the second indicator shown in Figure 4.12.

The Mplus `model` statement for estimating the LST model in Figure 4.12 is shown in Figure 4.13. Note that the identification of the latent variable mean structure is slightly more complicated in the LST model than in the LS model. This is the case at least if one is interested in estimating the mean of the latent trait factor. (A more detailed discussion of different options for including a latent mean structure in LST analyses can be found in Box 4.7.)

One way to identify the latent trait factor mean as well as the latent intercept parameters γ_{0k} is to fix the intercept parameters pertaining to the marker indicators to zero, that is, $\alpha_{11} = \alpha_{12} = \alpha_{13} = 0$.

In the next step, the intercept term pertaining to an LS factor chosen as reference indicator of the latent trait is set to zero as well—in our case, the intercept pertaining to *State 1* (i.e., $\gamma_{01} = 0$). This state factor is chosen for simplicity, because Mplus automatically sets the loading of this state factor on the trait factor to 1 (i.e., $\gamma_1 = 1$). This is because Mplus, by default, treats the *first* variable listed after the `by` statement as the reference variable and sets its loading to 1. As a consequence, the mean of the latent trait factor is then directly identified through the mean of the marker variable Y_{11}. Finally, the intercepts of the remaining state factors (in our case, γ_{02} and γ_{03}) are freely estimated. The mean of the `is2` factor

BOX 4.7. Latent Mean Structures in the LST Model

Whether or not a latent variable mean structure is of interest in an LST analysis depends on the specific research question. Many LST analyses focus exclusively on the covariance structure of the variables and completely ignore the mean structure. In some situations, however, researchers may be interested in studying mean structures as well—for example, when mean differences across time are of interest or are theoretically expected. In the text, I described a way to identify the latent mean structure in an LST model that allows estimating the mean of the latent trait factor. In addition to the model version discussed in the text, there are other, statistically equivalent options for specifying a mean structure in an LST model. If one is not interested in estimating the mean of the latent trait factor, one can simply follow the Mplus default, according to which the trait factor mean is fixed at 0, and estimate all three latent intercept parameters γ_{01}, γ_{02}, and γ_{03}. The complete model specification is then simplified, as shown in the following:

```
state1 by d11 d21;
state2 by d12 d22;
state3 by d13 d23;
trait by state1-state3;
is2 by d21 d22 d23;
is2 with state1-state3@0 trait@0;
[d11@0 d12@0 d13@0];
[state1 state2 state3];
```

This alternative equivalent parameterization has the advantage that the intercepts of the three state factors are now identical to the LS factor means (which is not the case for the parameterization discussed in the text). Latent mean comparisons could be conducted by comparing the intercepts. Keep in mind, however, that such a comparison would require at least strong factorial invariance of the measurement model (see Section 4.1.4).

Another (equivalent) possibility is to completely ignore the latent variable mean structure and to leave all latent means and latent intercepts fixed at zero (as is the default in Mplus). In this case, only the intercepts α_{ik} pertaining to the observed variables would be estimated. This parameterization would be obtained through the following `model` specification:

```
state1 by d11 d21;
state2 by d12 d22;
state3 by d13 d23;
trait by state1-state3;
is2 by d21 d22 d23;
is2 with state1-state3@0 trait@0;
```

Additional alternative mean structures are possible. Furthermore, it can be useful in practice to place restrictions on the mean structure to test specific assumptions, as shown in Section 4.1.4. The type of mean structure included in an LST analysis should depend on the substantive research questions. For example, if the process studied is hypothesized to be a pure variability process (with no trait change over time), there should not be any changes in the LS means over time. Hence, in such a model, strong factorial invariance would be assumed to hold over time for the Y_{ik} variables, all trait loadings γ_k would be expected to be 1, and all LS intercept parameters γ_{0k} would be expected to be 0. This restricted model could be tested against a model with free parameters to find out whether the process under study involves just variability and no trait changes.

again remains fixed at 0 (following the Mplus default settings) because this factor is defined as a residual factor.

From the fit statistics (see below) we can see that the LST model, in this particular case, shows the same fit as the LS model with configural invariance from Section 4.1.3. This finding can be explained by the fact that in this case, data from only three time points are analyzed. With only three time points, the higher-order covariance structure of the LS factors is saturated in the LST model because no overidentifying restrictions are included for the loadings of *State* 2 and *State* 3 on the trait factor.

The mean structure is saturated as well because no overidentifying restrictions were placed on the latent trait mean or the intercept parameters. Therefore, the structural model does not provide any additional *df*, so that the fit of the model is identical to the fit of the unrestricted LS model. This would be different if we were analyzing more than three time points. With four or more time points, the LST model implies testable restrictions for the covariance structure of the LS factors, so that the structural model is no longer saturated in these cases.

```
Chi-Square Test of Model Fit

        Value                              3.541
        Degrees of Freedom                     3
        P-Value                           0.3155

RMSEA (Root Mean Square Error Of Approximation)

        Estimate                           0.024
        90 Percent C.I.                    0.000  0.100
        Probability RMSEA <= .05           0.615
```

```
CFI/TLI

         CFI                                    1.000
         TLI                                    0.998

SRMR (Standardized Root Mean Square Residual)

         Value                                  0.008

Information Criteria

         Akaike (AIC)                        1085.741
         Bayesian (BIC)                      1176.404
         Sample-Size Adjusted BIC            1100.279
           (n* = (n + 2) / 24)
```

The Mplus parameter estimates (`MODEL RESULTS`) show that the state factors have fairly large and statistically significant loadings on the trait factor (see under `Trait by`). The estimated unstandardized loadings for *State 2* and *State 3* are $\hat{\gamma}_2$ and $\hat{\gamma}_3$ (z = 8.731 and 8.805, respectively; the loading of *State 1* was fixed to 1 for identification). The estimated standardized loadings are $\hat{\gamma}_1^{\text{standardized}} = .707$, $\hat{\gamma}_2^{\text{standardized}} = .782$, and $\hat{\gamma}_3^{\text{standardized}} = .739$. The size of the standardized loadings shows that a sizable proportion of true individual differences (individual differences on the state factors) is explained by stable influences (trait effects). This finding reflects the substantial correlations seen between the LS variables in the LS model. The amount of state factor variance that is explained by the trait factor can be found in the output under `R-SQUARE—Latent Variable` (under the standardized model results). The R^2 values for the latent variables (here the LS factors) are identical to the squared standardized loadings on the trait factor: $R_1^2 = .707^2 = .500$; $R_2^2 = .787^2 = .611$; $R_3^2 = .739^2 = .546$. Hence, between 50 and 61.1% of true individual differences in depression states can be explained by stable personality dispositions, whereas the remaining 38.9–50% are due to occasion-specific effects.

```
MODEL RESULTS

                                                          Two-Tailed
                      Estimate       S.E.  Est./S.E.      P-Value

 STATE1   BY
    DEPDAD11             1.000      0.000    999.000      999.000
    DEPDAD21             0.700      0.049     14.248        0.000
```

```
STATE2   BY
   DEPDAD12          1.000      0.000    999.000    999.000
   DEPDAD22          0.751      0.043     17.260      0.000

STATE3   BY
   DEPDAD13          1.000      0.000    999.000    999.000
   DEPDAD23          0.755      0.047     16.087      0.000

IS2      BY
   DEPDAD21          1.000      0.000    999.000    999.000
   DEPDAD22          0.612      0.375      1.629      0.103
   DEPDAD23          0.799      0.518      1.542      0.123

TRAIT    BY
   STATE1            1.000      0.000    999.000    999.000
   STATE2            1.168      0.134      8.731      0.000
   STATE3            1.067      0.121      8.805      0.000

IS2      WITH
   STATE1            0.000      0.000    999.000    999.000
   STATE2            0.000      0.000    999.000    999.000
   STATE3            0.000      0.000    999.000    999.000
   TRAIT             0.000      0.000    999.000    999.000

Means
   TRAIT             1.584      0.027     58.184      0.000

Intercepts
   DEPDAD11          0.000      0.000    999.000    999.000
   DEPDAD21          0.246      0.079      3.112      0.002
   DEPDAD12          0.000      0.000    999.000    999.000
   DEPDAD22          0.156      0.073      2.147      0.032
   DEPDAD13          0.000      0.000    999.000    999.000
   DEPDAD23          0.171      0.078      2.197      0.028
   STATE1            0.000      0.000    999.000    999.000
   STATE2           -0.209      0.214     -0.975      0.330
   STATE3           -0.060      0.194     -0.311      0.756

Variances
   TRAIT             0.103      0.019      5.553      0.000
   IS2               0.011      0.008      1.390      0.164

Residual Variances
   DEPDAD11          0.033      0.012      2.711      0.007
   DEPDAD21          0.028      0.009      3.091      0.002
   DEPDAD12          0.025      0.011      2.297      0.022
   DEPDAD22          0.036      0.007      5.351      0.000
   DEPDAD13          0.022      0.011      1.986      0.047
   DEPDAD23          0.035      0.008      4.592      0.000
   STATE1            0.103      0.016      6.308      0.000
   STATE2            0.089      0.017      5.146      0.000
   STATE3            0.098      0.017      5.901      0.000
```

```
STANDARDIZED MODEL RESULTS (STDYX Standardization)

                                                    Two-Tailed
                    Estimate       S.E.  Est./S.E.    P-Value

 STATE1   BY
    DEPDAD11           0.928      0.028     32.979      0.000
    DEPDAD21           0.849      0.029     29.046      0.000

 STATE2   BY
    DEPDAD12           0.950      0.023     41.661      0.000
    DEPDAD22           0.874      0.024     36.051      0.000

 STATE3   BY
    DEPDAD13           0.953      0.025     38.686      0.000
    DEPDAD23           0.862      0.026     32.966      0.000

 IS2      BY
    DEPDAD21           0.278      0.100      2.785      0.005
    DEPDAD22           0.155      0.062      2.502      0.012
    DEPDAD23           0.205      0.077      2.659      0.008

 TRAIT    BY
    STATE1             0.707      0.046     15.245      0.000
    STATE2             0.782      0.045     17.409      0.000
    STATE3             0.739      0.046     16.188      0.000

 IS2      WITH
    STATE1             0.000      0.000    999.000    999.000
    STATE2             0.000      0.000    999.000    999.000
    STATE3             0.000      0.000    999.000    999.000
    TRAIT              0.000      0.000    999.000    999.000

 Means
    TRAIT              4.937      0.453     10.909      0.000

 Intercepts
    DEPDAD11           0.000      0.000    999.000    999.000
    DEPDAD21           0.656      0.220      2.980      0.003
    DEPDAD12           0.000      0.000    999.000    999.000
    DEPDAD22           0.378      0.182      2.085      0.037
    DEPDAD13           0.000      0.000    999.000    999.000
    DEPDAD23           0.420      0.197      2.131      0.033
    STATE1             0.000      0.000    999.000    999.000
    STATE2            -0.435      0.440     -0.989      0.323
    STATE3            -0.130      0.416     -0.313      0.755

 Variances
    TRAIT              1.000      0.000    999.000    999.000
    IS2                1.000      0.000    999.000    999.000
```

```
Residual Variances
    DEPDAD11           0.139      0.052      2.668      0.008
    DEPDAD21           0.201      0.067      3.026      0.002
    DEPDAD12           0.098      0.043      2.267      0.023
    DEPDAD22           0.212      0.042      5.081      0.000
    DEPDAD13           0.092      0.047      1.966      0.049
    DEPDAD23           0.215      0.049      4.417      0.000
    STATE1             0.500      0.066      7.634      0.000
    STATE2             0.389      0.070      5.534      0.000
    STATE3             0.454      0.067      6.741      0.000


R-SQUARE

    Observed                                           Two-Tailed
    Variable        Estimate       S.E.  Est./S.E.    P-Value

    DEPDAD11           0.861      0.052     16.490      0.000
    DEPDAD21           0.799      0.067     11.993      0.000
    DEPDAD12           0.902      0.043     20.830      0.000
    DEPDAD22           0.788      0.042     18.925      0.000
    DEPDAD13           0.908      0.047     19.343      0.000
    DEPDAD23           0.785      0.049     16.155      0.000

     Latent                                            Two-Tailed
    Variable        Estimate       S.E.  Est./S.E.    P-Value

    STATE1             0.500      0.066      7.622      0.000
    STATE2             0.611      0.070      8.705      0.000
    STATE3             0.546      0.067      8.094      0.000
```

The latent mean structure is also shown in the output. In this model, the unstandardized latent trait mean is estimated to be 1.584. The intercepts of *State* 2 and *State* 3 are estimated to be $\hat{\gamma}_{02} = -0.209$ and $\hat{\gamma}_{03} = -0.060$. These values reflect slight mean differences relative to the first state factor. However, these mean differences are not significant ($p \geq .33$).

Further steps of an LST analysis may involve tests of measurement invariance to obtain more parsimonious and substantively meaningful models. Given that we have already discussed the basic principles of testing measurement invariance for the LS model in Section 4.1.4, I will not go into the details here. The procedure shown for the LS model can be easily transferred and applied to the LST model as well.

LST models were primarily developed as variability models to model systematic, occasion-specific fluctuations of measurements around a constant trait value. As we saw, these models can be used to estimate variance components to separate stable influences from occasion-specific influences on LS variables. In the following sections, we consider longitudinal models that are less concerned with occasion-specific fluctuations versus stable components of constructs, but rather focus on actual changes in constructs over time. Such change models are used particularly when it has to be assumed that an attribute has actually changed (rather than just showing fluctuations around a fixed set point). We first describe autoregressive models, which can be seen as "classical" models for measuring change within the framework of path analysis and SEM.

4.3 AUTOREGRESSIVE MODELS

For a long time, autoregressive models (e.g., Jöreskog, 1979a, 1979b) were seen as the "gold standard" of methodology for analyzing longitudinal data. With the development of latent growth curve models (LGCMs; see Section 4.5), autoregressive models have become somewhat less popular (for a critique of autoregressive models, see Hertzog & Nesselroade, 1987). Nonetheless, autoregressive models are useful to answer a variety of important research questions in longitudinal studies.

Autoregressive models are based on the (fairly plausible) idea that previous behavior is the best predictor of present behavior. For this reason, repeatedly measured manifest or latent variables are connected through so-called *autoregressions* in autoregressive models (as reflected in the path coefficients β_1–β_4 in the manifest autoregressive model shown in Figure 4.14). The strengths of autoregressive (or autopredictive) effects as well as the stability of individual differences across time can be examined by looking at the size of the autoregressive coefficients as well as the amount of residual variance (variance of the residual variables ε_{jk} in Figure 4.14). When the ratio of residual variance to total variance is large, this means that the autoprediction is rather weak—indicating individual differences in change over time. (In manifest autoregressive models that do not account for measurement error, such error can be an additional or even alternative explanation for a large residual variance.)

However, the goal of an analysis of autoregressive models is usually not only to determine the degree of stability of (or changes in) a single construct over time. Often, an additional goal is to predict individual differences not explained by the autoregressive effect(s) through external variables that are also included in the model. The impact of such additional variables can be examined by means of so-called *cross-lagged effects*

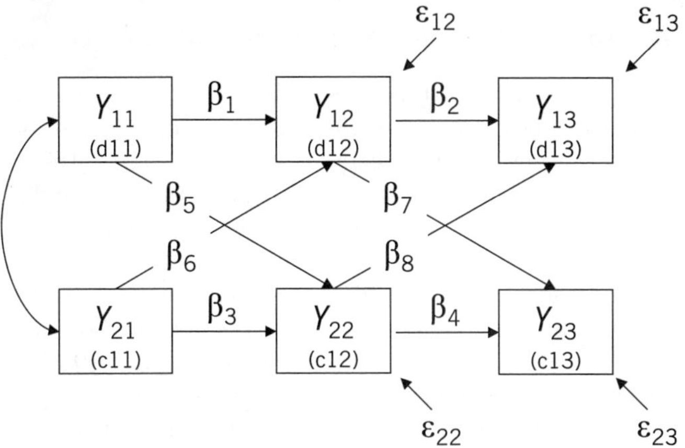

FIGURE 4.14. Manifest autoregressive model for two manifest variables Y_{jk} (j = construct, k = time point) measuring two constructs (j = 1, 2; depression and competence) on three measurement occasions (k = 1, 2, 3): β_1–β_4 = path coefficients representing autoregressive effects; β_5–β_8 = path coefficients representing cross-lagged effects; ε_{jk} = residual variables. The variable names used in Mplus appear in parentheses.

(see path coefficients β_5–β_8 in Figure 4.14). Cross-lagged effects are the effects of additional, temporally preceding variables that are included in the model in addition to the autoregressive effects. The goal is to explain at least part of the "leftover" variability that is not explained by the autoregressive effect(s). In other words, one attempts to explain the "unstable" part of individual differences by external variables that may be possible causes of change.

4.3.1 Manifest Autoregressive Models

Originally, autoregressive and/or cross-lagged models were often specified exclusively at the level of manifest variables (sometimes referred to as *single-indicator models*, as shown in Figure 4.14), and analyses with observed variables are still common. These models imply simple path analyses without latent variables (manifest path models for cross-sectional data are described in Section 3.5.2). In the following, I first describe the analysis of manifest autoregressive models in Mplus, and in Section 4.3.2, I discuss latent autoregressive models that explicitly account for measurement error.

BOX 4.8. *Example of Manifest Autoregressive Models*

Here we analyze a longitudinal data set with two constructs (self-reported depression and competencies, N = 586 children) on three measurement occasions.* There were 6 months between each time point. The data set, **depression-competence.dat**, contains summary data (means, standard deviations, and correlations) for six manifest variables. The first three variables pertain to a repeatedly administered depression scale (the Child Depression Inventory, CDI; Kovacs, 1985). The last three variables represent a summary score of various competencies (for details on this study, see Cole, Martin, & Powers, 1997, as well as Cole, Martin, Powers, & Truglio, 1996). Our goal is to estimate a manifest autoregressive model for the six manifest variables. In this model, we want to examine the stability of both constructs as well as potential cross-lagged effects.

*I would like to thank David A. Cole for providing the data used for this example.

Figure 4.15 shows the Mplus input file for the manifest autoregressive model with cross-lagged effects from Figure 4.14. The autoregressive and cross-lagged effects in the model are represented by partial regression coefficients (also referred to as *path coefficients*; cf. Section 3.5). Therefore, `on` statements are used in the Mplus `model` command to specify these effects. As noted above, the model represents a special case of a manifest path analysis, here specified for longitudinal data.

An important aspect in the model specification is that the residual variables shown in Figure 4.14 are assumed to be uncorrelated. This has

```
model: d12 on d11   ! autoregressive path to depression T2
              c11;  ! cross-lagged path to depression T2
       d13 on d12   ! autoregressive path to depression T3
              c12;  ! cross-lagged path to depression T3;

       c12 on c11   ! autoregressive path to competence T2
              d11;  ! cross-lagged path to competence T2
       c13 on c12   ! autoregressive path to competence T3
              d12;  ! cross-lagged path to competence T3

  d13 with c13@0;  ! Fix correlation between T3 residuals to zero
```

FIGURE 4.15. Mplus input file for the specification of the simple manifest autoregressive model for three measurement occasions shown in Figure 4.14.

to be explicitly specified for the residuals on the third time point, because Mplus otherwise estimates a residual correlation between these residuals by default. For this reason, we add the following command in the model specification:

```
d13 with c13@0;
```

This command overrides the Mplus default and sets the residual correlation for the final outcome variables to zero. All other residual correlations are automatically set to zero by Mplus. (As we will see shortly, the original model with uncorrelated residuals does not fit the data in this example, so that this restriction will be relaxed again in later analysis steps.)

The model fit indices reported by Mplus indicate a very bad fit of the model to the data, $\chi^2 = 201.90$, $df = 6$, $p < .001$, $CFI = 0.86$, $RMSEA = 0.24$, $SRMR = 0.09$ (the full output can be found on the companion website). The lack of fit can in this case be explained by the fact that the model does not allow the residuals at the same time point to be correlated. The estimation of these additional parameters is necessary in this example, because there are shared occasion-specific effects between the depression and competencies constructs at the same time point, in line with LST theory. In other words, children who rated themselves as more depressed also tended to report a lower level of competencies at the same time point. These situation-specific effects are not sufficiently accounted for in the standard autoregressive model with uncorrelated residual variables, shown in Figure 4.14. This can be changed by allowing the residual variables at the same time point to correlate (see Figure 4.16).

In addition to situation-specific effects, the present example also requires the inclusion of second-order autoregressive effects to achieve an acceptable fit. Second-order autoregressive effects are autoregressive effects between nonadjacent time points (represented by the path coefficients β_9 and β_{10} in Figure 4.16). The Mplus `model` statement for the extended model is shown in Figure 4.17. This model fits the data well, $\chi^2 = 2.74$, $df = 2$, $p = .25$, $CFI = 0.999$, $RMSEA = 0.03$, $SRMR = 0.01$. In addition, it fits significantly better than the original model with uncorrelated residual variables and no second-order autoregressive effects, $\Delta\chi^2 = 199.16$, $\Delta df = 4$, $p < .001$. The AIC value also indicates that the less restrictive model in Figure 4.16 ($AIC = 2493.08$) should be preferred (the AIC value for the model in Figure 4.14 was 2690.01). In the following, the parameter estimates for the extended model are presented.

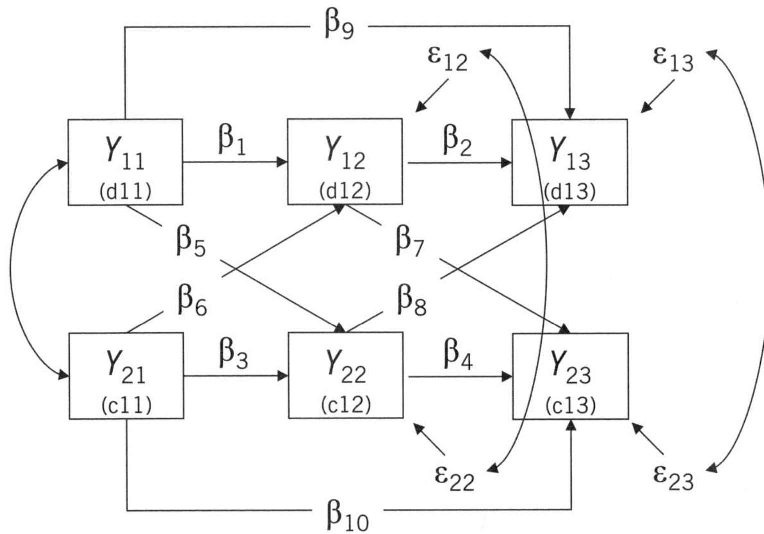

FIGURE 4.16. Manifest autoregressive model for two manifest variables Y_{jk} (j = construct, k = time point) measuring two constructs (j = 1, 2; depression and competence) on three measurement occasions (k = 1, 2, 3). β_1–β_4 = path coefficients representing first-order autoregressive effects; β_9 and β_{10} = latent path coefficients representing second-order autoregressive effects; β_5–β_8 = path coefficients representing cross-lagged effects; ε_{jk} = residual variables. In contrast to the model shown in Figure 4.14, this model allows for second-order autoregressive effects as well as correlated residual variables at the same measurement occasion. The variable names used in Mplus appear in parentheses.

```
model: d12 on d11   ! autoregressive path to depression T2
              c11;  ! cross-lagged path to depression T2
       d13 on d12 d11   ! autoregressive paths to depression T3
              c12;  ! cross-lagged path to depression T3;

       c12 on c11   ! autoregressive path to competence T2
              d11;  ! cross-lagged path to competence T2
       c13 on c12 c11   ! autoregressive paths to competence T3
              d12;  ! cross-lagged path to competence T3

  d12 with c12;  ! Residual correlation T2
  d13 with c13;  ! Residual correlation T3
```

FIGURE 4.17. Mplus `model` command for the specification of the extended autoregressive model with second-order autoregressive effects and correlated residual variables shown in Figure 4.16.

```
MODEL RESULTS

                                                    Two-Tailed
                   Estimate       S.E.  Est./S.E.     P-Value

 D12      ON
   D11                0.526      0.037     14.225      0.000
   C11               -0.085      0.020     -4.184      0.000

 D13      ON
   D12                0.510      0.040     12.782      0.000
   D11                0.156      0.035      4.411      0.000
   C12               -0.056      0.020     -2.749      0.006

 C12      ON
   C11                0.422      0.037     11.352      0.000
   D11               -0.392      0.068     -5.786      0.000

 C13      ON
   C12                0.386      0.044      8.797      0.000
   C11                0.192      0.037      5.181      0.000
   D12               -0.436      0.072     -6.066      0.000

 D12      WITH
   C12               -0.040      0.005     -8.067      0.000

 D13      WITH
   C13               -0.035      0.005     -7.868      0.000

 Intercepts
   D12                0.288      0.050      5.789      0.000
   D13                0.210      0.050      4.198      0.000
   C12                1.335      0.091     14.640      0.000
   C13                0.995      0.107      9.322      0.000

 Residual Variances
   D12                0.061      0.004     17.117      0.000
   D13                0.051      0.003     17.117      0.000
   C12                0.206      0.012     17.117      0.000
   C13                0.207      0.012     17.117      0.000


STANDARDIZED MODEL RESULTS (STDYX Standardization)

                                                    Two-Tailed
                   Estimate       S.E.  Est./S.E.     P-Value

 D12      ON
   D11                0.531      0.033     15.947      0.000
   C11               -0.156      0.037     -4.209      0.000
```

```
 D13        ON
    D12                  0.517      0.037     13.820      0.000
    D11                  0.160      0.036      4.426      0.000
    C12                 -0.100      0.036     -2.754      0.006

 C12        ON
    C11                  0.440      0.036     12.214      0.000
    D11                 -0.224      0.038     -5.872      0.000

 C13        ON
    C12                  0.361      0.040      9.128      0.000
    C11                  0.187      0.036      5.214      0.000
    D12                 -0.231      0.038     -6.150      0.000

 D12        WITH
    C12                 -0.353      0.036     -9.778      0.000

 D13        WITH
    C13                 -0.344      0.036     -9.434      0.000

 Intercepts
    D12                  0.909      0.159      5.718      0.000
    D13                  0.674      0.163      4.146      0.000
    C12                  2.386      0.197     12.142      0.000
    C13                  1.663      0.200      8.315      0.000

 Residual Variances
    D12                  0.610      0.031     19.374      0.000
    D13                  0.526      0.030     17.590      0.000
    C12                  0.657      0.032     20.657      0.000
    C13                  0.579      0.031     18.679      0.000

R-SQUARE

    Observed                                             Two-Tailed
    Variable        Estimate       S.E.  Est./S.E.         P-Value

    D12                0.390      0.031     12.403           0.000
    D13                0.474      0.030     15.875           0.000
    C12                0.343      0.032     10.800           0.000
    C13                0.421      0.031     13.602           0.000
```

It turns out that all autoregressive effects (including both first- and second-order effects) are statistically significant (see estimated path coefficients and *p*-values under D12 ON D11, D13 ON D12 D11, C12 ON C11, and C13 ON C12 C11). This indicates that a significant portion of individual differences remained stable over time for both depression and competencies. Nonetheless, individual differences were not perfectly stable over time. Part of the "instability" in depression and competencies is accounted for by temporally preceding scores on the other construct, respectively, as shown by significant cross-lagged coefficients. The significant cross-lagged effects can be interpreted in terms of less competent individuals showing higher depression scores at later time points, even when the prior level of depression is controlled for. Conversely, children reporting higher depression tend to report a lower level of competencies at later occasions of measurement, even when the prior level of competence is taken into account.

In this regard, it is particularly interesting that the estimated cross-lagged effects from depression to competence are larger (standardized path coefficients $\hat{\beta}^{\text{standardized}} = -0.224$ and -0.231) than the corresponding cross-lagged effects from competence to depression (standardized path coefficients $\hat{\beta}^{\text{standardized}} = -0.156$ and -0.100). Overall, the cross-lagged effects are relatively small in size compared to the autoregressive coefficients, indicating that cross-lagged effects account for only a small (albeit significant) amount of individual differences in the model.

The correlations between the residual variables are statistically significant and of medium size ($rs = -.35$ and $-.34$, $ps < .001$), indicating that there is a small amount of shared variance in the depression and competence scores at the same occasion of measurement, over and above what can be explained by autoregression and cross-lagged effects. These correlations are likely due to shared situation-specific effects that influence both constructs at the same time point.

The R^2 values indicate the amount of variability in the endogenous (T2 and T3) variables that can be explained by the sum of autoregressive and cross-lagged effects. It turns out that, overall, 39% of individual differences in depression and 47.4% of individual differences in competence scores can be explained at T2. At T3, the amount of explained variability is 34.3% for depression and 42.1% for competencies. The remaining percentages are due to other influences not represented in the model, shared occasion-specific effects and random measurement error. All these influences are represented by the residual variables ε_{jk}. Latent autoregressive models, which separate random measurement error from reliable individual differences, are discussed in the following section.

4.3.2 Latent Autoregressive Models

The models discussed in the previous section were based on manifest variables. As a consequence, these models are plagued by the same problems as other manifest regression or path models (see Sections 3.2 and

3.5.2), namely, that measurement error is not explicitly accounted for and that the path coefficients and their *SE*s may therefore be biased. In the context of autoregressive models this can lead to bias in the estimation of stability, change, and/or cross-lagged effects and corresponding tests of statistical significance.

Autoregressive models with latent variables (latent autoregressive models, LAMs) explicitly account for random measurement error by using multiple indicators at each time point. LAMs have the additional advantages that they allow testing of measurement models, modeling of indicator-specific effects, and examining of the degree of measurement invariance over time (cf. Section 4.1.4). These models were discussed in detail by Jöreskog (1979a, 1979b) as well as by Hertzog and Nesselroade (1987).

LAMs are based on the LS model described in Section 4.1.2. LAMs restrict the covariances of the LS variables by imposing an autoregressive structure. Cross-lagged models are based on multiconstruct versions of the basic LS model and additionally include cross-lagged effects between LS variables. Figure 4.18 shows a model for two constructs, each of which is measured by two manifest variables Y_{ijk} at each of three time points (i = indicator, j = construct, k = time point). Note that the structural model (containing the paths between the LS variables) is equivalent to the structure of the manifest first-order autoregressive model with uncorrelated residual variables in Figure 4.14.

A good starting point for a latent autoregressive analysis is the basic LS model discussed in Section 4.1. This model can be used to clarify technical issues such as (1) the question of whether the basic measurement

BOX 4.9. *Example of LAMs*

In the following, we show how a multiple-indicator LAM can be specified for the depression and competence data. In this example, we use two indicators for each LS at each time point, as illustrated in Figure 4.18. In order to obtain two indicators, the depression and competence scales were split into two test halves ("parcels") at each time point by assigning the items to two separate sum scores instead of a single one. The summary data for N = 569 children are provided in the file **depression-competence-latent.dat** on the companion website. Among other advantages, the LAM allows us (1) to clarify whether the effects in the manifest autoregressive model were partly biased due to random measurement error, (2) to more properly estimate the autoregressive and cross-lagged coefficients, and (3) to quantify the amount of (un)reliability in each scale.

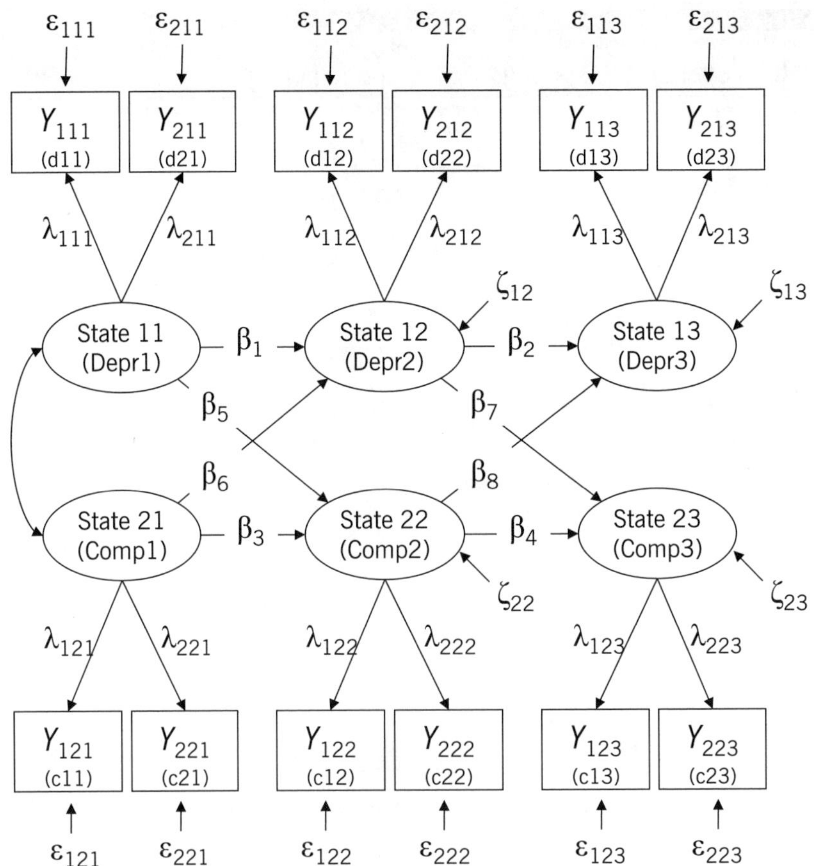

FIGURE 4.18. Latent autoregressive model for 12 manifest indicators Y_{ijk} (i = indicator, j = construct, k = time point) measuring two constructs (j = 1, 2; depression and competence) on three measurement occasions (k = 1, 2, 3). λ_{ijk} = state factor loadings; β_1–β_4 = latent path coefficients representing autoregressive effects; β_5–β_8 = latent path coefficients representing cross-lagged effects; ε_{ijk} = measurement error variables; ζ_{jk} = LS residual variable. The variable names used in Mplus appear in parentheses.

model fits for each construct, (2) whether indicator-specific factors need to be included due to indicator heterogeneity, and (3) which level of measurement invariance can be assumed across time for each construct. The final best-fitting LS model can then serve as the basis for specifying LAMs with or without cross-lagged effects.

Figure 4.19 shows the Mplus input file for the estimation of the LAM from Figure 4.18. For simplicity, we first show a simple model version without indicator-specific factors. Later on, we discuss a more complex model that accounts for indicator-specific effects.

```
title:  Latent autoregressive/cross-lagged model for depression and competence
        shown in Figure 4.18, 3 time points

data: file = depression-competence-latent.dat;
      type = means std corr;
      nobs = 569;

variable: names = d11 d21 ! depression scales T1
                  d12 d22 ! depression scales T2
                  d13 d23 ! depression scales T3
                  c11 c21 ! competence scales T1
                  c12 c22 ! competence scales T2
                  c13 c23 ! competence scales T3

model:! Measurement models depression and competence
       depr1 by d11
                d21; ! Depression T1
       depr2 by d12
                d22; ! Depression T2
       depr3 by d13
                d23; ! Depression T3

       comp1 by c11
                c21; ! Competence T1
       comp2 by c12
                c22; ! Competence T2
       comp3 by c13
                c23; ! Competence T3

   ! Structural model: Autoregressive model with cross-lagged effects
    depr2 on depr1 comp1;
    depr3 on depr2 comp2;
    comp2 on comp1 depr1;
    comp3 on comp2 depr2;

    depr3 with comp3@0; ! Fix correlation between latent residual variables at T3 to zero

output: sampstat stdyx;
```

FIGURE 4.19. Mplus input file for the specification of the simple latent autoregressive model for three measurement occasions shown in Figure 4.18.

The input shows that the basic measurement model specification is identical to the LS model. The only difference is that we now consider two constructs simultaneously. In the structural model, we include autoregressive and cross-lagged effects using `on` statements. The command `depr3 with comp3@0;` again ensures that the residual correlation for time point 3 is set to zero in the initial model. (Mplus would otherwise estimate this correlation as in the manifest model.)

The analysis of the model fit reveals that the model does *not* fit the data well: $\chi^2 = 408.42$, $df = 45$, $p < .001$, $CFI = 0.93$, $RMSEA = 0.12$, $SRMR = 0.05$. This is shown especially by the very large chi-square and *RMSEA* values. For this reason, we do not discuss the parameter estimates for this model here (the full output can be found on the companion website). The bad model fit can be explained by several factors. First, our analysis of the manifest autoregressive model already indicated that the inclusion of correlated residuals and second-order autoregressive effects was necessary. It is likely that these effects are also required in the LAM. Furthermore, in our multiple-indicator LAM there may be indicator-specific effects due to the use of the same indicators over time (cf. Section 4.1.3).

The LAM can be extended in a similar way as the manifest model. In addition, we can include indicator-specific factors as discussed for the LS model in Section 4.1.3. The extended model is shown in Figure 4.20 (p. 143). Figure 4.21 (p. 144) shows the corresponding Mplus `model` command.

Even though the extended model still shows a significant chi-square value, the fit of the model is much improved compared to the model in Figure 4.18, $\chi^2 = 46.72$, $df = 28$, $p = .02$; $CFI = 0.996$; $RMSEA = 0.03$; $SRMR = 0.02$. A comparison of the AIC values also reveals that the more complex model ($AIC = 2601.53$) should be preferred over the initial model ($AIC = 2929.24$). In the following, we show the parameter estimates obtained for the more complex model.

```
MODEL RESULTS

                                                          Two-Tailed
                    Estimate       S.E.  Est./S.E.          P-Value

 DEPR1      BY
    D11                1.000      0.000    999.000          999.000
    D21                0.957      0.032     29.972            0.000

 DEPR2      BY
    D12                1.000      0.000    999.000          999.000
    D22                0.909      0.030     30.500            0.000

 DEPR3      BY
    D13                1.000      0.000    999.000          999.000
    D23                0.924      0.028     32.900            0.000

 ISD        BY
    D21                1.000      0.000    999.000          999.000
    D22                1.093      0.277      3.941            0.000
    D23                1.385      0.425      3.256            0.001

 COMP1      BY
    C11                1.000      0.000    999.000          999.000
    C21                1.031      0.059     17.501            0.000
```

```
COMP2    BY
   C12              1.000      0.000    999.000    999.000
   C22              0.913      0.054     16.840      0.000

COMP3    BY
   C13              1.000      0.000    999.000    999.000
   C23              0.857      0.049     17.346      0.000

ISC      BY
   C21              1.000      0.000    999.000    999.000
   C22              1.167      0.165      7.084      0.000
   C23              1.151      0.172      6.685      0.000

DEPR2    ON
   DEPR1            0.720      0.055     13.141      0.000
   COMP1           -0.030      0.034     -0.878      0.380

DEPR3    ON
   DEPR2            0.590      0.063      9.406      0.000
   DEPR1            0.153      0.051      3.033      0.002
   COMP2           -0.049      0.033     -1.471      0.141

COMP2    ON
   COMP1            0.693      0.071      9.715      0.000
   DEPR1           -0.208      0.100     -2.080      0.037

COMP3    ON
   COMP2            0.597      0.101      5.930      0.000
   COMP1            0.195      0.073      2.679      0.007
   DEPR2           -0.243      0.104     -2.338      0.019

ISD      WITH
   DEPR1            0.000      0.000    999.000    999.000
   DEPR2            0.000      0.000    999.000    999.000
   DEPR3            0.000      0.000    999.000    999.000
   COMP1            0.000      0.002      0.151      0.880
   COMP2           -0.002      0.002     -1.089      0.276
   COMP3            0.000      0.002     -0.242      0.809

ISC      WITH
   COMP1            0.000      0.000    999.000    999.000
   COMP2            0.000      0.000    999.000    999.000
   COMP3            0.000      0.000    999.000    999.000
   DEPR1           -0.011      0.004     -2.823      0.005
   DEPR2           -0.007      0.003     -2.601      0.009
   DEPR3           -0.008      0.003     -3.122      0.002
   ISD             -0.002      0.001     -1.622      0.105

DEPR2    WITH
   COMP2           -0.035      0.004     -8.310      0.000

DEPR3    WITH
   COMP3           -0.036      0.004     -8.584      0.000
```

```
COMP1    WITH
   DEPR1              -0.093      0.008    -11.127      0.000

Intercepts
   D11                 0.306      0.013     22.757      0.000
   D21                 0.274      0.013     21.672      0.000
   D12                 0.274      0.013     20.497      0.000
   D22                 0.253      0.013     20.079      0.000
   D13                 0.283      0.013     21.352      0.000
   D23                 0.256      0.013     20.152      0.000
   C11                 2.074      0.024     85.370      0.000
   C21                 2.121      0.026     82.201      0.000
   C12                 2.091      0.024     88.301      0.000
   C22                 2.115      0.025     83.180      0.000
   C13                 2.082      0.025     82.382      0.000
   C23                 2.184      0.025     85.819      0.000

Variances
   DEPR1               0.085      0.006     13.491      0.000
   ISD                 0.003      0.001      2.508      0.012
   COMP1               0.225      0.021     10.628      0.000
   ISC                 0.054      0.012      4.578      0.000

Residual Variances
   D11                 0.018      0.002      8.220      0.000
   D21                 0.010      0.002      5.108      0.000
   D12                 0.014      0.002      6.928      0.000
   D22                 0.014      0.002      7.801      0.000
   D13                 0.010      0.002      5.251      0.000
   D23                 0.008      0.002      3.802      0.000
   C11                 0.111      0.012      9.473      0.000
   C21                 0.086      0.011      7.648      0.000
   C12                 0.084      0.011      7.546      0.000
   C22                 0.094      0.012      8.178      0.000
   C13                 0.087      0.013      6.982      0.000
   C23                 0.085      0.011      7.693      0.000
   DEPR2               0.039      0.003     11.783      0.000
   DEPR3               0.038      0.003     12.569      0.000
   COMP2               0.096      0.013      7.650      0.000
   COMP3               0.102      0.013      7.901      0.000

STANDARDIZED MODEL RESULTS (STDYX Standardization)

                                                     Two-Tailed
                    Estimate       S.E.  Est./S.E.    P-Value

DEPR1    BY
   D11                 0.909      0.013     72.457      0.000
   D21                 0.925      0.012     75.929      0.000

DEPR2    BY
   D12                 0.929      0.011     82.978      0.000
   D22                 0.896      0.013     71.363      0.000
```

```
DEPR3      BY
   D13                 0.948       0.011      90.229       0.000
   D23                 0.914       0.012      76.546       0.000

ISD        BY
   D21                 0.193       0.038       5.013       0.000
   D22                 0.211       0.041       5.215       0.000
   D23                 0.266       0.046       5.721       0.000

COMP1      BY
   C11                 0.818       0.022      36.435       0.000
   C21                 0.794       0.023      34.255       0.000

COMP2      BY
   C12                 0.858       0.021      40.148       0.000
   C22                 0.729       0.026      28.125       0.000

COMP3      BY
   C13                 0.871       0.021      42.281       0.000
   C23                 0.741       0.026      28.907       0.000

ISC        BY
   C21                 0.377       0.040       9.400       0.000
   C22                 0.446       0.043      10.403       0.000
   C23                 0.439       0.043      10.224       0.000

DEPR2      ON
   DEPR1               0.708       0.046      15.362       0.000
   COMP1              -0.048       0.055      -0.880       0.379

DEPR3      ON
   DEPR2               0.583       0.057      10.175       0.000
   DEPR1               0.149       0.049       3.048       0.002
   COMP2              -0.078       0.053      -1.475       0.140

COMP2      ON
   COMP1               0.678       0.057      11.966       0.000
   DEPR1              -0.125       0.060      -2.080       0.038

COMP3      ON
   COMP2               0.551       0.084       6.591       0.000
   COMP1               0.176       0.065       2.699       0.007
   DEPR2              -0.137       0.059      -2.330       0.020

ISD        WITH
   DEPR1               0.000       0.000     999.000     999.000
   DEPR2               0.000       0.000     999.000     999.000
   DEPR3               0.000       0.000     999.000     999.000
   COMP1               0.010       0.064       0.150       0.880
   COMP2              -0.091       0.082      -1.111       0.267
   COMP3              -0.020       0.083      -0.241       0.809
```

```
ISC      WITH
  COMP1               0.000        0.000      999.000      999.000
  COMP2               0.000        0.000      999.000      999.000
  COMP3               0.000        0.000      999.000      999.000
  DEPR1              -0.169        0.051       -3.295        0.001
  DEPR2              -0.157        0.059       -2.691        0.007
  DEPR3              -0.185        0.056       -3.307        0.001
  ISD                -0.152        0.087       -1.741        0.082

DEPR2    WITH
  COMP2              -0.570        0.051      -11.108        0.000

DEPR3    WITH
  COMP3              -0.570        0.049      -11.625        0.000

COMP1    WITH
  DEPR1              -0.675        0.032      -21.093        0.000

Intercepts
  D11                 0.954        0.051       18.870        0.000
  D21                 0.909        0.050       18.254        0.000
  D12                 0.859        0.049       17.521        0.000
  D22                 0.842        0.049       17.264        0.000
  D13                 0.895        0.050       18.049        0.000
  D23                 0.845        0.049       17.323        0.000
  C11                 3.579        0.114       31.374        0.000
  C21                 3.446        0.110       31.414        0.000
  C12                 3.702        0.117       31.514        0.000
  C22                 3.487        0.111       31.443        0.000
  C13                 3.454        0.111       31.226        0.000
  C23                 3.598        0.114       31.647        0.000

Variances
  DEPR1               1.000        0.000      999.000      999.000
  ISD                 1.000        0.000      999.000      999.000
  COMP1               1.000        0.000      999.000      999.000
  ISC                 1.000        0.000      999.000      999.000

Residual Variances
  D11                 0.174        0.023        7.652        0.000
  D21                 0.107        0.022        4.907        0.000
  D12                 0.136        0.021        6.538        0.000
  D22                 0.152        0.021        7.249        0.000
  D13                 0.101        0.020        5.060        0.000
  D23                 0.091        0.025        3.703        0.000
  C11                 0.331        0.037        9.004        0.000
  C21                 0.227        0.032        7.146        0.000
  C12                 0.265        0.037        7.219        0.000
  C22                 0.256        0.033        7.652        0.000
  C13                 0.241        0.036        6.702        0.000
  C23                 0.230        0.032        7.209        0.000
```

```
    DEPR2              0.450      0.034     13.290      0.000
    DEPR3              0.425      0.031     13.604      0.000
    COMP2              0.410      0.043      9.547      0.000
    COMP3              0.369      0.038      9.642      0.000

R-SQUARE

    Observed                                          Two-Tailed
    Variable        Estimate       S.E.  Est./S.E.    P-Value

    D11                0.826      0.023     36.229      0.000
    D21                0.893      0.022     41.054      0.000
    D12                0.864      0.021     41.489      0.000
    D22                0.848      0.021     40.347      0.000
    D13                0.899      0.020     45.115      0.000
    D23                0.909      0.025     36.837      0.000
    C11                0.669      0.037     18.218      0.000
    C21                0.773      0.032     24.327      0.000
    C12                0.735      0.037     20.074      0.000
    C22                0.744      0.033     22.263      0.000
    C13                0.759      0.036     21.141      0.000
    C23                0.770      0.032     24.147      0.000

     Latent                                           Two-Tailed
    Variable        Estimate       S.E.  Est./S.E.    P-Value

    DEPR2              0.550      0.034     16.267      0.000
    DEPR3              0.575      0.031     18.403      0.000
    COMP2              0.590      0.043     13.765      0.000
    COMP3              0.631      0.038     16.494      0.000
```

The parameter estimates pertaining to the structural model show some interesting differences compared to the manifest autoregressive model. Overall, we can see that the estimated R^2 values for the structural model (`R-SQUARE—Latent Variable`) are much larger in the LAM ($.55 \leq R^2 \leq .63$) than the corresponding values in the manifest model ($.39 \leq R^2 \leq .47$). In other words, the LAM can explain a much larger amount of variability in the T2 and T3 depression and competence constructs than the manifest model.

On the other hand, the cross-lagged effects from competence to depression that were found to be significant in the manifest path model turn out to be nonsignificant in the LAM (whereas the cross-lagged effects from depression to competence are still significant). The larger R^2 values in the LAM can primarily be explained by the fact that the first-order autoregressive effects are estimated to be larger in this model [standardized first-order latent autoregressive path coefficients: $0.55 \leq \hat{\beta}^{\text{standardized}}$

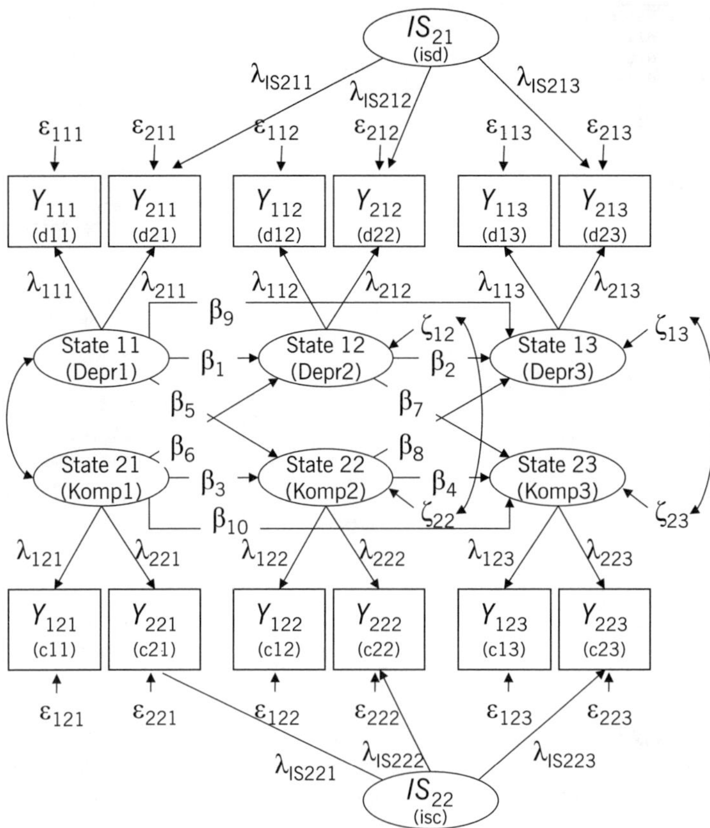

FIGURE 4.20. Latent autoregressive model for 12 manifest indicators Y_{ijk} (i = indicator, j = construct, k = time point) measuring two constructs (j = 1, 2; depression and competence) on three measurement occasions (k = 1, 2, 3). λ_{ijk} = state factor loadings; λ_{IS2jk} = loadings on the indicator-specific factors IS_{2j}; β_1–β_4 = latent path coefficients representing first-order autoregressive effects; β_9 and β_{10} = latent path coefficients representing second-order autoregressive effects; β_5–β_8 = latent path coefficients representing cross-lagged effects; ε_{ijk} = measurement error variables; ζ_{jk} = latent state residual variable. In contrast to the model shown in Figure 4.18, this model allows for second-order autoregressive effects, correlated residual variables at the same measurement occasion, and indicator-specific factors IS_{2j} for the second indicator. To avoid cluttering, not all possible correlations between variables are included in the picture. The variable names used in Mplus appear in parentheses.

```
model:! Measurement models depression and competence
      depr1 by d11
               d21; ! Depression T1
      depr2 by d12
               d22; ! Depression T2
      depr3 by d13
               d23; ! Depression T3

    isd by d21 d22 d23; ! indicator-specific factor depression
    isd with depr1-depr3@0; ! not correlated with the depression state/residual factors
    isd with comp1 comp2 comp3; ! can be corrrelated with the remaining factors/residuals

      comp1 by c11
               c21; ! Competence T1
      comp2 by c12
               c22; ! Competence T2
      comp3 by c13
               c23; ! Competence T3

   isc by c21 c22 c23; ! indicator-specific factor competence
   isc with comp1-comp3@0; ! not correlated with competence state/residual factors
   isc with depr1 depr2 depr3; ! can be correlated with the remaining factors/residuals

 ! Struktural model: Autoregressive model with cross-lagged effects
 ! including second-order autoregressive effects
   depr2 on depr1 comp1;
   depr3 on depr2 depr1 comp2;
   comp2 on comp1 depr1;
   comp3 on comp2 comp1 depr2;

   depr2 with comp2; ! allow correlation of latent residual variables at T2
   depr3 with comp3; ! allow correlation of latent residual variables at T3
```

FIGURE 4.21. Mplus `model` command for the specification of the extended latent autoregressive model with second-order autoregressive effects, correlated latent residual variables, and indicator-specific factors shown in Figure 4.20.

≤ 0.71; see results reported under `STANDARDIZED MODEL RESULTS (STDYX Standardization)`] compared to the manifest model ($0.36 \leq \hat{\beta}^{\text{standardized}} \leq 0.53$). This finding indicates an underestimation of the actual stability of individual differences in the manifest model, which is likely due to the fact that measurement error was not explicitly taken into account in the manifest model.

In summary, the analyses again illustrate the advantages of using latent variable models for analyzing longitudinal data. These models correct for measurement error and therefore allow for a more accurate analysis of complex relationships between variables. In the present example, especially, the scales measuring competencies show relatively low reliabilities ($.67 \leq R^2 \leq .77$; see values reported under `R-SQUARE—Observed Variable`, variables `C11–C23`). Likewise, the indicators of depression have high, albeit less than perfect, reliabilities ($.83 \leq R^2 \leq .91$; see `R-SQUARE—Observed Variable`, variables `D11–D23`).

Imperfect reliabilities are one reason for the differences seen in the results between the manifest and the latent autoregressive models. An additional reason may be the relatively large amounts of specific variance in the competence test halves (the competence scale is composed of rather heterogeneous items), as indicated by the relatively large occasion-specific effects (standardized loadings on the indicator-specific factor `ISC`: $.377 \leq \hat{\lambda}^{\text{standardized}} \leq .446$).

As in an LS analysis, the degree of invariance of the parameters of the measurement model over time should be examined for the LAM in subsequent analysis steps. (The possibility to test for measurement invariance is another advantage of the LAM over the manifest model.) I do not discuss such an analysis here in detail given that the principle of invariance testing was already illustrated in detail for the LS model in Section 4.1.4. The steps shown for the LS model can be transferred to the LAM. The companion website contains a sample input file for a version of the LAM assuming strong factorial invariance across time.

4.4 LATENT CHANGE MODELS

In latent change (LC) models (McArdle & Hamagami, 2001; Raykov, 1993; Steyer et al., 1997, 2000), change is not measured "indirectly" through the residual variables in autoregressions (as in autoregressive models), but directly through so-called *latent difference variables*. Latent difference variables represent interindividual differences in true intraindividual change over time—that is, change scores corrected for random measurement error. For this reason, these types of models have also been referred to as *true change models* (Steyer et al., 1997). Because latent difference variables are of key importance in this approach, LC models are sometimes also called *latent difference models*.

Latent difference variables can be included in SEMs in a relatively simple way by reformulating LS models (see Section 4.1). Figure 4.22 illustrates the reparameterization of an LS model (A) to an LC model (B) based on a single construct measured by two indicators on two measurement occasions. The basic idea of the LC model is that the LS variable at time 2 (*State 2*) is a function of (1 times) the initial LS variable (*State 1*) plus (1 times) change (in terms of the latent difference variable *State 2 – State 1*):

$$\textit{State 2} = 1\ \textit{State 1} + 1\ (\textit{State 2} - \textit{State 1})$$

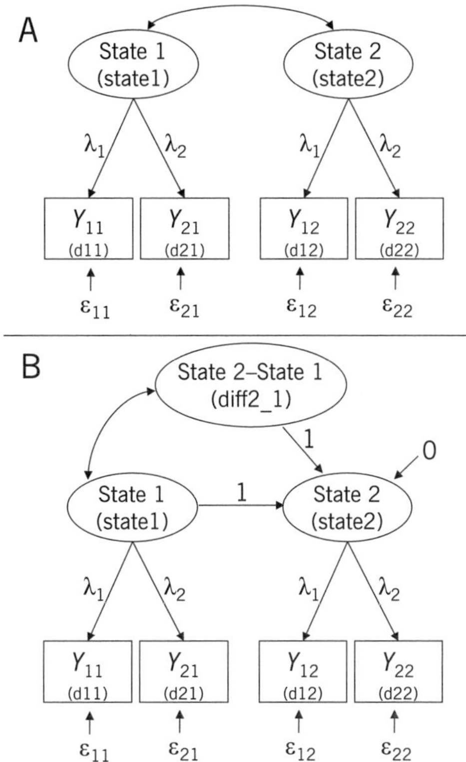

FIGURE 4.22. LS model and corresponding latent change (LC) model for depression measured by two indicators Y_{ik} (i = indicator, k = time point) on two measurement occasions: λ_i = time-invariant state factor loadings; ε_{ik} = measurement error variable. **A**: LS model. **B**: LC model. The variable names used in the Mplus appear in parentheses.

Note that this decomposition is not at all restrictive: We add one variable (the factor *State 1*) to another variable (here the factor *State 2*) and subtract this variable again at the same time. This decomposition into initial state plus change can be accomplished in an LS model through the inclusion of an additional latent variable, the latent difference variable (*State 2 – State 1*), as shown in Figure 4.22B. This means that the latent difference becomes an explicit part of the model in the form of an additional latent variable, which makes it possible to study interindividual differences in intraindividual change at the latent (error-free) level.

A latent difference variable can be used like any other latent variable in an SEM. For example, the latent difference variable can be correlated with other variables or it can serve as an exogenous (predictor) or endogenous (criterion) variable in extended SEMs. Often, researchers are interested in explaining individual differences in change over time (i.e., why do some people change more than others?). In such a case, the latent difference model could be used as an endogenous variable that is predicted (or "explained") by other variables. In addition, the mean of the latent difference variable can be estimated and used as a measure of mean differences across time (e.g., does significant mean change occur?).

Note that in the above equation, the variable *State 2* can be seen as being "regressed on" *State 1* as well as the latent difference variable (*State 2* – *State 1*). Technically, one can see this as a "perfect" (or deterministic) regression analysis, because there is no residual variable in the equation. This can also be seen by the fact that the path diagram in Figure 4.22B explicitly includes a residual of zero for the endogenous variable *State 2*. It is important to emphasize this aspect because it is relevant for the model specification in Mplus, in which the residual variance of each endogenous variable is estimated by default and thus has to be set to zero by the user, in this case.

Another important issue to consider when using LC models is that they require at least strong factorial invariance with regard to the measurement model (cf. Section 4.1.4). Strong factorial invariance is a prerequisite for a meaningful interpretation of latent difference scores, because it ensures that both *State 1* and *State 2* are measured in the same metric (equal loadings) and have the same origin of measurement (equal intercepts). Strong measurement invariance thus ensures that we are not subtracting apples from oranges.

BOX 4.10. *Example of LC Models*

As a substantive example, we once again consider the LS model for depression from Section 4.1. We might be interested in decomposing the Time 2 LS factor for depression (*Depression T2*) into initial state (factor *Depression T1*) plus change (*Depression T2* – *Depression T1*):

$$\textit{Depression T2} = \textit{Depression T1} + (\textit{Depression T2} - \textit{Depression T1})$$

This decomposition allows us to examine the degree of individual differences in change over time with regard to depression (by means of the variance of the latent difference factor). It also allows us to relate individual differences in change to external variables; for example, to explain why some people's depression scores changed more than others.

The assumption of time-invariant loadings (as one required aspect of strong factorial invariance) is reflected in Figure 4.22 by the fact that the loading parameters λ_i carry an index only for the variable, but not for the occasion of measurement (hence, they do not depend on the time point but are the same at each measurement occasion). The time-invariant intercepts are not shown in the figure. Implementing the assumption of strong factorial invariance is critical in the model specification in Mplus. Equality constraints, as discussed in detail in Section 4.1.4, have to be imposed to obtain time-invariant loadings and intercepts.

For more than two time points, Steyer et al. (1997, 2000) distinguish between a baseline and a neighbor change version of the LC model. In the baseline change version, change is assessed with regard to a specific baseline situation or time point (often the first time point). In this model, for example, change from the first to the second, the first to the third, the first to the fourth time point, and so on, is examined.

In contrast, neighbor change models always consider change between adjacent time points; for example, change between the first and the second, the second and the third, and the third and the fourth time points. Figure 4.23 shows a baseline (A) and a neighbor (B) LC model for three time points.

In this case, the difference between the baseline and the neighbor change version is that the third LS variable (*State 3*) is decomposed into initial state (*State 1*) plus change from time 1 to time 3 (*State 3 – State 1*) in the baseline change model:

BOX 4.11. *Data Example of LC Models in Mplus*

We use the LS model for depression from Section 4.1.4 (data set **depression.dat**) as the basis for our illustration of the analysis of LC models in Mplus. As the starting point, we use the LS model version with an indicator-specific factor for the second indicator and strong factorial invariance (in which the factor loadings and intercepts are assumed to be equal across time). Given that we have already tested the assumption of strong factorial invariance in Section 4.1.4 (and found that we did not have to reject it), we can directly start with the analysis of LC models. In general, the assumption of strong factorial invariance has to be tested first before one can start an LC analysis. The LS model is equivalent to both a baseline and a neighbor change model; that is, all three models imply the same mean and covariance structure. The reason is that the LC models are just reparameterizations of the LS model. Therefore, the fit of all three models is also identical.

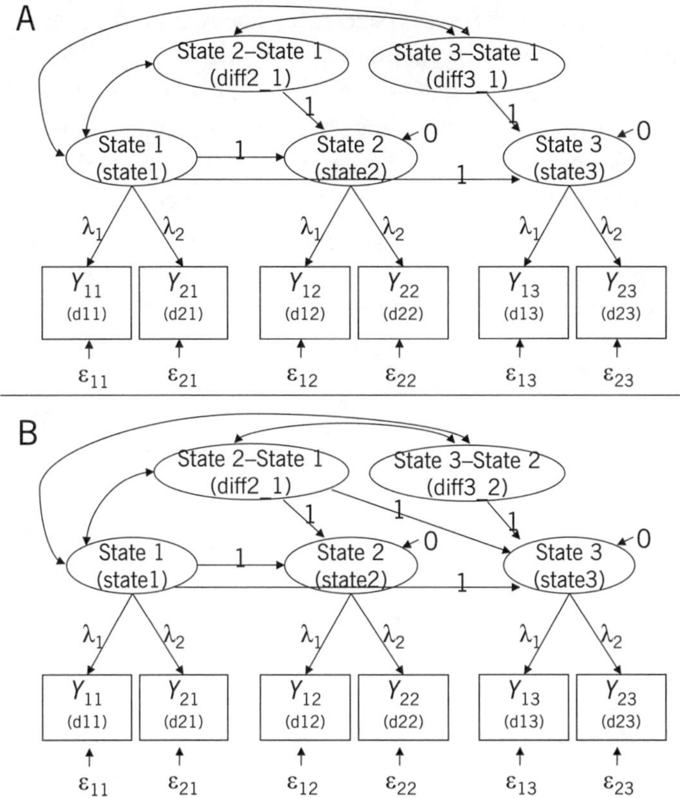

FIGURE 4.23. LC model for two indicators Y_{ik} (i = indicator, k = time point) and three measurement occasions. λ_i = time-invariant state factor loadings; ε_{ik} = measurement error variable. **A**: Baseline change model. **B**: Neighbor change model. The models are equivalent and equivalent to an LS model with invariant parameters. The (often required) indicator-specific factor for the second indicator is not shown here to save space. The variable names used in the Mplus input appear in parentheses.

$$State\ 3 = 1 \cdot State\ 1 + 1 \cdot (State\ 3 - State\ 1)$$

whereas in the neighbor change model, *State 3* is decomposed into the initial state plus two separate change components:

$$State\ 3 = 1 \cdot State\ 1 + 1 \cdot (State\ 2 - State\ 1) + 1 \cdot (State\ 3 - State\ 2)$$

Figure 4.24 shows the Mplus `model` command for the specification of the baseline change model. (The specification of the neighbor change model is shown in Figure 4.25, page 158.) The remaining input does not differ from the input for the LS model (cf. Figure 4.9).

The measurement models for the three LS factors are formulated in analogy to the LS model with time-invariant loadings. According to the parameterization in Figure 4.23, the latent difference variables are not directly connected with observed indicators. Steyer et al. (1997, 2000) discuss an alternative equivalent parameterization of LC models in which the latent difference variables are directly connected to observed indicators. For didactic reasons, I did not choose this parameterization here.

```
model: ! Latent state factors
state1 by d11
          d21 (1);

state2 by d12
          d22 (1);

state3 by d13
          d23 (1);

! Introduce the names of the latent difference factors
diff2_1 by d11@0;
diff3_1 by d11@0;

! Specifiy the latent difference model as a deterministic regression model
state2 on state1@1 diff2_1@1;
state3 on state1@1 diff3_1@1;

state2@0;
state3@0;

state2 with state3@0 diff3_1@0;
state3 with diff2_1@0;

! Indicator-specific (residual) factor for the second indicator
is2 by d21 d22@1 d23@1;

! Indicator-specific factor is not allowed to correlate with the state factors
is2 with state1@0 state2@0 state3@0 diff2_1@0 diff3_1@0;

! Fix the intercepts of the first indicator to zero
[d11@0 d12@0 d13@0];

! Estimate the means of the latent state and latent difference factors
[state1 diff2_1 diff3_1];

! Set the intercepts of the second indicator equal across time
[d21 d22 d23] (2);
```

FIGURE 4.24. Mplus `model` command for the specification of the baseline change model shown in Figure 4.23A. An additional indicator-specific factor for the second indicator was included in the model. (This factor is not shown in Figure 4.23.)

However, both types of parameterizations can be found in separate input files on the companion website.

Given that, in the parameterization chosen here, the latent difference variables diff2_1 and diff3_1 are not directly connected to the observed variables, we have to use a trick to include them in the model. The reason is that Mplus requires all latent variables to be defined via a by statement. In order to define the latent difference variables, we therefore simply choose an arbitrary observed variable that is listed under usevariables (e.g., d11) and specify that this variable has a loading of 0 on each latent difference variable:

```
diff2_1 by d11@0;
diff3_1 by d11@0;
```

These commands thus merely serve to introduce the names of the latent variables diff2_1 and diff3_1—they have no deeper implication for the model specification other than defining the names of the latent difference variables so that they can be used in the model. The relevant commands that assign the meaning as difference scores to these variables are shown next. We use on commands to specify that the LS variables at T2 and T3 are functions of the initial LS variable (state1) plus the latent difference, respectively:

```
state2 on state1@1 diff2_1@1;
state3 on state1@1 diff3_1@1;
```

The "regression coefficients" of these regressions are fixed to 1 using the command @1, because the implicit specification of the LC model is that, for example, state2 is equal to *one times* the initial LS variable (state1) plus *1 times* the latent difference diff2_1.

Furthermore, we have to fix the residuals of these regressions to zero because Mplus would otherwise automatically add a residual term to each regression equation (which would not be correct, given that state2 and state3 are *fully* determined by initial status and change in this model):

```
state2@0;
state3@0;
```

The latent difference variables diff2_1 and diff3_1 obtain their meaning as latent difference variables through the above specifications.

Given that the endogenous variables `state2` and `state3` are perfectly determined by initial state and change in this model, their residual variables were fixed to zero. As a consequence, the residual terms cannot be correlated with other variables. These correlations have to be suppressed in Mplus, because otherwise the model would be misspecified and would also, very likely, produce estimation problems:

```
state2 with state3@0 diff3_1@0;
state3 with diff2_1@0;
```

The following commands serve to specify the indicator-specific factor for the second indicator (`is2`), as in the LS model (cf. Section 4.1.3). All loadings on this factor are fixed to 1 to keep them invariant across time. The `with` command is used to set the correlations of the `is2` factor with all other latent variables to zero.

```
is2 by d21 d22@1 d23@1;
is2 with state1@0 state2@0 state3@0 diff2_1@0 diff3_1@0;
```

All remaining commands concern the mean structure of the model. We first set the intercepts of the reference indicators to 0 to identify the latent means (cf. Section 4.1.4):

```
[d11@0 d12@0 d13@0];
```

Next, we request the estimation of the latent means for `state1` as well as for the two latent difference variables `diff2_1` and `diff3_1` (otherwise, Mplus would keep these means fixed at 0 by default):

```
[state1 diff2_1 diff3_1];
```

Finally, the intercepts of the remaining (non-reference) indicators are set equal across time to establish strong factorial invariance:

```
[d21 d22 d23] (2);
```

As expected, the fit of the baseline change model is identical to the fit of the LS model with strong factorial invariance, $\chi^2 = 6.656$, $df = 9$, $p = .6729$, $RMSEA = .00$, $p(RMSEA \leq .05 = .95$, $SRMR = .014$, $CFI = 1.00$ (cf. Section 4.1.4; the complete output can be found on the companion website).

In the following MODEL RESULTS, we can see that the parameters of the measurement model are also the same as in the LS model with strong factorial invariance. The output now additionally contains the covariances (under MODEL RESULTS) and correlations [under STANDARDIZED MODEL RESULTS (STDYX Standardization)] of the latent difference variables diff2_1 and diff3_1 with the initial LS factor (state1) as well as between the two latent difference variables.

```
MODEL RESULTS (Baseline Change Model)

                                                   Two-Tailed
                  Estimate       S.E.  Est./S.E.    P-Value

 STATE1   BY
    D11              1.000      0.000    999.000    999.000
    D21              0.738      0.030     24.997      0.000

 STATE2   BY
    D12              1.000      0.000    999.000    999.000
    D22              0.738      0.030     24.997      0.000

 STATE3   BY
    D13              1.000      0.000    999.000    999.000
    D23              0.738      0.030     24.997      0.000

 DIFF2_1  BY
    D11              0.000      0.000    999.000    999.000

 DIFF3_1  BY
    D11              0.000      0.000    999.000    999.000

 IS2      BY
    D21              1.000      0.000    999.000    999.000
    D22              1.000      0.000    999.000    999.000
    D23              1.000      0.000    999.000    999.000

 STATE2   ON
    STATE1           1.000      0.000    999.000    999.000
    DIFF2_1          1.000      0.000    999.000    999.000

 STATE3   ON
    STATE1           1.000      0.000    999.000    999.000
    DIFF3_1          1.000      0.000    999.000    999.000

 STATE2   WITH
    STATE3           0.000      0.000    999.000    999.000
    DIFF3_1          0.000      0.000    999.000    999.000

 STATE3   WITH
    DIFF2_1          0.000      0.000    999.000    999.000
```

```
 IS2      WITH
    STATE1             0.000       0.000    999.000    999.000
    STATE2             0.000       0.000    999.000    999.000
    STATE3             0.000       0.000    999.000    999.000
    DIFF2_1            0.000       0.000    999.000    999.000
    DIFF3_1            0.000       0.000    999.000    999.000

 DIFF2_1  WITH
    STATE1            -0.077       0.015     -5.324      0.000

 DIFF3_1  WITH
    STATE1            -0.088       0.015     -5.856      0.000
    DIFF2_1            0.099       0.015      6.451      0.000

 Means
    STATE1             1.583       0.026     60.157      0.000
    DIFF2_1            0.056       0.027      2.078      0.038
    DIFF3_1            0.052       0.027      1.900      0.057

 Intercepts
    D11                0.000       0.000    999.000    999.000
    D21                0.187       0.049      3.861      0.000
    D12                0.000       0.000    999.000    999.000
    D22                0.187       0.049      3.861      0.000
    D13                0.000       0.000    999.000    999.000
    D23                0.187       0.049      3.861      0.000

 Variances
    STATE1             0.195       0.019     10.510      0.000
    DIFF2_1            0.193       0.021      9.385      0.000
    DIFF3_1            0.198       0.021      9.453      0.000
    IS2                0.007       0.002      3.433      0.001

 Residual Variances
    D11                0.040       0.009      4.477      0.000
    D21                0.028       0.005      5.425      0.000
    D12                0.022       0.009      2.453      0.014
    D22                0.035       0.006      6.299      0.000
    D13                0.019       0.009      2.192      0.028
    D23                0.037       0.006      6.608      0.000
    STATE2             0.000       0.000    999.000    999.000
    STATE3             0.000       0.000    999.000    999.000


STANDARDIZED MODEL RESULTS (STDYX Standardization)

                                                    Two-Tailed
                    Estimate       S.E.  Est./S.E.    P-Value

 STATE1   BY
    D11                0.911       0.021     43.988      0.000
    D21                0.867       0.022     39.895      0.000
```

```
STATE2   BY
   D12                0.956      0.018     52.311      0.000
   D22                0.867      0.020     43.500      0.000

STATE3   BY
   D13                0.959      0.019     50.014      0.000
   D23                0.854      0.021     41.331      0.000

DIFF2_1  BY
   D11                0.000      0.000    999.000    999.000

DIFF3_1  BY
   D11                0.000      0.000    999.000    999.000

IS2      BY
   D21                0.220      0.033      6.732      0.000
   D22                0.202      0.030      6.720      0.000
   D23                0.205      0.031      6.733      0.000

STATE2   ON
   STATE1             0.915      0.049     18.583      0.000
   DIFF2_1            0.909      0.049     18.466      0.000

STATE3   ON
   STATE1             0.946      0.052     18.195      0.000
   DIFF3_1            0.953      0.052     18.430      0.000

STATE2   WITH
   STATE3           999.000    999.000    999.000    999.000
   DIFF3_1          999.000    999.000    999.000    999.000

STATE3   WITH
   DIFF2_1          999.000    999.000    999.000    999.000

IS2      WITH
   STATE1             0.000      0.000    999.000    999.000
   STATE2           999.000    999.000    999.000    999.000
   STATE3           999.000    999.000    999.000    999.000
   DIFF2_1            0.000      0.000    999.000    999.000
   DIFF3_1            0.000      0.000    999.000    999.000

DIFF2_1  WITH
   STATE1            -0.399      0.054     -7.345      0.000

DIFF3_1  WITH
   STATE1            -0.446      0.052     -8.646      0.000
   DIFF2_1            0.508      0.050     10.167      0.000

Means
   STATE1             3.583      0.181     19.792      0.000
   DIFF2_1            0.127      0.061      2.069      0.039
   DIFF3_1            0.116      0.061      1.892      0.058
```

```
 Intercepts
    D11               0.000      0.000    999.000    999.000
    D21               0.498      0.134      3.706      0.000
    D12               0.000      0.000    999.000    999.000
    D22               0.456      0.124      3.677      0.000
    D13               0.000      0.000    999.000    999.000
    D23               0.465      0.126      3.686      0.000

 Variances
    STATE1            1.000      0.000    999.000    999.000
    DIFF2_1           1.000      0.000    999.000    999.000
    DIFF3_1           1.000      0.000    999.000    999.000
    IS2               1.000      0.000    999.000    999.000

 Residual Variances
    D11               0.171      0.038      4.532      0.000
    D21               0.200      0.036      5.535      0.000
    D12               0.086      0.035      2.448      0.014
    D22               0.208      0.033      6.332      0.000
    D13               0.081      0.037      2.191      0.028
    D23               0.228      0.034      6.767      0.000
    STATE2            0.000    999.000    999.000    999.000
    STATE3            0.000    999.000    999.000    999.000

R-SQUARE

    Observed                                        Two-Tailed
    Variable       Estimate       S.E.  Est./S.E.    P-Value

    D11               0.829      0.038     21.994      0.000
    D21               0.800      0.036     22.155      0.000
    D12               0.914      0.035     26.155      0.000
    D22               0.792      0.033     24.165      0.000
    D13               0.919      0.037     25.007      0.000
    D23               0.772      0.034     22.941      0.000

     Latent                                         Two-Tailed
    Variable       Estimate       S.E.  Est./S.E.    P-Value

    STATE2            1.000    999.000    999.000    999.000
    STATE3            1.000    999.000    999.000    999.000
```

In addition, we obtain the latent means of `state1`, `diff2_1`, and `diff3_1`. If we compare these values to the LS factor means obtained in the LS model with strong factorial invariance ($M_1 = 1.583$, $M_2 = 1.639$, $M_3 = 1.634$), we can see that (1) the mean of `state1` is identical, as expected, and that (2) the mean of `diff2_1` (0.056) is exactly equal to the difference between the means of `state2` and `state1`:

$$1.639 - 1.583 = 0.056$$

Likewise, the mean of `diff3_1` (0.052) is equal, within rounding error, to the mean difference between `state3` and `state1`:

$$1.634 - 1.583 = 0.051$$

The positive signs of the latent difference factor means indicate that the latent depression scores have (slightly) *increased* between time 1 and time 2 as well as between time 1 and time 3.

The estimated p-values for the latent difference factor means indicate that the mean difference between T1 and T2 is significantly different from zero at the .05 level for a two-tailed test, $z = 2.078$, $p = .038$, indicating that the increase in depression from T1 to T2 was statistically significant. The mean difference between T1 and T3 failed to reach statistical significance at the .05 level (at least for a two-tailed test), $z = 1.900$, $p = 0.057$.

The estimated variances of `state1` (0.195), `diff2_1` (0.193), and `diff3_1` (0.198) are significantly different from zero (all $ps < .001$), showing that there are individual differences in the initial latent depression state as well as in the LC scores. Notice that the R^2 values for `state2` and `state3` equal 1, reflecting the fact that these state factors are, by definition, perfectly determined by initial state plus change in this model.

Figure 4.25 shows the model statement for the specification of the neighbor change model for the same data example. The specification of the latent difference variable `diff2_1` is identical to the specification of this variable in the baseline change model. This variable still represents change from time 1 to time 2. The second latent difference variable in the model is now labeled `diff3_2` to make clear that in the neighbor change version, we consider change between the adjacent time points 2 and 3 (rather than between time 1 and 3). According to the path diagram in Figure 4.23B, the latent state variable `state3` is now determined by three components: (1) the initial state factor (`state1`), (2) LC between time 1 and time 2 (`diff2_1`), and (3) LC between time 2 and time 3 (`diff3_2`). Therefore, the `on` statement for `state3` now lists all three components and sets the paths of all these components to 1 (using the `@1` command). The remaining commands are analogous to the baseline change model.

The model fit of the neighbor change model is again identical to the fit of the LS model with strong factorial invariance as well as to the fit of the baseline change model (see Mplus outputs on the companion website

```
model: ! Latent state factors
state1 by d11
          d21 (1);

state2 by d12
          d22 (1);

state3 by d13
          d23 (1);

! Introduce the names of the latent difference factors
diff2_1 by d11@0;
diff3_2 by d11@0;

! Specifiy the latent difference model as a deterministic regression model
state2 on state1@1 diff2_1@1;
state3 on state1@1 diff2_1@1 diff3_2@1;

state2@0;
state3@0;

state2 with state3@0 diff3_2@0;

! Indicator-specific (residual) factor for the second indicator
is2 by d21 d22@1 d23@1;

! Indicator-specific factor is not allowed to correlate with the state factors
is2 with state1@0 state2@0 state3@0 diff2_1@0 diff3_2@0;

! Fix the intercepts of the first indicator to zero
[d11@0 d12@0 d13@0];

! Estimate the means of the latent state and latent difference factors
[state1 diff2_1 diff3_2];

! Set the intercepts of the second indicator equal across time
[d21 d22 d23] (2);
```

FIGURE 4.25. Mplus `model` command for the specification of the neighbor change model shown in Figure 4.23B. An additional indicator-specific factor for the second indicator was included in the model. (This factor is not shown in Figure 4.23.)

for details). The parameter estimates of the measurement model (loadings, intercepts, and residual variances) are also identical to the corresponding loadings in the LS and baseline change model. In the structural model, we now obtain the covariances and correlations between the initial state factor `state1` and the latent difference variables `diff2_1` (as in the baseline change model) and `diff3_2`. Furthermore, the covariances/correlations between `diff2_1` and `diff3_2` are estimated, as are the means of `state1`, `diff2_1`, and `diff3_2`. The means of `state1` and `diff2_1` are identical to the means in the baseline change model (M_1 = 1.583, M_{2-1} = 0.056). The mean of the latent difference variable `diff3_2` is estimated to M_{3-2} = –0.004. Within rounding error, this is equal to the difference in means between `state3` and `state2` in the LS model with strong factorial invariance. The mean difference of –0.004 is not statistically significant, z = –0.163, p = .871. We can conclude that the average level of depression has not significantly changed between T2 and T3.

In addition, we again obtain estimates for the variances of `state1` (0.195), `diff2_1` (0.193), and `diff3_2` (0.192). These variances indicate the degree to which individuals differ in their initial latent depression scores as well as in their LC scores. In additional analysis steps, one could add external variables (covariates) to the model that may be able to partly or fully explain individual differences in initial status and change (for a substantive example, see Steyer et al., 2000).

```
MODEL RESULTS

                                                        Two-Tailed
                    Estimate       S.E.  Est./S.E.     P-Value

 STATE1    BY
    D11                1.000      0.000    999.000     999.000
    D21                0.738      0.030     24.997       0.000

 STATE2    BY
    D12                1.000      0.000    999.000     999.000
    D22                0.738      0.030     24.997       0.000

 STATE3    BY
    D13                1.000      0.000    999.000     999.000
    D23                0.738      0.030     24.997       0.000

 DIFF2_1   BY
    D11                0.000      0.000    999.000     999.000

 DIFF3_2   BY
    D11                0.000      0.000    999.000     999.000

 IS2       BY
    D21                1.000      0.000    999.000     999.000
    D22                1.000      0.000    999.000     999.000
    D23                1.000      0.000    999.000     999.000

 STATE2    ON
    STATE1             1.000      0.000    999.000     999.000
    DIFF2_1            1.000      0.000    999.000     999.000
```

```
STATE3    ON
   STATE1              1.000      0.000    999.000    999.000
   DIFF2_1             1.000      0.000    999.000    999.000
   DIFF3_2             1.000      0.000    999.000    999.000

STATE2    WITH
   STATE3              0.000      0.000    999.000    999.000
   DIFF3_2             0.000      0.000    999.000    999.000

IS2       WITH
   STATE1              0.000      0.000    999.000    999.000
   STATE2              0.000      0.000    999.000    999.000
   STATE3              0.000      0.000    999.000    999.000
   DIFF2_1             0.000      0.000    999.000    999.000
   DIFF3_2             0.000      0.000    999.000    999.000

DIFF2_1  WITH
   STATE1             -0.077      0.015     -5.324      0.000

DIFF3_2  WITH
   STATE1             -0.010      0.012     -0.832      0.405
   DIFF2_1            -0.093      0.015     -6.142      0.000

Means
   STATE1              1.583      0.026     60.157      0.000
   DIFF2_1             0.056      0.027      2.078      0.038
   DIFF3_2            -0.004      0.026     -0.163      0.871

Intercepts
   D11                 0.000      0.000    999.000    999.000
   D21                 0.187      0.049      3.861      0.000
   D12                 0.000      0.000    999.000    999.000
   D22                 0.187      0.049      3.861      0.000
   D13                 0.000      0.000    999.000    999.000
   D23                 0.187      0.049      3.861      0.000

Variances
   STATE1              0.195      0.019     10.510      0.000
   DIFF2_1             0.193      0.021      9.385      0.000
   DIFF3_2             0.192      0.021      9.341      0.000
   IS2                 0.007      0.002      3.433      0.001

Residual Variances
   D11                 0.040      0.009      4.477      0.000
   D21                 0.028      0.005      5.425      0.000
   D12                 0.022      0.009      2.453      0.014
   D22                 0.035      0.006      6.299      0.000
   D13                 0.019      0.009      2.192      0.028
   D23                 0.037      0.006      6.608      0.000
   STATE2              0.000      0.000    999.000    999.000
   STATE3              0.000      0.000    999.000    999.000
```

```
STANDARDIZED MODEL RESULTS (STDYX Standardization)

                                                Two-Tailed
                    Estimate       S.E.  Est./S.E.    P-Value

 STATE1   BY
    D11                0.911      0.021     43.988      0.000
    D21                0.867      0.022     39.895      0.000

 STATE2   BY
    D12                0.956      0.018     52.311      0.000
    D22                0.867      0.020     43.501      0.000

 STATE3   BY
    D13                0.959      0.019     50.014      0.000
    D23                0.854      0.021     41.331      0.000

 DIFF2_1  BY
    D11                0.000      0.000    999.000    999.000

 DIFF3_2  BY
    D11                0.000      0.000    999.000    999.000

 IS2      BY
    D21                0.220      0.033      6.732      0.000
    D22                0.202      0.030      6.720      0.000
    D23                0.205      0.031      6.733      0.000

 STATE2   ON
    STATE1             0.915      0.049     18.583      0.000
    DIFF2_1            0.909      0.049     18.466      0.000

 STATE3   ON
    STATE1             0.946      0.052     18.195      0.000
    DIFF2_1            0.939      0.061     15.318      0.000
    DIFF3_2            0.939      0.054     17.503      0.000

 STATE2   WITH
    STATE3           999.000    999.000    999.000    999.000
    DIFF3_2          999.000    999.000    999.000    999.000

 IS2      WITH
    STATE1             0.000      0.000    999.000    999.000
    STATE2           999.000    999.000    999.000    999.000
    STATE3           999.000    999.000    999.000    999.000
    DIFF2_1            0.000      0.000    999.000    999.000
    DIFF3_2            0.000      0.000    999.000    999.000

 DIFF2_1  WITH
    STATE1            -0.399      0.054     -7.345      0.000
```

```
 DIFF3_2  WITH
    STATE1            -0.053       0.064      -0.835       0.403
    DIFF2_1           -0.485       0.052      -9.383       0.000

 Means
    STATE1             3.583       0.181      19.792       0.000
    DIFF2_1            0.127       0.061       2.069       0.039
    DIFF3_2           -0.010       0.060      -0.163       0.871

 Intercepts
    D11                0.000       0.000     999.000     999.000
    D21                0.498       0.134       3.706       0.000
    D12                0.000       0.000     999.000     999.000
    D22                0.456       0.124       3.677       0.000
    D13                0.000       0.000     999.000     999.000
    D23                0.465       0.126       3.686       0.000

 Variances
    STATE1             1.000       0.000     999.000     999.000
    DIFF2_1            1.000       0.000     999.000     999.000
    DIFF3_2            1.000       0.000     999.000     999.000
    IS2                1.000       0.000     999.000     999.000

 Residual Variances
    D11                0.171       0.038       4.532       0.000
    D21                0.200       0.036       5.535       0.000
    D12                0.086       0.035       2.448       0.014
    D22                0.208       0.033       6.332       0.000
    D13                0.081       0.037       2.191       0.028
    D23                0.228       0.034       6.767       0.000
    STATE2             0.000     999.000     999.000     999.000
    STATE3             0.000     999.000     999.000     999.000


R-SQUARE

    Observed                                                 Two-Tailed
    Variable        Estimate       S.E.  Est./S.E.    P-Value

    D11                0.829       0.038      21.994       0.000
    D21                0.800       0.036      22.155       0.000
    D12                0.914       0.035      26.155       0.000
    D22                0.792       0.033      24.165       0.000
    D13                0.919       0.037      25.007       0.000
    D23                0.772       0.034      22.941       0.000

     Latent                                                  Two-Tailed
    Variable        Estimate       S.E.  Est./S.E.    P-Value

    STATE2             1.000     999.000     999.000     999.000
    STATE3             1.000     999.000     999.000     999.000
```

The specific appeal of LC models lies in the fact that these models allow us to analyze "true" change over time (i.e., change scores that are corrected for measurement error) and to relate latent change variables to other variables. For example, we may try to explain why depression scores changed more in some individuals than in others. In addition, latent difference variables may serve as independent or mediator variables.

From a technical point of view, such extended analyses are easily carried out in Mplus by adding additional variables to the model and including additional `on` statements to either regress latent difference variables on external variables or use the latent difference variables themselves as predictors of other variables. For example, if age was another variable in the data set (which is not the case here), we could examine whether individual differences in latent change between time 1 and time 2 could be explained by age differences. The additional specification would look as follows, where `age` is an additional variable in the data set:

```
diff2_1 on age;
```

A substantive example of an LC analysis with multiple constructs can be found in Reuter et al. (2010).

4.5 LATENT GROWTH CURVE MODELS

LGCMs (Bollen & Curran, 2006; Duncan et al., 2006; Meredith & Tisak, 1984, 1990) are increasingly used in the social sciences to analyze longitudinal data. In contrast to the LC models that were discussed in the previous section, LGCMs explicitly focus on modeling the *form* of change over time. One key question in growth curve modeling is which mathematical function adequately describes individual latent growth trajectories over time (e.g., linear or quadratic growth). Important research questions that can be answered by LGCMs are (among others):

- How large is the latent mean with regard to an attribute on the first occasion of measurement (mean initial value)?
- Are there individual differences in the true initial value ("intercept") and, if yes, how large are they?
- Does the attribute change over time and, if yes, what is the form and strength of this change? On average, is there an increase or

decline in the attribute? Is change, for example, linear or curvilinear (quadratic)?

- How large is the mean slope (rate of the growth or decline)?
- Are there individual differences in the rate of change (e.g., do some individuals show a steeper slope than others?) and, if yes, how large are these differences?
- Are intercept and slope correlated? If yes, what is the direction and strength of this relationship?
- Are there other variables (covariates) that predict individual differences in intercept and/or slope?

Obviously, the research questions that can be addressed with LGCMs are similar (or even identical) to those addressed with LC models (see Section 4.4). For example, also with LC models, one is typically interested in examining (1) mean changes over time, (2) individual differences in initial value and change scores, and (3) relationships between initial value and change as well as external variables.

The main difference between LC models and LGCMs is that LGCMs typically imply explicit hypotheses as to the *form of change* over time (linear, quadratic, etc.), which is not the case for LC models. In this sense, LC models are less restrictive, because in these models, change over time does not have to follow a specific functional form. We first consider the formal background and application of first-order LGCMs, then in Section 4.5.2, second-order LGCMs.

4.5.1 First-Order LGCMs

First-order LGCMs are based on one single repeatedly measured indicator per construct (e.g., the repeatedly measured sum score of an anxiety scale). This indicator is used to directly measure one or more latent growth factors. In contrast, second-order LGCMs can (and should!) be used when multiple indicators (e.g., multiple items, parallel tests, or item parcels) are available for each time point. As discussed in Section 4.5.2, second-order LGCMs have a number of important advantages over first-order LGCMs.

4.5.1.1 Analysis of First-Order Linear LGCMs

For simplicity, we first consider linear LGCMs. In Section 4.5.1.3, I show an extension to a quadratic LGCM. Figure 4.26 shows a path diagram of a first-order LGCM for one construct measured by the same observed

BOX 4.12. *Example of First-Order LGCM*

To illustrate the analysis of longitudinal data with first-order LGCMs, we use data on the self-reported anxiety of children (N = 485) measured on four (equally spaced) time points T1–T4.* There was a time interval of approximately 6 months between the measurement occasions. With regard to the model shown in Figure 4.26, the variables Y_1–Y_4 represent repeatedly assessed anxiety sum scores.

The data are provided in the file **anxiety.dat**. This data set contains the individual scores of the children on four manifest variables `a1–a4`. The variables `a1–a4` represent the anxiety sum scores at T1–T4, respectively. The data set does not contain missing data.

*I would like to thank David A. Cole for providing the data used for this example.

variable Y_k on four measurement occasions, where k indicates the occasion of measurement.

In the linear LGCM in Figure 4.26, two latent factors have a direct effect on the observed variables Y_1–Y_4: the intercept factor and the linear slope factor. In addition, the model assumes that all measurements are influenced by random measurement error, as represented by the variables ε_1–ε_4.

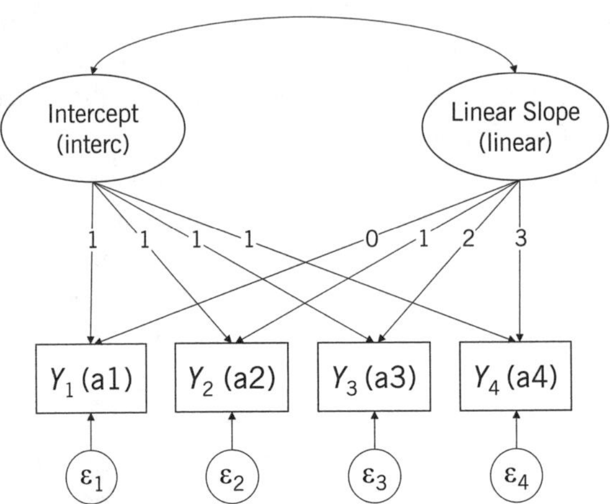

FIGURE 4.26. First-order LGCM for one observed variable Y_k (k = time point) measured on four occasions of measurement (k = 1, 2, 3, 4). ε_k = error variable. The model assumes linear growth and equal spacing between time points. The variable names used in the Mplus input appear in parentheses.

It can be seen in Figure 4.26 that all factor loadings in the model are set to specific values (i.e., the loadings are not estimated as free parameters, but are fixed a priori). This is done so that the factors can be interpreted as intercept (or "initial status") factor and linear slope factor.

Specifically, all Y_k variables have unit loadings on the intercept factor and zero intercepts (all constant intercept parameters α_k are set to 0; this is not explicitly shown in the figure). Furthermore, Y_1 loads only on the intercept factor (but not on the slope factor). The intercept factor can therefore be interpreted as the true score variable (τ_1) pertaining to Y_1 in the sense of classical test theory: $Y_1 = \tau_1 + \varepsilon_1 = \text{Intercept} + \varepsilon_1$. In other words, the intercept factor represents individual differences in the true (error-free) initial (T1) anxiety scores.

The linear slope factor can be interpreted as the true score difference variable between the true score variable pertaining to Y_2 and the true score variable pertaining to Y_1:

$$\text{Linear Slope} = \tau_2 - \tau_1$$

This is because Y_2 has unit loadings on *both* the intercept and linear slope factors (for more details on how to define factors in LGCMs based on true score theory see Geiser, Keller, & Lockhart, in press): $Y_2 = \tau_1 + (\tau_2 - \tau_1) + \varepsilon_2 = \text{Intercept} + \text{Linear Slope} + \varepsilon_2$. This definition parallels the definition of latent difference factors in LC models (see Section 4.4). In contrast to the LC factors considered in the previous section, however, the linear slope factor in LGCM represents true individual differences in *linear* change over time, because the loadings of the (equally spaced) measurements are set to 0, 1, 2, and 3, respectively.

With regard to our example, children with larger positive scores on the slope factor show a stronger linear increase in their anxiety scores than children with smaller slope factor scores. Children with negative slope factor scores show decreasing anxiety values over time. The double-headed arrow between the intercept and slope factors indicates that intercept and slope can be correlated. (Their correlation can be estimated as a separate model parameter in Mplus.) For example, individuals with larger initial anxiety scores may show different trajectories than those with smaller initial anxiety scores.

How can we answer the research questions discussed above with the linear LGCMs? The estimated mean of the intercept factor provides an answer to the question of what the mean true anxiety level was at T1. A large intercept factor mean indicates a high level of anxiety at T1. The variance of the intercept factor indicates to which extent individuals differed in their latent anxiety scores at T1. A large intercept factor variance indicates that there is a large amount of variability in the latent anxiety scores at T1.

The mean of the slope factor informs us about the average trajectory in the sample. Positive values indicate that, on average, there is an increase in latent anxiety scores over time, whereas negative values indicate a decline. A value of zero means that, on average, there is no change. The variance of the slope factor shows to which extent individual growth trajectories differ in their slopes. The larger the variance of the slope factor, the more the individual growth curves differ in their steepness.

The question about the relationship between initial status and change can be answered by estimating the correlation between intercept and slope. A positive correlation indicates that children with larger initial anxiety scores tend to show larger slope values than children with smaller initial anxiety scores. A negative correlation would indicate that children with larger initial values tend to show smaller slope factor values than children with smaller initial values.

The question concerning the influence of external variables on change (e.g., age, gender, personality, socioeconomic status) can be addressed by adding external variables (covariates) to the model. It is possible, for example, to regress the intercept and slope factor on covariates—similar to what can be done in LC models (see Section 4.4). In addition, the growth factors can also serve as independent variables predicting other variables. It could, for example, be interesting to study whether changes in anxiety can predict changes in other constructs, such as depression.

Figure 4.27 shows the Mplus input file for the specification of the linear first-order LCGM from Figure 4.26 for the four anxiety measurements as represented by the variables `a1`, `a2`, `a3`, and `a4`. From the model command, it can be seen that Mplus uses a special syntax for growth models that simplifies the specification of these types of models. With this special syntax, only one line of code is needed to specify the entire model:

```
model: interc linear | a1@0 a2@1 a3@2 a4@3;
```

In this command, the latent variables `interc` and `linear` represent the intercept and linear slope factors, respectively. The vertical line (|) is the sign that Mplus uses to indicate random slopes in multilevel models (see Chapter 5). In the context of LGCMs, *random slope* means that the

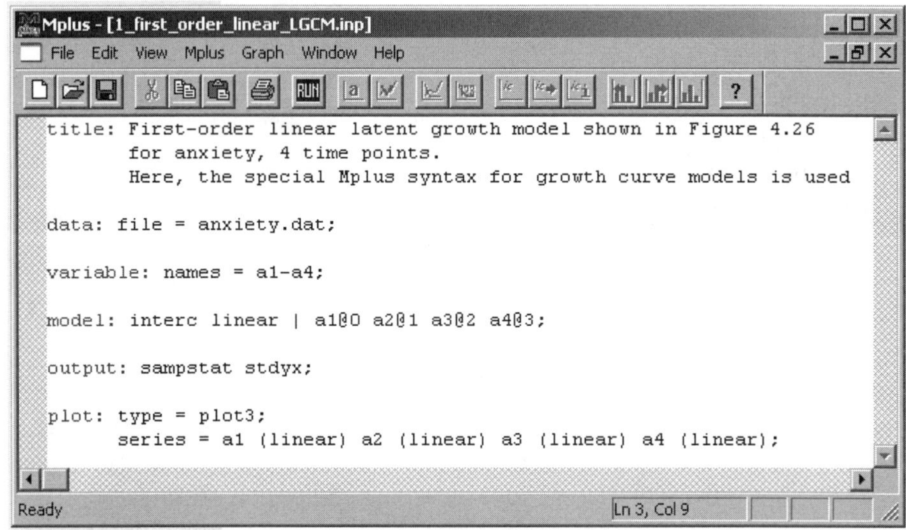

FIGURE 4.27. Mplus input file for the specification of the linear first-order LGCM for anxiety measured by one indicator across four measurement occasions shown in Figure 4.26. In this input file, the simplified syntax for LGCMs is used.

slope of the growth curve is a random effect that can vary across individuals (i.e., the slope is a variable, not a constant; individuals can differ in how much they change over time). The same is true for the intercept factor that also represents a random effect (i.e., individuals can differ in their true initial anxiety scores). (The distinction of random vs. fixed effects is revisited in Chapter 5, in which we discuss multilevel models.)

Behind the | sign, the repeatedly measured observed anxiety variables are listed that serve as indicators of the growth factors. The @ sign is used to fix the loadings of the indicators on the slope factor so that the slope factor properly represents the assumed form of the growth trajectories. In line with the assumption of linear growth over time, the loadings are fixed to 0, 1, 2, and 3 on the slope factor (cf. Figure 4.26).

In the default specification of growth curve models with the special syntax shown above, Mplus automatically fixes all loadings on the intercept factor to 1 and sets all constant intercept terms (α_k) to 0. In addition, Mplus automatically estimates the means of the intercept and slope factors. It is important to be aware of these default settings, because growth models can also be specified using the conventional Mplus syntax for standard CFA. If the conventional CFA syntax is used, the intercept parameters α_k have to be explicitly set to 0 by the user and the estimation

BOX 4.13. *Specification of LGCMs Using the Conventional Mplus Syntax for CFA Models*

LGCMs can also be specified using the standard Mplus syntax for confirmatory factor models. This alternative specification is slightly more complicated than using the special Mplus syntax for LGCMs, because the loading pattern for both the intercept and slope factors has to be explicitly specified, the intercepts α_k have to be explicitly set to 0, and the estimation of the latent growth factor means has to be explicitly requested by the user. On the other hand, this method makes the underlying specification of LGCMs more explicit and shows that these models are special cases of confirmatory factor models. In the following, we show the alternative equivalent specification of the same first-order LGCM for the anxiety data using the conventional Mplus syntax:

```
model: interc by a1@1 a2@1 a3@1 a4@1; ! Intercept factor
       linear by a1@0 a2@1 a3@2 a4@3; ! Slope factor
        [a1-a4@0]; ! set constant intercepts to zero
        [interc linear]; ! estimate growth factor means
```

The complete input files for both types of specifications are provided on the companion website.

of the latent growth factor means has to be explicitly requested (see Box 4.13).

The Mplus `plot` option is very useful in the analysis of LGCMs, because it can be used to analyze, for example, the individual observed and model-implied growth trajectories. The `plot` option also allows the plotting of the average observed trajectory along with the average model-implied trajectories. These curves can be useful, for example, to examine model fit. If, for instance, many individuals appear to deviate from a close-to-linear trajectory, this might be a sign that a linear growth model may not be appropriate for the data. Note that the plot option can be used only when individual data (and not summary data) are used as input for the analyses. (The difference between individual and summary data is explained in Chapter 2.)

In order to obtain plots of the growth curves, we request the Mplus plot type 3 (`type = plot3;`). Using the `series` option, we specify that the values of the variables `a1–a4` are to be plotted as a function of time (*linear* here refers to the name chosen for the linear slope factor in the `model` statement):

```
plot: type = plot3;
      series = a1 (linear) a2 (linear) a3 (linear) a4 (linear);
```

One obtains a set of graphs that can be opened in the Mplus output by selecting the menu option **Graph → View Graphs**, as described in detail in Section 4.5.1.2. Before looking at the graphs, we first examine the numerical output provided by Mplus. The model fit statistics indicate that the linear LGCM shows a rather mediocre fit to the anxiety data. This is shown especially by the large chi-square and *RMSEA* values: $\chi^2 = 27.288$, $df = 5$, $p < .001$, $CFI = 0.98$, $RMSEA = 0.096$, $SRMR = 0.061$.

For comparison, we can estimate a so-called *intercept-only* model in which only an intercept, but no slope factor, is assumed. This model implies that there is no true change in the latent anxiety scores over time. (According to the intercept-only model, any change seen in the observed scores over time is due only to measurement error.) By comparing the linear LGCM to the intercept-only model, we can see whether the LGCM at least fits better than a no-change model. Figure 4.28 shows the Mplus input file for the specification of the intercept-only model.

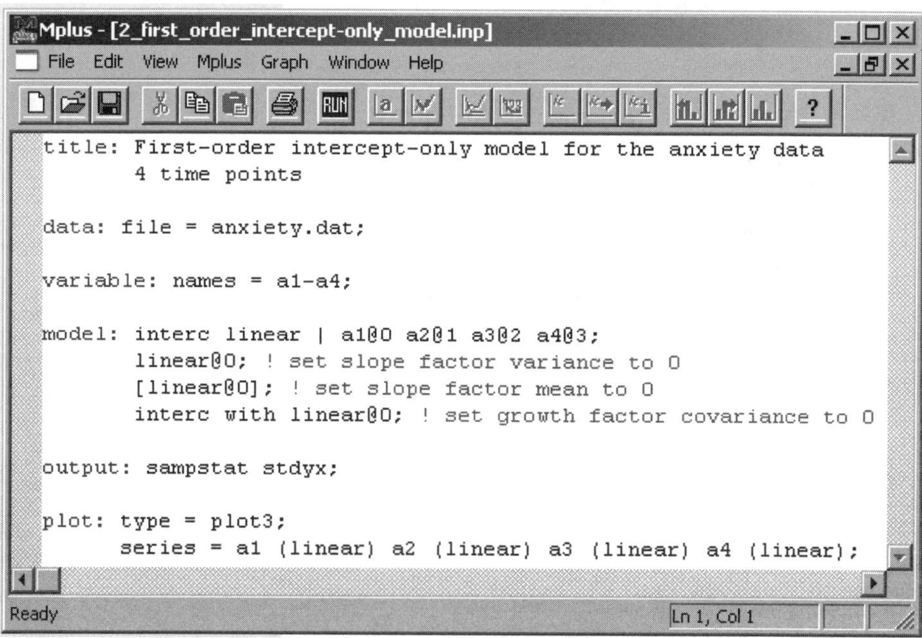

FIGURE 4.28. Mplus input file for the specification of the first-order intercept-only model for the anxiety data using the simplified syntax for LGCMs.

The basic model specification for LGCMs can be retained for the specification of the intercept-only model. Three additional commands are included to set the mean, variance, and covariance of the linear slope factor to zero, given that these parameters are not estimated in the intercept-only model. According to this specification, only the intercept factor remains in the model.

The plot option is unchanged, so that we can examine the model-implied latent growth curves in the intercept-only model as well and compare them to the model-implied growth curves in the linear LGCM. The model fit statistics for the intercept-only model reveal that (as expected) it shows a very poor fit to the data: $\chi^2 = 176.355$, $df = 8$, $p < .001$, $CFI = 0.857$, $RMSEA = 0.208$, $SRMR = 0.141$. (The full output for the intercept-only model can be found on the companion website.) A comparison of the *AIC* values indicates that the intercept-only model ($AIC = 1296.065$) fits worse than the linear LGCM ($AIC = 1152.997$). Hence, the assumption of linear change is at least preferred over the assumption of no change. (Nonetheless, the fit of the linear model is not optimal, indicating that the assumption of linear change for every individual in the sample may be too restrictive.)

In the following, we discuss the most important parameters for the first-order linear LGCM, despite its modest fit. Under `MODEL RESULTS` we see that the mean and variance of both the intercept and slope factor are significantly different from zero (assuming an alpha level of .05). This finding indicates that the mean initial latent level of anxiety is significantly different from zero ($M_{\text{INTERCEPT}} = 0.698$, $z = 34.866$, $p < .001$). There also is significant variability in the initial latent anxiety scores ($Var_{\text{INTERCEPT}} = 0.151$, $z = 11.996$, $p < .001$).

With regard to the slope factor, we can see that, on average, there is a significant linear decline in latent anxiety scores across time, because the estimated slope factor mean has a negative sign ($M_{\text{LINEAR}} = -0.062$, $z = -10.405$, $p < 0.001$). This means that the mean model-implied linear growth curve has a negative slope. In addition, there is a significant amount of individual differences in the slope values around the mean growth curve, as indicated by the significant slope factor variance ($Var_{\text{LINEAR}} = 0.007$, $z = 4.667$, $p < .001$). This means that the children differ not only in their initial latent anxiety scores, but also in their trajectories over time: Some children show a stronger increase (or decrease) in their anxiety scores than others. (This finding will be made clearer shortly when we look at individual growth trajectories in the requested plots.)

```
MODEL RESULTS

                                                      Two-Tailed
                    Estimate       S.E.  Est./S.E.    P-Value

 INTERC   |
    A1                 1.000      0.000    999.000    999.000
    A2                 1.000      0.000    999.000    999.000
    A3                 1.000      0.000    999.000    999.000
    A4                 1.000      0.000    999.000    999.000

 LINEAR   |
    A1                 0.000      0.000    999.000    999.000
    A2                 1.000      0.000    999.000    999.000
    A3                 2.000      0.000    999.000    999.000
    A4                 3.000      0.000    999.000    999.000

 L NEAR   WITH
    INTERC            -0.011      0.003     -3.485      0.000

 Means
    INTERC             0.698      0.020     34.866      0.000
    LINEAR            -0.062      0.006    -10.405      0.000

 Intercepts
    A1                 0.000      0.000    999.000    999.000
    A2                 0.000      0.000    999.000    999.000
    A3                 0.000      0.000    999.000    999.000
    A4                 0.000      0.000    999.000    999.000

 Variances
    INTERC             0.151      0.013     11.996      0.000
    LINEAR             0.007      0.001      4.667      0.000

 Residual Variances
    A1                 0.067      0.008      8.675      0.000
    A2                 0.048      0.004     10.965      0.000
    A3                 0.048      0.004     11.180      0.000
    A4                 0.040      0.006      6.545      0.000
```

The standardized model results [`STANDARDIZED MODEL RESULTS (STDYX Standardization)`] provide us with the standardized covariance (i.e., the correlation) between the intercept and slope factors. In our example, the intercept and slope factors are significantly negatively correlated ($r = -.349$, $z = -5.001$, $p < .001$). Furthermore, the values reported under `R-SQUARE—Observed Variable` show us that between 69.4 and 78.5% of observed individual differences are accounted for by the latent growth factors. The remaining variance is due to measurement error and systematic occasion-specific variance in this model.

(Second-order LGCMs, discussed in Section 4.5.2, allow us to separate error variance from occasion-specific variance; for a more detailed comparison of first- and second-order LGCMs, see Geiser et al., in press.)

```
STANDARDIZED MODEL RESULTS (STDYX Standardization)

                                                    Two-Tailed
                    Estimate       S.E.  Est./S.E.    P-Value

 INTERC    |
    A1                 0.833      0.019     43.608      0.000
    A2                 0.906      0.023     40.204      0.000
    A3                 0.911      0.030     29.912      0.000
    A4                 0.903      0.040     22.597      0.000

 LINEAR    |
    A1                 0.000      0.000    999.000    999.000
    A2                 0.193      0.021      9.160      0.000
    A3                 0.389      0.042      9.259      0.000
    A4                 0.578      0.065      8.861      0.000

 LINEAR   WITH
    INTERC            -0.349      0.070     -5.001      0.000

 Means
    INTERC             1.796      0.091     19.789      0.000
    LINEAR            -0.753      0.108     -6.965      0.000

 Intercepts
    A1                 0.000      0.000    999.000    999.000
    A2                 0.000      0.000    999.000    999.000
    A3                 0.000      0.000    999.000    999.000
    A4                 0.000      0.000    999.000    999.000

 Variances
    INTERC             1.000      0.000    999.000    999.000
    LINEAR             1.000      0.000    999.000    999.000

 Residual Variances
    A1                 0.306      0.032      9.622      0.000
    A2                 0.264      0.024     11.037      0.000
    A3                 0.265      0.023     11.747      0.000
    A4                 0.215      0.031      6.812      0.000

R-SQUARE

    Observed                                        Two-Tailed
    Variable        Estimate       S.E.  Est./S.E.    P-Value

    A1                 0.694      0.032     21.804      0.000
    A2                 0.736      0.024     30.789      0.000
```

```
A3                    0.735      0.023      32.541      0.000
A4                    0.785      0.031      24.941      0.000
```

The model could be extended by adding external variables as predictors of the intercept and slope factors that might explain why the children differ in their initial anxiety scores and in their rate of change. For example, variables such as parental support or changes in other variables such as personal competencies could be related to changes in anxiety. The inclusion of independent variables predicting initial state and/or growth is done by specifying one or more `on` statements, in addition to the growth specification; for example:

```
interc linear on x y z;
```

Using this command, the intercept and slope factors are regressed on three independent variables named `x`, `y`, and `z`. The growth factors could also serve as independent variables themselves. In this case, they would appear on the right-hand side of an `on` statement.

4.5.1.2 Graphical Analysis of Growth Curves

This section deals with the Mplus options used to retrieve graphics requested through the `plot` option. These graphics are useful for visualizing individual and average growth curves. Graphs are retrieved in the output window either by clicking on **Graph → View Graphs** (see Figure 4.29) or by clicking on the

symbol in the Mplus menu. Figure 4.30 shows different options available for viewing graphs. The option **Sample means** provides a plot of the observed anxiety means as a function of time. The option **Estimated means** results in a plot of the mean model-implied growth curve. When choosing **Sample and estimated means**, both the average sample and the average model-implied means are plotted in a single graph. **Observed individual values** yields the observed individual growth curves for all individuals in the sample. This option was chosen to produce the graph shown in Figure 4.32.

After clicking on **Observed individual values**, the window **Properties for viewing individual curves** appears (see Figure 4.31). Here the user can choose between different options for viewing individual growth

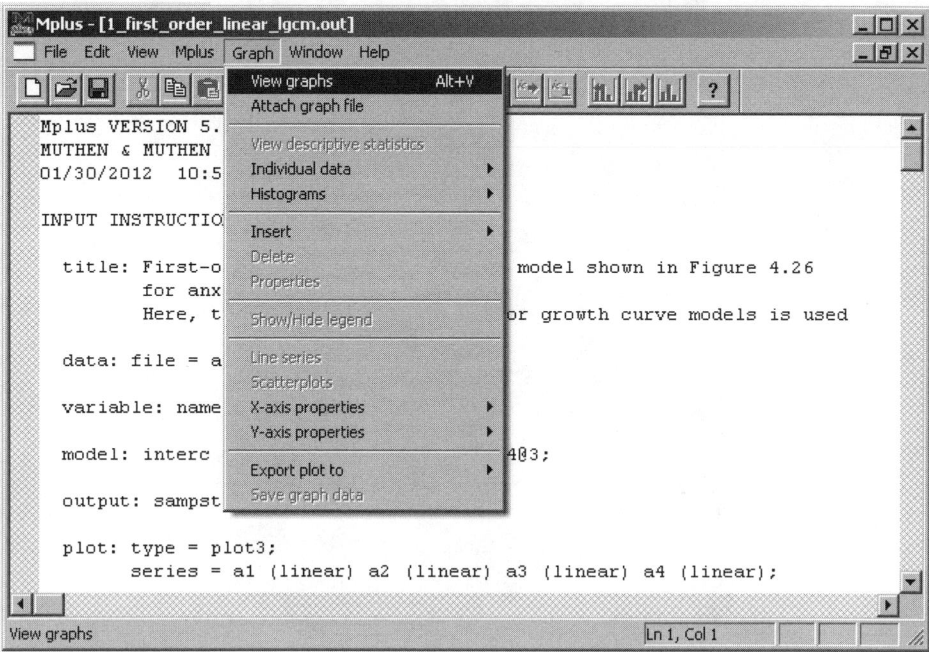

FIGURE 4.29. Opening requested graphs in the Mplus output window.

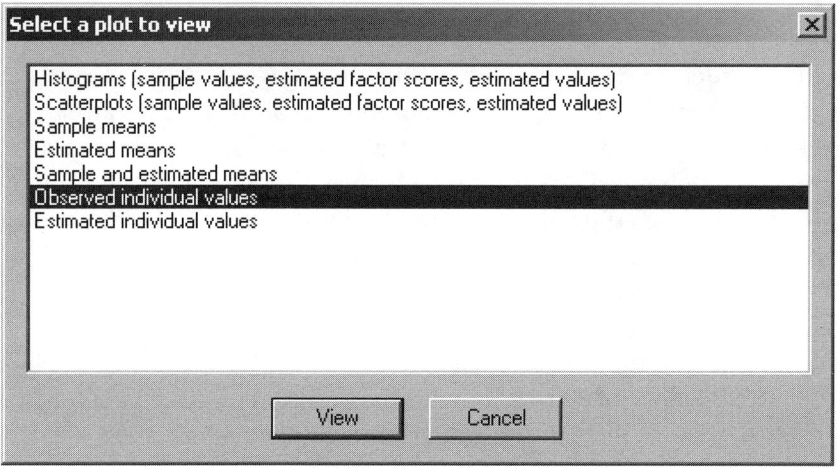

FIGURE 4.30. Choosing a specific graph in Mplus. In this case, we want to look at the observed individual growth curves.

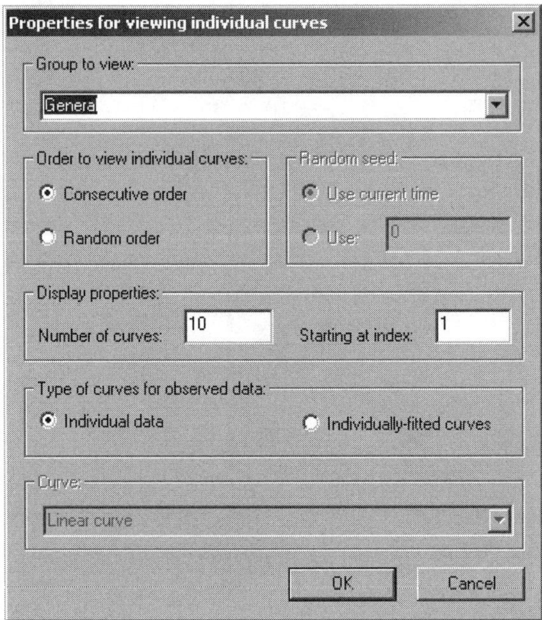

FIGURE 4.31. Choosing the type, number, and order of individual growth curves to be displayed. Here: curves based on observed data (**Individual data**), 10 curves per graph (**Number of curves: 10**), and consecutive order as in the data file, beginning with the first individual in the data set (**Consecutive order/Starting at index: 1**).

trajectories. The default is that growth curves are given in consecutive order (**Order to view individual curves → Consecutive order**), as extracted from the individual data file, and that only 10 curves are shown at a time to avoid cluttering (**Number of curves: 10**). In addition, as the default, the observed ("raw") data are shown without a specific curve-fitting procedure (**Type of curves for observed data → Individual data**). Specific curve-fitting procedures can be selected by choosing the option **Type of curves for observed data → Individually-fitted curves** (e.g., linear or quadratic fit).

By keeping the default options as shown in Figure 4.31, we obtain the graph in Figure 4.32 that contains the observed trajectories of the first 10 individuals in the data set **anxiety.dat**. By clicking on a specific data point, the curve of the corresponding individual is highlighted in bold and a label is shown that informs us about the number of the individual as well as the individual's actual observed numerical scores for all four time points. In Figure 4.32, the curve of the second individual in the data set is highlighted and the observed anxiety scores for this individual (1.643 at T1, 1.643 at T2, 1.214 at T3, and 1.929 at T4) are shown. This feature

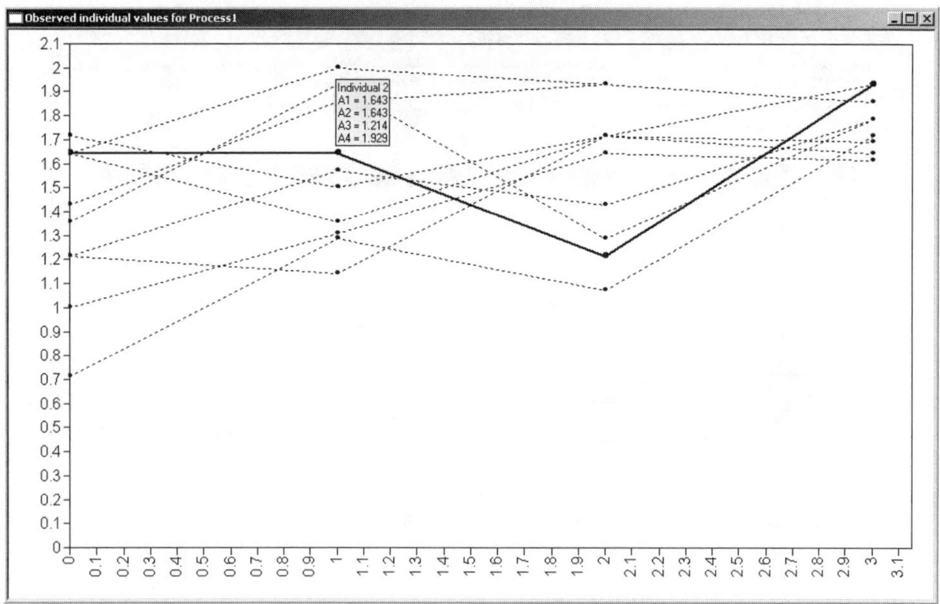

FIGURE 4.32. Individual growth curves of the first 10 individuals in the data set **anxiety.dat**. By moving the cursor over a specific data point, the number of the individual as well as his or her numeric scores for all time points are shown.

is useful, for example, to identify extreme cases or cases with aberrant growth trajectories relative to the remaining individuals in the sample.

The growth curves of the remaining individuals in the sample can be viewed by clicking on the symbol

that allows us to proceed to the next 10 curves. The symbol

allows us to return to the **Properties for viewing individual curves** options to change settings. By clicking on

a different type of plot can be selected; for example, the model-implied individual or the average growth curves. The graphs in Figures 4.34 and 4.35 were produced by choosing the option **Sample and estimated means**

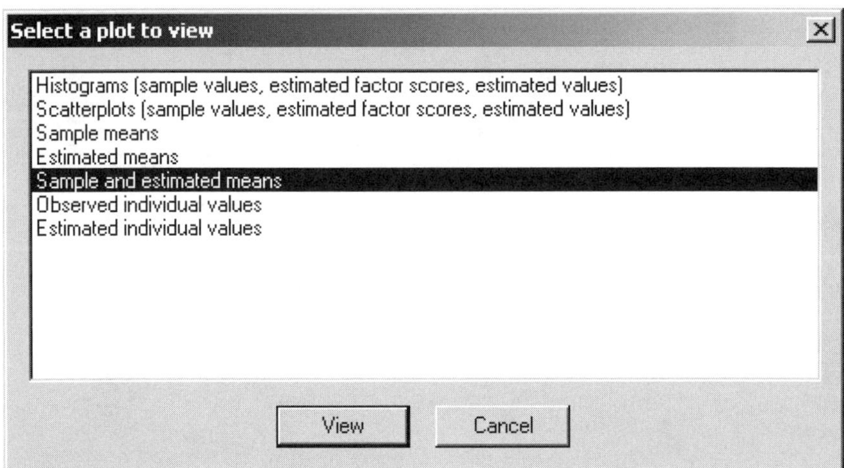

FIGURE 4.33. Choosing a specific graph in Mplus. In this case, we want to look at the observed and estimated mean growth curves.

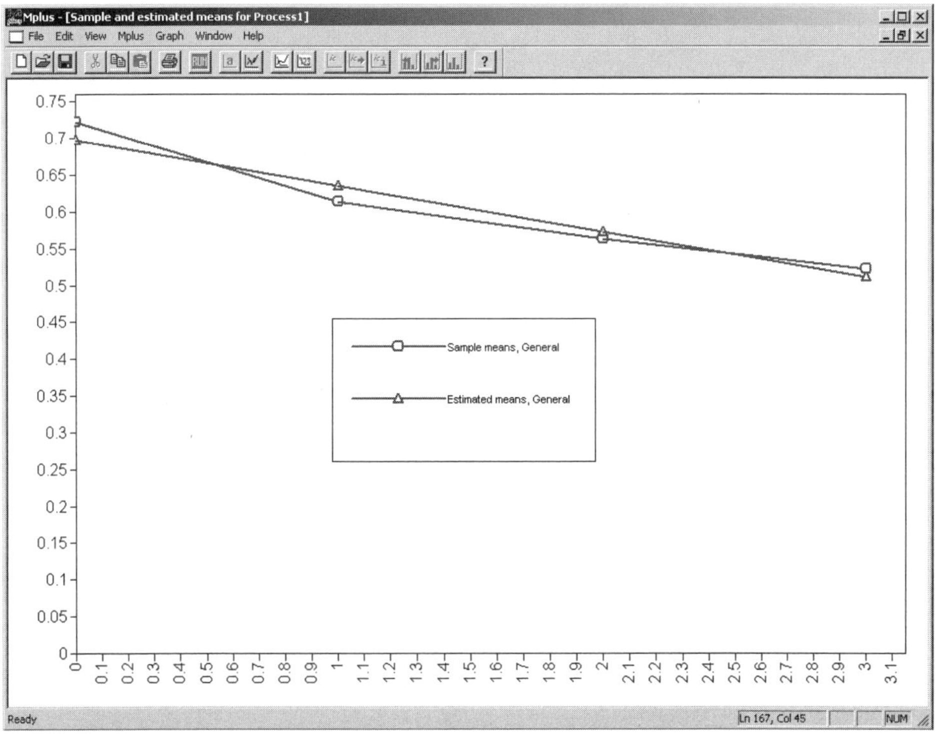

FIGURE 4.34. Mean observed (**Sample**) and mean model-implied (**Estimated**) growth curves in the first-order LGCM for the anxiety data.

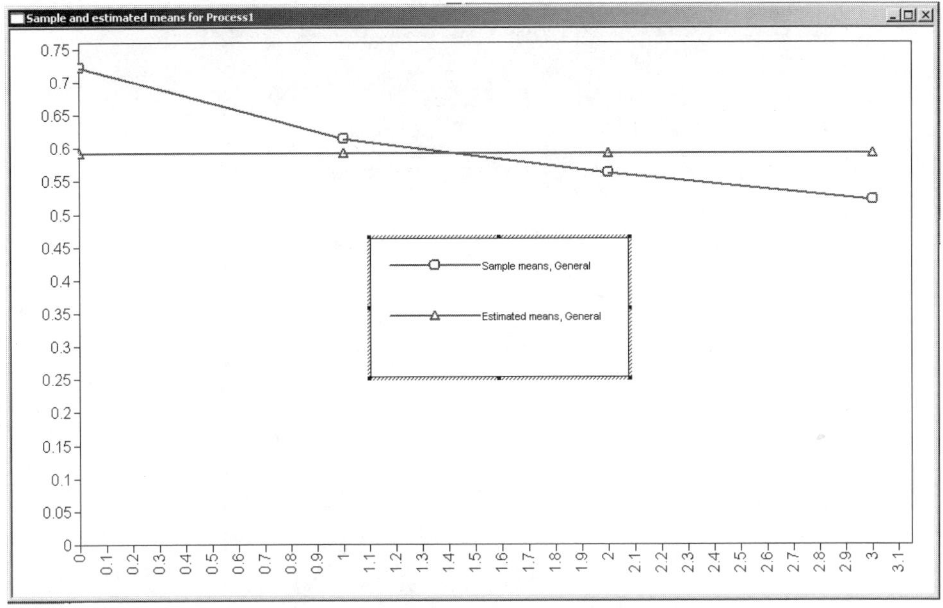

FIGURE 4.35. Mean observed (**Sample**) and mean model-implied (**Estimated**) growth curves in the first-order intercept-only model for the anxiety data.

(see Figure 4.33). Figure 4.34 shows the mean observed and the mean model-implied growth curves for the linear LGCM. Figure 4.35 shows the same curves for the intercept-only model, which assumes no change over time. Note that the model-implied curve in the intercept-only model is exactly parallel to the *x*-axis, a pattern that does not correspond well to the observed means (which clearly show a decline over time). Mplus graphs can be saved as a picture file in either *.DIB, *.EMF, or *.JPEG format. This can be done by choosing the menu option **Graph → Export plot to**, as shown in Figure 4.36.

4.5.1.3 Analysis of First-Order Quadratic LGCMs

The latent growth curve analysis discussed so far only contained a linear slope factor, restricting change to be linear for all individuals. To model other, nonlinear types of growth, the model can be extended by including additional growth factors. If one wants to test, for example, the hypothesis that growth is curvilinear, an additional factor can be included in the model that represents quadratic growth (see Figure 4.37).

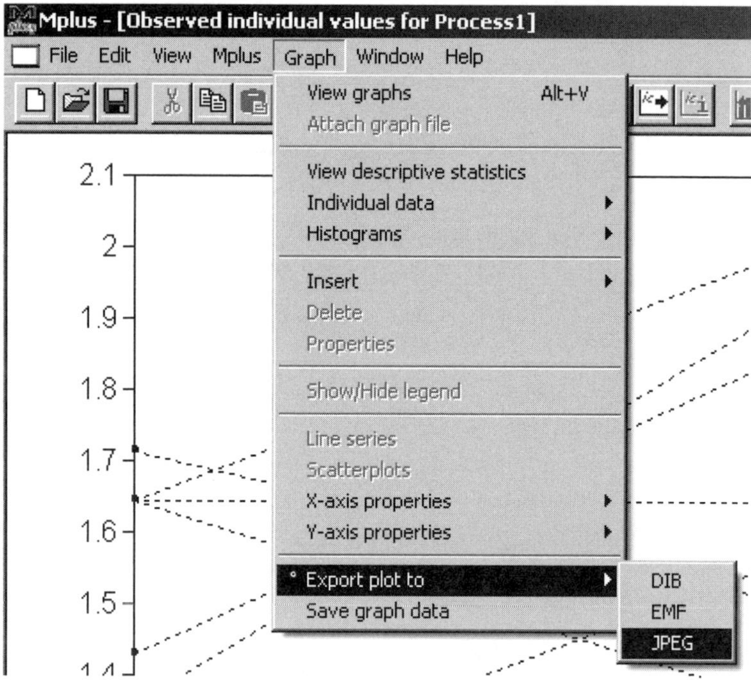

FIGURE 4.36. Exporting an Mplus graph (here as a *.JPEG file).

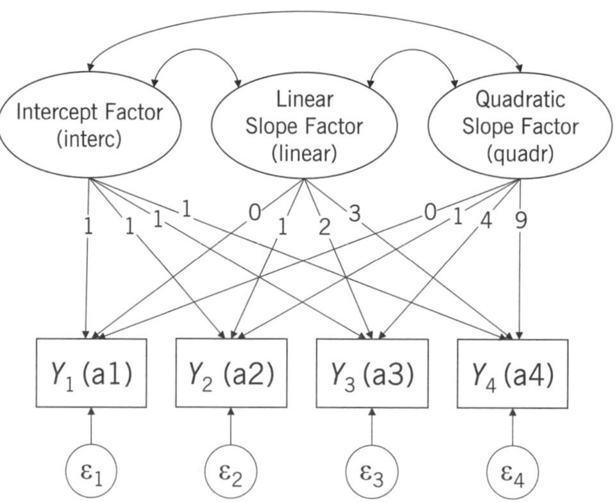

FIGURE 4.37. First-order LGCM for one observed variable Y_k (k = time point) measured on four occasions of measurement (k = 1, 2, 3, 4). ε_k = error variable. The model assumes curvilinear (quadratic) growth and equal spacing between time points. The variable names used in the Mplus input appear in parentheses.

The quadratic growth factor is again defined by a specific pattern of fixed loadings. For quadratic growth, the loadings are set to 0, 1, 4, and 9, respectively, as shown in Figure 4.37. If there are theoretical reasons to assume curvilinear change, and the quadratic growth model shows a better fit to the data than the linear growth model, then the quadratic model may be preferred. Other forms of change can also be tested. LGCMs are rather flexible in general and can be extended for various special cases (e.g., for nonequally spaced time points as well as specific growth components; e.g., see Mayer, Steyer, & Mueller, in press). Detailed discussions of special models can be found in Bollen and Curran (2006) as well as in Duncan et al. (2006).

Figure 4.38 shows the Mplus specification of a first-order quadratic LGCM for the anxiety data. The only difference in the model specification, compared to the linear LGCM, is that an additional growth factor (`quadr`) is introduced before the | sign:

```
model: interc linear quadr | a1@0 a2@1 a3@2 a4@3;
```

Mplus automatically treats the third factor `quadr` as a quadratic growth factor. In the estimation of the model parameters of the quadratic

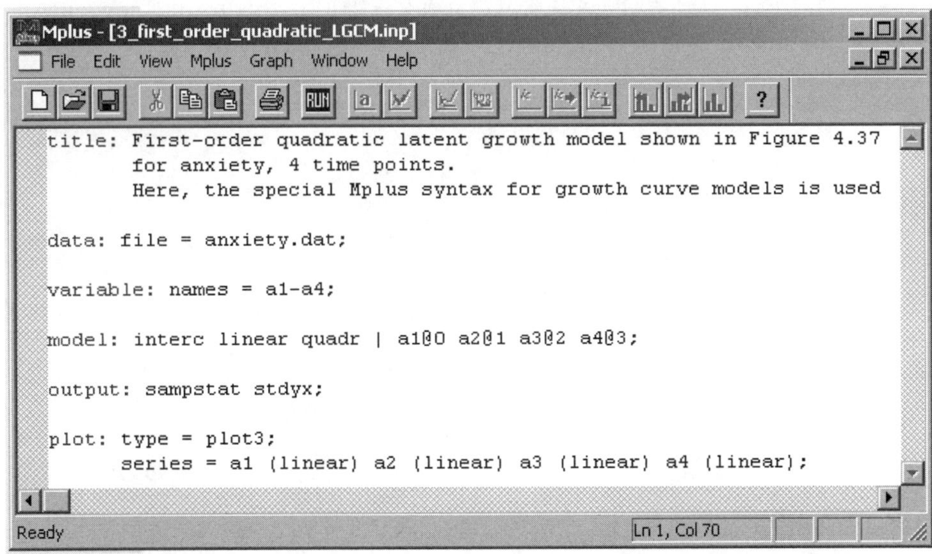

FIGURE 4.38. Mplus input file for the specification of the quadratic first-order LGCM for anxiety measured by one indicator across four measurement occasions shown in Figure 4.37. In this input file, the simplified syntax for LGCMs is used.

growth model for the anxiety data, an estimation problem is indicated by Mplus through the following warning message in the output:

```
WARNING:  THE LATENT VARIABLE COVARIANCE MATRIX (PSI) IS NOT
POSITIVE DEFINITE.  THIS COULD INDICATE A NEGATIVE
VARIANCE/RESIDUAL VARIANCE FOR A LATENT VARIABLE, A CORRELATION
GREATER OR EQUAL TO ONE BETWEEN TWO LATENT VARIABLES, OR A LINEAR
DEPENDENCY AMONG MORE THAN TWO LATENT VARIABLES. CHECK THE TECH4
OUTPUT FOR MORE INFORMATION. PROBLEM INVOLVING VARIABLE QUADR.
```

This warning message indicates that the covariance matrix of the latent growth factors is not a proper covariance matrix. This is often a sign that one or more factor variances were estimated to be zero or negative, that a correlation above |1| was estimated, or that a linear dependency among latent variables occurred. In our case, the problem is associated with the quadratic growth factor `quadr`. The table with the parameter estimates reveals that the variance of this variable is very small and not statistically significant (Var_{QUADR} = 0.001, z = 0.673, p = .501). In addition, the correlation between the linear and the quadratic growth factor was estimated to 1.205 (see the standardized model results), which is an inadmissible value for a correlation coefficient. This is the cause of the warning message output by Mplus. Even though the quadratic model shows a better global model fit than the linear model (χ^2 = 1.148, df = 1, p = .284, CFI = 1.00, $RMSEA$ = 0.017, $SRMR$ = 0.006), this result shows us that the assumption of quadratic growth may not be reasonable for these data.

```
MODEL RESULTS

                                                 Two-Tailed
                    Estimate         S.E.      Est./S.E.      P-Value

 INTERC    |
    A1                 1.000         0.000       999.000      999.000
    A2                 1.000         0.000       999.000      999.000
    A3                 1.000         0.000       999.000      999.000
    A4                 1.000         0.000       999.000      999.000

 LINEAR    |
    A1                 0.000         0.000       999.000      999.000
    A2                 1.000         0.000       999.000      999.000
    A3                 2.000         0.000       999.000      999.000
    A4                 3.000         0.000       999.000      999.000

 QUADR     |
    A1                 0.000         0.000       999.000      999.000
    A2                 1.000         0.000       999.000      999.000
    A3                 4.000         0.000       999.000      999.000
    A4                 9.000         0.000       999.000      999.000
```

```
LINEAR   WITH
    INTERC              -0.026        0.021       -1.201        0.230

QUADR    WITH
    INTERC               0.002        0.005        0.374        0.709
    LINEAR              -0.008        0.005       -1.565        0.117

Means
    INTERC               0.720        0.020       35.617        0.000
    LINEAR              -0.114        0.018       -6.452        0.000
    QUADR                0.016        0.005        3.113        0.002

Intercepts
    A1                   0.000        0.000      999.000      999.000
    A2                   0.000        0.000      999.000      999.000
    A3                   0.000        0.000      999.000      999.000
    A4                   0.000        0.000      999.000      999.000

Variances
    INTERC               0.163        0.022        7.441        0.000
    LINEAR               0.048        0.023        2.110        0.035
    QUADR                0.001        0.001        0.673        0.501

Residual Variances
    A1                   0.036        0.019        1.870        0.061
    A2                   0.053        0.007        7.720        0.000
    A3                   0.035        0.006        5.498        0.000
    A4                   0.072        0.019        3.890        0.000

STANDARDIZED MODEL RESULTS (STDYX Standardization)

                                               Two-Tailed
                      Estimate       S.E.    Est./S.E.      P-Value

...

LINEAR   WITH
    INTERC              -0.290        0.166       -1.746        0.081

QUADR    WITH
    INTERC               0.154        0.370        0.415        0.678
    LINEAR              -1.205        0.471       -2.558        0.011

Means
    INTERC               1.784        0.128       13.928        0.000
    LINEAR              -0.518        0.146       -3.552        0.000
    QUADR                0.514        0.415        1.237        0.216
```

4.5.2 Second-Order LGCMs

An important assumption in the application of LGCMs is measurement invariance of the measures over time (cf. Section 4.1.4). *Measurement invariance* means that properties of the measurement model (i.e., factor loadings, intercepts, and/or residual variances) have not changed over time

(Meredith, 1993; Meredith & Horn, 2001; Millsap & Meredith, 2007). As in LC models, at least strong measurement invariance is required for a meaningful interpretation of growth parameters. Otherwise, changes over time would be confounded with potential changes in the properties of the measurement instrument.

In first-order LGCMs discussed in the previous section, the assumption of strong measurement invariance is implicitly made, but is not testable in these models, because there is only a single indicator at each time point. One of the strengths of *second-order LGCMs* (*curve-of-factors models*; Geiser et al., in press; Hancock, Kuo, & Lawrence, 2001; McArdle, 1988; Sayer & Cumsille, 2001) is that these models use multiple indicators at each time point, so that the assumption of measurement invariance can be tested in the same way as, for example, in LS and LC models.

Figure 4.39 shows a second-order LGCM for anxiety measured at four time points using two indicators (e.g., two different scales or parallel test halves) at each time point. Note that the second-order model is based on more than just one observed variable per time point. Furthermore, in contrast to first-order LGCMs, the indicators in second-order LGCMs do not directly measure growth factors, but are indirectly related to the intercept and slope factors through LS factors. The LS factors represent the first-order factors in this model, whereas the growth factors are specified as second-order latent variables similar to the latent trait factor in LST models. In fact, Geiser et al. (in press) showed that second-order LGCMs can be formulated based on the fundamental concepts of LST theory.

The use of multiple indicators per time points makes it possible to empirically test the assumption of measurement invariance by constraining factor loadings, intercepts, and residual variables to be equal across time, as demonstrated for the LS model in Section 4.1.4. At least strong factorial invariance (equal loadings and intercepts across time) should hold for the growth parameters to be interpretable.

Another advantage of second-order LGCMs is that the use of multiple indicators makes it possible to separate reliable occasion-specific variance from variance due to the growth factors and measurement error. In second-order LGCMs, occasion-specific effects are explicitly represented by the LS residual variables (indicated as ζ_1–ζ_4 in Figure 4.39), whereas they are confounded with the error variables ε_k in first-order models. The reliabilities of the indicators therefore tend to be underestimated in first-order models (Geiser et al., in press). In the model shown in Figure 4.39, an indicator-specific residual factor (IS_2) was included to reflect stable specific variance in the second indicator not shared with the first indicator (cf. Section 4.1.3).

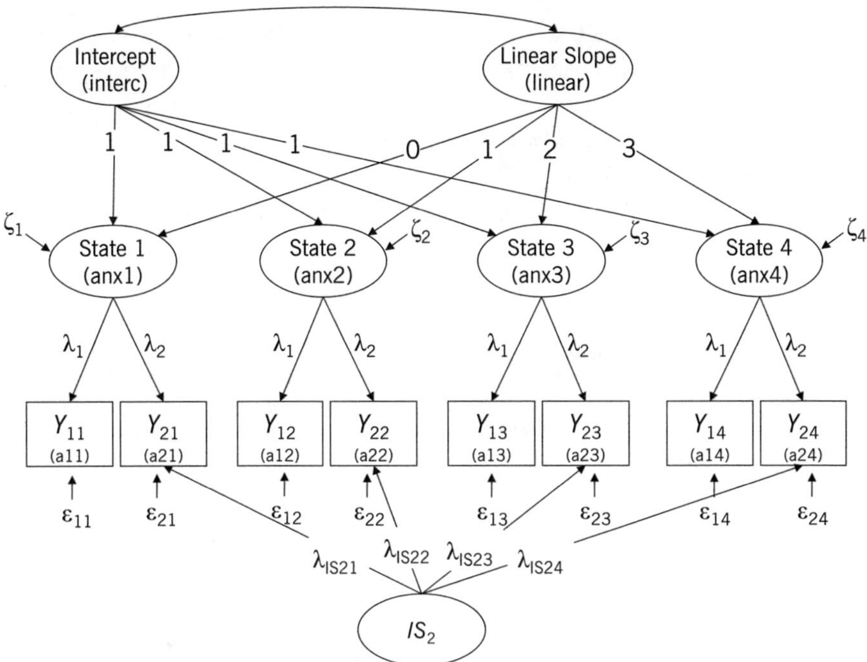

FIGURE 4.39. Second-order LGCM for two observed variables Y_{ik} (i = indicator, k = time point) measured on four occasions of measurement. ε_{ik} = measurement error variable; λ_i = time-invariant first-order state factor loading; ζ_k = LS residual variable. The model contains an indicator-specific (method) factor (IS_2) for the second indicator. The parameters λ_{IS2k} indicate factor loadings on the indicator-specific factor. The model assumes linear growth and equal spacing between time points. The change process is modeled at the level of the LS variables via second-order intercept and slope factors. The variable names used in Mplus appear in parentheses.

BOX 4.14. Example of Second-Order LGCMs

We illustrate the use of second-order LGCMs based on the anxiety data example that we used also for analyzing first-order LGCMs in Mplus. Instead of using just a single observed variable at each time point, we use two test halves ("parcels") constructed from the same scale. These test halves were constructed by assigning half of the items of the anxiety questionnaire to one test half and the other half to the second test half. The data of N = 484 children are in the file **anxiety_parcels.dat** on the companion website. This data set contains 2 × 4 = 8 variables (a11–a24).

Figure 4.40 shows the Mplus input for the specification of a second-order linear LGCM for the anxiety test halves. The variable names correspond to the names shown in parentheses in Figure 4.39. The first number indicates the test half ($i = 1, 2$), whereas the second index indicates the time point ($k = 1, 2, 3, 4$).

In practice, it is useful to first study the degree of measurement invariance of the indicators using a simple LS model (cf. discussion in Section 4.1) before imposing a restrictive growth structure on the LS variables. Given that the steps in testing measurement invariance were discussed in detail for the LS model, we proceed directly to the analysis of LGCMs, assuming strong measurement invariance for the indicators.

The first part of the model specification is identical to an LS model with equal loadings:

```
anx1 by a11
        a21 (1);
anx2 by a12
        a22 (1);
anx3 by a13
        a23 (1);
anx4 by a14
        a24 (1);
```

In the next part, the intercepts pertaining to the first indicator are fixed to zero to identify the means of the LS factors:

```
[a11@0 a12@0 a13@0 a14@0];
```

The intercepts pertaining to the second indicator are set equal across time so that—in conjunction with the constraints placed on the LS factor loadings—strong factorial invariance is maintained:

```
[a21 a22 a23 a24] (2);
```

The second-order factor structure that involves the growth factors `interc` and `linear` can be specified using the same syntax as for first-order LGCMs. The only difference is that the indicators of the growth factors now are the LS factors rather than the observed variables:

```
interc linear | anx1@0 anx2@1 anx3@2 anx4@3;
```

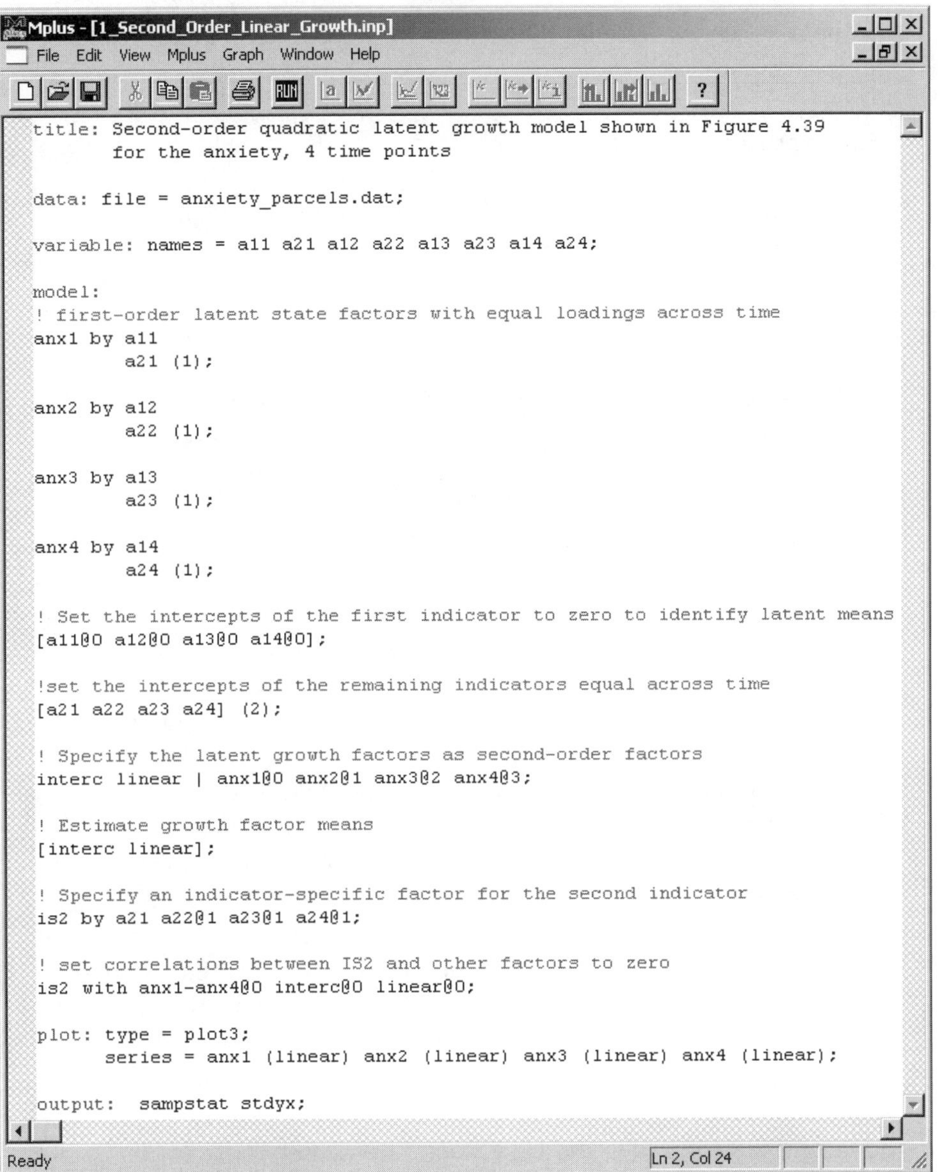

Mplus - [1_Second_Order_Linear_Growth.inp]

File Edit View Mplus Graph Window Help

```
title: Second-order quadratic latent growth model shown in Figure 4.39
       for the anxiety, 4 time points

data: file = anxiety_parcels.dat;

variable: names = a11 a21 a12 a22 a13 a23 a14 a24;

model:
! first-order latent state factors with equal loadings across time
anx1 by a11
        a21 (1);

anx2 by a12
        a22 (1);

anx3 by a13
        a23 (1);

anx4 by a14
        a24 (1);

! Set the intercepts of the first indicator to zero to identify latent means
[a11@0 a12@0 a13@0 a14@0];

!set the intercepts of the remaining indicators equal across time
[a21 a22 a23 a24] (2);

! Specify the latent growth factors as second-order factors
interc linear | anx1@0 anx2@1 anx3@2 anx4@3;

! Estimate growth factor means
[interc linear];

! Specify an indicator-specific factor for the second indicator
is2 by a21 a22@1 a23@1 a24@1;

! set correlations between IS2 and other factors to zero
is2 with anx1-anx4@0 interc@0 linear@0;

plot: type = plot3;
      series = anx1 (linear) anx2 (linear) anx3 (linear) anx4 (linear);

output:  sampstat stdyx;
```

Ready   Ln 2, Col 24

FIGURE 4.40. Mplus input file for the specification of linear second-order LGCM for anxiety measured by two indicators across four measurement occasions shown in Figure 4.39. In this input file, the simplified syntax for LGCMs is used.

In the next step, we request the estimation of the intercept and slope factor means:

```
[interc linear];
```

An indicator-specific factor is included for the second test half to account for indicator-specific variance:

```
is2 by a21 a22@1 a23@1 a24@1;
```

Defined as a residual factor, this factor is not allowed to correlate with any of the remaining latent variables in the model. Therefore, these correlations have to be set to zero:

```
is2 with anx1-anx4@0 interc@0 linear@0;
```

Even though the chi-square test is significant, the second-order linear LGCM shows an otherwise acceptable fit: $\chi^2 = 55.372$, $df = 24$, $p = .0003$, $CFI = 0.993$, $RMSEA = 0.052$, $SRMR = 0.050$. Interestingly, it appears to fit better than the first-order linear LGCM that did not account for occasion-specific fluctuations in the anxiety ratings.

The parameter estimates reveal similar results with regard to the growth process as the first-order LGCM. The mean latent anxiety value is significantly different from zero: $M_{INTERC} = 0.693$, $z = 35.827$, $p < .001$. There is also significant variability in the initial latent scores ($Var_{INTERC} = 0.141$, $z = 11.993$, $p < .001$). As in the first-order LGCM, the mean of the latent slope factor is negative and significantly different from zero ($M_{LINEAR} = -0.059$, $z = \_10.593$, $p < .001$). This again shows that there is a tendency for anxiety scores to decrease over time. The slope factor variance is also significant, $Var_{LINEAR} = 0.007$, $z = 5.408$, $p < .001$, indicating significant variability in the slopes of the individual growth curves (i.e., anxiety is not reduced to the same extent in all children).

```
MODEL RESULTS

                                                        Two-Tailed
                   Estimate       S.E.   Est./S.E.       P-Value

 INTERC    |
    ANX1              1.000      0.000     999.000       999.000
    ANX2              1.000      0.000     999.000       999.000
    ANX3              1.000      0.000     999.000       999.000
    ANX4              1.000      0.000     999.000       999.000
```

```
LINEAR   |
   ANX1              0.000     0.000   999.000   999.000
   ANX2              1.000     0.000   999.000   999.000
   ANX3              2.000     0.000   999.000   999.000
   ANX4              3.000     0.000   999.000   999.000

ANX1     BY
   A11               1.000     0.000   999.000   999.000
   A21               0.987     0.018    55.720     0.000

ANX2     BY
   A12               1.000     0.000   999.000   999.000
   A22               0.987     0.018    55.720     0.000

ANX3     BY
   A13               1.000     0.000   999.000   999.000
   A23               0.987     0.018    55.720     0.000

ANX4     BY
   A14               1.000     0.000   999.000   999.000
   A24               0.987     0.018    55.720     0.000

IS2      BY
   A21               1.000     0.000   999.000   999.000
   A22               1.000     0.000   999.000   999.000
   A23               1.000     0.000   999.000   999.000
   A24               1.000     0.000   999.000   999.000

IS2      WITH
   ANX1              0.000     0.000   999.000   999.000
   ANX2              0.000     0.000   999.000   999.000
   ANX3              0.000     0.000   999.000   999.000
   ANX4              0.000     0.000   999.000   999.000
   INTERC            0.000     0.000   999.000   999.000
   LINEAR            0.000     0.000   999.000   999.000

LINEAR   WITH
   INTERC           -0.008     0.003    -2.875     0.004

Means
   INTERC            0.693     0.019    35.827     0.000
   LINEAR           -0.059     0.006   -10.593     0.000

Intercepts
   A11               0.000     0.000   999.000   999.000
   A21               0.028     0.012     2.263     0.024
   A12               0.000     0.000   999.000   999.000
   A22               0.028     0.012     2.263     0.024
   A13               0.000     0.000   999.000   999.000
   A23               0.028     0.012     2.263     0.024
   A14               0.000     0.000   999.000   999.000
   A24               0.028     0.012     2.263     0.024
```

```
    ANX1              0.000       0.000     999.000     999.000
    ANX2              0.000       0.000     999.000     999.000
    ANX3              0.000       0.000     999.000     999.000
    ANX4              0.000       0.000     999.000     999.000

 Variances
    IS2               0.009       0.001       7.336       0.000
    INTERC            0.141       0.012      11.993       0.000
    LINEAR            0.007       0.001       5.408       0.000

 Residual Variances
    A11               0.021       0.004       5.561       0.000
    A21               0.025       0.004       6.720       0.000
    A12               0.019       0.003       6.491       0.000
    A22               0.023       0.003       7.844       0.000
    A13               0.019       0.003       7.209       0.000
    A23               0.017       0.003       6.718       0.000
    A14               0.020       0.003       7.352       0.000
    A24               0.016       0.003       6.003       0.000
    ANX1              0.048       0.007       7.063       0.000
    ANX2              0.031       0.004       7.922       0.000
    ANX3              0.030       0.004       8.199       0.000
    ANX4              0.017       0.005       3.339       0.001
```

The standardized parameters under STANDARDIZED MODEL RESULTS (STDYX Standardization) show us that the correlation between the intercept and slope factors was estimated to –.259, which is somewhat lower than the estimate in the first-order LGCM.

Overall, the second-order growth factors account for between 74.6 and 90.3% of the variance in the latent anxiety states, as represented by the LS factors anx1–anx4 (see values reported under R-SQUARE–Latent Variable). This indicates a good fit of the linear growth model to the data. The remaining 25.4 (first time point) to 9.7% (last time point) of the LS factor variance is due to reliable occasion-specific variability. This shows that occasion-specific fluctuations were more important at the beginning than toward the end of the study.

With regard to the measurement model, we find that both indicators have high loadings on the LS factors on all measurement occasions with values between .911 and .947. These values suggest that the indicators are rather homogeneous and have high reliabilities. The loadings of the second indicator on the indicator-specific factor are fairly small (between .208 and .224), albeit statistically significant. Therefore, only 4.3–5.0% of the observed score variability is due to indicator-specific effects.

The reliabilities of the observed variables (R-SQUARE–Observed Variable) were estimated to values between .88 and .918. These are substantially higher than in the first-order LGCM, in which the estimated reliabilities varied between .694 and .785. Furthermore, reliabilities seemed to increase over time in the first-order LGCM, whereas they are almost perfectly stable according to the second-order LGCM. These discrepancies are explained by the fact that the first-order model confounds unreliability with occasion specificity. First, this leads to an underestimation of indicator reliabilities in first-order LGCMs whenever occasion-specific effects are present. Second, *changes* in the amount of occasion specificity (as observed in the present data set in which occasion specificity decreased over time) are erroneously reflected in "changes" in the indicator reliabilities in first-order LGCMs. These findings illustrate that first-order LGCMs should be used only when constructs are perfectly trait-like, whereas second-order models are less restrictive and yield meaningful results also when constructs contain both state and trait components (for a detailed discussion of this issue, see Geiser et al., in press).

```
STANDARDIZED MODEL RESULTS (STDYX Standardization)

                                                      Two-Tailed
                    Estimate       S.E.  Est./S.E.    P-Value

 INTERC    |
    ANX1               0.864      0.019     46.518      0.000
    ANX2               0.932      0.021     43.447      0.000
    ANX3               0.922      0.030     31.217      0.000
    ANX4               0.909      0.039     23.222      0.000

 LINEAR    |
    ANX1               0.000      0.000    999.000    999.000
    ANX2               0.205      0.020     10.387      0.000
    ANX3               0.405      0.038     10.669      0.000
    ANX4               0.600      0.059     10.193      0.000

 ANX1     BY
    A11                0.949      0.010     99.540      0.000
    A21                0.918      0.010     90.264      0.000

 ANX2     BY
    A12                0.947      0.009    110.162      0.000
    A22                0.911      0.009     97.051      0.000

 ANX3     BY
    A13                0.947      0.008    125.147      0.000
    A23                0.927      0.009    108.099      0.000

 ANX4     BY
    A14                0.946      0.008    123.294      0.000
    A24                0.932      0.009    106.026      0.000
```

```
IS2      BY
   A21                0.208      0.015     13.758      0.000
   A22                0.223      0.016     13.928      0.000
   A23                0.224      0.016     13.857      0.000
   A24                0.223      0.016     13.532      0.000

IS2      WITH
   ANX1               0.000      0.000    999.000    999.000
   ANX2               0.000      0.000    999.000    999.000
   ANX3               0.000      0.000    999.000    999.000
   ANX4               0.000      0.000    999.000    999.000
   INTERC             0.000      0.000    999.000    999.000
   LINEAR             0.000      0.000    999.000    999.000

LINEAR   WITH
   INTERC            -0.259      0.071     -3.659      0.000

Means
   INTERC             1.844      0.092     20.014      0.000
   LINEAR            -0.720      0.095     -7.582      0.000

Intercepts
   A11                0.000      0.000    999.000    999.000
   A21                0.059      0.027      2.230      0.026
   A12                0.000      0.000    999.000    999.000
   A22                0.064      0.029      2.226      0.026
   A13                0.000      0.000    999.000    999.000
   A23                0.064      0.029      2.221      0.026
   A14                0.000      0.000    999.000    999.000
   A24                0.064      0.029      2.219      0.027
   ANX1               0.000      0.000    999.000    999.000
   ANX2               0.000      0.000    999.000    999.000
   ANX3               0.000      0.000    999.000    999.000
   ANX4               0.000      0.000    999.000    999.000

Variances
   IS2                1.000      0.000    999.000    999.000
   INTERC             1.000      0.000    999.000    999.000
   LINEAR             1.000      0.000    999.000    999.000

Residual Variances
   A11                0.099      0.018      5.460      0.000
   A21                0.115      0.017      6.746      0.000
   A12                0.104      0.016      6.363      0.000
   A22                0.120      0.015      7.793      0.000
   A13                0.103      0.014      7.176      0.000
   A23                0.090      0.014      6.465      0.000
   A14                0.106      0.015      7.310      0.000
   A24                0.082      0.014      5.696      0.000
   ANX1               0.254      0.032      7.910      0.000
   ANX2               0.188      0.023      8.188      0.000
```

```
    ANX3              0.180      0.021      8.648      0.000
    ANX4              0.097      0.028      3.446      0.001

R-SQUARE

    Observed                                       Two-Tailed
    Variable       Estimate        S.E.  Est./S.E.    P-Value

    A11          0.901      0.018      49.770      0.000
    A21               0.885      0.017     52.066      0.000
    A12               0.896      0.016     55.081      0.000
    A22               0.880      0.015     57.118      0.000
    A13               0.897      0.014     62.574      0.000
    A23               0.910      0.014     65.336      0.000
    A14               0.894      0.015     61.647      0.000
    A24               0.918      0.014     63.977      0.000

     Latent                                        Two-Tailed
    Variable       Estimate        S.E.  Est./S.E.    P-Value

    ANX1              0.746      0.032     23.259      0.000
    ANX2              0.812      0.023     35.357      0.000
    ANX3              0.820      0.021     39.311      0.000
    ANX4              0.903      0.028     32.101      0.000
```

Using the `plot` option, we generated a plot of the mean model-implied mean growth curve that can be viewed using the **Graph → View graphs** option (see Figure 4.41 on page 194). Graphs of individual growth curves are currently not available for second-order LGCMs in Mplus.

In the same way as first-order LGCMs, second-order LGCMs can be extended in various ways. For example, in addition to linear growth, we can also study quadratic or other forms of growth by adding additional growth factors to the model. The specification of a quadratic growth factor is analogous to the first-order LGCMs and is therefore not described in detail here.

In addition, covariates of change can also be included in second-order LGCMs. In this regard, second-order models are, once again, more flexible than first-order LGCMs. Second-order LGCMs allow researchers not only to include covariates of change, but also of occasion-specific variability, as represented by the LS residual variables.

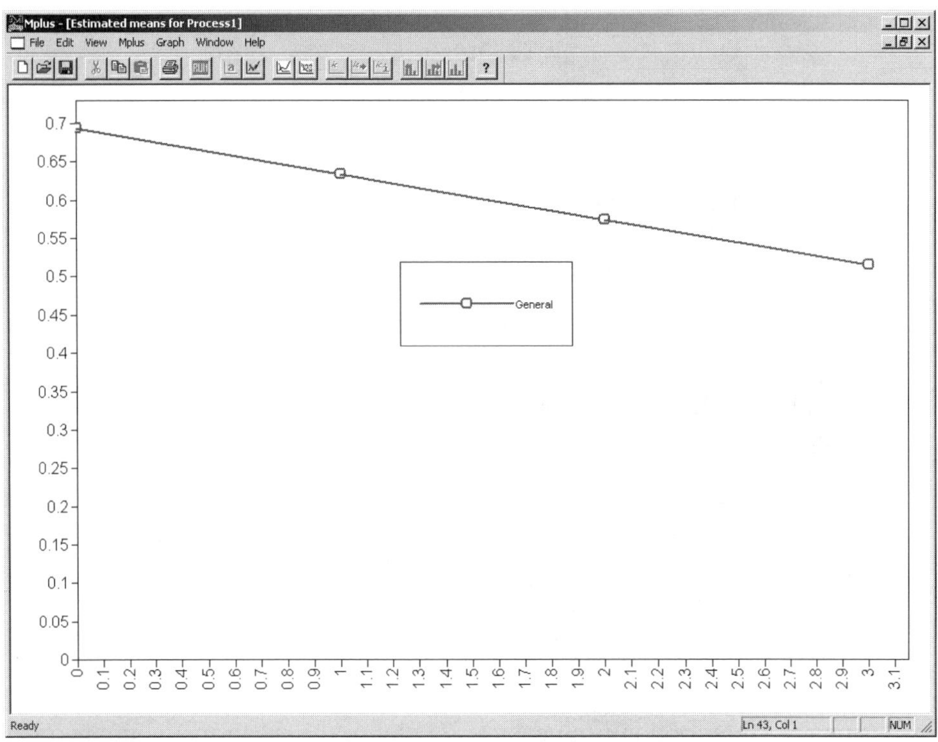

FIGURE 4.41. Mean model-implied growth curve for the linear second-order LGCM for the anxiety data generated via the Mplus `plot` option.

5

Multilevel Regression Analysis

5.1 INTRODUCTION TO MULTILEVEL ANALYSIS

Multilevel models (also referred to as *hierarchical linear models*, *random coefficient models*, or *mixed models*) are used to analyze clustered data, that is, data with a hierarchical (or cluster) structure. Clustered data occur, for example, when students from different school classes are selected for a study in such a way that some students share the same school class (with the associated common peer environment, teachers, etc.). In this case, the observational units (the students) are nested (or "clustered") within school classes. In a two-level sampling design, one distinguishes between level-1 and level-2 units. In our example, the students represent the level-1 units (units of the lower, so-called *micro level*) and the school classes represent the level-2 units (units of the *macro level*). Depending on the sampling design, there could be additional, higher levels (e.g., schools, districts, cities, counties, states, countries). In our examples, we consider only two levels.

Nested data structures also occur with longitudinal data in which measurement occasions (or time points) are nested within individuals. Therefore, multilevel analysis can also be used to analyze longitudinal data (e.g., see Bryk & Raudenbush, 1987; Singer & Willett, 2003).

Taking the hierarchical structure of clustered data into account is important for at least two reasons. First, clustered sampling, by definition, violates the assumption of independence of observations that is made by many traditional statistical approaches such as ordinary least squares (OLS) regression analysis and analysis of variance (ANOVA; Cohen et al.,

2003). Second, independent variables or predictors may act at different levels of analysis. For example, teacher-related variables such as teaching style or gender would be variables at level-2 and should be properly modeled as such.

In random samples (without cluster structure) the assumption of independence of observations is met. In clustered samples, however, there often are dependencies among observations from the same cluster. With regard to our student example, we might expect students within the same class to be more similar to each other with respect to certain attributes (e.g., knowledge about certain topics, school achievement in general) than students who belong to a different class. The reason is that students in the same class are, in part, subject to the same influences. For example, they typically share the same teacher(s) and are exposed to the same group dynamics within the class.

Using conventional statistical approaches to analyze clustered data without proper adjustment can lead to biased results. In particular, the standard errors of the model parameters (e.g., regression coefficients) may be underestimated, because dependencies in the data due to clustering lead to an overestimation of the effective sample size (Cohen et al., 2003; Snijders & Bosker, 1999). Undesirable consequences of the underestimation of standard errors are biased statistical inference (specifically, an increase in the alpha error rate) and incorrectly estimated confidence intervals around the parameter estimates. The *p*-values associated with tests of statistical significance will generally be too small, leading to a too-frequent rejection of the null hypothesis that a parameter is equal to zero in the population. Moreover, confidence intervals will be too small, suggesting a greater level of precision in parameter estimation than is actually present.

The second reason why the multilevel structure of the data should be taken into account is that modeling variables at different levels—as well as their interaction—is often of substantive interest. For example, in many cases, variables at the individual level (e.g., attributes of the students) as well as variables at the cluster level (e.g., attributes at the level of the class) are relevant for the prediction of an outcome variable (e.g., school achievement). At the level of the students, variables such as intelligence, industriousness, and motivation could be relevant for explaining school performance. At the class level, variables such as the size of the class, the class climate, and teacher attributes (teaching style, gender of the teacher, etc.) could be interesting predictor variables. In addition to studying the main effects of predictors at different levels, multilevel models allow us to model

BOX 5.1. *Summary of the Most Important Advantages of Multilevel Regression Analysis*

The most important advantages of multilevel regression analysis can be summarized as follows:

- Multilevel models appropriately account for the hierarchical data structure that causes dependencies in the data.
- Multilevel modeling avoids standard error bias due to clustering that leads to inflated type-I error rates and incorrect confidence intervals.
- Multilevel models allow analyzing variables at different levels as well as the analysis of cross-level interactions.
- Multilevel analysis is more flexible and requires fewer assumptions than traditional statistical methods such as, for example, repeated measures of ANOVA.

interactions between variables at different levels (so-called *cross-level interactions*; e.g., see Luke, 2004, as well as Section 5.5.2).

More detailed descriptions of multilevel analysis can be found in the textbooks by Hox (2002), Kreft and de Leeuw (1998), Luke (2004), Raudenbush and Bryk (2002), Singer and Willett (2003), as well as Snijders and Bosker (1999). A superb introductory chapter on multilevel analysis is also available in the book by Cohen et al. (2003, their Chapter 14). The use of multilevel models to analyze longitudinal data is discussed in Bryk and Raudenbush (1987) as well as in Singer and Willett (2003).

5.2 SPECIFICATION OF MULTILEVEL MODELS IN Mplus

The specification of multilevel models in Mplus is carried out by using the `analysis: type = twolevel;` option. In order to use this option, either the "multilevel add-on" or the "combination add-on" upgrades are required in addition to the Mplus base program (for details, see *www.statmodel.com*). As of version 6, Mplus is able to model variables at only two levels. An exception is longitudinal data, for which a multivariate approach can be used. *Multivariate* means that the two-level structure caused by repeated measurement (time points nested within individuals) is accounted for by using (single-level) LGCMs in which there are one or

BOX 5.2. *Example Multilevel Regression Analysis*

We use a simple cross-sectional data set to illustrate the analysis of multilevel regression models in Mplus. In this example, the outcome (or dependent) variable is mathematics achievement of German students. In our example, there are N = 503 students (level-1 units) nested within 34 school classes (level-2 units). Each student took a mathematics test (variable **math**) as well as the German Kognitiver Fähigkeitstest (cognitive ability test KFT; Heller et al., 1976; variable **kft**). The variables **math** and **kft** represent level-1 variables, because they were measured at the level of the students (each student can potentially have a different score on each test).

In addition, the school type (conventional German high school vs. German gymnasium) was recorded and dummy-coded (variable **stype**; 0 = conventional high school, 1 = gymnasium). School type is a level-2 variable because it can vary for different classes, but not for students within the same class.

Figure 5.1 shows part of the SPSS data set named **math_kft.sav**. Note that an individual data set is required for the multilevel analysis in Mplus and that this individual data set needs to contain a so-called *cluster variable* to indicate membership in a specific level-2 unit (here, the school classes). In our example, the cluster variable is named **class** and enumerates the school classes from 1 through 34.

more outcome variables at each time point (see Section 4.5). A third level (e.g., individuals nested within organizations or school classes) can then again be accounted for using the `type = twolevel;` option. Therefore, a total of three levels can be modeled in Mplus if one of the levels is defined by repeated observations.

5.3 OPTION `TwoLevel BASIC`

A useful option in Mplus is the so-called `twolevel basic` option that can be used at the beginning of a multilevel analysis to check whether the data are read correctly by Mplus (see also Chapter 2). The `twolevel basic` option also provides an overview of the cluster structure in the data and the degree of dependence of observations. The degree of dependence of observations is often measured by the *intraclass correlation coefficient* (*ICC*). An *ICC* of zero indicates that observations are independent of cluster membership. The larger the *ICC*, the more individual differences

BOX 5.3. *Formal Notation for Multilevel Regression Models Used in This Chapter*

The following common notation is used in this chapter to indicate the parameters estimated in multilevel regression models. Note that actual estimates based on sample data are indicated with a hat (^) to make clear that they are sample estimates of population parameters.

Y_{ij} = value of a person *i* belonging to cluster *j* on the dependent variable

β_{0j} = random intercept in the level-1 regression equation

β_{1j} = random slope in the level-1 regression equation

X_{ij} = value of a person *i* belonging to cluster *j* on a level-1 predictor variable

r_{ij} = level-1 residual score

$\sigma^2_{r_{ij}}$ = level-1 residual variance (also denoted as σ^2_W for `within` in the intercept-only model)

γ_{00} = grand mean/intercept for the random intercept coefficient on level 2

γ_{01} = slope coefficient for the random intercept on level 2

γ_{10} = intercept for the random slope on level 2

γ_{11} = slope coefficient for the random slope on level 2

W_j = value of a level-2 unit (e.g., a school class) on a level-2 predictor variable

u_{0j} = residual score for the random intercept on level 2

u_{1j} = residual score for the random slope on level 2

$\sigma^2_{u_{0j}}$ = level-2 residual variance for the random intercept (also denoted as σ^2_B for `between` in the intercept-only model)

$\sigma^2_{u_{1j}}$ = level-2 residual variance for the random slope

τ_{01} = level-2 (residual) covariance between random intercept and random slope

ρ_{IC} = intraclass correlation coefficient

are due to differences between clusters. Mplus automatically outputs the *ICC* in a multilevel analysis. In other multilevel regression analysis programs, the *ICC* sometimes has to be calculated manually based on variance parameter estimates of the so-called *null* or *intercept-only model* (see Section 5.4.1).

The *ICC* ρ_{IC} is defined as the ratio of the variance between the clusters (level-2 variance σ_B^2, "B" for "between clusters") to the total of variance ($\sigma_B^2 + \sigma_W^2$), where σ_W^2 indicates the (level-1) variance within the clusters ("W" for "within clusters"):

$$\rho_{IC} = \frac{\sigma_B^2}{\left(\sigma_W^2 + \sigma_B^2\right)}$$

Even very small *ICC* values of, say, .05 or .10 can lead to considerable bias in the results of tests of statistical significance in conventional OLS regression analyses and ANOVA, which do not take the dependence of observations into account (e.g., Cohen et al., 2003, p. 538). In a `two-level basic` analysis, Mplus outputs the *ICC* as well as the estimated level-1 (within clusters) and level-2 (between clusters) variances for all variables included in the analysis (i.e., for all variables listed under `use-variables`).

The individual data shown in Figure 5.1 were exported to an ASCII file named **math_kft.dat** for use in Mplus following the procedure described in Section 2.1. The Mplus input file for the specification of the `twolevel basic` analysis for the variables **math** and **kft** is shown in Figure 5.2. The cluster variable **class** has to be specifically defined using the subcommand `cluster = class;` to inform Mplus that the level-2 units (here the school classes) are defined based on this variable. The cluster variable does not have to appear under the `usevariables` list, because this variable is a variable with a special function and is neither used as an independent nor a dependent variable in the model.

Below, the most important part of the Mplus output for the `two-level basic` analysis is shown. Under `SUMMARY OF ANALYSIS`, we can see that $N = 503$ students (level-1 units) and two variables (**math** and **kft**) were used in the analysis. Mplus also informs us that the variable **class** served as the cluster variable in this analysis, as intended. This allows us to once again check that our level-2 units are correctly defined (the level-2 variable `stype` is included in the analysis in Sections 5.4.3 and 5.5.2).

math_kft.sav [DataSet3] - IBM SPSS Statistics Data Editor

	class	mathe	kft	stype
377	30	14	66	conventional high school
378	30	15	77	conventional high school
379	30	15	78	conventional high school
380	30	16	81	conventional high school
381	30	17	76	conventional high school
382	30	17	83	conventional high school
383	30	17	92	conventional high school
384	30	23	90	conventional high school
385	31	18	77	gymnasium
386	31	19	82	gymnasium
387	31	20	84	gymnasium
388	31	20	98	gymnasium
389	31	21	74	gymnasium
390	31	21	94	gymnasium
391	31	22	81	gymnasium
392	31	22	92	gymnasium
393	31	23	84	gymnasium
394	31	23	99	gymnasium
395	31	23	107	gymnasium
396	31	24	79	gymnasium
397	31	24	85	gymnasium
398	31	25	90	gymnasium
399	31	26	92	gymnasium
400	31	27	99	gymnasium

FIGURE 5.1. Screen shot of the sample data set **math_kft.sav**. The variable **class** indicates the different school classes and is used as cluster variable in Mplus. The variable **math** is the continuous dependent variable, **kft** is a continuous level-1 predictor variable, and **stype** is a dummy-coded dichotomous level-2 predictor variable.

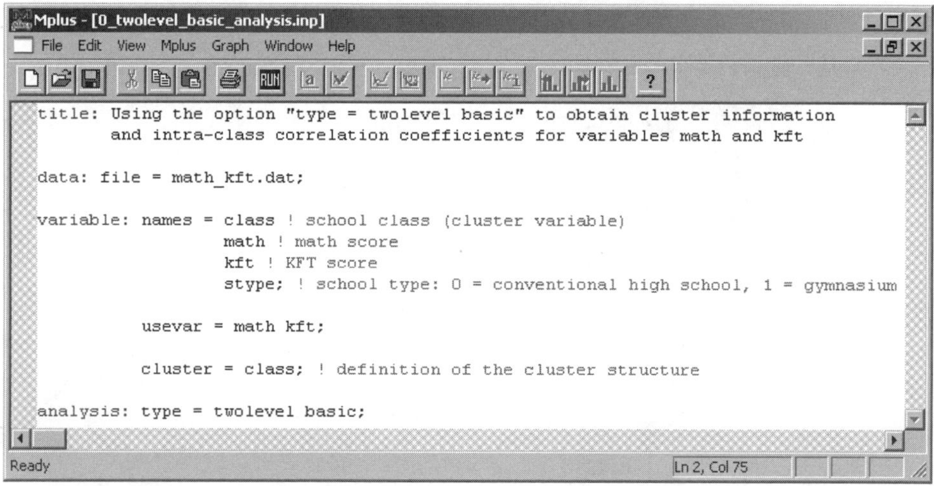

```
title: Using the option "type = twolevel basic" to obtain cluster information
       and intra-class correlation coefficients for variables math and kft

data: file = math_kft.dat;

variable: names = class ! school class (cluster variable)
                  math ! math score
                  kft ! KFT score
                  stype; ! school type: 0 = conventional high school, 1 = gymnasium

          usevar = math kft;

          cluster = class; ! definition of the cluster structure

analysis: type = twolevel basic;
```

FIGURE 5.2. Mplus input file for a `twolevel basic analysis` for the variables **math** and **kft**.

```
SUMMARY OF ANALYSIS

Number of groups                                                1
Number of observations                                        503

Number of dependent variables                                   2
Number of independent variables                                 0
Number of continuous latent variables                           0

Observed dependent variables

  Continuous
   MATH        KFT

Variables with special functions

  Cluster variable      CLASS
```

Under the rubric `SUMMARY OF DATA` we obtain more detailed information about the cluster structure present in the data. Here, we are dealing with 34 clusters (school classes = level-2 units). Mplus informs us abou the distribution of the cluster sizes in a stem-and-leaf type of plot. We can see that there is one cluster that contributed five students (the school class with the number 22), one cluster that contributed eight students (class number 18), and so on. The mode is 13 students per cluster (school classes number 14, 2, 5, 23, and 13). The class that provides the most students is class number 7 (24 students stem from this class). Under the plot, Mplus reports the average cluster size (here, 14.794 students per class).

```
SUMMARY OF DATA

     Number of clusters                          34

       Size (s)    Cluster ID with Size s

          5        22
          8        18
          9        19
         10        16 21 12 25
         11        20 3
         12        8
         13        14 2 5 23 13
         14        4
         15        17 24 1
         16        6 28 30
         17        11 27
         18        29 26 35 36
         19        33
```

```
        20          31
        21          34
        22          10
        23          32
        24           7

    Average cluster size          14.794
```

Mplus next outputs the estimated *ICCs* for both the **kft** and **math** variables. The values of ρ_{IC} = .44 for **kft** and ρ_{IC} = .378 for **math** indicate that class membership accounts for a substantial portion of individual differences in both the math and KFT test scores. In other words, a non-trivial amount of the variance in math and KFT scores is due to average performance differences between the school classes. This also shows us that in this example it makes sense to consider predictor variables at the class level, because there is a considerable amount of variability at this level. The inclusion of level-2 predictors would not make sense if there were no differences between the classes.

```
    Estimated Intraclass Correlations for the Y Variables

                Intraclass                 Intraclass
    Variable   Correlation    Variable   Correlation

    MATH           0.440      KFT            0.378
```

Below is the Mplus output of descriptive statistics (means, covariances, and correlations) separately for level 1 and level 2. Note that the (grand) means of the variables are estimated at level 2 (the between level). The estimated grand means are $\hat{\gamma}_{00}$ = 11.930 for **math** and $\hat{\gamma}_{00}$ = 66.716 for **kft**. Given that the level-1 means (or cluster means) are a function of level-2 parameters (the grand means plus the cluster-specific deviations from the grand means), the means at level 1 (within level) are output as 0.000 in Mplus. The estimated variances of the variables at the individual level are $\hat{\sigma}_W^2$ = 26.484 for **math** and $\hat{\sigma}_W^2$ = 235.735 for **kft**. At the class level, the estimated variances are $\hat{\sigma}_B^2$ = 20.806 for **math** and $\hat{\sigma}_B^2$ = 142.985 for **kft**.

```
RESULTS FOR BASIC ANALYSIS
NOTE:  The sample statistics for within and
between refer to the maximum-likelihood estimated
within and between covariance matrices,
respectively.
```

```
     ESTIMATED SAMPLE STATISTICS FOR WITHIN

           Means
              MATH          KFT
              ________      ________
 1               0.000         0.000

           Covariances
              MATH          KFT
              ________      ________
 MATH           26.484
 KFT            52.327       235.735

           Correlations
              MATH          KFT
              ________      ________
 MATH            1.000
 KFT             0.662         1.000

     ESTIMATED SAMPLE STATISTICS FOR BETWEEN

           Means
              MATH          KFT
              ________      ________
 1              11.930        66.716

           Covariances
              MATH          KFT
              ________      ________
 MATH           20.806
 KFT            49.983       142.985

           Correlations
              MATH          KFT
              ________      ________
 MATH            1.000
 KFT             0.916         1.000
```

The variance estimates can be used to calculate the estimated *ICCs* (this is not really necessary, given that Mplus automatically outputs the ρ_{IC} values):

For **math**: $$\hat{\rho}_{IC} = \frac{\hat{\sigma}_B^2}{\hat{\sigma}_W^2 + \hat{\sigma}_B^2} = \frac{20.806}{26.484 + 20.806} = 0.44$$

For **kft**: $$\hat{\rho}_{IC} = \frac{\hat{\sigma}_B^2}{\hat{\sigma}_W^2 + \hat{\sigma}_B^2} = \frac{142.985}{235.735 + 142.985} = 0.378$$

In addition, we see that the correlation between **math** and **kft** at the individual level is $r = .662$, whereas the relationship at the level of the school classes is much higher ($r = .916$). In summary, we find that the use of a multilevel analysis to analyze the present data must be highly recommended, given the large amount of variability between school classes. If we used a conventional OLS regression analysis without taking the cluster structure into account, we would have to expect a significant underestimation of the standard errors of the regression coefficients and therefore a substantial increase of our type-I error rate as well as biased confidence intervals. We now consider different types of multilevel regression models following the taxonomy of Luke (2004; see his Table 2.1). We begin with so-called *random coefficient regression models*, the most basic of which is the *null* or *intercept-only model*.

5.4 RANDOM INTERCEPT MODELS

5.4.1 Null Model (Intercept-Only Model)

The *null* or *intercept-only model* is often estimated in the first step of a multilevel regression analysis because it can be used to estimate the *ICC* for the dependent variable. In Mplus, this step is not strictly necessary, because the level-1 and level-2 variances as well as the *ICC* are directly output whenever the analysis option `type = twolevel` (or `twolevel basic`) is used. We still discuss the intercept-only model here for didactic reasons because it is one of the simplest multilevel models, and having an understanding of this basic model and its specification in Mplus facilitates understanding of the analysis of more complex multilevel models in Mplus.

In the intercept-only model, there is no predictor variable of the dependent variable on either level 1 or level 2. At level 1, the individual scores Y_{ij} are decomposed into the cluster mean β_{0j} plus the individual-specific deviation (or residual score) from the cluster mean r_{ij}:

$$\text{Level 1:} \quad Y_{ij} = \beta_{0j} + r_{ij}$$

In terms of our data example, we decompose the math score of an individual student i (e.g., David) who belongs to school class j into the mean of David's school class (cluster mean) plus the deviation of David's math score from the class average. The variance $\sigma^2_{r_{ij}}$ characterizes the amount of within-class (level-1) variability:

$$\sigma^2_{r_{ij}} = \sigma^2_W$$

Large values of $\sigma^2_{r_{ij}}$ indicate that there are substantial individual differences in the math scores among students who belong to the same class. From the `twolevel basic` analysis (see Section 5.3) we already know that $\hat{\sigma}^2_{r_{ij}} = \hat{\sigma}^2_W = 26.484$ for the math test score. The same estimate will also be obtained based on the intercept-only model. At level 2, variability in the cluster means β_{0j} is modeled. The cluster means are decomposed into the grand mean across all school classes (γ_{00}) plus the deviations of the cluster means from the grand mean (u_{0j}):

$$\text{Level 2:} \quad \beta_{0j} = \gamma_{00} + u_{0j}$$

The level-2 equation shows that in the intercept-only model, the cluster means are variables that have a mean γ_{00} and a variance $\sigma^2_{u_{0j}}$, both of which are parameters at level 2. This also explains the name *random intercept model*: Whereas in conventional OLS regression analysis the intercept is a constant (fixed effect), the intercept β_{0j} in the random intercept model can vary across clusters and therefore represents a random effect. In our example, the math test means are not constant, but can vary across school classes.

The variance $\sigma^2_{u_{0j}}$ characterizes differences in the cluster means across level-2 units (between clusters):

$$\sigma^2_{u_{0j}} = \sigma^2_B$$

that is, the degree of differences between the school classes. Large values of $\sigma^2_{u_{0j}}$ indicate that there are large differences in the mean math scores between school classes. From the `twolevel basic` analysis, we know that $\hat{\sigma}^2_{u_{0j}} = \hat{\sigma}^2_B = 20.806$ for the math test score. A similar estimate is also obtained in the intercept-only model. Because in this model the variability in the math test means across classes is not explained by external variables (the level-2 equation does not contain any predictor variables), the intercept-only model is sometimes referred to as *unconditional cell means model*, *unconstrained model*, *empty model*, or *null model*.

In summary, we obtain Mplus estimates for the following three types of parameters in the intercept-only model:

- At level 1 (`WITHIN`):
  - —The variance of the individual scores around the cluster means, $\sigma^2_{r_{ij}} = \sigma^2_{\mathrm{W}}$
- At level 2 (`BETWEEN`):
  - —The grand mean γ_{00}
  - —The variance of the cluster means around the grand mean, $\sigma^2_{u_{0j}} = \sigma^2_{\mathrm{B}}$

Figure 5.3 shows the Mplus input file for the estimation of the intercept-only model using the outcome variable **math**. It is only necessary to list the variable **math** under `usevariables`, specify the relevant cluster variable (here, **class**), and request `analysis: type = twolevel`. A specific model statement is not required for the "null model." After running the input file, the following Mplus warning message occurs in the output:

```
*** WARNING in MODEL command
All variables are uncorrelated with all other
variables in the model. Check that this is
what is intended.
   1 WARNING(S) FOUND IN THE INPUT INSTRUCTIONS
```

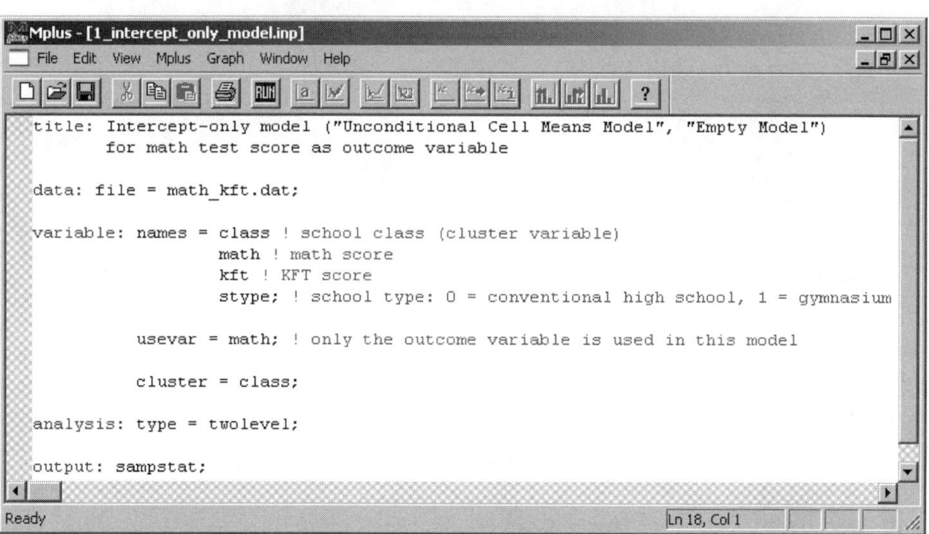

FIGURE 5.3. Mplus input file for the specification of the intercept-only model for the variable **math**.

This message occurs due to the fact that we did not specify any relations between variables. This is in line with our null model, however, which does not relate either the individual scores or the cluster means to any external variables. Therefore, the warning message can be ignored in this particular case. (Note that in other models, the same or similar messages may indicate a potentially serious model misspecification and should therefore not be generally ignored.)

The Mplus output provides us with the estimate of the level-1 variance under `MODEL RESULTS—Within Level` ($\hat{\sigma}^2_{r_{ij}}$ = 26.480). Under `Between Level` we obtain estimates of the grand mean ($\hat{\gamma}_{00}$ = 11.933) and the level-2 variance $\hat{\sigma}^2_{u_{0j}}$ = 20.853. The estimated values are only slightly different from the values that were estimated in the `twolevel basic` analysis (see Section 5.3). In addition, the intercept-only model also provides us with standard errors of the model parameter estimates as well as test statistics (z-scores) and corresponding p-values.

```
MODEL RESULTS

                                                       Two-Tailed
                    Estimate       S.E.  Est./S.E.      P-Value

Within Level

 Variances
    MATH              26.480      2.450     10.809        0.000

Between Level

 Means
    MATH              11.933      0.808     14.776        0.000

 Variances
    MATH              20.853      6.017      3.466        0.001
```

BOX 5.4. *Estimation of Standard Errors under* `type = twolevel` *in Mplus*

Under `type = twolevel` the standard errors of the model parameters are estimated by default using robust maximum likelihood estimation (`estimator = mlr;`) in Mplus. Conventional maximum likelihood estimation can be requested by using the following specification:

```
analysis: estimator = ml;
```

The intercept-only model provides only the level-1 and level-2 variances that can be used for the calculation of the *ICC*. The model does not contain any additional independent variables ("empty model"). Therefore, variability in the scores at the individual level or the group means is not accounted for by other variables in this model. In the following, we discuss more complex multilevel models in which additional independent variables are present (1) only at level 1 (so-called *random effects analysis of covariance* [ANCOVA] *model*), (2) only at level 2 (so-called *means-as-outcomes models*), or (3) at both level 1 and level 2 (so-called *intercepts-and-slopes-as-outcomes models*).

5.4.2 One-Way Random Effects ANCOVA

We now discuss the case that a researcher (1) wants to predict an outcome variable (e.g., math score) using a continuous level-1 predictor variable only (e.g., KFT score) and (2) wants to control for differences in the KFT means between school classes without assuming differences in the slopes of the level-1 regressions across clusters. The resulting model consists of a level-1 regression equation with a random intercept (β_{0j}) and a constant slope ($\beta_{1j} = \gamma_{10}$). This model is equivalent to a one-factorial analysis of covariance with a random factor (so-called *one-way random effects ANCOVA*; Luke, 2004), where the random factor, in our case, is the school class:

$$\text{Level 1:} \quad Y_{ij} = \beta_{0j} + \beta_{1j} \cdot X_{ij} + r_{ij}$$

$$\text{Level 2:} \quad \beta_{0j} = \gamma_{00} + u_{0j}$$

$$\beta_{1j} = \gamma_{10}$$

The level-2 equations show that in this model, the intercept β_{0j} from the level-1 regression of math score on KFT score can vary across school classes (level-2 units). In contrast, the level-1 slope coefficient β_{1j} is assumed to be constant across school classes. This can be seen from the fact that there is no residual score in the level-2 equation for β_{1j}, whereas for the intercept β_{0j}, a residual term u_{0j} is included. Note that this model is too restrictive if the slopes of the level-1 regressions actually do vary across school classes, because no such variation is allowed in the model. In Section 5.5 we consider models that allow for variation in both the intercept and slope coefficients across clusters.

In Mplus, we obtain the parameters of the one-way random effects ANCOVA model in the following way:

- At level 1 (`WITHIN`):
  —The constant slope (fixed effect) $\beta_{1j} = \gamma_{10}$
  —The residual variance $\sigma^2_{r_{ij}}$
- At level 2 (`BETWEEN`):
  —The mean intercept γ_{00} across clusters
  —The variance $\sigma^2_{u_{0j}}$ of the intercepts across clusters

Before we consider the results for this model in detail, I introduce a concept that is of great importance in multilevel analysis: that of *centering predictor variables*. Centering was briefly discussed in the Section 3.2 on OLS regression analysis (cf. Box 3.4). For simplicity, we return to simple OLS regression analysis to revisit the issue of centering:

$$Y = \beta_0 + \beta_1 \cdot X + \varepsilon$$

where β_0 indicates a fixed intercept and β_1 indicates a fixed slope coefficient in the regression of a criterion variable Y on a single predictor variable X, and ε denotes a residual variable. The estimated OLS regression equation for our example is

$$\text{math} = -6.486 + 0.279 \cdot \text{kft} + \text{residual}$$

Note that the estimated OLS regression coefficients do not take clustering into account and therefore should not be used. The negative intercept term in this equation ($\hat{\beta}_0 = -6.486$) means that for students who obtained a KFT score of 0, we would expect a math test score of –6.486. There are two problems associated with this estimate for our interpretation of the results. First, negative scores lie outside of the possible range of values for the outcome variable **math** (the smallest possible score on the math test is 0 points). Second, a KFT raw score of 0 is very unlikely to be observed for any student (and, in fact, was not observed in the present study). Therefore, a substantively meaningful interpretation of the intercept is not possible in this example—at least not with uncentered variables. By centering the independent variable **kft** before the analysis, the zero point of this variable becomes more meaningful. Centering means that a meaningful constant (usually a type of mean) is subtracted from each raw score. In the analysis, the centered (or deviation) scores are then used instead of the raw scores.

A frequently used form of centering is *grand mean centering*, in which the grand mean $\overline{X}_{..}$ is subtracted from all raw scores X_{ij}:

$$X_{ij}^{C} = X_{ij} - \overline{X}_{..}$$

where X_{ij}^{C} indicates the centered variable. If the student, for example, has a score of 0 on the grand-mean-centered KFT variable, this means that the KFT score of this student is exactly identical to the average in the entire sample. Negative values on the centered variable indicate that a student scored below average on the KFT, whereas positive values indicate scores above average in the sample.

In the OLS regression model, centering leads to a different intercept estimate that typically has a more meaningful interpretation when independent variables have no meaningful zero point or when the value of 0 is meaningful, but did not occur in the data (cf. Section 3.2). The intercept in the regression equation with a centered predictor variable provides the expected value of the dependent variable for an individual with an *average* value on the independent variable. The slope is unaffected by centering in the simple regression model. The OLS regression equation for the math–KFT example changes as follows when centered, instead of uncentered, KFT scores are used:

$$\text{math} = 12.533 + 0.279 \cdot \text{kft} + \text{residual}$$

We see that only the intercept, but not the slope of the regression equation, has changed. The new intercept is 12.533, which means that for students with an average KFT score, we expect a math test score of 12.533 based on the linear regression of **math** on **kft**. Substantively, this represents a more meaningful result than the negative intercept estimate in the uncentered regression equation.

In Mplus, centering of variables is performed by adding the single additional subcommand `centering` in the `variable` command. This means that the independent variables do not have to be manually centered prior to the analysis in Mplus. Mplus offers two options for centering variables: (1) centering at the grand mean (*grand mean centering*) and (2) centering at the cluster mean (*group mean centering*). Grand mean centering can be requested in Mplus with the following specification:

```
variable: centering = grandmean (kft);
```

Group mean centering is requested as follows:

```
variable: centering = groupmean (kft);
```

Detailed recommendations on the use of different forms of centering in multilevel models can be found in Enders and Tofighi (2007), Hofmann and Gavin (1998), as well as Kreft, de Leeuw, and Aiken (1995). Figure 5.4 shows the Mplus input for the specification of the one-way random effects ANCOVA model for our example. Of importance, the predictor variable **kft** is defined as a level-1 variable, because in our example, this variable is only used at level 1:

```
within = kft;
```

In addition, we use grand mean centering for the variable **kft**, as demonstrated above. In the `model` command, we specify the regression equation at level 1. Since level 1 is referred to as the `within` level in Mplus, we have to include a command that makes clear that this equation refers to this level:

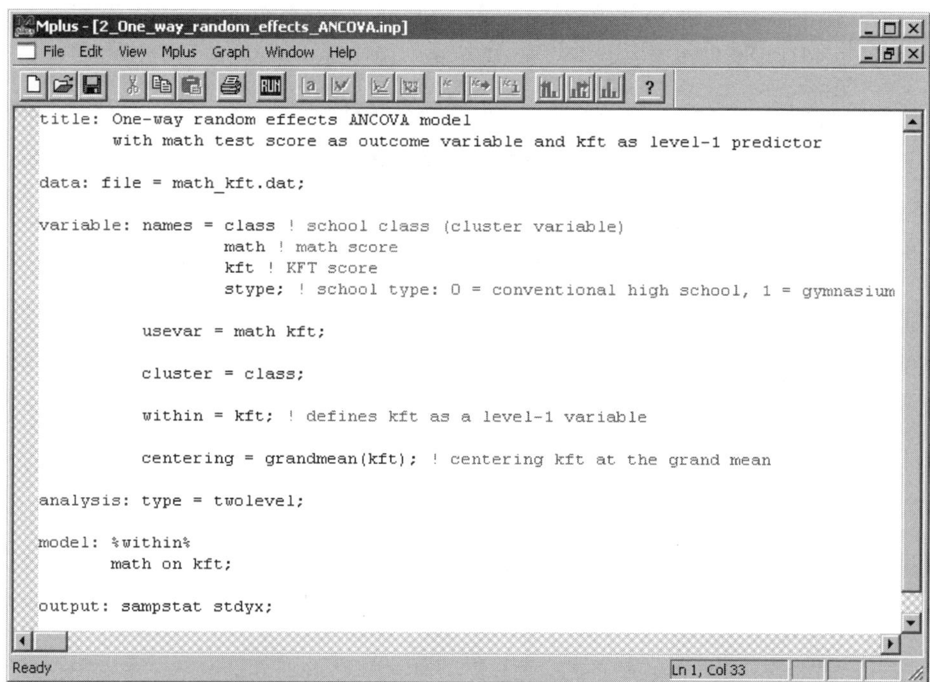


```
title: One-way random effects ANCOVA model
       with math test score as outcome variable and kft as level-1 predictor

data: file = math_kft.dat;

variable: names = class ! school class (cluster variable)
                  math ! math score
                  kft ! KFT score
                  stype; ! school type: 0 = conventional high school, 1 = gymnasium

          usevar = math kft;

          cluster = class;

          within = kft; ! defines kft as a level-1 variable

          centering = grandmean(kft); ! centering kft at the grand mean

analysis: type = twolevel;

model: %within%
       math on kft;

output: sampstat stdyx;
```

FIGURE 5.4. Mplus input file for the specification of the one-way random effects ANCOVA model for the outcome variable **math** and the level-1 predictor variable **kft**.

```
model:    %within%
          math on kft;
```

Because in our model, the level-2 equations only contain a random intercept and a fixed slope with no additional structure, nothing has to be specified for the `between` level. Mplus automatically estimates the parameters γ_{00} and $\sigma^2_{u_{0j}}$ at level 2. (The fixed slope $\beta_{1j} = \gamma_{10}$ is treated as a level-1 parameter in Mplus.) The subcommand `stdyx` in the output command is used to request the fully standardized solution. Under `MODEL RESULTS—Within Level` Mplus provides the estimated slope coefficient $\hat{\beta}_{1j} = \hat{\gamma}_{10} = 0.234$ as well as the estimated level-1 residual variance $\hat{\sigma}^2_{r_{ij}} = 14.883$. Under `Between Level`, the mean intercept ($\hat{\gamma}_{00} = 12.310$) and the level-2 residual variance for the random intercept ($\hat{\sigma}^2_{u_{0j}} = 5.403$) are given.

```
MODEL RESULTS

                                                    Two-Tailed
                    Estimate       S.E.  Est./S.E.    P-Value

Within Level

 MATH       ON
    KFT                0.234      0.012     20.042      0.000

 Residual Variances
    MATH              14.883      1.052     14.141      0.000

Between Level

 Means
    MATH              12.310      0.437     28.142      0.000

 Variances
    MATH               5.403      1.612      3.352      0.001
```

It can be seen that the level-1 residual variance (14.883) is substantially smaller than the corresponding (unconditional) level-1 variance estimated in the intercept-only model (26.48) that did not contain any level-1 predictor variable (see Section 5.4.1). This shows that a substantial amount of the variability in the math test scores can be explained by differences in individual KFT scores. (Since we used grand mean centering, these differences reflect both within and between class differences; see

Enders & Tofighi, 2007, for details.) More detailed information on the size of this effect is provided under the standardized solution (`STDYX Standardization`). We can see that the standardized level-1 regression coefficient for the regression of math on KFT was estimated to 0.773. The estimated R^2 value for the level-1 regression is .598, which shows that almost 60% of the variability in individual math test scores is accounted for by individual and group differences in the KFT scores.

```
STANDARDIZED MODEL RESULTS (STDYX Standardization)

                                                      Two-Tailed
                    Estimate       S.E.  Est./S.E.    P-Value

Within Level

 MATH        ON
   KFT                 0.773      0.020     38.617      0.000

 Residual Variances
   MATH                0.402      0.031     12.987      0.000

Between Level

 Means
   MATH                5.296      0.763      6.938      0.000

 Variances
   MATH                1.000      0.000    999.000    999.000


R-SQUARE

Within Level

   Observed                                           Two-Tailed
   Variable         Estimate       S.E.  Est./S.E.    P-Value

   MATH                0.598      0.031     19.309      0.000
```

5.4.3 Means-as-Outcomes Model

In the previous section, we discussed a random intercept model with one level-1 predictor and no level-2 predictors. We now consider a model in which there is no level-1 predictor but one level-2 predictor. Such a model can be useful when one is interested in only explaining differences in the cluster means on the dependent variable (Luke, 2004). For example, one might be interested in explaining differences in the math test cluster means through macro variables such as, for example, characteristics of the teacher or the type of school students attend. The equations for a model with no level-1 and one level-2 predictor, W_j, can be written as follows:

$$\text{Level 1:} \quad Y_{ij} = \beta_{0j} + r_{ij}$$

$$\text{Level 2:} \quad \beta_{0j} = \gamma_{00} + \gamma_{01} \cdot W_j + u_{0j}$$

The level-1 equation contains only the simple decomposition of an observed score into the cluster mean plus an individual deviation from the cluster mean. This part of the model is identical to the intercept-only model (see Section 5.4.1). In contrast to the intercept-only model, the level-2 equation in the means-as-outcomes model is structured such that at level 2, differences in the cluster means are explained through the level-2 predictor W_j. The parameters γ_{00} and γ_{01} are fixed level-2 regression coefficients for the regression of the cluster means on the level-2 predictor. The term u_{0j} reflects that part of the cluster mean β_{0j} that cannot be predicted by W_j. Because this model focuses on the explanation of differences between clusters in terms of level-2 variables, it has been referred to as *means-as-outcomes model* by Luke (2004).

With regard to our data example, the means-as-outcomes model allows us to examine the question of whether differences in the math scores at the level of the school classes can be explained by *school type* (standard high school vs. gymnasium). The variable **stype** is a level-2 variable because it varies between, but not within, school classes. We can use **stype** in our model as a level-2 predictor (W_j). Mplus provides us with the following parameter estimates for the means-as-outcomes model:

- At level 1 (`WITHIN`):
  —The residual variance $\sigma^2_{r_{ij}}$
- At level 2 (`BETWEEN`):
  —The fixed intercept γ_{00} for the regression of β_{0j} on W_j
  —The fixed slope γ_{01} for the regression of β_{0j} on W_j
  —The residual variance $\sigma^2_{u_{0j}}$

In our example, the coefficients γ_{00} and γ_{01} have a special meaning, because our level-2 predictor school type is a dichotomous variable with the categories 0 = standard high school and 1 = gymnasium. For this reason, γ_{00} gives the expected mean math score for the standard high school group. The slope coefficient γ_{01} represents the expected mean difference in math scores (gymnasium minus high school). Note that the interpretation of the coefficients would change if we used a different coding scheme for the categories of the variable school type (e.g., effect or contrast coding; for details see Chapter 8 in Cohen et al., 2003).

Figure 5.5 shows the Mplus input for the means-as-outcomes model for math test scores. It is important to note that the variable **stype** has to be defined as a level-2 only variable. This is accomplished through the following specification in the `variable` command:

```
between = stype;
```

Note that `between` level variables can vary only between, but not within clusters. If variables defined as `between` level variables show variation within any of the clusters, Mplus issues a warning message in the output. Further note that it is not necessary to center the variable **stype**, because the value of 0 is generally meaningful for a dummy-coded variable (in our case, it refers to the group *conventional high school*). In the model statement, we specify that the math test score (variable **math**) is predicted by the variable school type at level 2:

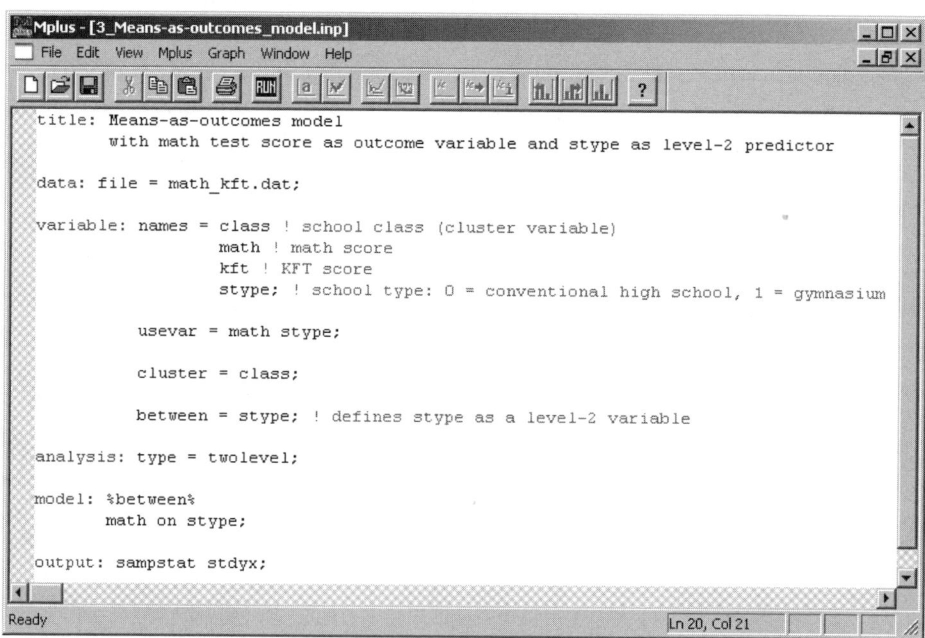

```
title: Means-as-outcomes model
       with math test score as outcome variable and stype as level-2 predictor

data: file = math_kft.dat;

variable: names = class ! school class (cluster variable)
                  math ! math score
                  kft ! KFT score
                  stype; ! school type: 0 = conventional high school, 1 = gymnasium

          usevar = math stype;

          cluster = class;

          between = stype; ! defines stype as a level-2 variable

analysis: type = twolevel;

model: %between%
       math on stype;

output: sampstat stdyx;
```

FIGURE 5.5. Mplus input file for the specification of the means-as-outcomes model for the outcome variable **math** and the level-2 predictor variable **stype**.

```
model:    %between%
          math on stype;
```

Because there is only a random intercept and otherwise no structure at level 1, no statement for the `within` level is required in this model. Mplus automatically estimates the residual variance for the `within` level. We again request that the fully standardized solution be output by including the `stdyx` keyword in the `output` command. In the output we obtained the following parameter estimates:

```
MODEL RESULTS

                                                           Two-Tailed
                    Estimate       S.E.  Est./S.E.           P-Value

Within Level

 Variances
    MATH              26.467      2.450     10.802             0.000

Between Level

 MATH        ON
    STYPE             10.641      1.188      8.957             0.000

 Intercepts
    MATH              10.003      0.441     22.671             0.000

 Residual Variances
    MATH               3.980      0.887      4.488             0.000
```

For level 1, Mplus estimates only the level-1 residual variance ($\hat{\sigma}^2_{r_{ij}}$ = 26.467). For level 2, the slope coefficient $\hat{\gamma}_{10}$ is estimated at 10.641. This means that the expected mean difference in math test scores between the group gymnasium and the group standard high school is 10.641. This value is statistically significant ($z = 8.957$, $p < .001$). We can conclude that the mean math score in group gymnasium is significantly larger than in group standard high school. Hence, the variable **stype** accounts for a significant portion of the differences seen in the mean math scores across school classes.

The intercept term of the level-2 regression is estimated to be $\hat{\gamma}_{00}$ = 10.223. This means that the expected average math test score in the group standard high school is 10.003 points. The estimated mean for group gymnasium can be calculated as the sum of the level-2 intercept plus the level-2 slope coefficient: $\hat{\gamma}_{00} + \hat{\gamma}_{01} = 10.003 + 10.641 = 20.644$.

The level-2 residual variance in this model is estimated at $\hat{\sigma}^2_{u_{0j}}$ = 3.98. This shows that the level-2 residual variance has decreased considerably through adding the predictor school type in comparison to the intercept-only model, in which the estimated (unconditional) level-2 variance was 20.853 (see Section 5.4.1). This again indicates that the level-2 predictor school type accounts for a considerable amount of difference in the math test scores between school classes. The graph in Figure 5.6 illustrates this finding. The circles and boxes indicate the (unweighted) means in each of the 34 school classes (the unweighted cluster means). The error bars indicate one standard deviation above and below each cluster mean, respectively. Circles indicate the cluster means in the standard high school group, whereas boxes indicate the cluster means for the group gymnasium. The solid horizontal line represents the estimated intercept coefficient $\hat{\gamma}_{00}$, that is, the estimated mean for the group high school based on the Mplus multilevel analysis. The dotted horizontal line shows the estimated mean for the group gymnasium (the sum of the estimated coefficients $\hat{\gamma}_{00} + \hat{\gamma}_{01} = 20.644$). The graph illustrates the large difference

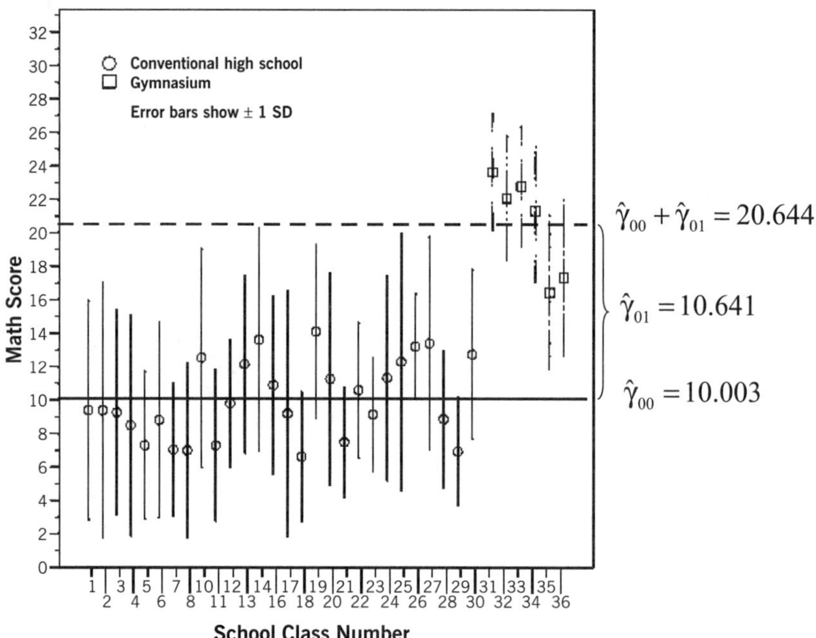

FIGURE 5.6. Error bar plot for illustrating the relationship between cluster-level math performance and school type. The figure also illustrates the meaning of the level-2 regression coefficients estimated in the means-as-outcomes model.

in the estimated means of 10.641 points in the math test performance between high school and gymnasium. This mean difference leads to the significant slope coefficient $\hat{\gamma}_{01}$ in the means-as-outcomes model and results in a large reduction of the level-2 variance after inclusion of the predictor school type.

The estimated proportion of explained variability can be found in the Mplus output under the standardized solution (`stdyx`). We can see that the standardized level-2 regression coefficient of 0.897 is very large. The R^2 value is estimated to be 0.805 by Mplus. This indicates that approximately 80.5% of the differences in the math test means between school classes are accounted for by differences between school types. The remaining variability in math scores across school classes remains unexplained in the model.

```
STANDARDIZED MODEL RESULTS

STDYX Standardization

                                                          Two-Tailed
                    Estimate       S.E.  Est./S.E.    P-Value

Within Level

 Variances
    MATH               1.000      0.000    999.000    999.000

Between Level

 MATH       ON
    STYPE              0.897      0.033     27.184      0.000

 Intercepts
    MATH               2.213      0.246      9.013      0.000

 Residual Variances
    MATH               0.195      0.059      3.287      0.001


R-SQUARE

Within Level

Between Level

    Observed                                          Two-Tailed
    Variable        Estimate       S.E.  Est./S.E.    P-Value

    MATH               0.805      0.059     13.592      0.000
```

5.5 RANDOM INTERCEPT AND SLOPE MODELS

So far, we have discussed multilevel regression models in which only the intercept (but not the slope) of a level-1 regression was allowed to vary across level-2 units. Often, however, it is also of interest to analyze possible variation in the level-1 slope coefficients across clusters—that is, to analyze models with random slopes.

Figure 5.7 demonstrates at a descriptive level that simple OLS regression analyses of math test scores on KFT by school class show regression lines that differ with regard to both the intercepts (the regression lines intersect with the *y*-axis at different levels) and slopes (the regression lines have different rates of change), even though at this point, it is not clear whether these differences are statistically significant. It seems interesting to examine variability in the slopes across level-2 units as well. Models in which both the intercepts and slopes of level-1 regressions can vary across level-2 units are often referred to as *random coefficient regression models* (Cohen et al., 2003; Luke, 2004). Models in which differences in the intercepts and

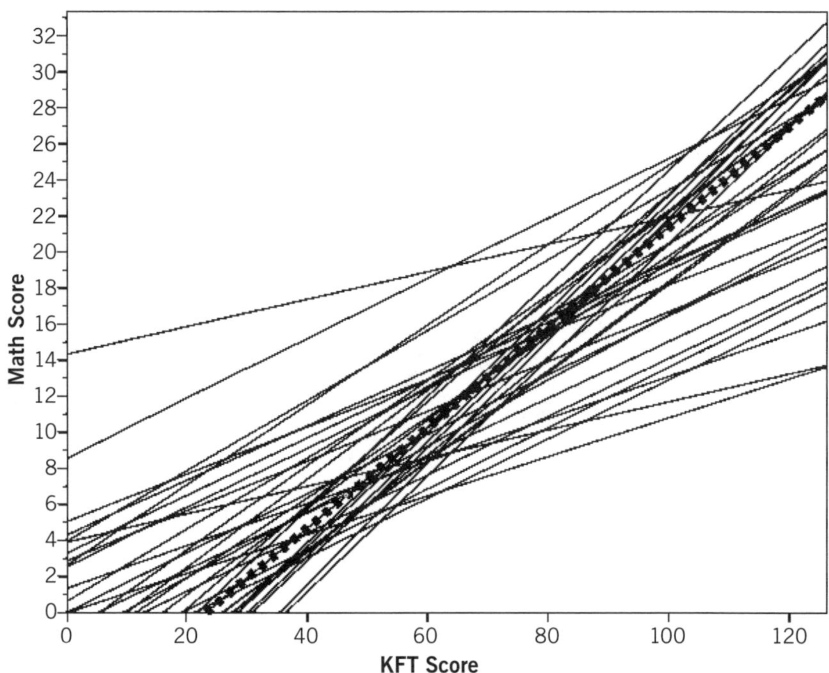

FIGURE 5.7. OLS regression of math score on KFT score by school class. Each line refers to the regression in one of the 34 school classes. The thick dotted line represents the (uncentered) average OLS regression line across all school classes.

slopes across clusters are explained by level-2 predictor variables have been referred to as *intercepts-and-slopes-as-outcomes models* by Luke (2004).

5.5.1 Random Coefficient Regression Analysis

In order to allow for differences in both the intercept and slope of a level-1 regression across clusters, the one-way random effects ANCOVA model (see Section 5.4.2) is extended as follows:

$$\text{Level 1:} \quad Y_{ij} = \beta_{0j} + \beta_{1j} \cdot X_{ij} + r_{ij}$$

$$\text{Level 2:} \quad \beta_{0j} = \gamma_{00} + u_{0j}$$
$$\beta_{1j} = \gamma_{10} + u_{1j}$$

The level-2 equations show that variability is now allowed for both the intercept and the slope, since residual terms are now included in both level-2 equations. Such a random coefficient regression model, without any level-2 predictors, is useful, for example, when a researcher is exclusively interested in level-1 predictor variables, but in addition wants to account for the effects of clustered data. If, in such a case, the researcher used a conventional OLS regression analysis without taking the clustering of observations into account, he or she would have to expect bias in the estimated standard errors of the regression coefficients and, consequently, inaccurate tests of significance and confidence intervals. In the random coefficient regression model, in contrast, the dependencies among observations are taken into account and the standard errors, test statistics, *p*-values, and confidence intervals are more accurate.

Note that the only difference between the one-way random effects ANCOVA model and the random coefficient regression model is that now there is also a residual term in the level-2 equation for the level-1 slope coefficient. For our example, this means that the regression lines for the regressions of math scores on KFT scores can now have a different intercept *and* a different slope in each school class, as illustrated in Figure 5.7. Mplus provides the following parameter estimates for the random coefficient regression model:

- At Level 1 (`WITHIN`):
  —The residual variance $\sigma^2_{r_{ij}}$
- At level 2 (`BETWEEN`):
  —The mean intercept γ_{00} across clusters
  —The variance $\sigma^2_{u_{0j}}$ in the intercepts across clusters

—The mean slope coefficient γ_{10} across clusters
—The variance $\sigma^2_{u_{1j}}$ in the slopes across clusters
—The covariance τ_{01} between intercept and slope (needs to be specifically requested in Mplus)

Figure 5.8 shows the specification of the random coefficient regression model for our example. The predictor variable KFT is again defined as a level-1 variable using the `within` subcommand and is entered into the model in grand-mean-centered form to allow for a more straightforward interpretation of the results (see Section 5.4.2):

```
within = kft;
centering = grandmean (kft);
```

At level 1, math test performance is predicted by KFT test performance. Intercept and slope of the level-1 regression are considered random coefficients that can vary across level-2 units. In order to analyze

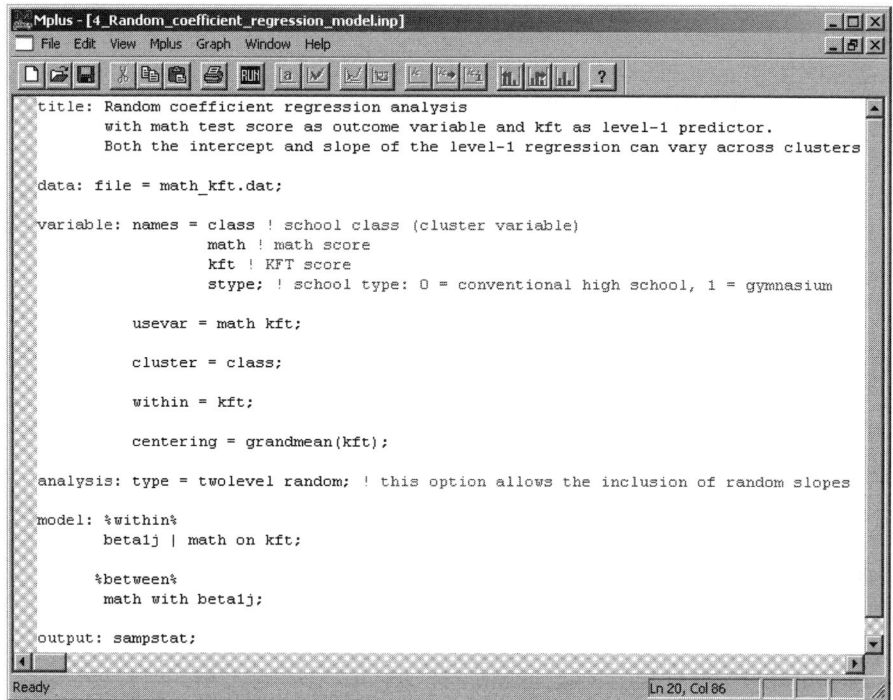


```
title: Random coefficient regression analysis
       with math test score as outcome variable and kft as level-1 predictor.
       Both the intercept and slope of the level-1 regression can vary across clusters

data: file = math_kft.dat;

variable: names = class ! school class (cluster variable)
                  math ! math score
                  kft ! KFT score
                  stype; ! school type: 0 = conventional high school, 1 = gymnasium

          usevar = math kft;

          cluster = class;

          within = kft;

          centering = grandmean(kft);

analysis: type = twolevel random; ! this option allows the inclusion of random slopes

model: %within%
       beta1j | math on kft;

      %between%
       math with beta1j;

output: sampstat;
```

FIGURE 5.8. Mplus input file for the specification of the random coefficient regression model for the outcome variable **math** and the level-1 predictor variable **kft**.

random slopes in Mplus, the `analysis` command has to be changed to `type = twolevel random`. Subsequently, the relevant random slope has to be defined in the `model` statement. Mplus treats a random slope as if it were a latent variable, such that the random slope automatically has a variance at level 2. In the syntax file, this is specified as follows:

```
model: %within%
       beta1j | math on kft;
```

In this specification, `beta1j` denotes the (arbitrary) label chosen for the random slope coefficient. This line of command means that the slope of the level-1 regression of math test scores on KFT scores is treated as a latent variable that can vary across level-2 units. At level 2, we include a command for the estimation of the covariance τ_{01} between the random intercept and the random slope, because this parameter is not estimated by default in Mplus:

```
%between%
math with beta1j;
```

In the Mplus output, we obtain the following parameter estimates (note that for `analysis: type = twolevel random`, Mplus currently does not provide standardized parameter estimates):

```
MODEL RESULTS

                                                          Two-Tailed
                    Estimate       S.E.  Est./S.E.         P-Value

Within Level

 Residual Variances
    MATH              14.862      1.091     13.627           0.000

Between Level

 MATH       WITH
    BETA1J             0.050      0.032      1.572           0.116

 Means
    MATH              12.195      0.456     26.771           0.000
    BETA1J             0.233      0.012     19.401           0.000

 Variances
    MATH               4.801      1.356      3.542           0.000
    BETA1J             0.001      0.001      0.672           0.502
```

The level-1 residual variance is estimated at $\hat{\sigma}^2_{r_{ij}} = 14.862$. This is a considerably smaller value than in the intercept-only model (20.853) in which the predictor of KFT was not included. For the `between` level, we first obtain estimates of the mean intercept ($\hat{\gamma}_{00} = 12.195$) and the mean slope ($\hat{\gamma}_{10} = 0.233$) across clusters. Therefore, the "average" regression equation across all school classes can be written as:

$$\text{Math} = 12.195 + 0.233 \cdot \text{kft\_centered} + \text{residual}$$

For comparison purposes, we again consider the OLS regression analysis that does not account for the cluster structure in the data:

$$\text{Math} = 12.533 + 0.279 \cdot \text{kft\_centered} + \text{residual}$$

We can see that the results are very similar. Nonetheless, the random coefficient regression model is the preferred method in this case because it takes the dependencies among observations into account that arise due to clustering, such that the standard errors are correctly estimated and potential differences in the intercepts and slopes across classes are permitted.

Variability in the intercepts and slopes can be analyzed by the variance estimates for the `between` level. Once again, we can see that there is variability in the intercepts ($\hat{\sigma}^2_{u_{0j}} = 4.801$). It can be seen that the variance in the slopes ($\sigma^2_{u_{1j}} = 0.001$) is rather small. Nonetheless, one should not rule out the possibility that differences in the slopes between school classes may be explained through level-2 predictor variables if such effects are theoretically predicted. Predicting differences in the slopes across clusters can be done by specifying so-called *intercepts-and-slopes-as-outcomes models*, which are described in the next section. Finally, the estimated covariance between intercept and slope is $\hat{\tau}_{01} = 0.050$, which is statistically nonsignificant ($z = 1.572$, $p = .116$).

5.5.2 Intercepts-and-Slopes-as-Outcomes Model

Often, researchers are interested in the influence of variables at both the individual level (micro variables, level-1 predictors) and the cluster level (macro variables, level-2 predictors). Thus far, we have discussed only models in which there were either no predictor variables at all (intercept-only model, Section 5.4.1) or there were predictor variables only at level 1 (one-way random effects ANCOVA, Section 5.4.2; random coefficient regression model, Section 5.5.1) or only at level 2 (means-as-outcomes model, Section 5.4.3). We now want to learn about a more general model in which both random intercepts and random slopes are specified and in which there are both level-1 and level-2 predictor variables at the same time. Following Luke (2004), we refer to this model as *intercepts-and-slopes-as-outcomes model*. As an example, we use the KFT score as a level-1 predictor and school type as a level-2 predictor of math performance. Below are the formal equations for an intercepts-and-slopes-as-outcomes model with one level-1 and one level-2 predictor:

$$\text{Level 1:} \quad Y_{ij} = \beta_{0j} + \beta_{1j} \cdot X_{ij} + r_{ij}$$

$$\text{Level 2:} \quad \beta_{0j} = \gamma_{00} + \gamma_{01} \cdot W_j + u_{0j}$$
$$\beta_{1j} = \gamma_{10} + \gamma_{11} \cdot W_j + u_{1j}$$

In our example, we again consider the regression of the individual math test scores on the individual KFT scores at level 1. The intercept β_{0j} and the slope β_{1j} in this regression are allowed to vary across school classes (as in the random coefficient regression model discussed in Section 5.5.1). The residual term r_{ij} refers to differences in the math test performance between students that cannot be explained through the level-1 predictor.

At level 2, the intercept and slope coefficients from level 1 are regressed on the level-2 predictor school type (W_j). (Note that it is also possible to include a predictor variable for only one of the two level-1 coefficients—e.g., only for the intercept term.) The parameter γ_{00} represents the expected intercept when the level-2 predictor takes on the value of zero. In our example, γ_{00} therefore indicates the intercept in the group that is coded zero, which is the conventional high school group.

The parameter γ_{01} gives the expected change in the intercept for a 1-unit change in the level-2 predictor variable. In our case, the level-2 predictor `stype` is dichotomous with values 0 = conventional high school and 1 = gymnasium. Therefore, γ_{01} gives us the expected difference in the intercepts between group gymnasium and group high school. If $\gamma_{01} = 0$, there would be no difference in the intercepts between school types. If $\gamma_{01} > 0$, the intercept in group gymnasium would be larger than the intercept in group high school. If $\gamma_{01} < 0$, the intercept in group high school would be larger than in group gymnasium.

The interpretation of the parameters γ_{10} and γ_{11} follows a similar principle, except that those coefficients refer to the slope of the regression line. The parameter γ_{10} gives the estimated slope in the group that is coded zero (high school). The parameter γ_{11} indicates the difference in the slopes (gymnasium minus high school). If $\gamma_{11} = 0$, there is no difference in the slopes between the school types. If $\gamma_{11} > 0$, the slope in group gymnasium is larger than the slope in group high school. If $\gamma_{11} < 0$, the slope in group high school is larger than the slope in group gymnasium.

The parameter γ_{11} is often of particular interest because this coefficient reflects a potential interaction effect between the level-1 predictor (here, KFT score) and the level-2 predictor (here, school type). This is often referred to as a *cross-level interaction*, and it means that the relationship between the level-1 predictor and the outcome varies depending upon the values of the level-2 predictor. In our example, this would mean that if a cross-level interaction is present, the regression of **math** on **kft** would be different for different school types. A significant γ_{11} coefficient would indicate a significant cross-level interaction.

The residual terms u_{0j} and u_{1j} reflect differences in the intercept and slope coefficients between school classes that cannot be explained through the level-2 predictor school type. In summary, we obtain the following estimates for the intercepts-and-slopes-as-outcomes model in Mplus:

- At level 1 (`WITHIN`):
  - —The residual variance $\sigma^2_{r_{ij}}$
- At level 2 (`BETWEEN`):
  - —The fixed intercept γ_{00} for the regression of the random intercept β_{0j} on W_j
  - —The fixed slope γ_{01} for the regression of the random intercept β_{0j} on W_j
  - —The fixed intercept γ_{10} for the regression of the random slope β_{1j} on W_j
  - —The fixed slope γ_{11} for the regression of the random slope β_{1j} on W_j
  - —The residual variance $\hat{\sigma}^2_{u_{0j}}$ for the random intercepts
  - —The residual variance $\sigma^2_{u_{1j}}$ for the random slopes
  - —The residual covariance τ_{01} between the random intercept and random slope (provided only upon request in Mplus)

The Mplus input file for the specification of the intercepts-and-slopes-as-outcomes model is shown in Figure 5.9. Note that the variable **kft** was again defined as a level-1 variable. Furthermore, the variable **kft**

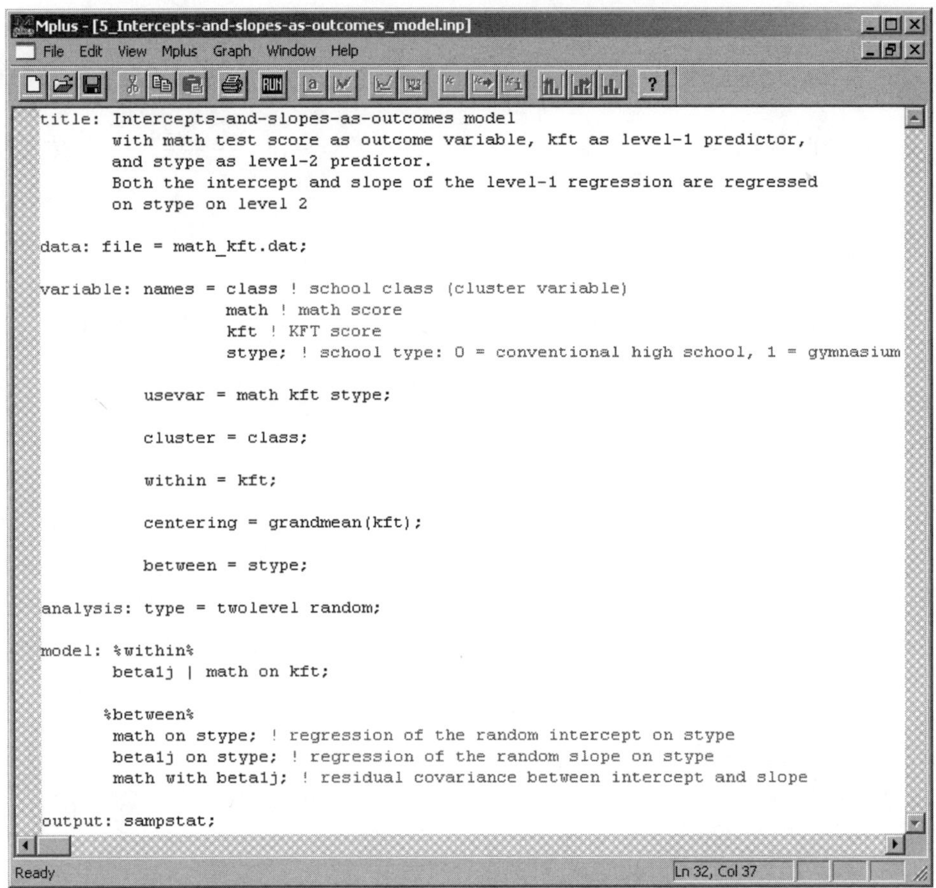

Mplus - [5_Intercepts-and-slopes-as-outcomes_model.inp]
File Edit View Mplus Graph Window Help
RUN
title: Intercepts-and-slopes-as-outcomes model
with math test score as outcome variable, kft as level-1 predictor,
and stype as level-2 predictor.
Both the intercept and slope of the level-1 regression are regressed
on stype on level 2
data: file = math_kft.dat;
variable: names = class ! school class (cluster variable)
math ! math score
kft ! KFT score
stype; ! school type: 0 = conventional high school, 1 = gymnasium
usevar = math kft stype;
cluster = class;
within = kft;
centering = grandmean(kft);
between = stype;
analysis: type = twolevel random;
model: %within%
beta1j | math on kft;
%between%
math on stype; ! regression of the random intercept on stype
beta1j on stype; ! regression of the random slope on stype
math with beta1j; ! residual covariance between intercept and slope
output: sampstat;
Ready
Ln 32, Col 37

FIGURE 5.9. Mplus input file for the specification of the intercepts-and-slopes-as-outcomes model for the outcome variable **math**, the level-1 predictor variable **kft**, and the level-2 predictor variable **stype**.

was centered at the grand mean to allow for a meaningful interpretation of the results. The variable **stype** was defined as a level-2 variable, so that this variable can only be used at level 2. In the model statement for level 1 (`%within%`) the slope for the regression of **math** on **kft** is again defined as a random effect (named `beta1j`):

```
model: %within%
       beta1j | math on kft;
```

At level 2 (`%between%`), the regression of the random intercept on the level-2 predictor **stype** is requested by the command

```
%between%
math on stype;
```

Subsequently, it is specified that the random slope `beta1j` is also regressed on school type:

```
beta1j on stype;
```

The command `math with beta1j;` is included to request estimation of the residual covariance τ_{01} between the random intercept and slope. All relevant residual variances are estimated by default. In the Mplus output we obtain the following parameter estimates for our example:

```
MODEL RESULTS

                                                          Two-Tailed
                    Estimate       S.E.  Est./S.E.       P-Value

Within Level

 Residual Variances
    MATH              14.608      1.070     13.658         0.000

Between Level

 BETA1J       ON
    STYPE             -0.058      0.018     -3.139         0.002

 MATH         ON
    STYPE              5.394      0.969      5.568         0.000

 MATH       WITH
    BETA1J             0.035      0.022      1.567         0.117

 Intercepts
    MATH              11.536      0.396     29.149         0.000
    BETA1J             0.226      0.013     17.258         0.000

 Residual Variances
    MATH               3.022      0.724      4.171         0.000
    BETA1J             0.001      0.001      0.509         0.611
```

The level-1 residual variance is estimated to be $\hat{\sigma}^2_{r_{ij}} = 14.608$. At level 2, Mplus first outputs the estimated regression coefficient $\hat{\gamma}_{11}$ for the regression of the random slope β_{1j} on school type. In the present example, the estimated coefficient $\hat{\gamma}_{11}$ gives the difference in the estimated mean regression slopes (gymnasium minus high school). The value of $\hat{\gamma}_{11}$ is –0.058 which is statistically significant at the .01 level (z = –3.139, p = .002). This means that the slope of the regression line in the regression of math score on KFT score differs significantly between group gymnasium and group high school.

This cross-level interaction effect is illustrated in Figure 5.10 in a scatter plot that shows the conventional OLS regression lines by school type. Figure 5.10 shows that the regression line for the group gymnasium (dotted line) has a flatter slope than the corresponding regression line for the group high school (solid line). According to the z-test for $\hat{\gamma}_{11}$, this difference in the slopes of the regression lines is statistically significant. The negative sign of $\hat{\gamma}_{11}$ shows us that the average slope coefficient is smaller (less steep) in group gymnasium than in group high school, because gymnasium is coded 1 and high school is coded 0. (A positive sign of $\hat{\gamma}_{11}$ would have indicated a steeper slope in group gymnasium than in group high school.)

Next, Mplus reports the estimated regression coefficient $\hat{\gamma}_{01}$ for the regression of the random intercept on school type. In our case, the coefficient $\hat{\gamma}_{01}$ gives the difference in the estimated mean intercepts (gymnasium

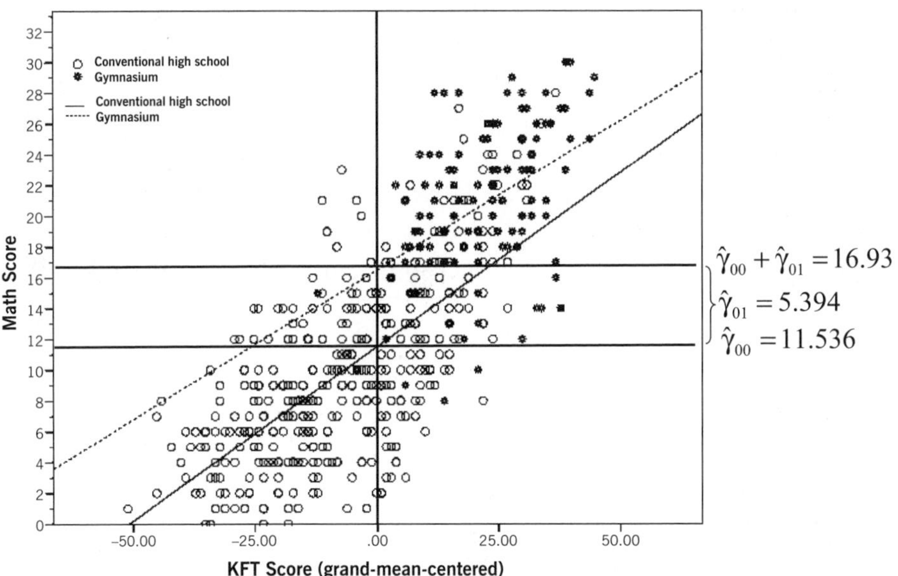

FIGURE 5.10. OLS regression of math score on grand-mean-centered KFT score by school class and illustration of the estimated level-2 regression intercept coefficients in the intercepts-and-slopes-as-outcomes model.

minus high school). The value of $\hat{\gamma}_{01}$ is 5.394, which is also statistically significant ($z = 5.568$, $p < .001$). In summary, the level-2 predictor school type explains differences in both the intercept and slope coefficients between school classes. Given that the predictor variable **kft** has been centered at the grand mean, the estimated value of 5.394 indicates that students with an average KFT score (relative to the entire sample) are expected to have 5.394 points more on the math test if they belong to the group gymnasium than if they belong to the group high school. The difference in the intercepts is also illustrated in Figure 5.10. The regression lines for the two school types intersect the zero point of the grand-mean-centered **kft** variable at different levels (the dotted line for the gymnasium cuts the zero point above the solid line of the high school group).

Under `Intercepts` we first obtain the estimated intercept, $\hat{\gamma}_{00}$, for the regression of the random intercept, β_{0j}, on school type ($\hat{\gamma}_{00} = 11.536$). This value tells us that the estimated intercept for the regression of math performance on KFT score in group high school is 11.536 (cf. Figure 5.10). Therefore, for high school students with an average KFT value, a math test score of 11.536 is expected. The sum of the coefficients $\hat{\gamma}_{00}$ + $\hat{\gamma}_{01}$ equals the expected intercept for students in the group gymnasium: 11.536 + 5.394 = 16.93. Consequently, for students in the gymnasium with an average KFT score, a math test score of 16.93 is expected.

In addition, the estimated intercept $\hat{\gamma}_{10}$ for the regression of the random slope, β_{1j}, on school type is estimated ($\hat{\gamma}_{10} = 0.226$). This value gives the estimated slope of the regression line for the regression of the math score on the KFT score in group high school ($\hat{\gamma}_{10}$; this coefficient is approximately equal to the slope of the solid OLS regression line in Figure 5.10). Therefore, we can now also calculate the expected slope in group gymnasium, which is equal to the sum of $\hat{\gamma}_{10} + \hat{\gamma}_{11} = 0.226 + (-0.058) = 0.168$. This shows that the slope of the regression line is flatter for students in the group gymnasium than in the group high school. At level 2, Mplus additionally estimated the residual variances for the intercept ($\hat{\sigma}^2_{u_{0j}} = 3.022$) and the slope ($\hat{\sigma}^2_{u_{1j}} = 0.001$) as well as the residual covariance between intercept and slope ($\hat{\tau}_{01} = 0.035$).

Note that Mplus can also be used to analyze multilevel regression models with more than one level-1 and/or more than one level-2 predictor. In such extended models, some or all intercepts and slopes can be specified as random coefficients. For predictors for which the slopes are not supposed to be random coefficients, a separate `on` statement needs to be included in the `model` command, in which the | sign as well as the name of the random slope is omitted. Consider the following example:

```
model: %within%
       beta1J | y on x1;
       y on x2;
```

In this example, only the slope of the regression of the variable Y on X_1 (`beta1J | y on x1;`) would be a random slope, whereas the slope of the regression of Y on X_2 (`y on x2;`) would be fixed. The slope of the regression of Y on X_2 is a constant (fixed) effect in this example that does not vary between clusters.

A particular strength of Mplus is that not only univariate multilevel regression models (models with a single dependent variable), as discussed in this book, can be analyzed, but also multivariate regression models, in which multiple dependent variables are considered at the same time. This means that in case of a multilevel data structure, researchers can also analyze path analyses, CFAs, SEMs (see Chapter 3), LGCMs (see Section 4.5), and latent class models (see Chapter 6) as two-level models using the option `analysis: type = twolevel`. The analysis of more complex multivariate multilevel models in Mplus is discussed in Geiser et al. (2012).

6

Latent Class Analysis

6.1 INTRODUCTION TO LATENT CLASS ANALYSIS

Latent class analysis (LCA) or latent structure analysis (Goodman, 1974; Lazarsfeld & Henry, 1968) is a statistical procedure that can be used to classify individuals into homogeneous subgroups (latent classes, latent types). The starting points for the classification are the observed response patterns of individuals across a set of categorical (nominal or ordinal) test or questionnaire items (e.g., intelligence test items solved/not solved; symptoms present vs. absent; questionnaire items measured on a Likert scale). In an LCA, the relationships between the items are explained by the presence of a priori unknown subpopulations (the latent classes). In other words, individual differences in observed item response patterns are explained by differences in latent class membership, where each class shows a characteristic, class-specific response profile.

As an example, consider individuals who solve only certain item types for measuring spatial ability with a high probability, but not others. If different items can be solved with different solution strategies, this might explain these differences. Hence, individuals showing this specific response profile could be assigned to a latent class that represents the specific solution strategy used by these individuals. Similarly, individuals who guess and thus give random answers in a test may form a "guessing class" in an LCA. In the field of clinical psychology, patients with distinct symptom patterns could be assigned to different latent classes representing different types of disorders or diseases. As an example from personality research, individuals could also be classified according to their personality type. The main goals of LCA are summarized in Box 6.1.

BOX 6.1. *Important Goals of an LCA*

- Determine the number of classes necessary to sufficiently explain differences in the observed response patterns and summarize the data in a substantively meaningful way (exploratory LCA). The model should be parsimonious, that is, use as few latent classes as possible to explain the data.
- Examine what the classes are like: How can the classes be interpreted substantively, and in which way do they differ from one another?
- Test hypotheses about typological structures (confirmatory LCA).
- Evaluate the reliability of the classification based on a specific LCA solution.
- Determine the most likely latent class membership of one or more individuals for diagnostic purposes.
- Analyze relationships between class membership and external variables (e.g., age, sex, personality variables, intelligence).

The above examples point to similarities between LCA and exploratory factor analysis (EFA). Both approaches can be used for data reduction. In EFA, the relationships between continuous variables are "explained" by a smaller number of continuous latent variables (factors). In classical LCA, the relationships between categorical variables are "explained" by membership in one of several latent classes. One of the main differences between LCA and EFA is that EFA uses continuous latent variables ("factors") and metrical indicators, whereas LCA uses one categorical latent variable (a latent class variable with several categories = latent classes) to explain the relationships between categorical indicators.

LCA cannot only be used in an exploratory way, but also as a confirmatory analysis technique. For example, LCA allows us to test theories about typological differences between individuals (e.g., differences in attachment style, personality types, solution strategies) by assuming a specific number of classes and/or imposing parameter restrictions (e.g., with regard to the properties or sizes of the classes). Using model tests and/or model comparisons, we can test whether the hypothesized typological model fits the observed data. This is similar to using model tests in CFA and SEMs (see Chapter 3).

For simplicity, we consider only the analysis of dichotomous variables using exploratory LCA in this book. The procedure can be easily generalized to polytomous variables and analyses that are more confirmatory in nature. For a dichotomous variable, the LCA model for a single item can be written as follows (e.g., see Collins & Lanza, 2010; Rost, 2004):

$$p(X_{vi} = 1) = \sum_{g=1}^{G} \pi_g \, \pi_{ig}$$

In this equation, $p(X_{vi} = 1)$ denotes the unconditional probability that a randomly selected individual v obtained a score of $X = 1$ on item i, $i = 1, \ldots, I$ (e.g., correctly solved a test item or endorsed a questionnaire item). The class size parameter π_g indicates the unconditional probability of belonging to latent class g ($g = 1, \ldots, G$). The model assumes that each individual belongs to one and only one latent class. Therefore, the sum of all class-size parameters equals 1:

$$\sum_{g=1}^{G} \pi_g = 1$$

The parameter π_{ig} indicates the conditional probability of a score of 1 on item i given membership in class g:

$$\pi_{ig} = p(X_{vi} = 1 | G = g)$$

This probability is often referred to as a *conditional response* or *conditional solution probability*. The LCA model therefore states that an individual's response probability for item i depends on both the latent class prevalences and the class-specific response probabilities of the item. Box 6.2 gives an overview of the parameters that are estimated in an LCA model.

Note that the number of classes that is necessary to appropriately account for the observed response patterns is not a model parameter to be estimated. Similarly to EFA, the number of classes in exploratory LCA is usually determined by means of certain fit criteria and model comparisons. Models with different numbers of classes are fit to the same data set. Using statistical indices, the fit of the models is compared. The model with the best fit is selected, if this solution is also proper and easily interpretable in terms of the estimated parameters. Criteria for assessing model fit and for statistical model comparisons are discussed in Section 6.3.

More detailed descriptions of LCA as well as extensions of the basic model can be found in Clogg (1995), Collins and Lanza (2010), Hagenaars

BOX 6.2. *Summary of Parameters Estimated in an LCA Model for Dichotomous Variables*

- π_g = class size or class proportion parameter. $G - 1$ class size parameters π_g are estimated. The size of the last class is not an independent model parameter because of the assumption that $\sum_{g=1}^{G} \pi_g = 1$.
- π_{ig} = conditional response probabilities for item i in class g. For dichotomous indicators, $G \cdot I$ conditional response probabilities π_{ig} are estimated (the corresponding probability for the second category of each item is given by $1 - \pi_{ig}$).
- Mplus also outputs all parameters of the LCA model in an equivalent logistic threshold parameterization (e.g., see Hagenaars, 1993). The conversion of the logistic threshold parameters into probabilities is discussed in Chapter 13 of the *Mplus User's Guide* (Muthén & Muthén, 1998–2007).

(1993), Hagenaars and McCutcheon (2002), Langeheine and Rost (1988), McCutcheon (1987), Rost and Langeheine (1997), as well as on the homepage of John Uebersax (*http://www.john-uebersax.com/stat/soft.htm*). The use of LCA for comparisons of multiple groups (multigroup LCA) is discussed in Eid, Langeheine, and Diener (2003) in the context of cross-cultural research. An applied example of a multigroup LCA, including sample Mplus syntax, can be found in Geiser, Lehmann, and Eid (2006).

6.2 SPECIFICATION OF LCA MODELS IN Mplus

The specification of LCA models in Mplus requires the module for the analysis of mixture distribution models (option `analysis: type = mixture`). Either the mixture or the combination add-on upgrades are needed to analyze LCA models in Mplus in addition to the Mplus base version. Box 6.3 introduces the data example used in this chapter.

Figure 6.1 shows the Mplus input file for an LCA model with three latent classes. (My rationale for preferring a three-class solution will become clear in later sections when we discuss model fit.) The data set used here has the name **computergames.dat**. It contains the subject ID number (variable `id`) as well as the responses on the eight computer game questionnaire items (variable names: `c1–c8`). Using the command `variable: auxiliary = id;` we tell Mplus that the variable `id`

BOX 6.3. *Data Example Used in This Chapter*

We illustrate the analysis of an LCA in Mplus using the data set **computer-games.dat**. This data set contains the item responses of N = 861 German children, who answered a questionnaire on their computer game preferences. In the following, an English translation of this questionnaire is shown:

How often do you play the following computer games?		
	Never or rarely	Often or very often
1. Adventure games		
2. Action games		
3. Sport games		
4. Fantasy role-playing games		
5. Logic games		
6. Skill-training games		
7. Simulation games		
8. Driving simulator games		

Quaiser-Pohl, Geiser, and Lehmann (2006) applied LCA to the dichotomous item responses to find out whether different types of computer game players could be identified based on the eight computer game items above. More specifically, they wanted to find out how many distinct latent classes would emerge and how each latent class would be interpreted. In addition, they were interested in finding out how reliably children could be classified into distinct computer game player types. For information on additional research questions examined in this study, see Quaiser-Pohl et al. (2006).

is used as an auxiliary variable that does not play a role in the statistical analysis as such, but that should still be included in a newly generated data set containing the individual class assignment probabilities produced by Mplus on request (see description of the `savedata` command on p. 239). Without the auxiliary command, the subject ID would not be saved to the new data set. This could be a disadvantage when, for example, LCA is used for individual diagnostic purposes. Specific individuals in the data set could no longer be linked to the estimated class membership information if there is no ID variable. The command `categorical`

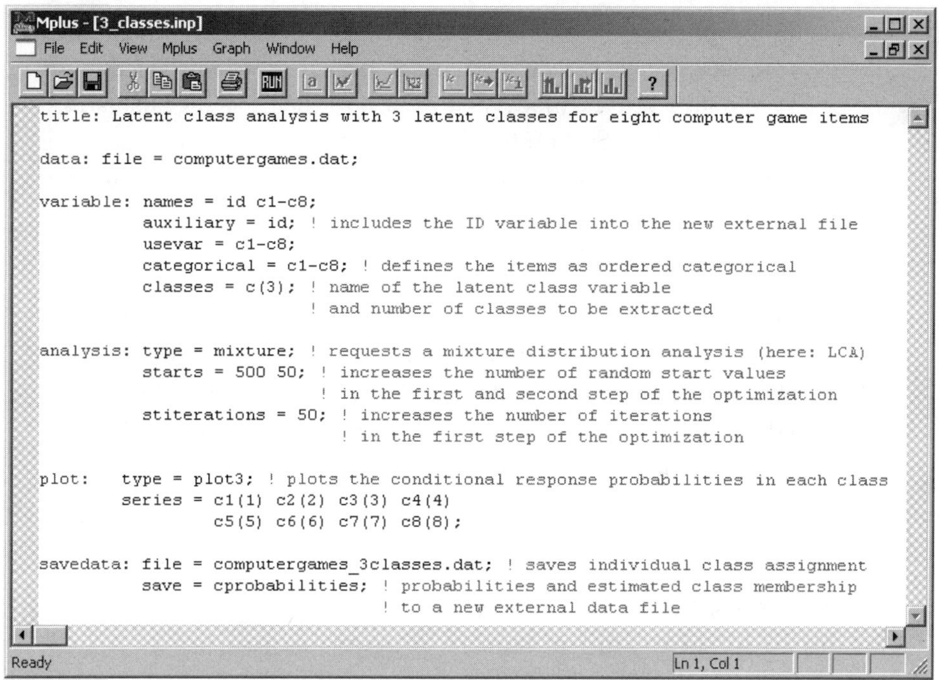

```
title: Latent class analysis with 3 latent classes for eight computer game items

data: file = computergames.dat;

variable: names = id c1-c8;
          auxiliary = id; ! includes the ID variable into the new external file
          usevar = c1-c8;
          categorical = c1-c8; ! defines the items as ordered categorical
          classes = c(3); ! name of the latent class variable
                          ! and number of classes to be extracted

analysis: type = mixture; ! requests a mixture distribution analysis (here: LCA)
          starts = 500 50; ! increases the number of random start values
                           ! in the first and second step of the optimization
          stiterations = 50; ! increases the number of iterations
                             ! in the first step of the optimization

plot:   type = plot3; ! plots the conditional response probabilities in each class
        series = c1(1) c2(2) c3(3) c4(4)
                 c5(5) c6(6) c7(7) c8(8);

savedata: file = computergames_3classes.dat; ! saves individual class assignment
          save = cprobabilities; ! probabilities and estimated class membership
                                 ! to a new external data file
```

FIGURE 6.1. Mplus input file for the specification of an LCA with three classes for the eight computer game items.

= `c1-c8;` defines the eight computer game items as (ordered) categorical (here, dichotomous). The same command would also be used if ordered categorical items with more than two categories (ordered polytomous items) were used. (For unordered categorical [nominal] variables, the command `nominal =` would be used.) Using the command `classes = c(3);` we specify that the latent categorical (or latent class) variable has the name `c` and three categories (i.e., three latent classes). This means that a three-class solution will be extracted. Using the command `analysis: type = mixture;` we tell Mplus that a mixture distribution analysis (here LCA) is to be carried out. *Mixture distribution* means that the population of students is assumed to consist of distinct subgroups (latent classes reflecting distinct computer game types). The goal of LCA is to "unmix" the population into homogeneous subgroups.

Similarly to CFA and SEMs, the parameter estimates as well as model fit statistics (see Section 6.3) for an LCA are determined using an iterative estimation procedure that is based on the maximum likelihood (ML) estimation method by default in Mplus. The goal is to maximize the likelihood function to find the solution with the largest possible log likelihood value. The *log likelihood value* is a measure of the probability of the observed data given the model and is used as the basis for calculating various fit statistics (see Section 6.3).

One complication for iterative estimation procedures that is particularly relevant to LCA (and mixture distribution analyses in general) is that, often, a single set of parameter starting values will not allow us to find the solution with the best possible log likelihood value. The consequence may be that the model estimation terminates at a so-called *local likelihood maximum*, which is often associated with inaccurate parameter estimates. Such a local solution can, for example, be associated with incorrect fit statistics and biased parameter estimates (e.g., see Uebersax, 2000). Local solutions should therefore be avoided (cf. Box 6.4).

If only a few sets of starting values are tried in an LCA, there is a relatively high chance of encountering a local likelihood maximum. Moreover, studies indicate that local maxima occur frequently in empirical applications, even if only four or five classes are extracted (Uebersax, 2000). The use of a sufficient number of random sets of starting values increases the chances that an LCA program will find the optimal solution with the highest log likelihood value. In fact, for relatively simple, clearly identified LCA models with few classes, the use of a large number of start values usually guarantees that the true maximum will be found.

The Mplus default setting is that 10 sets of random starting values are generated by the program and used in the model estimation. This relatively small number of start value sets can be insufficient in practice, especially for more complex models when more than two or three latent classes are extracted. To be on the safe side, we encourage users to specify a larger number of starting value sets. A relatively safe setting is to request at least 500 sets of start values in the first step of the optimization (for complex models, an even larger number may be necessary). The command `analysis: starts =` can be used to increase the number of starting values in Mplus. The specification `starts = 500 50;` causes Mplus to use 500 sets of start values in the first step of the optimization (instead of only 10) and to pick the 50 starting value sets that show the largest log likelihood values in the first step for the second step of the optimization process, until a convergence criterion (in Mplus the default is a parameter change of less than 0.000001) is reached. The solution with the highest log likelihood value is then output by Mplus as the final solution.

In addition to increasing the number of start value sets, it is also recommended to choose a sufficient number of iterations for the initial stage of the optimization (Uebersax, 2000). In Mplus, the command `analysis: stiterations` = can be used to increase the number of iterations in the first step of the optimization (the Mplus default is only 10 iterations in the first step). The command `stiterations = 50;` increases the number of initial stage iterations from the default of 10 to 50.

In general, if the best log likelihood value was not found by Mplus for at least two sets of starting values, Mplus issues a warning message. The model should be rerun with a larger number of starting values in this case, before any parameter estimates are interpreted. If the best log likelihood value cannot be replicated by at least one other starting value set, even for a very large number of starting value sets (say, 2,000), the results should be interpreted with great caution. The model may not be identified in this case or it may not be well defined for the data at hand (e.g., due to a too-small sample). Box 6.4 summarizes the most important strategies for avoiding local maxima in an LCA.

The `plot` option is useful to visualize the estimated conditional response probabilities in different classes. In LCA this is often done by means of a line graph, in which the items are shown on the *x*-axis and the conditional response probabilities are shown on the *y*-axis. Different classes are represented by separate lines. In this way, one obtains a profile of the items in each class that often allows for an easier interpretation of the classes. Such a diagram can be obtained in Mplus using the option `plot: type = plot3;`. Using the `series` option, it is specified in which order the items will be shown on the *x*-axis:

```
series = c1 (1) c2 (2) c3 (3) c4 (4) c5 (5) c6 (6)
c7 (7) c8 (8);
```

The resulting plot is shown below, where we discuss the Mplus output for an LCA.

Based on the estimated LCA model parameters, the probability with which each individual belongs to each of the extracted classes can be estimated. On the basis of these individual class assignment probabilities, one can estimate the most likely class membership for each individual for diagnostic purposes. An individual is assigned to the class for which his or her assignment probability is highest. In Mplus, the `savedata` command can be used to save individual class assignment probabilities and the most likely latent class membership information to an external file. In order to save these values to an external file, we specify:

```
savedata: file = computergames_3classes.dat;
save = cprobabilities;
```

BOX 6.4. *Avoiding Local Likelihood Maxima in LCA*

Local likelihood maxima are frequently encountered in practical applications of LCA. Following the recommendations below can help to avoid local solutions (see also Uebersax, 2000):

- *Use a sufficient number of different start values.* In the estimation of LCA models with more than two classes, a sufficient number of random sets of start values should be used (say, at least 500 in the first and the best 50 in the second step of the optimization; with complex models 1,000/100 or more should be used) → `analysis: starts = 500 50;` or `starts = 1000 100;`
- *Use a sufficient number of initial stage iterations.* It is also recommended to choose a larger number of initial stage iterations than Mplus uses as the default (e.g., `analysis: stiterations = 50;`).
- *Check the replicability of the best log likelihood value.* Users of LCA should check that the largest (best) log likelihood value was the result of at least two different sets of start values. This can easily be checked in the Mplus output (see discussion in the text).
- *Prefer models with fewer latent classes.* If possible, users should avoid the extraction of a large number of latent classes, because local maxima are more likely to occur in models with more classes as compared to models with fewer classes. Already with four or more classes, local maxima tend to be more frequently observed.
- *Use a tight convergence criterion.* The Mplus criterion for convergence is 0.000001. If in doubt, one should choose the smaller convergence criterion to avoid local maxima (e.g., `analysis: convergence = 0.0000001;`).
- *Avoid solutions that contain many boundary parameter estimates.* If many conditional response probabilities are estimated to exactly 0 or 1 in a solution (so-called *boundary estimates*; cf. Box 6.5), this can be a sign of an invalid solution and/or indicate that too many classes were extracted.
- *Replicate the model parameter estimates in one or more additional LCA programs.* It can be reassuring to compare the estimates across different software programs, especially when analyzing complex models with many classes. Ideally, the best log likelihood value should be found by all programs.
- *Replicate the model with additional data.* Another sign of the validity of a class solution is if this solution can be replicated with a fresh data set.

Through this command, Mplus saves a new file with the name **computergames_3classes.dat** to the same directory that also contains the input file. The new file contains the eight computer game variables, the ID variable `id` (because we defined this variable as an auxiliary variable earlier under the variable command), the individual class assignment probabilities (new variables named `CPROB1`, `CPROB2`, and `CPROB3` to be generated by Mplus in the analysis), and the estimated class membership (new variable `C` to be generated by Mplus).

For an LCA, Mplus by default estimates the parameters using ML estimation with robust standard errors. Conventional ML standard errors can be requested using the command `analysis: estimator = ml;`.

In the following, the most important part of the Mplus output for the three-class solution of the computer game example is shown. First of all, we obtain the unconditional item response probabilities for each category in the total sample. It can be seen that overall, the category never/rarely was chosen more frequently in all items. Of interest to us is whether the

BOX 6.5. *Boundary Parameter Estimates*

Boundary parameter estimates are estimates at the border of the theoretically admissible parameter space. For probabilities (such as the π_{ig} parameters in LCA) the admissible range lies between 0 and 1 (which corresponds to values of +15 and –15 in the Mplus threshold parameterization, respectively). Boundary estimates are more likely to occur when the data are sparse (e.g., due to the use of many items and/or a small sample), as well as in solutions with many classes. Boundary estimates are often a sign that too many classes were extracted, but can also sometimes be a symptom of a local maximum or an identification problem. For this reason, boundary solutions should be interpreted with caution. In Mplus, the occurrence of a boundary solution is indicated through the following warning message:

```
IN THE OPTIMIZATION, ONE OR MORE LOGIT THRESHOLDS APPROACHED AND
WERE SET AT THE EXTREME VALUES.  EXTREME VALUES ARE -15.000
AND 15.000.
     THE FOLLOWING THRESHOLDS WERE SET AT THESE VALUES:
     * THRESHOLD 1 OF CLASS INDICATOR C1 FOR CLASS 2 AT ITERATION 35
     * THRESHOLD 1 OF CLASS INDICATOR C4 FOR CLASS 2 AT ITERATION 38
     * THRESHOLD 1 OF CLASS INDICATOR C2 FOR CLASS 2 AT ITERATION 58
     * THRESHOLD 1 OF CLASS INDICATOR C3 FOR CLASS 3 AT ITERATION 66
     * THRESHOLD 1 OF CLASS INDICATOR C8 FOR CLASS 3 AT ITERATION 69
```

This message indicates that in the estimation process, one or more conditional response probabilities were estimated and set to boundary values of 0 or 1 (which corresponds to threshold values of +15 and –15 in Mplus).

conditional response probabilities show a different pattern in subgroups, that is, in the three extracted latent classes.

```
SUMMARY OF CATEGORICAL DATA PROPORTIONS

    C1
      Category 1     0.822
      Category 2     0.178
    C2
      Category 1     0.727
      Category 2     0.273
    C3
      Category 1     0.746
      Category 2     0.254
    C4
      Category 1     0.816
      Category 2     0.184
    C5
      Category 1     0.739
      Category 2     0.261
    C6
      Category 1     0.746
      Category 2     0.254
    C7
      Category 1     0.649
      Category 2     0.351
    C8
      Category 1     0.674
      Category 2     0.326
```

Next is a summary of the log likelihood values for the 50 sets of start values that showed the largest log likelihood values after the initial step of the optimization (ordered from the best to the worst log likelihood values), together with the associated seeds (*seed* = random start number for generating start values) and the number of the corresponding starting value set. It can be seen that the same log likelihood value of –3463.814 was found for each of the 50 best sets of start values from the first step. This is a good sign because it shows that the solution is replicable across a variety of different start values. This indicates that local maxima are apparently not an issue for this solution. Such a result is typical for well-defined models with a relatively small number of classes.

```
RANDOM STARTS RESULTS RANKED FROM THE BEST TO THE
WORST LOGLIKELIHOOD VALUES

Final stage loglikelihood values at local maxima,
seeds, and initial stage start numbers:
```

```
-3463.814  605358        321
-3463.814  57226         208
-3463.814  714455        476
-3463.814  965639        463
-3463.814  798821        423
-3463.814  85734         411
-3463.814  926797        406
-3463.814  973369        202
-3463.814  7959          256
-3463.814  987090        70
-3463.814  137305        379
-3463.814  732596        320
-3463.814  900268        327
-3463.814  319575        499
-3463.814  576596        99
-3463.814  772131        407
-3463.814  100874        108
-3463.814  377504        294
-3463.814  694303        282
-3463.814  741888        138
-3463.814  582296        452
-3463.814  344422        296
-3463.814  340112        126
-3463.814  937225        394
-3463.814  848890        95
-3463.814  695155        150
-3463.814  455617        242
-3463.814  168762        200
-3463.814  846194        93
-3463.814  347515        24
-3463.814  970689        266
-3463.814  21345         199
-3463.814  652266        490
-3463.814  971853        402
-3463.814  81117         305
-3463.814  417035        149
-3463.814  570908        98
-3463.814  655497        376
-3463.814  637345        19
-3463.814  736574        414
-3463.814  923437        398
-3463.814  782821        272
-3463.814  315029        471
-3463.814  850840        232
-3463.814  972873        157
-3463.814  860102        495
-3463.814  793035        187
-3463.814  414828        322
-3463.814  483369        270
-3463.814  529496        343
```

By default Mplus informs the user of the issue of local maxima with the following message, which is always printed under the list of log likelihood values:

```
WARNING: WHEN ESTIMATING A MODEL WITH MORE THAN TWO CLASSES,
IT MAY BE NECESSARY TO INCREASE THE NUMBER OF RANDOM STARTS
USING THE STARTS OPTION TO AVOID LOCAL MAXIMA.
```

In the present example, this message can be ignored, because we have clearly used a sufficient number of random starts for the three-class model, as seen above.

In models with more latent classes, one often finds that there are slight differences among the log likelihood values in the Mplus list. In this case, it is reassuring when the best log likelihood value was found for at least two different sets of start values. If this is not the case, Mplus issues the following warning message:

```
WARNING:  THE BEST LOGLIKELIHOOD VALUE WAS NOT REPLICATED.
THE SOLUTION MAY NOT BE TRUSTWORTHY DUE TO LOCAL MAXIMA.
INCREASE THE NUMBER OF RANDOM STARTS.
```

As recommended by Mplus, in this case one should increase the number of random starts and/or the number of iterations in the first step of the optimization (see above) until the best log likelihood value is reliably identified by multiple sets of start values. If the best log likelihood value cannot be replicated even with an increased number of start values, this may indicate that the model is not well defined for the data. Subsequently, only the following message (and no additional error messages) should appear:

```
THE MODEL ESTIMATION TERMINATED NORMALLY
```

If the model converged properly, the best log likelihood value for the final solution is output once again under `MODEL FIT INFORMATION`:

```
MODEL FIT INFORMATION

Loglikelihood

          H0 Value                                -3463.814
```

This log likelihood value is identical to the best value that appears on the very top of the previous listing of log likelihood values for different sets

BOX 6.6. *Excursion* `optseed` *Option*

The listing of the log likelihood values in Mplus can also be useful for replicating the solution with the best log likelihood value in subsequent analyses steps. This allows the user to reproduce the best solution without having to generate a large number of start value sets again, which can be time-consuming for complex models. This approach can be useful, for example, when one wants to request additional output for a solution that has not been requested initially. Using the so-called `optseed` option in Mplus, one can replicate a specific solution on the basis of the specific seed number associated with this solution. In the current example, we could specify the following in the input:

```
analysis: optseed = 605358;
```

where the number 605358 refers to the seed number that pertains to the starting value set with the number 321, which is the starting value set that is ranked first in the list of log likelihood values:

```
RANDOM STARTS RESULTS RANKED FROM THE BEST TO THE WORST
LOGLIKELIHOOD VALUES

Final stage loglikelihood values at local maxima, seeds,
and initial stage start numbers:

           -3463.814  605358           321
```

This starting value set is among those sets that produced the best log likelihood value of –3463.814. Note that in this example one could have chosen any one of the 50 seed numbers, because all 50 start value sets resulted in the same best log likelihood value. This, however, is not always the case, especially for models with more classes. Using the `optseed` command as specified above, Mplus will replicate the exact same solution that has been found based on the seed 605358, although this should be verified in the subsequent output file.

of start values. Following are different model fit statistics, which are discussed in detail in Section 6.3:

```
Information Criteria

         Number of Free Parameters                  26
         Akaike (AIC)                         6979.628
         Bayesian (BIC)                       7103.338
```

```
          Sample-Size Adjusted BIC              7020.769
            (n* = (n + 2) / 24)

Chi-Square Test of Model Fit for the Binary and
Ordered Categorical
(Ordinal) Outcomes

          Pearson Chi-Square

          Value                                  386.883
          Degrees of Freedom                         229
          P-Value                                 0.0000

          Likelihood Ratio Chi-Square

          Value                                  340.605
          Degrees of Freedom                         229
          P-Value                                 0.0000
```

Next, Mplus provides information about the estimated sizes of the latent classes in the model. The following table contains the class sizes in terms of the estimated $\hat{\pi}_g$ parameters:

```
FINAL CLASS COUNTS AND PROPORTIONS FOR THE LATENT
CLASSES BASED ON THE ESTIMATED MODEL

    Latent
   Classes

       1        149.48776          0.17362
       2        327.71918          0.38063
       3        383.79305          0.44575
```

According to these estimates, Class 3 is the largest class with approximately 44.6% ($\hat{\pi}_3$ = .44575). Relative to our sample, this corresponds to approximately N = 384 participants. Class 2 has a size of approximately 38.1% ($\hat{\pi}_2$ = .38063, approximately N = 328 participants). Class 1 is the smallest class with approximately 17.4% ($\hat{\pi}_1$ = .17362, approximately N = 150). Note that the order of the classes is arbitrary. This means, for example, that if we run the same three-class solution on the same data but different computers, we might obtain solutions that differ with regard to the order of the classes. However, the solution would still show the same log likelihood value, and the parameter estimates would not be different.

Mplus also outputs class size estimates based on the estimated posterior probabilities. In this example, these estimates are close to identical to the class proportions based on the estimated model:

```
FINAL CLASS COUNTS AND PROPORTIONS FOR THE LATENT
CLASS PATTERNS BASED ON ESTIMATED POSTERIOR
PROBABILITIES

    Latent
   Classes

       1        149.48771          0.17362
       2        327.71923          0.38063
       3        383.79307          0.44575
```

The entropy statistic is a summary measure for the quality of the classification. Values close to 1 indicate high classification accuracy, whereas values close to 0 indicate low classification certainty.

```
CLASSIFICATION QUALITY

     Entropy                         0.731
```

Somewhat more informative are the average class assignment probabilities for individuals that were assigned to a specific class. For each person, LCA allows estimating the probability with which each individual belongs to each of the three extracted classes. As mentioned above, for diagnostic (or other) purposes, a person can be assigned to the class for which he or she has the greatest probability according to his or her observed response pattern. Mplus first outputs the class sizes that are based on this kind of manifest classification:

```
CLASSIFICATION OF INDIVIDUALS BASED ON THEIR MOST
LIKELY LATENT CLASS MEMBERSHIP

Class Counts and Proportions

    Latent
   Classes

       1              152          0.17654
       2              317          0.36818
       3              392          0.45528
```

The class sizes that are estimated based on the manifest classification deviate slightly from the estimated class portions $\hat{\pi}_g$ in our example. A certain amount of discrepancy between these two kinds of class proportion estimates is usually observed, because the manifest classification of persons using the maximum class assignment probability is almost always associated with some amount of estimation error. The reason is that each person has a certain (nonzero) membership probability for each class, which is not taken into account when people are assigned to the one latent class for which the probability is highest. For this reason, the $\hat{\pi}_g$ parameters should generally be preferred as estimates of the latent class sizes.

Following are the average latent class assignment probabilities for individuals assigned to each class. These are important indicators of the quality of an LCA solution. Values close to 1 on the main diagonal of the classification matrix indicate a high precision or reliability of the classification. High values on the main diagonal of this matrix mean that individuals, on average, are classified with high certainty into their most likely latent class. In contrast, moderate to low values indicate that there is a high uncertainty of the class assignment, on average. According to Rost (2006), the values on the main diagonal should be .8 or larger for a good class solution. In our example, we obtained high class assignment probabilities for Classes 2 and 3 (.913 and .922, respectively), whereas the mean assignment probability for members of Class 1 is only .76, which is relatively low. Apparently, there is somewhat more uncertainty with regard to the assignment to Class 1 compared to Classes 2 and 3. Members of Class 1 also have a relatively high average probability of belonging to Class 2 (.146). Therefore, there is a certain degree of overlap between these two classes. Nonetheless, the classification quality for Class 1 can still be seen as satisfactory.

```
Average Latent Class Probabilities for Most Likely
Latent Class Membership (Row) by Latent Class
(Column)

             1          2          3

    1    0.760      0.146      0.094
    2    0.061      0.913      0.025
    3    0.037      0.041      0.922
```

The more latent classes are extracted, the lower in general are the mean class assignment probabilities. The reason is that with many extracted classes, there are more possibilities for an incorrect classification. The classes often are not as clearly separated any more.

Under `MODEL RESULTS`, Mplus first provides the parameters of the LCA model in the logistic threshold parameterization. First are the estimated threshold parameters that correspond to the conditional response probabilities $\hat{\pi}_{ig}$. Under `Categorical Latent Variables—Means`,

Mplus outputs the threshold parameters that correspond to the class sizes $\hat{\pi}_g$. The conversion of these parameters into probabilities is explained in Chapter 13 of the *Mplus User's Guide* (Muthén & Muthén, 1998–2012).

```
MODEL RESULTS

                                                    Two-Tailed
                    Estimate       S.E.  Est./S.E.    P-Value

Latent Class 1

 Thresholds
    C1$1               1.398      0.506      2.761      0.006
    C2$1               1.920      0.706      2.717      0.007
    C3$1               1.675      0.423      3.961      0.000
    C4$1               1.489      0.523      2.850      0.004
    C5$1              -0.981      0.406     -2.413      0.016
    C6$1              -1.480      0.654     -2.263      0.024
    C7$1               0.187      0.357      0.524      0.600
    C8$1               0.685      0.334      2.052      0.040

Latent Class 2

 Thresholds
    C1$1               0.555      0.144      3.852      0.000
    C2$1              -0.591      0.191     -3.101      0.002
    C3$1              -0.097      0.163     -0.593      0.553
    C4$1               0.463      0.143      3.244      0.001
    C5$1               1.154      0.247      4.681      0.000
    C6$1               1.542      0.291      5.290      0.000
    C7$1              -0.628      0.152     -4.134      0.000
    C8$1              -0.576      0.159     -3.633      0.000

Latent Class 3

 Thresholds
    C1$1               4.582      0.780      5.872      0.000
    C2$1               4.334      0.804      5.388      0.000
    C3$1               2.723      0.322      8.455      0.000
    C4$1               4.583      0.927      4.947      0.000
    C5$1               2.216      0.300      7.391      0.000
    C6$1               2.166      0.366      5.924      0.000
    C7$1               2.873      0.326      8.817      0.000
    C8$1               2.845      0.410      6.937      0.000

Categorical Latent Variables

 Means
    C#1               -0.943      0.247     -3.817      0.000
    C#2               -0.158      0.151     -1.048      0.294
```

More readily interpretable is the output of the LCA results in terms of the estimated probability parameters $\hat{\pi}_g$ and $\hat{\pi}_{ig}$. The estimates of the $\hat{\pi}_g$ parameters were already output earlier under `FINAL CLASS COUNTS AND PROPORTIONS FOR THE LATENT CLASSES BASED ON THE ESTIMATED MODEL`. Estimates of the conditional response probabilities $\hat{\pi}_{ig}$ (as well as $1 - \hat{\pi}_{ig}$) are obtained under the rubric `RESULTS IN PROBABILITY SCALE`. Under `Category 1`, Mplus outputs the conditional response probabilities for the lower category ($1 - \hat{\pi}_{ig}$), respectively. In our case, the lower category is coded zero and labeled "never/rarely." Under `Category 2`, the conditional response probabilities $\hat{\pi}_{ig}$ for the higher category (in our case, the category that is coded 1: "often/very often") are output.

```
RESULTS IN PROBABILITY SCALE

Latent Class 1

 C1
    Category 1        0.802        0.080        9.968        0.000
    Category 2        0.198        0.080        2.463        0.014
 C2
    Category 1        0.872        0.079       11.068        0.000
    Category 2        0.128        0.079        1.623        0.105
 C3
    Category 1        0.842        0.056       14.991        0.000
    Category 2        0.158        0.056        2.808        0.005
 C4
    Category 1        0.816        0.078       10.399        0.000
    Category 2        0.184        0.078        2.345        0.019
 C5
    Category 1        0.273        0.081        3.383        0.001
    Category 2        0.727        0.081        9.020        0.000
 C6
    Category 1        0.185        0.099        1.878        0.060
    Category 2        0.815        0.099        8.247        0.000
 C7
    Category 1        0.547        0.088        6.179        0.000
    Category 2        0.453        0.088        5.125        0.000
 C8
    Category 1        0.665        0.074        8.941        0.000
    Category 2        0.335        0.074        4.508        0.000

Latent Class 2

 C1
    Category 1        0.635        0.033       19.021        0.000
    Category 2        0.365        0.033       10.915        0.000
```

```
C2
   Category 1          0.356        0.044        8.152        0.000
   Category 2          0.644        0.044       14.721        0.000
C3
   Category 1          0.476        0.041       11.727        0.000
   Category 2          0.524        0.041       12.916        0.000
C4
   Category 1          0.614        0.034       18.144        0.000
   Category 2          0.386        0.034       11.423        0.000
C5
   Category 1          0.760        0.045       16.916        0.000
   Category 2          0.240        0.045        5.332        0.000
C6
   Category 1          0.824        0.042       19.466        0.000
   Category 2          0.176        0.042        4.165        0.000
C7
   Category 1          0.348        0.034       10.094        0.000
   Category 2          0.652        0.034       18.917        0.000
C8
   Category 1          0.360        0.037        9.847        0.000
   Category 2          0.640        0.037       17.521        0.000

Latent Class 3

C1
   Category 1          0.990        0.008      126.531        0.000
   Category 2          0.010        0.008        1.295        0.195
C2
   Category 1          0.987        0.010       96.062        0.000
   Category 2          0.013        0.010        1.259        0.208
C3
   Category 1          0.938        0.019       50.383        0.000
   Category 2          0.062        0.019        3.309        0.001
C4
   Category 1          0.990        0.009      106.680        0.000
   Category 2          0.010        0.009        1.090        0.276
C5
   Category 1          0.902        0.027       33.919        0.000
   Category 2          0.098        0.027        3.699        0.000
C6
   Category 1          0.897        0.034       26.596        0.000
   Category 2          0.103        0.034        3.049        0.002
C7
   Category 1          0.947        0.017       57.362        0.000
   Category 2          0.053        0.017        3.242        0.001
C8
   Category 1          0.945        0.021       44.386        0.000
   Category 2          0.055        0.021        2.580        0.010
```

On the basis of the estimated conditional response probabilities, we can see that children who were assigned to Class 1 have fairly low probabilities to endorse the category "often/very often," except for items C5 (logic games) and C6 (skill-training games). Apparently, Class 1 represents the group of children who prefer logic and skill-training games, whereas they report playing other types of games rarely or never. As seen above, approximately 17.4% of children belong to this latent class.

Children in Class 2 show a different pattern of conditional response probabilities. They generally show a higher probability for the category "often/very often" than do children in Class 1. Specifically, members of Class 2 have high response probabilities for items C2 (action games), C3 (sport games), C7 (simulation games), and C8 (driving simulator games). Therefore, Class 2 represents a group of children who play computer games more often in general, and in particular prefer action and simulation games. As we have seen, based on the estimated class proportion parameters, approximately 38.1% of children belong to this group.

The largest class (Class 3, 44.6%) is characterized by a pattern of very low probabilities for the category "often/very often" for all items. Therefore, we can interpret Class 3 as a class of nonplayers, that is, as a group of children who do not play any of the computer games listed in the questionnaire often or very often.

For a clear and easy interpretation, it is useful to visualize the conditional response probabilities $\hat{\pi}_{ig}$ in each class using a so-called *class profile plot*. In this way, it is easier to assess the meaning of the classes as well as the quality of a class solution. For example, a good class solution is typically characterized by classes that show mostly low or high conditional response probabilities, so that the classes have an unequivocal interpretation. We can view the line graph that we requested through the `plot` option via the Mplus point-and-click menu using **GRAPH → View Graphs** in the output. Under **Select a plot to view**, we choose **Estimated probabilities** (see Figure 6.2).

Subsequently, one has to specify whether the probabilities for the first or the second category should be shown in the graph (see Figure 6.3). Although arbitrary for dichotomous variables, the plot is usually easier to interpret if the probabilities for the higher category ($\hat{\pi}_{ig}$; here, "often/very often") are plotted (because this category indicates agreement) rather than the probabilities for the lower category ($1 - \hat{\pi}_{ig}$, which indicates disagreement). One obtains the line graph shown in Figure 6.4, in which the estimated class proportions are also given again in terms of percentages.

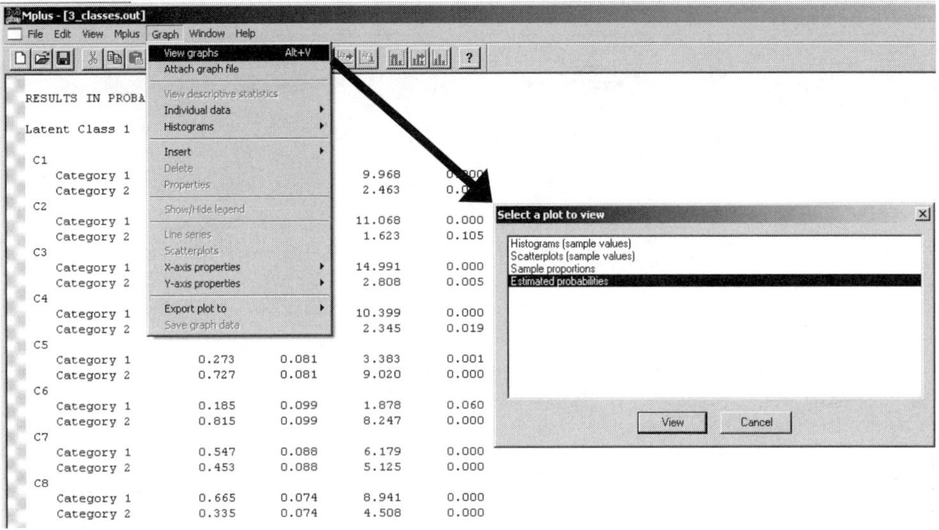

FIGURE 6.2. First step in viewing the item profile plot in Mplus.

Given that there are limited options to edit the Mplus line graph (e.g., it does not contain labels for the *y*- and *x*-axes), it is useful for a first inspection of the class solution, but not suitable for inclusion in publications, presentations, etc. It is therefore usually a good idea to plot the relevant conditional response probabilities again in an external graphics program that allows for more nicely designed graphs. As an example, Figure 6.5 shows the solution in a Microsoft Excel® line graph. In this

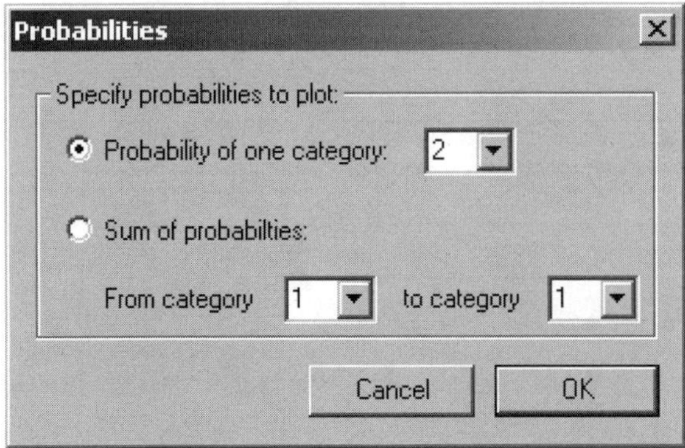

FIGURE 6.3. Specification of the types of conditional response probabilities to be shown in the profile plot. In this example, the probabilities for the second category ("often/very often") are selected.

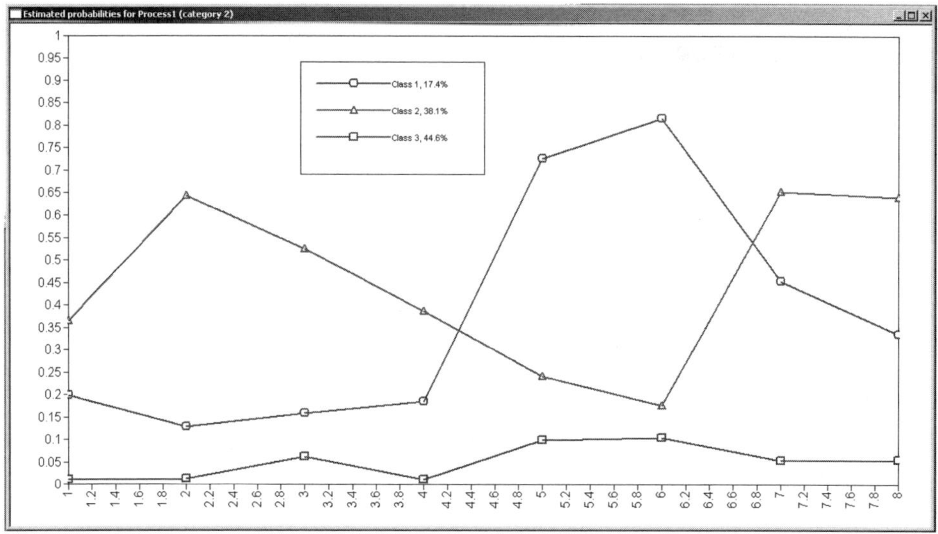

FIGURE 6.4. Mplus profile plot showing the conditional response probabilities for the second category of the computer game items in each of the three latent classes. The items are on the *x*-axis, whereas the *y*-axis shows the conditional probability of endorsing the category "often/very often."

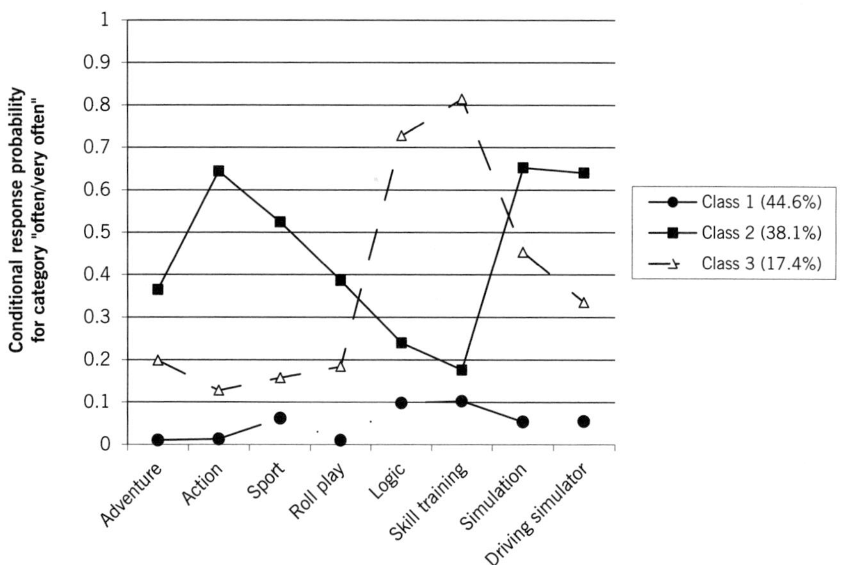

FIGURE 6.5. Microsoft Excel line graph for the same data shown in Figure 6.4.

example, the order of classes was changed from "largest first" to "smallest last," so that the smallest class in the Mplus solution is now Class 3 and the largest class is now Class 1. In addition, the *x*-axis was labeled according to the item content to facilitate the interpretation of the solution.

Using the class profile plot, we can once again see how the classes differ from one another: The largest class (now Class 1) is the class of nonplayers, in which members have very low probabilities for the category "often/very often" across all items. The second largest class (Class 2) represents the group of children who play more often in general and who have a specific preference for action, sport, and simulation games. The smallest class (now Class 3) consists of logic and skill-training game players.

In addition to the class profile plot, we have also requested that the individual class assignment probabilities and estimated class membership based on the maximum class assignment probability be saved to an external file. At the end of the Mplus output file, we obtain a list of the old and new variables that were saved to the new file by Mplus as well as information on the format of the variables in the new data file. This information is important, because it tells us the order in which the variables (columns) appear in the new data file, so that the data can be processed correctly in further analyses in external statistic programs such as, for example, SPSS. As an example, note that the variable ID (subject ID) now is no longer the first variable in the data set, but is now the ninth variable:

```
SAVEDATA INFORMATION

  Order and format of variables

    C1          F10.3
    C2          F10.3
    C3          F10.3
    C4          F10.3
    C5          F10.3
    C6          F10.3
    C7          F10.3
    C8          F10.3
    ID          F10.3
    CPROB1      F10.3
    CPROB2      F10.3
    CPROB3      F10.3
    C           F10.3
```

```
Save file
  computergames_3classes.dat

Save file format
  13F10.3

Save file record length    5000
```

The four new variables that Mplus added to the data file are CPROB1, CPROB2, CPROB3, and C. The newly created data file is named **computergames_3classes.dat** (the name was specified in the input file) and can be used for further analyses. For instance, one could use the class membership information saved by Mplus to find out about the preferences of specific children in the data set. To which computer game class is a specific child most likely to belong? This and similar questions can be answered based on the individual class assignment probabilities that Mplus saved for each child. Figure 6.6 shows an excerpt from that part of the newly created data file (after it was read into SPSS) that contains the four newly generated variables CPROB1, CPROB2, CPROB3, and C. An SPSS syntax file for reading the data set generated by Mplus can be found on the companion website.

The variables CPROB1, CPROB2, and CPROB3 indicate the estimated probability of class membership for each child for Classes 1, 2, and 3, respectively. For example, based on his or her response pattern, the first child in the data set (first row) has a probability of .218 of belonging to Class 1, .028 of belonging to Class 2, and .754 of belonging to Class 3. Note that the sum of the probabilities is 1. This is because LCA assumes that each child belongs to one (and only one) of the extracted latent classes. Given that this child's probability is largest for Class 3, the child is assigned to this class and therefore obtains the value of 3 on the variable C, which indicates the most likely latent class membership for each child.

The second child (second row) has the highest assignment probability for Class 1 (.988) and is therefore assigned to Class 1, etc. In this way, one can (1) examine how reliably each individual can be classified and (2) obtain an estimate of the most likely latent class membership for each individual based on the estimated class assignment probabilities. The average latent class assignment probabilities for the most likely latent class membership that Mplus reports in the standard output are calculated based on these individual class assignment probabilities.

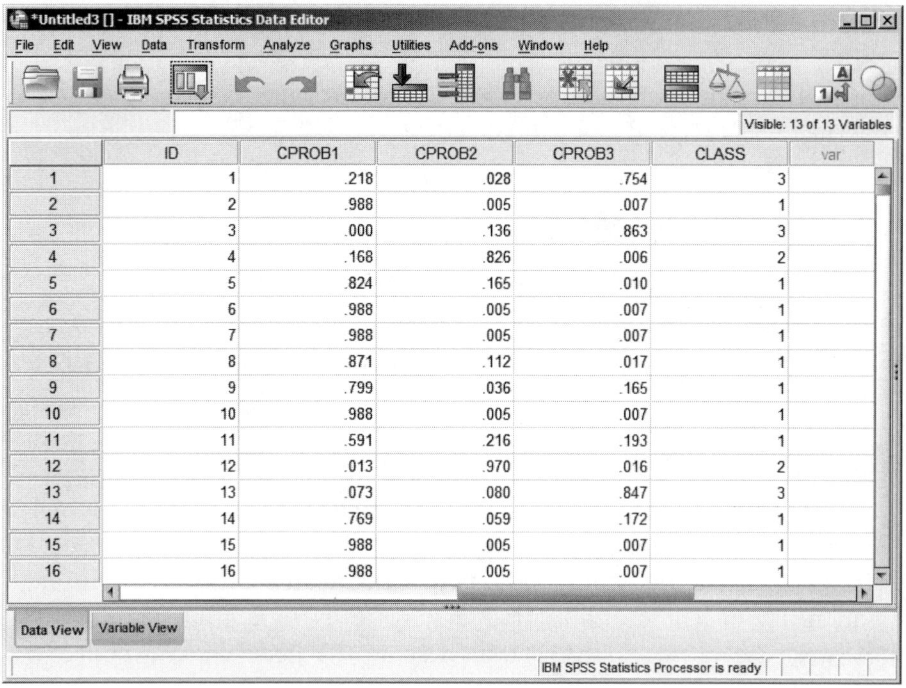

*Untitled3 [] - IBM SPSS Statistics Data Editor

File Edit View Data Transform Analyze Graphs Utilities Add-ons Window Help

Visible: 13 of 13 Variables

	ID	CPROB1	CPROB2	CPROB3	CLASS	var
1	1	.218	.028	.754	3	
2	2	.988	.005	.007	1	
3	3	.000	.136	.863	3	
4	4	.168	.826	.006	2	
5	5	.824	.165	.010	1	
6	6	.988	.005	.007	1	
7	7	.988	.005	.007	1	
8	8	.871	.112	.017	1	
9	9	.799	.036	.165	1	
10	10	.988	.005	.007	1	
11	11	.591	.216	.193	1	
12	12	.013	.970	.016	2	
13	13	.073	.080	.847	3	
14	14	.769	.059	.172	1	
15	15	.988	.005	.007	1	
16	16	.988	.005	.007	1	

Data View Variable View

IBM SPSS Statistics Processor is ready

FIGURE 6.6. Excerpt from the data set **computergames_3classes.sav**, which contains the individual estimated class assignment probabilities (variables CPROB1–CPROB3) and the most likely class membership (variable C).

6.3 MODEL FIT ASSESSMENT AND MODEL COMPARISONS

Often, researchers do not have a strong theory that allows them to make a firm assumption about the number of classes to extract. Given that the number of classes is not a model parameter to be estimated in LCA, the number of classes has to be determined indirectly through model tests and/or model comparisons. In practice, this means that researchers usually estimate a series of LCA models with different numbers of classes (e.g., the two- to five-class solutions) and then compare the absolute and relative fit of these models. The model with the best model fit is usually selected.

For the selection of the best fitting model, a number of different criteria are available. Here I discuss only those criteria that are available in Mplus. One can distinguish between indices for evaluating absolute fit (how well does a model fit the observed data in absolute terms?) and indices for evaluating relative fit (how well does a model fit compared to other models?). More detailed information on indices for evaluating model fit in LCA can be found in Collins, Fidler, Wugalter, and Long (1993), Formann (2003), and Rost (2004).

6.3.1 Absolute Model Fit

6.3.1.1 Likelihood Ratio and Pearson X^2 Statistic

Absolute model fit refers to the degree to which a class solution can reproduce the observed response patterns. In Mplus, two different test statistics are available for this purpose: the likelihood ratio (LR) test and the Pearson X^2 test. Both statistics are based on the comparison of the observed response pattern frequencies to the model-implied response pattern frequencies and are output by default when analyzing LCA. Under optimal conditions (see discussion below), both statistics follow a chi-square distribution under the null hypothesis that the model is true in the population. Significant values indicate a statistically significant discrepancy between the model and the data. In this case, the model does not perfectly reproduce the observed data (e.g., because too few classes were extracted).

Unfortunately, the LR and Pearson statistics follow a chi-square distribution only under fairly restrictive conditions. Specifically, relatively large sample sizes in combination with a relatively small number of items are needed to obtain reliable *p*-values from these statistics (Collins et al., 1993; Langeheine, Pannekoek, & van de Pol, 1996; von Davier, 1997). In practice, however, one often has to deal with a relatively large number of items, but a rather small sample size, so that the asymptotic conditions of the LR and Pearson statistics are not met. In these cases, one speaks of "data sparseness" or "sparse tables." One consequence of data sparseness may be that the *p*-values (which are based on the theoretical chi-square distribution) obtained for the LR and Pearson statistics may not be reliable (Rost, 2004).

As a rule of thumb, the *p*-values should not be trusted if there is a large discrepancy between the values of the LR and the Pearson test statistics for the same model. If the values are very different, this indicates that at least one of the two statistics does not follow the theoretical chi-square distribution. Collins et al. (1993) as well as Langeheine et al. (1996) proposed the use of a parametric bootstrap method in these cases, which can be used to approximate the empirical distribution of the test statistic that is valid for the application at hand.

Unfortunately, as of version 6.1, the parametric bootstrap has been implemented in Mplus only for relative model fit assessment (bootstrap LR difference test; see Section 6.3.2.1), but not for absolute fit assessment. Currently, a parametric bootstrap for global model fit assessment can be obtained only indirectly in Mplus through a Monte Carlo simulation study (see Muthén & Muthén, 2002, as well as Geiser et al., 2012). For our data example, the Pearson X^2 and LR statistics with conventional p-values are as follows:

```
MODEL FIT INFORMATION

Chi-Square Test of Model Fit for the Binary and Ordered
Categorical (Ordinal) Outcomes

          Pearson Chi-Square

          Value                              386.883
          Degrees of Freedom                     229
          P-Value                             0.0000

          Likelihood Ratio Chi-Square

          Value                              340.605
          Degrees of Freedom                     229
          P-Value                             0.0000
```

The values of the test statistics are relatively similar (LR = 386.883; Pearson X^2 = 340.605), so that we can suspect that the asymptotic conditions for the two tests are approximately met. As a consequence, the *p*-values can be interpreted, albeit with caution.

Both statistics show significant *p*-values in our example. Therefore, the three-class solution would have to be rejected based on these statistics. However, neither the LR nor the Pearson X^2 value is extremely large relative to their degrees of freedom ($df = 229$). This indicates that the degree of misfit of the model is not extremely large. In addition, we are using a relatively large sample size ($N = 861$), so that there is considerable statistical power to detect even relatively minor misspecifications. Additional model fit indices as well as model comparisons should be used to obtain a more precise picture of the fit of the model.

6.3.1.2 Residual Statistics (`tech10` Output)

Residual statistics are useful to assess which response patterns contribute particularly to the misfit of the model in terms of their contribution to the

Pearson X^2 statistic and log likelihood value. Residual statistics also allow us to detect "outliers," that is, cases with unique or aberrant response patterns. Residual statistics indicate the contribution of each observed response pattern to the global Pearson X^2 value and the log likelihood. In addition, Mplus outputs standardized residuals (z-scores) for each pattern. Large absolute z-values indicate response pattern frequencies that are particularly under- or overestimated by the model. Residual statistics are not part of the Mplus standard output, but can be requested using the following line of code in the Mplus input file:

```
output: tech10;
```

To save time, we use the `optseed` function (see Box 6.6) to reestimate the model with the additional request for the `tech10` output. For this purpose, we specify the seed that was associated with the best log likelihood value in our previous analysis, so that Mplus automatically reproduces the best solution (without having to iterate through all 500 sets of start values again):

```
analysis: optseed = 605358;
```

The complete input file can be found on the companion website. We now obtain additional output (`TECHNICAL 10 OUTPUT`) under the estimated model parameters. Mplus first provides us with a detailed overview of the observed response patterns. Each observed response pattern across the eight computer game items is listed and enumerated by Mplus. In our example, a total of 163 (of the total of $2^8 = 256$ possible) response patterns were actually observed. For example, the pattern with the number 1 (00100001) refers to the pattern in which the children selected the second category ("often/very often") only for the third (C3) and last item (C8). In pattern number 2 (00000000), the category "often/very often" was not selected for any of the eight items, and so on.

```
TECHNICAL 10 OUTPUT

     MODEL FIT INFORMATION FOR THE LATENT CLASS INDICATOR MODEL PART

     RESPONSE PATTERNS

     No.  Pattern      No.  Pattern      No.  Pattern      No.  Pattern
       1  00100001       2  00000000       3  11000101       4  00001100
       5  00000100       6  00001000       7  00000001       8  00101000
       9  00001110      10  10000001      11  00000010      12  00010000
      13  10011111      14  01001100      15  01001010      16  11101011
```

17	11001100	18	01011110	19	00011110	20	00001101
21	10011100	22	10001100	23	01001111	24	00101100
25	10111111	26	11100111	27	01000011	28	00010010
29	10000000	30	00011000	31	10001110	32	10101110
33	00001010	34	00011111	35	01000110	36	00100101
37	10010111	38	00011100	39	10010100	40	11011100
41	00100011	42	01000000	43	00000110	44	00000101
45	00001001	46	00001111	47	10000110	48	00100000
49	00010001	50	11111111	51	10111011	52	00100100
53	01000010	54	11000000	55	10101111	56	11010001
57	01100010	58	01110000	59	01100000	60	00111111
61	01011001	62	00110000	63	01110111	64	01001011
65	01100011	66	00101011	67	01010001	68	11100010
69	11000111	70	11000001	71	11100001	72	01110011
73	01100111	74	01101000	75	11000010	76	11111011
77	11010111	78	11110011	79	11100011	80	11101111
81	01100001	82	10010010	83	01101111	84	11101001
85	11001000	86	00101001	87	10110010	88	11110001
89	00011010	90	00000011	91	11101010	92	01010011
93	11110111	94	10001011	95	00000111	96	11000011
97	01010010	98	11010011	99	11001001	100	00100111
101	10010011	102	00110010	103	10001010	104	00011011
105	01010100	106	11110010	107	11111000	108	00101110
109	01101011	110	11011110	111	11001011	112	01100110
113	01000100	114	00001011	115	01100101	116	11011011
117	01010000	118	01001110	119	10100011	120	00010100
121	00101111	122	11010010	123	11011001	124	10000010
125	10110111	126	10010000	127	00110011	128	10010110
129	00110001	130	10100000	131	10000011	132	10011000
133	10111101	134	10100010	135	00101101	136	10001111
137	01011000	138	01110010	139	11011000	140	10100001
141	10111010	142	00010110	143	01000001	144	01101001
145	10000100	146	01010111	147	00010111	148	11110110
149	00100010	150	01111010	151	11001111	152	01011011
153	00101010	154	01011111	155	11011111	156	11010000
157	00111011	158	11011010	159	01110101	160	01110001
161	10010001	162	11010101	163	01001000		

Subsequently, Mplus provides us with a list of the observed and corresponding model-implied response pattern frequencies for all 163 observed response patterns. In order to save space, only the first 44 patterns are shown here (the full output is available on the companion website). For example, the first pattern (00100001) was observed for 13 children in our sample, but was expected for about only four to five children under the three-class model. This discrepancy between the observed and the model-implied pattern frequencies results in a relatively large z-score of 4.09 for pattern number 1. This shows that the observed frequency of this response pattern is "too high" and thus contributes significantly to the global misfit of the model.

Overall, the largest z-value in our example is observed for the response pattern number 40 (11011100; z = 8.47). Apparently, children who show this pattern are particularly hard to classify based on the three-class solution. In addition to the z-statistics, we also obtain the contributions of each pattern to the overall Pearson X^2 statistic and log likelihood value. For our pattern number 1, we find relatively large contributions of 16.68 Pearson X^2 statistic and 28.07 for the log likelihood. These values have a similar interpretation as do modification indices in SEMs (cf. Box 3.7). If, for example, pattern number 1 had not been observed, the overall Pearson X^2 value would decrease by 16.68. Residual statistics can provide valuable information about outliers (e.g., "unscalable" cases) and other peculiarities in the data. However, these statistics should never be used to exclude cases with "inconvenient" response patterns in a purely data-driven way.

RESPONSE PATTERN FREQUENCIES AND CHI-SQUARE CONTRIBUTIONS

Response Pattern	Frequency Observed	Frequency Estimated	Standardized Residual (z-score)	Chi-square Contribution Pearson	Chi-square Contribution Loglikelihood
1	13.00	4.42	4.09	16.68	28.07
2	261.00	255.07	0.44	0.14	12.00
3	1.00	0.78	0.25	0.06	0.51
4	27.00	18.73	1.93	3.65	19.75
5	32.00	35.06	-0.53	0.27	-5.84
6	29.00	31.54	-0.46	0.20	-4.87
7	14.00	18.34	-1.02	1.03	-7.56
8	5.00	3.05	1.12	1.24	4.93
9	11.00	13.22	-0.62	0.37	-4.04
10	2.00	2.05	-0.03	0.00	-0.10
11	19.00	18.53	0.11	0.01	0.96
12	3.00	3.94	-0.48	0.23	-1.64
13	1.00	0.50	0.71	0.50	1.39
14	1.00	2.52	-0.96	0.91	-1.85
15	3.00	2.26	0.49	0.24	1.70
16	1.00	2.05	-0.73	0.54	-1.43
17	4.00	0.68	4.03	16.22	14.18
18	2.00	0.67	1.63	2.65	4.38
19	2.00	3.03	-0.59	0.35	-1.66
20	9.00	8.18	0.29	0.08	1.71
21	2.00	0.90	1.15	1.33	3.18
22	2.00	3.92	-0.97	0.94	-2.69
23	4.00	1.64	1.85	3.40	7.14
24	5.00	3.23	0.99	0.97	4.37
25	1.00	0.22	1.67	2.77	3.03
26	2.00	1.40	0.51	0.26	1.43
27	9.00	10.32	-0.41	0.17	-2.47
28	5.00	2.40	1.68	2.83	7.35
29	4.00	3.88	0.06	0.00	0.24
30	1.00	1.41	-0.35	0.12	-0.69
31	4.00	3.30	0.39	0.15	1.55
32	2.00	0.73	1.49	2.21	4.03
33	4.00	5.48	-0.63	0.40	-2.52
34	3.00	1.70	1.00	1.00	3.41
35	2.00	1.96	0.03	0.00	0.09
36	4.00	1.37	2.25	5.04	8.57
37	2.00	0.57	1.89	3.55	5.00
38	1.00	3.59	-1.37	1.87	-2.56
39	1.00	0.46	0.80	0.64	1.56
40	4.00	0.20	8.47	71.73	23.92

```
 41        8.00       6.40       0.64       0.40       3.57
 42        7.00       6.57       0.17       0.03       0.89
 43        9.00       7.12       0.71       0.49       4.21
 44        8.00       5.25       1.20       1.44       6.74
 . . .     . . .      . . .      . . .      . . .      . . .
```

At the end of the residual statistics table, Mplus also provides the overall contribution to the global Pearson X^2 value that stems from model-implied response patterns that were not observed in the actual data (so-called "empty cells"):

```
THE TOTAL PEARSON CHI-SQUARE CONTRIBUTION FROM EMPTY CELLS IS     77.39
```

In addition, `tech10` includes univariate and bivariate model fit information (not shown here) that can also be useful to examine model fit in LCA.

6.3.2 Relative Model Fit

Given the complications of evaluating absolute model fit using the Pearson X^2 and LR statistic, due to the frequent violation of the asymptotic conditions for those statistics (cf. Section 6.3.1.1), researchers often evaluate model fit in LCA more in terms of the relative fit of a model compared to competing models (often models with more or fewer classes than the target model). Upon request, Mplus offers two different statistical tests that can be used to directly compare the fit of models with different numbers of classes: the bootstrap LR difference test (`tech14`) and the Vuong–Lo–Mendell–Rubin test (`tech11`). In addition, similar to other statistical models, LCA models can be compared using information criteria (in Mplus: *AIC*, *BIC*, and sample-size-adjusted *BIC*).

6.3.2.1 Bootstrap LR Difference Test (`tech14` Output)

Using the bootstrap LR difference test, one can compare a model with G latent classes against a model with $G - 1$ classes. Hereby, the difference in the LR values between the G and the $G - 1$ class model is calculated. Using a parametric bootstrap procedure (e.g., Langeheine et al., 1996; von Davier, 1997), approximate p-values for the LR difference are estimated by fitting both the G and the $G - 1$ model to each bootstrap sample and computing LR difference values for each bootstrap sample. This procedure results in an empirical distribution of LR difference values under the null hypothesis that the $G - 1$ class model is the true model. A significant

p-value indicates that the model with G classes fits the data better than the more parsimonious model with one class less. For a nonsignificant p-value, the more parsimonious model with one class less is preferred.

In our example, we first test the three-class model against a two-class solution. The bootstrap LR difference test procedure is requested in Mplus by adding the following command to the input file for the three-class model in Figure 6.1:

```
output: tech14;
```

To select the desired number of bootstrap samples (e.g., 500), we additionally specify:

```
analysis: lrtbootstrap = 500;
```

Five hundred bootstrap samples are often sufficient to obtain a reasonably precise estimate of the approximate p-value for the LR difference test. To ensure that no local maxima occur during the analysis of each parametric bootstrap sample, we increase the number of random start value sets for the estimation of both the G and the $G - 1$ class model to 50 in the first and 20 in the second step of the optimization:

```
analysis: lrtstarts = 50 20 50 20;
```

For more complex models, it is highly recommended to further increase the number of random starts used in the bootstrap analysis, even if this may lead to a considerable increase in the required computing time. The Mplus default (`lrtstarts = 0 0 20 5`) is often not sufficient to obtain valid bootstrap results due to the problem of local maxima (cf. Box 6.4). We obtain the following additional output in Mplus:

```
TECHNICAL 14 OUTPUT

Random Starts Specifications for the k-1 Class Analysis Model
        Number of initial stage random starts                   10
        Number of final stage optimizations                      2

Random Starts Specification for the k-1 Class Model for Generated Data
        Number of initial stage random starts                   50
        Number of final stage optimizations                     20
Random Starts Specification for the k Class Model for Generated Data
        Number of initial stage random starts                   50
        Number of final stage optimizations                     20
     Number of bootstrap draws requested                       500
```

```
PARAMETRIC BOOTSTRAPPED LIKELIHOOD RATIO TEST FOR 2 (H0) VERSUS 3 CLASSES

          H0 Loglikelihood Value                          -3522.517
          2 Times the Loglikelihood Difference              117.407
          Difference in the Number of Parameters                  9
          Approximate P-Value                                0.0000
          Successful Bootstrap Draws                            500
```

The log likelihood value for the $G - 1$ model (here, the two-class model that is tested against the three-class model) is –3522.517 (it can be found under `H0 Loglikelihood Value`). It is important to compare the log likelihood value for the $G - 1$ model to the log likelihood value found in a previous run of the $G - 1$ model that used a large number of start values to make sure that the model estimated in the bootstrap procedure does not represent a local maximum. The output for the separate analysis of the two-class model is not shown here, but can be found on the companion website. It turns out that the separate estimation of the two-class solution with 500 sets of start values resulted in the same overall log likelihood value, which indicates that we can trust the present bootstrap results.

Mplus also reports the LR difference value, which is equal to the difference in LR values between the two models. For the two-class model, the LR value is 458.012 (see output on the companion website). For the three-class model, we obtained an LR value of 340.605 (see Section 6.3.1.1). Hence, the LR difference is 117.407. In the three-class model, nine additional parameters are estimated, compared to the two-class model (one additional class size parameter and eight additional conditional response probabilities). The LR difference of 117.407 is significant according to the bootstrap p-value (`Approximate P-Value`), which is smaller than .0001. Therefore, according to this criterion, the three-class model fits significantly better than the two-class model.

For the comparison of three versus four classes, we additionally have to estimate the four-class solution, including `tech14` output (see companion website for the detailed input specification). We obtain the following result (only the most relevant output is shown):

```
PARAMETRIC BOOTSTRAPPED LIKELIHOOD RATIO TEST FOR 3 (H0) VERSUS 4 CLASSES

          H0 Loglikelihood Value                          -3463.814
          2 Times the Loglikelihood Difference               54.239
          Difference in the Number of Parameters                  9
          Approximate P-Value                                0.0000
          Successful Bootstrap Draws                            500
```

We can see that the loglikelihood value for the three-class model (–3463.814) has again been replicated exactly, so that we can trust the bootstrap results. It turns out that the difference in the LR values between the three- and the four-class solution is also significant, $LR_{\Delta} = 54.239$, $df = 9$, $p < .0001$. According to this criterion, we would prefer the four-class model over the three-class solution. However, the decision as to the number of classes to retain should not be based only on statistical, but also on substantive criteria and interpretability of a solution. In our example, it turns out that the three-class solution is easier to interpret than the four-class solution (see Section 6.3.3).

6.3.2.2 Vuong–Lo–Mendell–Rubin Test (`tech11` Output)

The Vuong–Lo–Mendell–Rubin (VLMR) test (Lo, Mendell, & Rubin, 2001) is based on a principle similar to the LR difference test. A significant value of the VLMR test shows that the estimated model fits significantly better than the model with one class less. Two versions of the VLMR test are obtained through the command `output: tech11;` in Mplus. In our example, the VLMR test provides the following result for two versus three latent classes:

```
TECHNICAL 11 OUTPUT

Random Starts Specifications for the k-1 Class Analysis Model
        Number of initial stage random starts                  10
        Number of final stage optimizations                     2

VUONG-LO-MENDELL-RUBIN LIKELIHOOD RATIO TEST FOR 2 (H0) VERSUS 3 CLASSES

          H0 Loglikelihood Value                        -3522.517
          2 Times the Loglikelihood Difference            117.407
          Difference in the Number of Parameters                9
          Mean                                             19.334
          Standard Deviation                               20.559
          P-Value                                          0.0035

LO-MENDELL-RUBIN ADJUSTED LRT TEST

          Value                                           115.508
          P-Value                                          0.0038
```

It is again important to check that the likelihood value listed under `H0 Loglikelihood Value` is compared to the log likelihood value obtained for the $G - 1$ class model in a separate run with a sufficient number of sets of start values (here the values are identical, as desired). In this case, like the bootstrap LR difference test, the VLMR test favors the three-class model over the two-class model ($p = .0035$ for the VLMR test and $p = .0038$ for the adjusted version). In contrast, the comparison of three versus four classes (using an extended input file for the four-class model with `tech11`; see companion website) yields a result different from the bootstrap LR difference test:

```
TECHNICAL 11 OUTPUT

VUONG-LO-MENDELL-RUBIN LIKELIHOOD RATIO TEST FOR 3 (H0) VERSUS 4 CLASSES

          H0 Loglikelihood Value                          -3463.814
          2 Times the Loglikelihood Difference               54.239
          Difference in the Number of Parameters                  9
          Mean                                               18.229
          Standard Deviation                                 28.354
          P-Value                                            0.0896

LO-MENDELL-RUBIN ADJUSTED LRT TEST

          Value                                              53.362
          P-Value                                            0.0925
```

The p-values associated with both the VLMR test and its adjusted version are nonsignificant ($p = .0896$ and $p = .0925$, respectively). This means that according to these tests, the four-class model does not fit significantly better than the more parsimonious three-class solution. (In contrast, the bootstrap LR test found the four-class model to fit significantly better than the three-class model.)

The results of a simulation study by Nylund, Asparouhov, and Muthén (2007) indicate that, in general, the bootstrap LR test is a more accurate indicator of the number of classes than the VLMR test. Therefore, the bootstrap LR test should be preferred in practical applications.

6.3.2.3 Information Criteria

Information criteria (IC) are descriptive indices for model comparisons. They take into account both the goodness of fit of a model to the data and model parsimony (the number of estimated parameters). Models with more classes tend to fit the data better than models with fewer classes. On the other hand, with each additional class, the number of model parameters to be estimated increases (and parsimony decreases). In terms of the IC, the best model is the one that fits well and uses as few parameters as possible. In a series of models, the model with the smallest *AIC*, *BIC*, or sample-size-adjusted *BIC* (*aBIC*) value is preferred. In our example, we obtain the following IC values for the three-class model in the Mplus default output:

```
MODEL FIT INFORMATION

Information Criteria

          Number of Free Parameters                   26
          Akaike (AIC)                          6979.628
          Bayesian (BIC)                        7103.338
          Sample-Size Adjusted BIC              7020.769
            (n* = (n + 2) / 24)
```

These values are not meaningful in an absolute sense. However, they can be compared to the corresponding IC values calculated for other models. For example, we can compare them to the IC values obtained for the two- and four-class solutions. The IC values for all three solutions are shown in Table 6.1. It can be seen that the *BIC* index is smallest for three classes, whereas *AIC* and *aBIC* favor four (or even more) classes. Based on their simulation study, Nylund et al. (2007) recommend the *BIC* index for determining the number of classes in LCA (in addition to the bootstrap LR test; see Section 6.3.2.1).

6.3.3 Interpretability

For model fit evaluation and model comparisons in LCA, not only statistical criteria play an important role. Equally important is the interpretability of a solution (Collins & Lanza, 2010). This point can be illustrated using the data sample discussed in this chapter. Even though the bootstrap LR test indicated that the four-class solution fit the data better than the three-class solution, close inspection of the latent class profiles in the four-class solution reveals that one of the classes in the four-class solution

TABLE 6.1. IC for Different Class Solutions for the Computer Game Example

Model	*AIC*	*BIC*	*aBIC*
Two classes	7079.035	7159.923	7105.935
Three classes	6979.628	**7103.338**	7020.769
Four classes	**6943.389**	7109.922	**6998.771**

Note. *AIC*, Akaike's information criterion; *BIC*, Bayesian information criterion; *aBIC*, sample-size-adjusted BIC. Smallest values are printed in **boldface**.

BOX 6.7. *Overview of the Most Important Criteria for Evaluating Model Fit in LCA*

Tests of Significance for Evaluating Absolute Fit. The LR and Pearson X^2 statistics are reported by default in Mplus. A practical problem with these statistics is that they follow the theoretical chi-square distribution only when the number of items is small and the sample size is large. A parametric bootstrap can be used to generate an empirical test distribution that may yield more reliable *p*-values in cases where data are sparse (in Mplus indirectly available via a Monte Carlo simulation study).

Analysis of Model Residuals. Model residuals (`output: tech10;`) can help a researcher to figure out why a model shows a bad overall fit. Specifically, a researcher can use residuals to find out which response patterns contribute most to the global misfit. This can be helpful, for example, to detect outliers or individuals with aberrant response patterns.

Statistical Model Comparisons. Information criteria (IC; e.g., *AIC*, *BIC*, *aBIC*) can be used for descriptive model comparisons. The model with the smallest IC value is selected. *BIC* tends to perform well for determining the number of classes. Statistical tests (VLMR test → `tech11` output and bootstrap LR test → `tech14` output) are also available in Mplus. The bootstrap LR test is especially recommended.

Mean Class Assignment Probabilities. For a good class solution, the mean class assignment probabilities should be equal to or larger than .8.

Entropy. Summary measure for the quality of the classification in an LCA model. Values close to 1 indicate good classification accuracy, whereas values close to 0 indicate lack of accuracy. The entropy index is part of the Mplus default output.

Number of Classes. A parsimonious solution uses as few classes as possible. For solutions with one or more very small classes, one might consider selecting a model with fewer classes (unless the small classes are of substantive interest).

Number of Boundary Parameter Estimates. If many conditional response probabilities are estimated to exactly 0 or 1, this can be a sign for the extraction of too many classes, a local maximum, an identification problem, or an otherwise unreliable solution. Mplus issues a warning message in the output if boundary parameters occurred in an analysis.

Interpretation. Each latent class should have a clear interpretation. In general, interpretation is easiest when all items show either high or low conditional response probabilities within a class. Interpretable and theoretically meaningful solutions should be preferred to uninterpretable solutions.

Replicability/Stability of a Solution. It is a good sign for the validity and generalizability of the findings if an exploratory LCA solution can be replicated with fresh data, preferably samples that show different characteristics from the original sample (e.g., different age group or nationality).

is difficult to interpret, because this class shows primarily medium-size conditional response probabilities for the computer game items. Therefore, it is not clear how one would interpret this class.

In general, an easy-to-interpret class solution is typically characterized by the majority of conditional response probabilities being either close to 1 or close to 0, whereas medium-size conditional response probabilities do not occur. Classes that show medium-size conditional response probabilities for many items are often difficult to interpret, because individuals in this class would have a "fifty-fifty" chance of endorsing the higher category of an item. An exception are dichotomous test items, for which the answer can be either right or wrong. For such items, a probability of .5 corresponds to the probability of guessing an answer. Therefore, classes with around .5 conditional response probabilities for some or all items might be meaningfully interpreted as a class of individuals who use a guessing strategy under certain conditions.

Another argument against the four-class solution in the present example is that this solution contains a boundary estimate (one conditional response probability is estimated to be exactly 0). Therefore, the three-class solution appears to provide a more reasonable representation of the data, because it is easier to interpret (and also more parsimonious). Box 6.7 summarizes the most important criteria for evaluating model fit in LCA.

Appendix A

Summary of Key Mplus Commands Discussed in This Book

Command	Meaning/ explanation	Comments	Chapters/ Section
`title:`	Title of the analysis	Not a required command	2
`data: file =` <name_of_data_file. dat >;	Specification of the name and location of the file that contains the data to be analyzed	The complete path does not have to be specified if the data set is located in the same directory as the input file	2
`data: listwise = on;`	Using listwise deletion of missing values	The Mplus default, as of version 5, is FIML estimation with missing data	2
`data: type =` <type of summary data >;	Specification of the kind of summary data to be analyzed	Example 1 (means, standard deviations, and correlation matrix): `data: type = means std corr;`	2

Command	Meaning/ explanation	Comments	Chapters/ Section
		Example 2 (covariance matrix): `data: type = cova;`	
`data: nobservations =` <sample size >`;`	Specification of the sample size (required when summary data are used in the analysis)	Not required when individual data are analyzed; in this book, I also use the abbreviation `nobs` instead of `nobservations`	2
`variable: names =` <list of all variable names >`;`	Specification of the variable names	Variable names cannot be longer than eight characters	2
`variable: categorical =` <list of ordered categorical variables to be used in the analysis >`;`	Specification of variables in the analysis that are ordered categorical (ordinal) or dichotomous		6
`variable: nominal =` <list of nominal variables to be used in the analysis >`;`	Specification of variables as unordered categorical (nominal)		6
`variable: usevariables =` <list of all variables used in the statistical model >`;`	Specification of all variables that are used in the statistical model	Not required when all variables in the data set are used in the statistical model; in the book, I mainly use the abbreviation `usevar`	2

Command	Meaning/ explanation	Comments	Chapters/ Section
variable: missing = <variable name (missing value code) >;	Specification of the missing value code	missing = all(Missing-Value-Code); defines the same missing value code for all variables	2
variable: cluster = <cluster variable >;	Definition of a variable that indicates cluster membership	Required when nested data (e.g., children nested within school classes) are analyzed using multilevel modeling techniques	5
variable: within = <name of the level-1 variable(s) in the analysis >;	Definition of a variable that is used only at level 1 of a multilevel analysis		5
variable: between = < name of the level-2 variable(s) in the analysis>;	Definition of a variable that is used only at level 2 of a multilevel analysis		5
variable: centering = grandmean × (<variable name >);	Centering of a variable at the grand mean		3; 5
variable: centering = groupmean × (<variable name >);	Centering of a variable at the cluster mean (group mean centering)		5

Command	Meaning/ explanation	Comments	Chapters/ Section
`variable: classes =` <name of the latent class variable > (<number of latent classes >);	Specification of the name of a latent class variable and the number of classes to be extracted	Used in LCA and other types of mixture distribution analyses	6
`variable: auxiliary =` <name of the auxiliary variable >;	Specification of an auxiliary variable (e.g., the subject ID variable)	Can be used to save additional variables to an external file generated by Mplus, even if those variables are not used in the actual analysis	6
`analysis: type = basic;`	Basic analysis	Used to check the data; provides only descriptive statistics	2
`analysis: type = general;`	Type of analysis used for conventional regression, path, and SEM analyses	Default type of analysis in Mplus	3; 4
`analysis: type = twolevel;`	Two-level analysis	Used in connection with the specification of a cluster variable to carry out a multilevel analysis with two levels	5
`analysis: type = twolevel random;`	Two-level analysis with random slopes	Used in multilevel analyses with random slopes	5.5

Command	Meaning/ explanation	Comments	Chapters/ Section
`analysis: type = mixture;`	Mixture distribution analysis	Used to specify an LCA or other type of mixture distribution analysis in connection with `variable: classes =` <name of the latent class variable > (<number of latent classes >)`;`	6
`analysis: estimator =` <type of estimator >`;`	Specification of the method of estimation to be used in the analysis (e.g., `ml` for maximum likelihood estimation)	Can be used to select a different estimator rather than the default	Various chapters
`model:`	Specification of a model		3–6
`model: y on x;`	Regression of variable `y` on variable `x`		3–5
`model: y with x;`	Covariance/ correlation between `y` and `x`		3; 4
`model: f by y;`	Factor loading of an indicator `y` on a latent factor `f`	The loading of the first indicator listed after `by` is fixed to 1 for identification as the default; in the example, the loading of `y` on `f` would be fixed to 1	3

Command	Meaning/ explanation	Comments	Chapters/ Section
<parameter >*	Setting a fixed parameter free	Example: `f by y*;` this command sets the loading of `y` on `f` free	3
<parameter >* <starting value >	Assigning a user-defined starting value to a parameter	Also sets a fixed parameter free (and at the same time assigns a starting value)	3
<parameter >@ <number >	Fixation of a parameter to a specific value	Example: `f by y1*1 y2@1;` this command sets the loading of `y1` on `f` free (and assigns the starting value of 1 to this loading) and fixes the loading of `y2` on the same factor to 1	3
<parameter >(label)	Assigning a label to a parameter	The label can be a numeric or string; this command is often used to set parameters equal to other parameters or to refer to parameters in the so-called *model constraint command*	4
	Specification of growth factors or random slopes	Used in growth curve modeling and multilevel modeling with random slopes	4.5; 5.5

Command	Meaning/ explanation	Comments	Chapters/ Section
`model: %within%` <model specification >	Specification of the level-1 part of a two-level analysis		5
`model:` `%between%` <model specification >	Specification of the level-2 part of a two-level analysis		5
<name of the random slope > | `y on x;`	Specification of a random slope for the regression of `y` on `x` in a multilevel model	Used in multilevel modeling with random slopes	5.5
`model indirect:`	Request for a summary of direct, indirect, and total effects in a path model	Relevant especially in statistical mediation analysis (path analysis with indirect effects)	3.5
`model indirect:` `y ind x;`	Output of all indirect effects from `x` to `y`		3.5
`output:`	Request for additional output that is not provided as the default		Various chapters
`output:` `sampstat;`	Descriptive statistics		Various chapters
`output:` `patterns;`	Observed missing data patterns and missing data pattern frequencies (when FIML estimation is used)	Not available under `data: listwise = on;`	2

Command	Meaning/ explanation	Comments	Chapters/ Section
output: standardized;	All standardized solutions		Various chapters
output: stdyx;	Only the fully standardized solution		Various chapters
output: cinterval;	Confidence intervals for all parameter estimates		3.5
output: residual;	Model-implied covariance and mean structure and residual statistics		
output: modindices;	Model modification indices		
plot:	Output of graphs		4.5; 6
savedata: file = <name of the new data set >;	Saves new or modified data sets/ external files		6
savedata: save = <information to be saved >;	Specification of the information to be saved to an external file	Can be used, for example, to request that the individual class assignment probabilities be saved as new variables in LCA	6

Appendix B

Common Mistakes in the Mplus Input Setup and Troubleshooting

Problem	Possible cause	Potential remedy
Error messages in the output; no model computed.	• Data set could not be found by Mplus.	• Check that the name and location of the data set were correctly specified.
	• Data set could not be correctly read by Mplus.	• Check that the number and order of the variables were correctly specified.
	• Input line exceeds 80 or 90 characters.	• Use return to break too-long input lines into smaller lines.
	• One or more semicolons (;) missing in the input file.	• Insert a semicolon (;) at the end of each command.
	• Incorrect specification of the `usevar` command (e.g., too many or too few variables listed under `usevar`) or `usevar` command not specified in the input.	• Check whether the `usevar` command is specified correctly.

Problem	Possible cause	Potential remedy
	• Variable names incorrectly spelled (in the `usevar` or `model` command).	• Check whether the `model` command is specified correctly.
Incorrect or implausible descriptive statistics/model results; estimation or convergence problems, etc.	• Missing values not properly coded or missing value code incorrectly specified.	• Properly code missing values and specify missing value code in the `variable` command using the subcommand `missing =`.
	• Incorrect processing of the data set by Mplus.	• Check the data set; if necessary save new data set from SPSS; run a `basic` analysis to check proper processing of the data in Mplus.
	• Order or number of the variables in the data set is different from what is specified under `variable: names`.	• Check the number and correct order of the variables in the `variable` command.
The following error message appears in the output: **At least one variable is uncorrelated with all other variables in the model. Check that this is what is intended.**	• `Usevar` command not specified (in this case Mplus assumes that all variables are used in the model).	• Add `usevar` command unless all variables in the data set should be used in the model.
	• `Usevar` command incorrectly specified (more variables listed than are actually used in the model).	• List only those variables under `usevar` that are actually used in the analysis.

Problem	Possible cause	Potential remedy
Data could not be read by Mplus or were incorrectly read; for this reason no output or incorrect/implausible results.	• Data set contains commas instead of dots as decimal signs.	• Make sure that decimal points are indicated by dots.
	• Data set contains string variables that cannot be processed by Mplus.	• Avoid string variables or transform them into numeric variables prior to saving a data set for Mplus.
	• Missing values have not been coded with a missing value code.	• Assign a missing value code to all missing values. A numeric missing value code (e.g., –99) seems to work best. Can be easily done in SPSS using the RECODE command.
	• Variable names appear in the data set.	• Delete variable names in the data file or save data file again without adding the variable names to the file.
	• Data were not saved in tab-delimited format but in fixed ASCII format.	• Save data in tab-delineated format.
	• Data set was not found because it is not in the same directory as the input file or because an incorrect path was specified under `data`.	• Make sure the data set is located in the directory that you specified.
	• Order or number of `variables under variable: names =` does not match the order/number of variables in the data set.	• Make sure the order and number of variables listed in the `names` command are correct.

Problem	Possible cause	Potential remedy
	• One or more input lines exceed 80 or 90 characters.	• Break input lines that are too long using the return key.
Mplus does not estimate the model even though all input commands are correct and the data are correctly processed by Mplus.	• `analysis: type = basic;` is specified. Under the basic option, no actual model parameters are estimated by Mplus.	• Replace `type = basic;` by `type = general;` or another relevant type of analysis.

Appendix C

Further Readings

A .pdf version of the *Mplus User's Guide* can be downloaded for free from the Mplus homepage (*http://www.statmodel.com*).

Muthén, L. K., & Muthén, B. O. (1998–2007). *Mplus user's guide, fifth edition*. Los Angeles: Muthén & Muthén. *http://www.statmodel.com/ugexcerpts.shtml*.

The following book by Barbara Byrne introduces basic and advanced structural equation modeling with Mplus:

Byrne, B. M. (2011). *Structural equation modeling with Mplus: Basic concepts, applications, and programming*. New York: Routledge.

The following book deals with more complex analyses in Mplus:

Geiser, C., Crayen, C., & Enders, K. (2012). *Advanced data analysis with Mplus*. Wiesbaden: VS Verlag für Sozialwissenschaften. (Manuscript in preparation)

Specific readings that deal with the specific statistical details of methods discussed in the book can be found at the beginning of each chapter.

References

Aiken, L. S., & West, S. G. (1991). *Multiple regression: Testing and interpreting interactions*. Newbury Park, CA: Sage.

Baron, R. M., & Kenny, D. A. (1986). The moderator–mediator variable distinction in social psychological research: Conceptual, strategic, and statistical considerations. *Journal of Personality and Social Psychology, 51*, 1173–1182.

Bollen, K. A. (1989). *Structural equations with latent variables*. New York: Wiley.

Bollen, K. A., & Curran, P. J. (2006). *Latent curve models: A structural equation perspective*. New York: Wiley.

Bollen, K. A., & Long, S. (Eds.). (1993). *Testing structural equation models*. Newbury Park, CA: Sage.

Bryk, A. S., & Raudenbush, S. W. (1987). Application of hierarchical linear models to assessing change. *Psychological Bulletin, 101*, 147–158.

Byrne, B. M., Shavelson, R. J., & Muthén, B. O. (1989). Testing for the equivalence of factor covariance and mean structures: The issue of partial measurement invariance. *Psychological Bulletin, 105*, 456–466.

Chen, F., Bollen, K. A., Paxton, P., Curran, P., & Kirby, J. (2001). Improper solutions in structural equation models: Causes, consequences, and strategies. *Sociological Methods and Research, 29*, 468–508.

Clogg, C. C. (1995). Latent class models: Recent developments and prospects for the future. In G. Arminger, C. C. Clogg, & M. E. Sobel (Eds.), *Handbook of statistical modeling in the social sciences* (pp. 311–359). New York: Plenum Press.

Cohen, J., Cohen, P., West, S. G., & Aiken, L. S. (2003). *Applied multiple regression/correlation analysis for the behavioral sciences*. Mahwah, NJ: Erlbaum.

Cole, D. A., Martin, J. M., & Powers, B. (1997). A competency-based model of child depression: A longitudinal study of peer, parent, teacher, and self-evaluations. *Journal of Child Psychology and Psychiatry and Allied Disciplines, 38*, 505–514.

Cole, D. A., Martin, J. M., Powers, B., & Truglio, R. (1996). Modeling causal relations between academic and social competence and depression: A multitrait–multimethod longitudinal study of children. *Journal of Abnormal Psychology, 105*, 258–270.

Cole, D. A., & Maxwell, S. E. (2003). Testing mediational models with longitudinal data: Questions and tips in the use of structural equation modeling. *Journal of Abnormal Psychology, 112*, 558–577.

Collins, L. M., Fidler, P. L., Wugalter, S. E., & Long, J. D. (1993). Goodness-of-fit testing for latent class models. *Multivariate Behavioral Research, 28*, 375–389.

Collins, L. M., & Lanza, S. T. (2010). *Latent class and latent transition analysis with applications in the social, behavioral, and health sciences*. New York: Wiley.

Crayen, C. (2010). *Chi-square distributions calculator version 3* [Computer software]. Berlin: Freie Universitat.

Duncan, T. E., Duncan, S. C., & Strycker, L. A. (2006). *An introduction to latent variable growth curve modeling: Concepts, issues, and applications* (2nd ed.). Mahwah, NJ: Erlbaum.

Eid, M. (2000). A multitrait–multimethod model with minimal assumptions. *Psychometrika, 65*, 241–261.

Eid, M., Courvoisier, D. S., & Lischetzke, T. (2011). Structural equation modeling of ambulatory assessment data. In M. R. Mehl & T. S. Connor (Eds.), *Handbook of research methods for studying daily life* (pp. 384–406). New York: Guilford Press.

Eid, M., Gollwitzer, M., & Schmitt, M. (2010). *Forschungsmethoden und Statistik* [Research methods and statistics]. Weinheim, Germany: Beltz.

Eid, M., Langeheine, R., & Diener, E. (2003). Comparing typological structures across cultures by multigroup latent class analysis. *Journal of Cross-Cultural Psychology, 34*, 195–210.

Eid, M., Lischetzke, T., & Nussbeck, F. W. (2006). Structural equation models for multitrait–multimethod data. In M. Eid & E. Diener (Eds.), *Handbook of multimethod measurement in psychology* (pp. 283–299). Washington, DC: American Psychological Association.

Eid, M., Nussbeck, F. W., Geiser, C., Cole, D. A., Gollwitzer, M., & Lischetzke, T. (2008). Structural equation modeling of multitrait–multimethod data: Different models for different types of methods. *Psychological Methods, 13*, 230–253.

Eid, M., Schneider, C., & Schwenkmezger, P. (1999). Do you feel better or worse?: The validity of perceived deviations of mood states from mood traits. *European Journal of Personality, 13*, 283–306.

Enders, C. K. (2010). *Applied missing data analysis*. New York: Guilford Press.

Enders, C. K., & Tofighi, D. (2007). Centering predictor variables in cross-sectional multilevel models: A new look at an old issue. *Psychological Methods, 12*, 121–138.

Finney, S. J., & DiStefano, C. (2006). Non-normal and categorical data in structural equation modeling. In G. R. Hancock & R. O. Mueller (Eds.), *Structural equation modeling: A second course* (pp. 269–314). Greenwich, CT: Information Age.

Formann, A. K. (2003). Latent class model diagnostics: A review and some proposals. *Computational Statistics and Data Analysis*, *41*, 549–559.

Geiser, C. (2009). *Multitrait–multimethod–multioccasion modeling.* Munich: AVM.

Geiser, C., Crayen, C., & Enders, C. K. (2012). *Datenanalyse mit Mplus für Fortgeschrittene* [Advanced data analysis with Mplus]. Wiesbaden, Germany: VS Verlag für Sozialwissenschaften. (Manuscript in preparation)

Geiser, C., Eid, M., & Nussbeck, F. W. (2008). On the meaning of the latent variables in the CT-C(M–1) model: A comment on Maydeu-Olivares & Coffman (2006). *Psychological Methods*, *13*, 49–57.

Geiser, C., Keller, B. T., & Lockhart, G. (in press). First- versus second-order latent growth curve models: Some insights from latent state–trait theory. *Structural Equation Modeling.*

Geiser, C., Lehmann, W., & Eid, M. (2006). Separating "rotators" from "nonrotators" in the mental rotations test: A multigroup latent class analysis. *Multivariate Behavioral Research*, *41*, 261–293.

Geiser, C., & Lockhart, G. (2012). A comparison of four approaches to account for method effects in latent state–trait analyses. *Psychological Methods*, *17*, 255–283.

Goodman, L. A. (1974). Exploratory latent structure analysis using both identifiable and unidentifiable models. *Biometrika*, *61*, 215–231.

Hagenaars, J. A. (1993). *Loglinear models with latent variables.* Beverly Hills, CA: Sage.

Hagenaars, J. A., & McCutcheon, A. L. (Eds.). (2002). *Applied latent class analysis.* Cambridge, UK: Cambridge University Press.

Hancock, G. R., Kuo, W., & Lawrence, F. R. (2001). An illustration of second-order latent growth models. *Structural Equation Modeling*, *8*, 470–489.

Heller, K., Gaedicke, A.-K., & Weinläder, H. (1976). *Kognitiver Fahigkeitstest (KFT 4–13)* [Cognitive Ability Test (KFT 4-13)]. Weinheim, Germany: Beltz.

Hertzog, C., & Nesselroade, J. R. (1987). Beyond autoregressive models: Some implications of the trait–state distinction for the structural modeling of developmental change. *Child Development*, *58*, 93–109.

Hofmann, D. A., & Gavin, M. B. (1998). Centering decisions in hierarchical linear models: Implications for research in organizations. *Journal of Management*, *24*, 623–641.

Hox, J. J. (2002). *Multilevel analysis: Techniques and applications.* Mahwah, NJ: Erlbaum.

Hu, L., & Bentler, P. M. (1999). Cutoff criteria for fit indexes in covariance structure analysis: Conventional criteria versus new alternatives. *Structural Equation Modeling*, *6*, 1–55.

Jöreskog, K. G. (1979a). Statistical models and methods for analysis of longitudinal data. In K. G. Jöreskog & D. Sörbom (Eds.), *Advances in factor analysis and structural equation models* (pp. 129–169). Cambridge, MA: Abt.

Jöreskog, K. G. (1979b). Statistical estimation of structural models in longitudinal–developmental investigations. In J. R. Nesselroade & P. B. Baltes (Eds.), *Longitudinal research in the study of behavior and development* (pp. 303–351). New York: Academic Press.

Kaplan, D. (2009). *Structural equation modeling: Foundations and extensions* (2nd ed.). Newbury Park, CA: Sage.

Kline, R. B. (2011). *Principles and practice of structural equation modeling* (3rd ed.). New York: Guilford Press.

Kovacs, M. (1985). The Children's Depression Inventory (CDI). *Psychopharmacology Bulletin, 21*, 995–998.

Kreft, I. G. G., & de Leeuw, J. (1998). *Introducing multilevel modeling*. London: Sage.

Kreft, I. G. G., de Leeuw, J., & Aiken, L. S. (1995). The effect of different forms of centering in hierarchical linear models. *Multivariate Behavioral Research, 30*, 1–21.

Lance, C. E., Noble, C. L., & Scullen, S. E. (2002). A critique of the correlated trait–correlated method and correlated uniqueness models for multitrait–multimethod data. *Psychological Methods, 7*, 228–244.

Langeheine, R., Pannekoek, J., & van de Pol, F. (1996). Bootstrapping goodness-of-fit measures in categorical data analysis. *Sociological Methods and Research, 24*, 249–264.

Langeheine, R., & Rost, J. (Eds.). (1988). *Latent trait and latent class models*. New York: Plenum.

Lazarsfeld, P. F., & Henry, N. W. (1968). *Latent structure analysis*. Boston: Houghton Mifflin.

Lo, Y., Mendell, N. R., & Rubin, D. B. (2001). Testing the number of components in a normal mixture. *Biometrika, 88*, 767–778.

Loehlin, J. C. (1998). *Latent variable models: An introduction to factor, path, and structural analysis*. Mahwah, NJ: Erlbaum.

Luke, D. A. (2004). *Multilevel modeling*. Thousand Oaks, CA: Sage.

MacKinnon, D. P. (2008). *Introduction to statistical mediation analysis*. Mahwah, NJ: Erlbaum.

MacKinnon, D. P., Lockwood, C. M., Hoffman, J. M., West, S. G., & Sheets, V. (2002). A comparison of methods to test mediation and other intervening variable effects. *Psychological Methods, 7*, 83–104.

MacKinnon, D. P., Lockwood, C. M., & Williams, J. (2004). Confidence limits for the indirect effect: Distribution of the product and resampling methods. *Multivariate Behavioral Research, 39*, 99–128.

Marsh, H. W., Wen, Z., & Hau, K. T. (2006). Structural equation models of latent interaction and quadratic effects. In G. Hancock & R. Mueller (Eds.), *Structural equation modeling: A second course* (pp. 225–265). Greenwich, CT: Information Age.

Mayer, A., Steyer, R., & Mueller, H. (in press). A general approach to defining latent growth components. *Structural Equation Modeling*.

McArdle, J. J. (1988). *Dynamic but structural equation modeling of repeated measures data*. In R. B. Cattell & J. Nesselroade (Eds.), *Handbook of multivariate experimental psychology* (pp. 561–614). New York: Plenum Press.

McArdle, J. J., & Hamagami, F. (2001). Latent difference score structural models for linear dynamic analysis with incomplete longitudinal data. In L. M. Collins & A. G. Sayer (Eds.), *New methods for the analysis of change* (pp. 137–175). Washington, DC: American Psychological Association.

McCutcheon, A. L. (1987). *Latent class analysis*. Beverly Hills, CA: Sage.

Meredith, W. (1993). Measurement invariance, factor analysis and factorial invariance. *Psychometrika*, *58*, 525–543.

Meredith, W., & Horn, J. (2001). The role of factorial invariance in modeling growth and change. In L. M. Collins & A. G. Sayer (Eds.), *New methods for the analysis of change* (pp. 203–240). Washington, DC: American Psychological Association.

Meredith, W., & Tisak, J. (1984, June). *On "Tuckerizing" curves*. Paper presented at the annual meeting of the Psychometric Society, Santa Barbara, CA.

Meredith, W., & Tisak, J. (1990). Latent curve analysis. *Psychometrika*, *55*, 107–122.

Millsap, R. E., & Meredith, W. (2007). Factorial invariance: Historical perspectives and new problems. In R. Cudeck & R. MacCallum (Eds.), *Factor analysis at 100* (pp. 131–152). Mahwah, NJ: Erlbaum.

Mulaik, S. A., & Millsap, R. E. (2000). Doing the four-step right. *Structural Equation Modeling*, *7*, 36–74.

Muthén, B. O. (2002). Beyond SEM: General latent variable modeling. *Behaviormetrika*, *29*, 81–117.

Muthén, L. K., & Muthén, B. O. (2002). How to use a Monte Carlo study to decide on sample size and power. *Structural Equation Modeling*, *9*, 599–620.

Muthén, L. K., & Muthén, B. O. (2010). *Mplus 6* [Computer software]. Los Angeles: Muthén & Muthén. *http://statmodel.com*.

Muthén, L. K., & Muthén, B. O. (1998–2012). *Mplus user's guide, sixth edition*. Los Angeles: Muthén & Muthén. *http://statmodel.com/ugexcerpts.shtml*.

Nylund, K., Asparouhov, T., & Muthén, B. O. (2007). Deciding on the number of classes in latent class analysis and growth mixture modeling: A Monte Carlo simulation study. *Structural Equation Modeling*, *14*, 535–569.

Pinquart, M. (2001). Correlates of subjective health in older adults: A meta-analysis. *Psychology and Aging*, *16*, 414–426.

Quaiser-Pohl, C., Geiser, C., & Lehmann, W. (2006). The relationship between computer-game preference, gender, and mental rotation ability. *Personality and Individual Differences*, *40*, 609–619.

Radloff, L. S. (1977). The CES-D Scale: A self-report depression scale for research in the general population. *Applied Psychological Measurement*, *1*, 385–401.

Raffalovich, L. E., & Bohrnstedt, G. W. (1987). Common, specific, and error variance components of factor models: Estimation with longitudinal data. *Sociological Methods and Research*, *15*, 385–405.

Raudenbush, S. W., & Bryk, A. S. (2002). *Hierarchical linear models* (2nd ed.). Thousand Oaks, CA: Sage.

Raykov, T. (1993). On estimating true change interrelationships with other variables. *Quality and Quantity, 27*, 353–370.

Raykov, T., & Marcoulides, G. A. (2006). *A first course in structural equation modeling* (2nd ed.). Mahwah, NJ: Erlbaum.

Reuter, T., Ziegelmann, J. P., Wiedemann, A. U., Geiser, C., Lippke, S., Schüz, B., et al. (2010). Changes in intentions, planning, and self-efficacy predict changes in behaviors: An application of latent true change modeling. *Journal of Health Psychology, 15*, 935–947.

Roosa, M. W., Liu, F., Torres, M., Gonzales, N., Knight, G., & Saenz, D. (2008). Sampling and recruitment in studies of cultural influences on adjustment: A case study with Mexican Americans. *Journal of Family Psychology, 22*, 293–302.

Rost, J. (2004). *Lehrbuch Testtheorie–Teskonstruktion* (2nd ed.) [Textbook test theory and test construction]. Bern, Germany: Huber.

Rost, J. (2006). Latent-Class-Analyse [Latent class analysis]. In F. Petermann & M. Eid (Eds.), *Handbuch de Psycologischen Dianostik* [Handbook of Psychological Assessment] (pp. 275–287). Göttingen, Germany: Hogrefe.

Rost, J., & Langeheine, R. (Eds.). (1997). *Applications of latent trait and latent class models in the social sciences*. Munster, Germany: Waxmann.

Sayer, A. G., & Cumsille, P. E. (2001). Second-order latent growth models. In L. M. Collins & A. G. Sayer (Eds.), *New methods for the analysis of change* (pp. 177–200). Washington, DC: American Psychological Association.

Schafer, J. L., & Graham, J. W. (2002). Missing data: Our view of the state of the art. *Psychological Methods, 7*, 147–177.

Schermelleh-Engel, K., Moosbrugger, H., & Müller, H. (2003). Evaluating the fit of structural equation models: Test of significance and descriptive goodness-of-fit measures. *Methods of Psychological Research—Online, 8*, 23–74. *http://www.dgps.de/fachgruppen/methoden/mpr-online*.

Schumacker, R. E., & Lomax, R. G. (1996). *A beginner's guide to structural equation modeling*. Mahwah, NJ: Erlbaum.

Singer, J. D., & Willett, J. B. (2003). *Applied longitudinal data analysis: Modeling change and event occurrence*. New York: Oxford University Press.

Snijders, T. A. B., & Bosker, R. J. (1999). *Multilevel analysis: An introduction to basic and advanced multilevel modeling*. London: Sage.

Sobel, M. E. (1982). Asymptotic confidence intervals for indirect effects in structural equation models. In S. Leinhardt (Ed.), *Sociological methodology 1982* (pp. 290–312). Washington, DC: American Sociological Association.

Sörbom, D. (1975). Detection of correlated errors in longitudinal data. *British Journal of Mathematical and Statistical Psychology, 28*, 138–151.

Steyer, R. (1988). *Experiment, Regression und Kausalitat: Die logische Struktur kausaler Regressionsmodelle* [Experiment, regression, and causality: On the logical structure of causal regression models]. Unpublished habitation thesis, University of Trier, Trier, Germany.

Steyer, R., Eid, M., & Schwenkmezger, P. (1997). Modeling true intraindividual change: True change as a latent variable. *Methods of Psychological Research—Online*, *2*, 21–33. *http://www.dgps.de/fachgruppen/methoden/mpr-online.*

Steyer, R., Ferring, D., & Schmitt, M. J. (1992). States and traits in psychological assessment. *European Journal of Psychological Assessment*, *8*, 79–98.

Steyer, R., Partchev, I., & Shanahan, M. (2000). Modeling true intra-individual change in structural equation models: The case of poverty and children's psychosocial adjustment. In T. D. Little, K. U. Schnabel, & J. Baumert (Eds.), *Modeling longitudinal and multiple-group data: Practical issues, applied approaches, and specific examples* (pp. 109–126). Hillsdale, NJ: Erlbaum.

Steyer, R., Schmitt, M. J., & Eid, M. (1999). Latent state–trait theory and research in personality and individual differences. *European Journal of Personality*, *13*, 389–408.

Uebersax, J. (2000). *A brief study of local maximum solutions in latent class analysis.* Available at *http://www.johnuebersax.com/stat/local.htm.*

von Davier, M. (1997). Bootstrapping goodness-of-fit statistics for sparse categorical data: Results of a Monte Carlo study. *Methods of Psychological Research—Online*, *2*, 29–48.

Ware, J. E., & Sherbourne, C. D. (1992). The MOS 36-item short-form health survey (SF-36): I. Conceptual framework and item selection. *Medical Care*, *30*, 473–483.

Whitelaw, N. A., & Liang, J. (1991). The structure of the OARS physical health measures. *Medical Care*, *29*, 332–347.

Widaman, K. F., & Reise, S. P. (1997). Exploring the measurement invariance of psychological instruments: Applications in the substance use domain. In K. J. Bryant, M. Windle, & S. G. West (Eds.), *The science of prevention: Methodological advances from alcohol and substance abuse research* (pp. 281–324). Washington, DC: American Psychological Association.

Author Index

T

U

V

W

Subject Index

Note. Page numbers followed by *b, t,* and *f* indicate boxes, tables, and figures. Commands and subcommands appear in `Courier` font.

D

E

M

N

O

P

Q

R

S

T

U

V

About the Author

Christian Geiser, PhD, is Assistant Professor in the Department of Psychology at Utah State University in Logan. His methodological research focuses on the development, evaluation, and application of latent variable psychometric models for longitudinal and multimethod data. In his substantive research, he focuses on individual differences in spatial abilities and how they can be explained.